Illuminate Publishing

WJEC Eduqas
GCSE
Film Studies

Jackie Newman
Dave Fairclough
Kelly Fincham
Julie Patrick

Published in 2017 by Illuminate Publishing Ltd, PO Box 1160,
Cheltenham, Gloucestershire GL50 9RW

Orders: Please visit www.illuminatepublishing.com
or email sales@illuminatepublishing.com

© Jackie Newman, Dave Fairclough, Kelly Fincham and Julie Patrick

The moral rights of the authors have been asserted.
All rights reserved. No part of this book may be reprinted, reproduced or utilised in any
form or by any electronic, mechanical, or other means, now known or hereafter invented,
including photocopying and recording, or in any information storage and retrieval
system, without permission in writing from the publishers.

British Library Cataloguing-in-Publication Data

A catalogue record for this book is available from the British Library
ISBN 978-1-911208-02-0

Printed by Standartų Spaustuvė, Lithuania

5.19

The publisher's policy is to use papers that are natural, renewable and recyclable
products made from wood grown in sustainable forests. The logging and manufacturing
processes are expected to conform to the environmental regulations of the country
of origin.

Every effort has been made to contact copyright holders of material produced in this book. Great care has
been taken by the authors and publisher to ensure that either formal permission has been granted for the
use of copyright material reproduced, or that copyright material has been used under the provision of fair-
dealing guidelines in the UK – specifically that it has been used sparingly, solely for the purpose of criticism
and review, and has been properly acknowledged. If notified, the publisher will be pleased to rectify any
errors or omissions at the earliest opportunity.

This material has been endorsed by WJEC and offers high quality support for the
delivery of WJEC qualifications. While this material has been through a WJEC quality
assurance process, all responsibility for the content remains with the publisher.

WJEC examination questions are reproduced by permission from WJEC.

Editor: Dawn Booth
Layout: Kamae Design
Cover and text design: Nigel Harriss
Cover image: iStock.com / baronvsp

Contents

How to use this book — 5
Knowledge and understanding — 5
Part 1: Exploring film — 5
Part 2: Film form — 6
The case studies — 6
Part 3: Component 1: US film — 7
Part 4: Component 2: Global film — 7
Part 5: Component 3: Production
   Filmmaking and screenwriting — 7
Part 6: Exam skills — 7

Part 1: Exploring Film — 8
Studying film — 8
Why do we study film? — 8
What do we study and why do we study it? — 9

Part 2: Film form — 10
Introduction — 10
How films communicate: the key
   elements of film form — 11
Cinematography — 12
   The close-up — 13
   Basic 4-point lighting — 17
   Bird's-eye view — 18
   Point-of-view shot — 18
   Camera movement — 19
Sound — 21
   Soundtrack — 23
   Dialogue — 24
   Sound effects — 24
   Music — 25
   Musical motifs — 26
Editing — 27
   Types of edit — 27
Mise-en-scène — 32
   Setting — 33
   Props, costume and make-up — 35
   Framing and body language — 38
How film form is used: the structural
   elements of film form — 41
Genre — 42
   Why is genre important? — 42
   Tracking typicality: investigating genre — 43
   Typical settings — 45
   Characters — 46
   Style — 47
   Genre narratives — 49
   Genre – a dynamic paradigm — 50

Writing about genre — 52
Narrative — 53
   Story and plot — 53
   Narrative structure — 54
   Narrative viewpoint — 56
   Voice-over narration — 56
   Narrative time and space — 59
   Narrative theory — 61
   Alternative narratives — 64
   Planning a narrative analysis — 64
How is film form used? — 65
Representation — 65
   The representation of gender — 68
   The representation of ethnicity and
     culture — 72
   The representation of age — 74
The aesthetic qualities of film — 76
   Aesthetics and popular culture — 77
   Style and aesthetics — 79
   Sound and aesthetics — 83
How we make sense of film — 84
   Context — 84
   Context – films made in the US — 85
   Context – US independent films — 88
   Context – global films — 90
   Context – global non-English language
     films — 93
   The two-point study plan — 94
   Context – contemporary UK films — 98
Specialist writing on film, including film
   criticism — 100
   Thinking, talking and writing about
     film — 100
   Film form and specialist writing — 102
   Cinematography source: *Me and Earl and
     the Dying Girl* — 102
   Film review source — 103
   Indie cinema source — 104

Part 3: Component 1: Films made in the USA — 106

Sections A & B: The comparative study and key developments in film and film technology
Content — 106
Why study mainstream American film? — 107
Introduction – mainstream Hollywood — 108
Introducing the industry and its context — 110
   Film timeline – Part 1 — 110

Film in the 1950s — 113
Film after the 1950s — 114
   Film timeline – Part 2 — 114
Film in the 1980s — 117
Film after the 1980s — 120
   Film timeline – Part 3 — 120
Two decades and beyond
   Hollywood in the 21st century — 124
The wider social, political and
   economic context — 126
   America in the 1950s — 126
   America in the 1980s — 128
Context – a brief comparison — 130
Case study: *Invasion of the
   Body Snatchers* and *E.T.
   the Extra-Terrestrial* — 131
Introduction — 132
The key elements of film form — 132
Cinematography in *Invasion of the
   Body Snatchers* — 133
Cinematography in *E.T. the
   Extra-Terrestrial* — 135
Mise-en-scène in *Invasion of the
   Body Snatchers* — 137
Mise-en-scène in *E.T. the
   Extra-Terrestrial* — 138
Editing in *Invasion of the
   Body Snatchers* — 139
Editing in *E.T. the Extra-Terrestrial* — 140
Sound in *Invasion of the
   Body Snatchers* — 141
Sound in *E.T. the Extra-Terrestrial* — 142
Concluding aesthetics — 144
The structural elements of film form — 146
   Genre and science fiction — 146
   Representation — 151
   Invasion of the Body Snatchers
     and *E.T. the Extra-Terrestrial* — 151
Further reading — 154

Section C: US independent films
Introduction — 155
Why study American independent film? — 155
Case study: *The Hurt Locker* — 156
What do we understand by US
   indie film? — 157
   Applying this to *The Hurt Locker* — 158

Context	159
Iraq	159
What else was going on?	160
Film in 2009	160
Studying the key elements of film form	162
Introduction	162
Cinematography and lighting	162
Studying the key elements of film form	162
Introduction	162
Cinematography and lighting	162
Slow motion	167
Lighting	168
Mise-en-scène	170
Setting	170
Performance	171
Positioning of characters and objects	172
Costume, hair and make-up	173
Props	174
Editing	175
Sound	176
Talking and writing about films	178
Reviews	178
Academic study	180

Part 4: Component 2: Global film   182

Introduction	183
Suggested approach	184

Section A: Global English language films

Case Study: *District 9*	185
Introduction	185
Key contexts	186
The key elements of film form	189
Cinematography and mise-en-scène	190
Sound	193
Editing	194
Narrative	195

Section B: Global non-English language films

Case study: *Let the Right One In*	202
Introduction	202
Key contexts	202
The key elements of film form	204
Cinematography and mise-en-scène	204
Sound	206
Editing	208
Representation	213
Gender	213
Age	216
Vampires	218

Section C: Global films: Contemporary UK films

Contemporary British cinema: an introduction	220
2009–2017: a golden age?	220
Case study: *Submarine*	221
Introduction	221
Key contexts	222
Historical and political context	222
Social and cultural context	222
Technological and institutional context	223
Awards	225
Submarine and the key elements of film form	226
Mise-en-scène	228
Oliver and Jordana	228
Costume: Oliver and Lloyd	230
Cinematography	234
Sound	238
The voice-over	238
Music	238
Recurring sounds and silence	239
Editing	241
Representation	244
Narrative	245
Style and aesthetics	248
Style in *Submarine*: intertextuality and post-modernism	248
Submarine as art: the poetry of language	251
The aesthetics of music and poetry	252
Film form – working together to create something special	253

Part 5: Component 3: Production   255

Introduction	255
The brief	255
Assessment	256
Suggested approach	256
Screenwriting option	257
Formatting	257
Writing action	258
Writing style	261
The key elements of film form	264
Cinematography and mise-en-scène	264
Editing	266
Sound	268
Representation	269
Adding dialogue	269
Final checklist	270
Shooting script	272
Filmmaking option	273
The key elements of film form	274
Cinematography and mise-en-scène	275
Editing	281
Sound	282
Representation	283
Evaluative analysis	283

Part 6: Exam skills   288

Component 1: Key developments in US film	288
Section A: US film 1930–1960	288
Section A: US film 1961–1990	290
Section A: The US film comparative study	291
Section B: Key developments in film and film technology	293
Section C: US independent films	294
Component 2: Global film: narrative, representation and film style	297
Time management	297
Section A: Global English language films (produced outside the US)	298
Section B: Global non-English language films	299
Section C: Contemporary UK films (produced after 2010)	301

Glossary	305
Index	313
Acknowledgements	319

How to use this book

This student book has been written especially for the new WJEC Eduqas GCSE Film Studies course. It has been designed to give you clear guidance through each element of the new specification by providing helpful information, tips and ideas. These will help you to deepen your knowledge and understanding of film form and provide a strong structure on which to base your study of global film.

Knowledge and understanding

The contents of this book are designed to enrich your knowledge and understanding of a variety of films that have been important both in the development of film and film technology. In addition, they will provide opportunities for you to apply your knowledge and understanding creatively to screenwriting and filmmaking. Your learning will be supported by a variety of features including:

- Task boxes designed to stimulate and encourage research. These also involve the close analysis of key areas through direct reference to film sequences, stills, criticism, reviews and screenwriting.
- Definitions of key terms with examples of the ways that these should be used in your analyses.
- Quick questions that test, enhance or clarify your understanding of the key areas covered in each subsection.
- Top tips created to help you improve your examination technique and support your production work.

You need to enrich your knowledge of films.

Part 1: Exploring film

Part 1 gives an introduction to why we study film and overview of the new specification.

CE N'EST PAS UNE IMAGE JUSTE, C'EST JUSTE UNE IMAGE

Part 2: Film form

Part 2 of this book aims to provide a strong foundation for your study of a variety of films made in different places and at different times during the history of film. It is divided into six areas, each of which allows a close focus on the specific elements of film form. These elements will provide a framework for studying all of your chosen films. They are as follows:

1. film form (cinematography, mise-en-scène, editing and sound)
2. structural elements of film form (genre and narrative, including screenplays)
3. representation of people and ideas
4. aesthetic qualities of film
5. **contexts of film** (social, cultural, historical, political and institutional) including key aspects of the history of film and film technology
6. specialist writing on film, including film criticism.

You will explore each of the above areas separately using examples/evidence from the broad range of film options offered in the specification. However, there is also a consistent emphasis on ways in which all the elements of film form work together to create meaning and response. Your understanding of these elements and ability to analyse how film form creates meaning – both in isolation and together – is a core skill in Film Studies at any level. This section is designed to enhance and consolidate these core skills.

> *Key term*
>
> **Context (film)**
> Where and when a film is made and set. What is communicated about culture, history, society, institutions or politics.

The case studies

The case studies in Parts 3 and 4 for both Component 1 and Component 2 may not feature the specific films you have chosen from the set list. However, they allow an in-depth exploration of key elements of film form across a range of films. The tasks set are specifically designed to give you ways into a close study of how films are constructed and used, their aesthetic qualities and how they communicate ideas. They also highlight how an understanding of social, historical, political and institutional context can illuminate and enrich our responses to the films we study.

How to use this book

Part 3: Component 1: US film

This section contains:

- A comparative case study for Section A, which focuses on one pair of US **mainstream** films (*Invasion of the Body Snatchers* and *E.T. the Extra-Terrestrial*).
- A case study for Section B focusing on one US Independent film (*The Hurt Locker*).

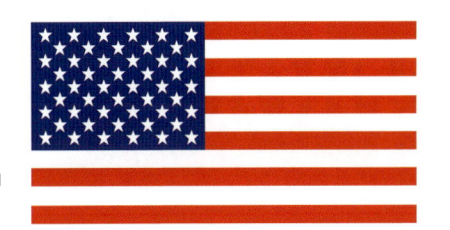

> ### Key term
> **Mainstream**
> Mainstream films can be defined as commercial films that know a wide release and play in first-run cinemas. Hollywood films are usually considered mainstream and blockbusters are mainstream films.

Part 4: Component 2: Global film

This section contains:

- A case study for Section A, which focuses on one global English language film (*District 9*).
- A case study for Section B, which focuses on one recent global non-English language film (*Let the Right One In*).
- A case study for Section C, which focuses on one contemporary UK film produced since 2010 (*Submarine*).

Part 5: Component 3: Production

Filmmaking and screenwriting

This section focuses on ways to help you tackle your production work (the non-examination assessment). It will give technical tips for those of you who are creating a film extract. It also contains advice on the appropriate format for both shooting scripts and screenplays should you choose the screenwriting option. Your production work should be built on your understanding of genre, genre conventions and narratives gained through your close study of the six set films. This section aims to reinforce this knowledge and understanding, and provide guidance on how this can be evidenced through your production work and your evaluative analysis of each stage of the production process.

Part 6: Exam skills

Tasks and tips throughout this student book will provide opportunities to think about and practise your exam skills and techniques. This section will also provide you with more examples of professional writing, allowing you to analyse and compare it to your own work. You will be given advice on the ways in which you can move from shorter to longer, more detailed answers, building your response step by step.

Part 1
Exploring film

Studying film

Quick Question 1.1

Think about the last film you watched. Did it educate or provoke debate in any way or did it simply entertain you? Do you believe films should make you think about important issues or simply provide an escape from them?

Why do we study film?

Film is often considered as the most important art form of the 20th century. The use of film and its explorations have progressed steadily since the 1800s. It is a major industry in most developed countries and an important part of people's cultural experience. It has become a huge influence on society today. Films entertain and **educate** us, and provoke **debate**. They affect the way we live, the way we speak, the way we act and more. We watch films, talk about them, write and read about them. Those who choose to study film usually bring with them a passion and enthusiasm for the subject.

There can be no doubt that film is a powerful medium that can inspire a range of responses from the 'emotional' to the 'reflective'. Viewers are drawn into the world of the characters, their stories and the issues that are raised. Film offers a powerful **audio-visual** experience incorporating the power of the visual image with the power of the music and sound.

Key term

Educate
The knowledge and understanding acquired by an individual after studying particular subject matters or experiencing life lessons.

Debate
Discussions between people in which they express different opinions.

Audio-visual
Using both sight and sound, typically in the form of images and recorded speech or music.

Part 1:
Exploring film

There are many academic reasons for studying film. Certainly, it is one of today's most important media and art forms and has the power to reach massive global markets; so it is vital that you understand how and what it communicates to that mass audience. However, let's not forget one of the most important reasons for studying film. It may be the reason that you chose it. One film studies student expressed it in the following terms, I really hope you feel the same way:

> *Because we love it. We love it so much that we want to know and understand everything about it, to investigate it inside and out. We want to understand how a shift in lighting, a line of dialogue, a note of music can change a scene. We want to build meaning out of it; not just the meaning of the plot, but the meaning that lies below the plot, that lies with every choice the director, the actor, the cinematographer and the scriptwriter made. What's more, we want to build multiple meanings, multiple understandings of the same work of art. We want to understand how cinema affects our lives, our culture. It is the art form of the 20th century, and like any art it does mean something beyond its entertainment value.*

What do we study and why do we study it?

The WJEC Eduqas GCSE Film Studies specification has been designed to build on your enthusiasm and interest in film. It covers a wide variety of cinematic experience by focusing on films that have been important at different points during the development of film and film technology. You will study one US mainstream film made in the 1950s and one from the 1970s or 1980s in order to focus on the ways in which Hollywood has developed over time. You will also study at least four recent films – these may be films you have already seen and liked (or disliked) or they may be films you have never heard of before. One will be a US independent film; the others will have been made in other countries, including the UK, South Africa and Sweden.

You will be encouraged to develop your knowledge and understanding of these films by analysing how they are constructed and organised into structure, and how they are used artistically as a way of communicating ideas/issues. You will also explore how key aspects of the history of film, its relevant contexts and specialist writing on film can help the viewer to make sense of what they are watching.

Given the power and scope of film in today's **global society**, it's little wonder that the study of film as an academic discipline is an important option in our education system. A report commissioned by the British Government in 2012, called 'A Future for British Film: It Begins with the Audience …' (www.theaco.net/images/Articles/260.pdf), advised that young people in every school should be taught the mechanics of filmmaking in order to encourage a new generation of scriptwriters, directors, and behind-the-camera technicians. The course you have opted for is designed to motivate you to broaden your knowledge of film and film technology. It may, or may not, encourage you to go on to a career in the film industry, but it will certainly make you aware of the strength and breadth of film as an industry and art form in today's world.

Given all these reasons to the question 'Why do we study film?' perhaps the definitive answer is 'Because we love it, it inspires and excites us and we want to learn more about it.'

Quick Question 1.2

Write down the reasons you have chosen to study film. Share some of the reasons with the rest of the group.

Key terms

Global society
A society that has been created in modern times where people of the world acknowledge that they have a good deal in common with one another. The idea of a global society helps people to understand the links between their own lives and those of people throughout the world.

Part 2: Film form

Introduction

Studying film is not simply a matter of watching a film and discussing why you thought it was good – although in some ways this is very important. In order to fully express a detailed knowledge about films and the way they work, it is important to have a vocabulary in which you can discuss why and how a film tells its story.

There are so many different ways a camera can now move and, combined with computer-generated imagery (CGI), there are not many places the camera cannot go, and not many amazing, fantastical places that cannot be visualised by cinematography. However, within your studies of film you will need to piece together how all of these different visual elements, combined with the other key elements of film form, make you feel and react. Naturally, you will need to be able to **contextualise** your thoughts and responses. Some of the films, maybe most of the films you are going to be studying, are films that are unfamiliar to you – perhaps because of the time during which they were produced or because they may feature a language you do not understand so have to read the subtitles.

Films such as *Singin' in the Rain* (1952, Gene Kelly and Stanley Donen), *Rebel Without a Cause* (1956, Nicholas Ray) and *Invasion of the Body Snatchers* (1956, Don Siegel) were all made before 1960, so the filmmaking techniques used at this time reflected, not only technical limitations but also new **innovations** and ideas. During the 1950s and 1960s, screens were becoming wider and colour became much more widely used. These changes obviously made a difference to cinematography because of the impact more sophisticated cameras, lighting, colour and the 'wide screen' brought with them. Although you will be discussing themes and representation, where historical context is much more important, you also need to take into account the importance of historical time to the style of filmmaking, otherwise you cannot appreciate each film in the comprehensive way necessary.

Computer generated imagery (CGI) creates an alien (*E.T. the Extra-Terrestrial*, 1982, Steven Spielberg).

Key terms

Contextualise
To think about or provide information about the situation in which something happens.

Innovation
The creation of something new or the development of a new method of doing something, e.g. computer generated imagery (CGI).

Rebel Without a Cause: wider screens, new ideas, iconic performances.

Part 2:
Film form

How films communicate: the key elements of film form

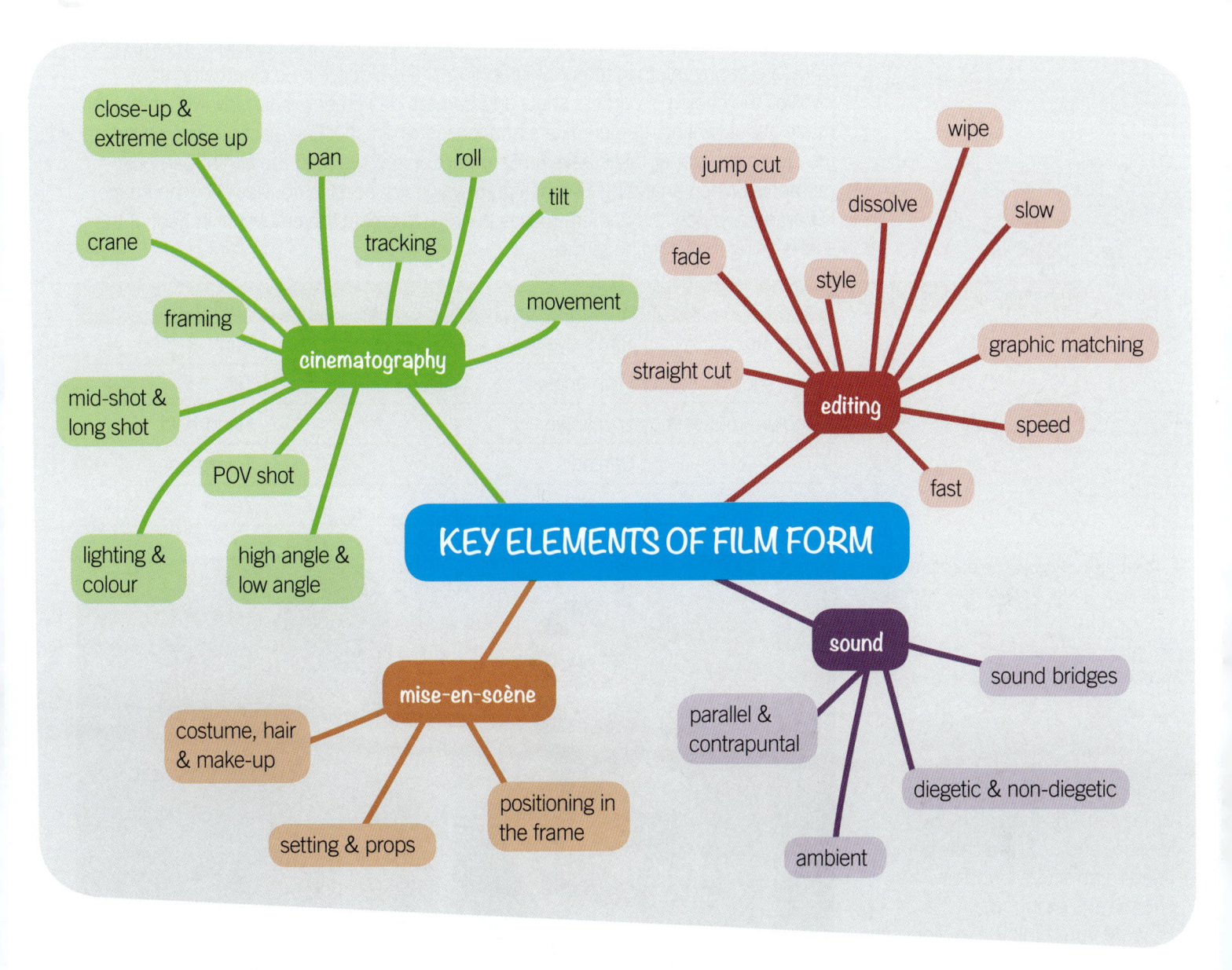

KEY ELEMENTS OF FILM FORM

- **cinematography**
  - close-up & extreme close up
  - pan
  - roll
  - tilt
  - tracking
  - crane
  - framing
  - movement
  - mid-shot & long shot
  - POV shot
  - lighting & colour
  - high angle & low angle

- **editing**
  - jump cut
  - wipe
  - dissolve
  - slow
  - fade
  - style
  - straight cut
  - graphic matching
  - speed
  - fast

- **mise-en-scène**
  - costume, hair & make-up
  - setting & props
  - positioning in the frame

- **sound**
  - parallel & contrapuntal
  - sound bridges
  - diegetic & non-diegetic
  - ambient

Film both reflects and creates the emotions of audiences and this is achieved not only through narrative content and ideas, but also by the technical elements of film production.

In your studies of film, focusing on **film** language and how to analyse it is going to be a key area with each of the films that you look at. These key elements are: cinematography (which includes lighting), mise-en-scène, editing and sound.

In this part each of these will be considered with reference to some of the films from the set lists. You will need to be able to apply your knowledge of these elements by analysing how they have been used to create meaning and response in each of the films you choose to study.

Key term

Film
A story or event recorded by a camera as a set of moving images.

11

GCSE Film Studies

Cinematography

The term cinematography comes from combining two Greek words: *kinema*, which means movement, and *graphein*, which means to record, write or paint. In film, cinematography refers to the photographing of the film itself. So cinematography involves the choice of camera shots and camera movement, it also involves decisions made about lighting, camera filters and lenses when shooting a scene. The shots the cinematographer takes have a big impact of how we read the film at particular moments. When analysing cinematography you will need to consider how an image is framed and how the camera moves in order to create the emotional impact of the scene using the following terms:

Cinematography toolkit	Types of shot	Camera angles	Depth of field	Camera movement
	Close-up	Bird's-eye view	Shallow	Pan
	Long shot	High angle	Deep	Tilt
	Medium mid-shot	Low angle		Hand-held
		Canted		Tracking
				Zoom

'Your little girl gave me the "stink eye" in class' (Juno, 2007, Jason Reitman).

Quick Question 2.1

Look at these three film stills. What camera shots can you identify and how are they being used to effectively portray the character's emotions?
How do you think the audience is meant to respond to these shots?

'Kiss me' (Slumdog Millionaire, 2008, Danny Boyle).

(continued)

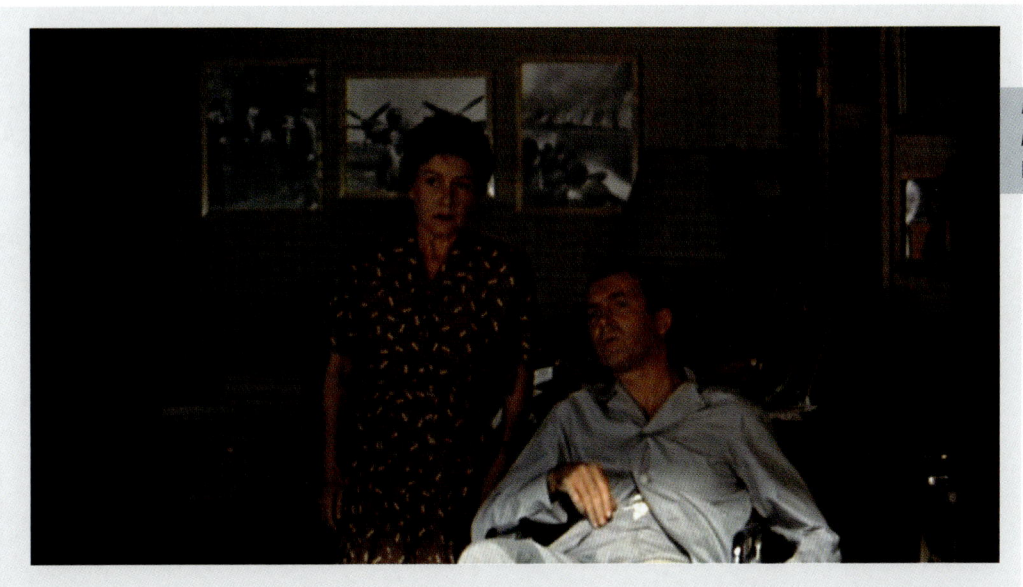

Part 2: Film form

I think, if I'm right, I've solved a murder' (*Rear Window*, 1954, Alfred Hitchcock).

Camera shots are probably the main element in a film, which draw our attention to emotions and also create strong emotional responses in audiences. Film is a visual medium and, although the sounds and pace of a film have their own way of creating impact on audiences, what we see is more likely to shock us, make us laugh or make us cry. So how do they do this?

The close-up

The **close-up** shot brings our attention to a character's facial expression, causes a reaction or focuses our attention on a significant prop. It is used to draw us into how a character is feeling about a particular narrative event that has just occurred. It brings us closer to their reaction than we would ever get in real life, therefore maybe offering the audience an insight into the character's motivations that other characters in the film might not see.

Key term

Close-up
A shot that focuses in on the head and shoulders and therefore draws our attention to a character's emotions. (Can also be a close-up of an object that is significant to the plot.)

Task 2.1

Watch the opening sequence of *Tsotsi* (2005, Gavin Hood). How many close-ups are used and what are they of? Why do you think the close-ups are used here?

The thug – a man of few words (*Tsotsi*).

GCSE Film Studies

Key term

Foreshadow
An event or clue in the narrative that signals a major event.

The close-ups in this opening sequence are significant and chosen for a particular reason. You will notice that all the characters are looking towards Tsotsi; the close-ups of their expressions as they look at him emphasise his important role. The close-up of the dice affirms the theme of chance, which is significant to the narrative of *Tsotsi* and its conclusion.

Task 2.2

Complete the sentences below using the correct shot name:

- The .... of Butcher's knife **foreshadows** its use in the upcoming sequence.
- An .... is used to focus on Tsotsi's eyes when he spots the man the gang are going to steal from.
- An .... showing the shanty town reveals the overcrowded nature and poverty surrounding Tsotsi's shack.
- The shanty town is revealed bit by bit using a sweeping ....
- We first see Tsotsi in a ...., which reveals him waist-up silhouetted against the light from his doorway.

Write one more sentence for each of the above, which explores the possible meanings created by this shot at this particular point in the sequence.

Key terms

Long shots
Enable us to view a character, or group of characters, within a setting, so we gain clues as to the coming action within the narrative and their role within it. There may be a number of things happening relevant to the plot within a long shot. A long shot can also show the whole of a person from head to toe, or the equivalent view of a building, landscape or prop.

Panning
The camera moves slowly from one area of the setting to another. If done quickly this is known as a whip pan.

In the opening of *Rabbit-proof Fence*, **long shots**, **panning** the wilds of the Australian outback, allow the audience to see the setting from the perspective of Molly, the central protagonist. This is to emphasise how important the land is to the Aborigines and how Molly and her people feel part of it. This makes it all the more painful when she is taken from this land and separated, both from her mother and the land she feels such a strong bond with.

'Don't look back' (*Rabbit-proof Fence*, 2002, Phillip Noyce).

Quick Question 2.2

Why do you think the filmmaker chose this long shot in *Rabbit-proof Fence*?

What is the purpose of this long shot in *Skyfall* (2012, Sam Mendes)?

'Home at last' (*Skyfall*).

14

Part 2:
Film form

The use of particular shots can create a number of different meanings. For example, the **mid-shot**, which conventionally shows a character from the waist up, is often used when dialogue is the most important factor in the scene, or when the director needs to fit more than one person in a shot but does not want the background to distract us from what is going on between them. Again, this could be due to the need for audiences to concentrate on important elements of the narrative, or to reveal the tension or emotion between the characters.

Key term

Mid-shot
Frames the character from the waist up or down.

Task 2.3

Although characters are often foregrounded in mid-shots, the setting can remain significant. Look carefully at the stills from *Rear Window* (1954, Alfred Hitchcock) below then answer the following questions.
1. Why do you think Hitchcock uses mid-shots in the stills below?
2. What detail did he include and why?
3. Consider the use of lighting and where the characters are positioned – what atmosphere does this create?

'What happened to me?' (Rear Window).

'You may want to open up a studio of your own one day' (Rear Window).

Shots can also be angled above and below the subject being filmed in order to create additional effects and meanings.

A **low angle shot** means that the camera is placed below the subject being filmed, making it appear bigger and therefore potentially dominant. In contrast, a **high angle shot** shows the subject from above and makes it look smaller, less significant and weaker.

This, of course, is not a rule and filmmakers often like to go against our expectations in order to stop the film becoming stale or too predictable, and to keep the audience 'on their toes'. We may know what we like but, even so, eventually we may tire of watching the same thing repeatedly – a fresh 'take', for example, on an old genre can often attract new audiences while still providing old pleasures for lovers of that genre.

Key terms

Low angle shot
The camera is placed below the subject making it look bigger and dominant.

High angle shot
The camera is positioned above the subject to make it look smaller and therefore weaker.

GCSE Film Studies

Low angle: 'You scrub up well' (Skyfall).

A low angle shot is sometimes used to draw our attention to attractive characters, emphasising their glamour and beauty. Or just to show us something that is higher up.

High angle: 'Don't look down!' (Skyfall).

A high angle shot, especially one that looks down on a character in a precarious situation, creates excitement and tension for the audience. In the still above we see just how far Bond may fall if he loses his footing.

Lighting and camera framing are also important elements of cinematography that you should analyse when studying your focus films.

There are two main ways to discuss lighting: **high key lighting** and **low key lighting**. However, having a simple understanding of how lights are used within the framing of a shot will also help you to understand how meaning is created. It is rare that lighting is not manipulated within a shot; even in broad daylight, lights might be used to affect the **colour palette** of a sequence or to manipulate where shadows do, or do not, fall.

> ## Key terms
>
> **High key lighting**
> When bright colour is created through the use of lots of filler lights.
>
> **Low key lighting**
> When less filler lights are used to create pools of shadows.

Blue is the colour (Skyfall).

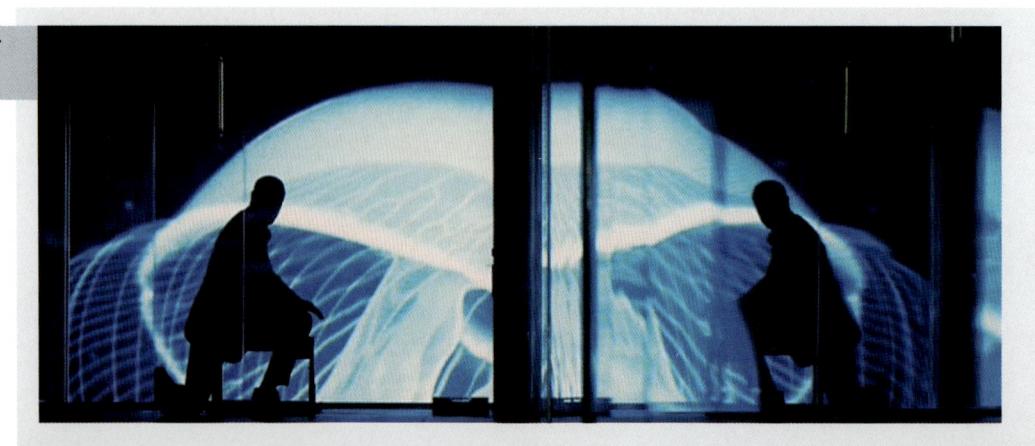

16

Part 2:
Film form

'I'm always trying to keep it real, I'm in love and that's how I feel' (Juno).

Quick Question 2.3

Analyse how colour and lighting are used in the image from *Skyfall* on the previous page and the one from *Juno* (opposite). What colours have been chosen and why? How does the lighting affect the mood and give clues as to the narrative?
Why do you think the shots have been framed in this way?

Basic 4-point lighting

4. Background light: lights the background, so the subject can be easily seen.

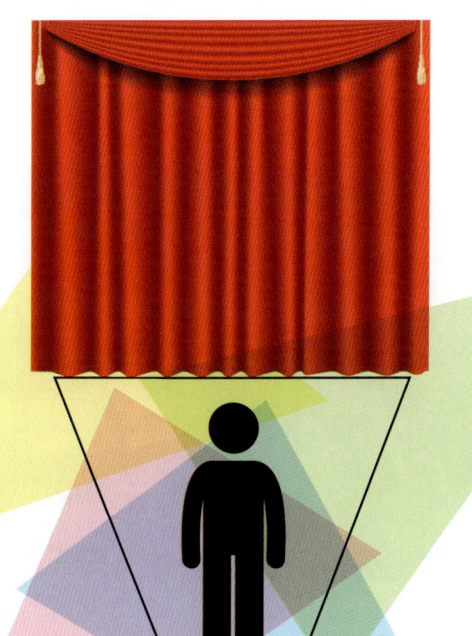

3. Back light: illuminates the back of the subject creating a 3D figure, so subject 'pops out' from the background.

1. Key light: the main light, often the brightest, on which placement of all other lights is based.

2. Fill light: the shadows created by the key light are filled in by this and shadows are eliminated.

Lighting and colour are often used to create atmosphere within a setting and together they create the overall **colour palette**. This refers to the main colours seen within one film and they often link to genre.

Key term

Colour palette
The 'look' of the film as created by the choice of colours.

17

GCSE Film Studies

The colour palette used in *Rabbit-proof Fence* consists of sandy browns and oranges, clearly designed to portray the hot, dryness of the outback.

In *Slumdog Millionaire*, lighting is clearly a strong indicator of narrative. Often the use of colour and lighting is strong and vibrant, representing Indian culture, but in the darker moments low key lighting is used to portray the dark, narrative themes.

You may also need to consider the use of focus within cinematography, which is categorised as either **deep focus** or **shallow focus**. Shallow focus is the most commonly used as it replicates what our eyes do. Basically, shallow focus closes in on the subject at the front of the frame, ignoring the background, this allows us to concentrate on the main action or dialogue. If deep focus is used, we are equally aware of the setting, or action, in the background; this signals that it has narrative significance.

Key terms

Deep focus
When all of the background and foreground details are in focus.

Shallow focus
When the camera only focuses on the subject in the foreground and the background is blurred out.

Bird's-eye view
The camera is placed directly above a subject, looking straight down.

Bird's-eye view

The overhead shot camera angle is one of the most interesting and specialised of all the camera angles. It is also called the **bird's-eye view**. It's not just a high angle shot, in this angle the scene is shown from almost directly (or directly) above the subject. Both *Slumdog Millionaire* and *Rabbit-proof Fence* use a bird's-eye view shot in the opening sequence in order to offer the viewer an interesting perspective of the setting.

'They can't touch me, can't even catch me' (*Slumdog Millionaire*).

Quick Question 2.4

Why do you think the bird's-eye view shot was chosen here?

Point-of-view shot

Point-of-view (POV) shots have been used since the early days of filmmaking. The camera emulates the gaze of a particular character and we see the world through his or her eyes. This subjective camera shot is still commonly used to put us in the characters' shoes, we can't know what is going on in their heads but we can see what they are seeing.

An **eye-level shot** works in the same way as a POV. The camera is placed 1.5 to 2 metres from the ground, corresponding to the height of an observer on the scene (lower if the observer is shorter or in a lower position, e.g. sitting on the floor). So the camera puts the audience on the same level as the character, showing them things much more from the scene observer's perspective.

Key term

Eye-level shot
The camera is placed at the same eye level as a character.

> **Task 2.4**
>
> Create a storyboard for a film sequence, using as many different camera shots as you can to create a dramatic or emotional part of a story.

Camera movement

The way the camera moves brings an audience into the action in particular ways. The main ways the camera moves are as follows:

zoom in or out **hand-held camera**
← pan (side to side) → **TRACKING SHOTS**
tilt (up and down) **canted angle**

A camera **panning** or tilting basically represents something we would do when looking at something. Panning around, allows the audience to see more of a setting – a whole room, a landscape, a group of alien spaceships about to attack Earth.

Tilting up from the floor allows us take in the size of a monstrous dinosaur or a huge skyscraper, both of these things we would naturally do if we were ever in a similar situation.

However, a **zoom in or out** works in a way our eye could not, and so it is therefore a narrative device, saying 'here, look at this a bit more closely', or if zooming out 'let's get away'. This sort of movement allows the filmmaker to draw our attention to important aspects of the action that will enhance our understanding of the situation.

A **canted angle** (sometimes called an oblique or Dutch angle) refers to an angle that is deliberately slanted to one side. This tilt is often used to show us that things are not quite right in the scene because, of course, it doesn't feel right when we view a setting from an unusual angle. The canted angle is sometimes used for dramatic effect to help portray, for example, unease, disorientation, frantic or desperate action, and intoxication or madness. It might be used to represent a character's emotional or physical disturbance caused by drugs or alcohol. Of course, a canted angle might simply be used to show us an actual physical change – a ship going down or a building after an earthquake.

A **tracking shot** tracks the action, so runs alongside it. A tracking shot is when a camera follows a person or an object, physically moving with the subject. In earlier days of filmmaking this involved the camera moving along on specially designed tracks, which 'tracked' the action. As cameras became more sophisticated, developments such as the Steady-cam allowed the filmmaker much more freedom. Today, cameras can be mounted on helicopters and, increasingly, on drones, but remember that these are very modern techniques.

> **Key terms**
>
> **Panning**
> To horizontally move the camera from a fixed point so that it sweeps across a scene.
>
> **Tilt (up and down)**
> The shot moves up or down.
>
> **Zoom in or out**
> The camera shot moves closer to or further away from the subject.
>
> **Canted angle**
> When the image is on an angle rather than on a straight horizontal line.
>
> **Tracking shot**
> The camera moves alongside the subject it is filming.

Part 2: Film form

GCSE Film Studies

'They're currently on the roof of the Grand Bazaar' (Skyfall).

Although filmmakers have been experimenting with hand-held cameras since the dawn of cinema, their use as an intentional aesthetic choice developed during *the cinéma vérité* style of the 1960s French New Wave movement, in films such as Luc Godard's *Breathless* (1960). Since then, the technique has been used to heighten tension and give realism to countless films. Today, new technologies are allowing filmmakers to push the boundaries of cinematography. One of the 'hallmarks' of director Danny Boyle's particular style of filmmaking is his frequent use of the hand-held camera (and canted angles). When making *Slumdog Millionaire*, Boyle and his cinematographer, Anthony Mantle, helped to develop and use an experimental silicon imaging HD (high definition) camera, this enabled Mantle to run along with the impoverished kids in the slums of Mumbai, on natural locations using the available light. This spirit of experimentation helped *Slumdog Millionaire* to win the very first Academy Award for HD Cinematography.

The use of a **hand-held camera** is becoming increasingly important in some genres, or in some aspects of narrative action. For example, if a character is running away, or if a fight sequence is filmed, hand-held cameras can give the viewer more of a sense of being part of this dramatic moment. Some films have gone even further and used this shaky camera technique throughout the whole film, thus giving the impression that **found footage** has been used.

Key terms

Hand-held camera
When the shot does not remain still but is shaky.

Found footage
Fictional, filmed material presented as if it is a documentary or factual footage.

Task 2.5

Discuss:

1. Why do you think the hand-held camera technique is popular in some modern films?
2. Which films have you seen it being used in?
3. Is it more suitable a technique for some genres rather than others?

Task 2.6

Watch the opening sequence of *Slumdog Millionaire* and make notes on the different types of camera movement used and how you think this impacts on the audience.

Sound

When analysing sound you will need to consider everything you hear when watching a film. Although dialogue is important, music and sound effects can also create meaning and response – indeed, they can often communicate as much as dialogue does in terms of the film's narrative and emotional appeal.

The 1920s saw a gradual move from silent cinema to the 'talkies'. The arrival of sound created great upheaval in the history of the motion picture industry. However, the move from silent films to sound films wasn't abrupt. Most major Hollywood studios began to make two versions of their motion picture releases. Sometimes, they even changed the plots in each version, perhaps by changing an ending or the editing sequence. For example, *All Quiet on the Western Front* (1930, Lewis Milestone) was produced in two versions – one silent version with music and effects, and one sound version.

The big Hollywood studios had obstacles to overcome with the advent of sound, which included:

- The restricted market for English-language talkies.
- The fact that silent-screen actors did not necessarily have good speaking voices or any real theatrical experience.
- In terms of technology, the noisy, bulky cameras of the time created a lot of unwanted background noise. One solution was to 'house' them in a soundproof booth but this restricted the ways in which they could be moved. The soundproof camera cover (blimp) was one inventive way of overcoming the problem but it was far from ideal.
- Artistically, acting suffered when studios attempted to record live dialogue, as stationary or hidden microphones (in either their costumes or other stage props) impeded the movement of actors.

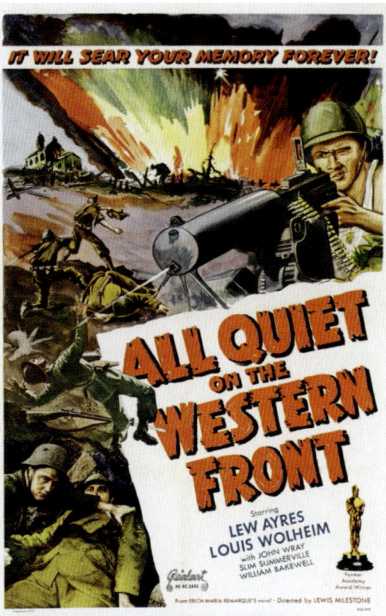

All Quiet on the Western Front poster.

Task 2.7

Answer the following questions:

1. Why was the market for English language films 'restricted' by the arrival of sound in the 1920s?
2. Give two reasons why the quality of acting in the new 'talkie' movies was poor.
3. Spend some time researching the move from silent cinema to sound cinema. Write a short paragraph exploring the technological and artistic issues involved when studios moved from silent films to the 'talkies'.

Given the problems explored above, we can't get away from the fact that some of the films made during the 1920s and 1930s were laughably bad, primitive and self-conscious. They had very little **artistic merit** and were simply designed to capitalise on the novelty of sound. One of the first Hollywood films to have real artistic merit while using sound was *The Jazz Singer* (1927, Alan Crossland and Gordon Hollingshead), produced by Warner Bros, starring Al Jolson. Of course, it made perfect sense that early films with sound should contain a lot of music, especially because people were used to seeing musical shows at the theatre.

Key term

Artistic merit
A term used by critics to judge, appreciate or evaluate a cultural product (in this case film) as a work of art. Critics and academics frequently view a film's artistic merit as more important than its entertainment value.

GCSE Film Studies

'Whacka Do, Whacka Do, Whacka Day' (Singin' in the Rain).

Singin' in the Rain, one of the focus films, is about the introduction of sound into film and looks back on the impact it had on performers and producers, in a light-hearted way.

FILM SOUND TERMINOLOGY

DIEGETIC SOUND
- Sound effects ① (Explosion, etc.)
- Ambient sound (Noises present in the environment)
- Dialogue (Characters speaking)
- Music represented as coming from objects in the story

Sound whose source is visible on the screen or whose source is implied to be present by the action fo the film

ACTUAL SOUND

Mode of address / direct address (Characters in the scene speak directly to the audience)

Synchronised sound (Lip sync) (Sound recorded while filming – usually involves footage of people speaking)

NON-DIEGETIC SOUND
- Theme tune (James Bond, Mission impossible, etc.)
- Incidental music (Used to create particular emotions, e.g. fear at key moments)
- Voice-over (Added dialogue) → Narrator's commentary

Sound whose source is neither visable nor has been implied to be present in the action

COMMENTARY SOUND

Sound effects ② (Added for dramatice effect)

22

The first way to break down the use of sound in film is into the terms – **non-diegetic** and **diegetic**.

Basically, sound that is diegetic is heard within the world of the film and non-diegetic sound can only be heard by the audience – usually music and narrative voice-overs. Diegetic sound includes sound effects and dialogue. Diegetic sound is important to creating the 'realism' of the scene, i.e. providing all the sounds that help you to 'believe' in the scene, even if it is set on an alien spaceship.

Although sound can be broken down into these parts for analytical purposes, they work together to create the atmosphere and tension within sequences, again to influence and manipulate our responses. Also be aware of **sound levels**. Diegetic sound within a sequence won't always be at the same level, or you would never be able to pick out dialogue. Noises such as shotguns and punches are often emphasised for dramatic effect.

> **Key terms**
>
> **Non-diegetic sound**
> Sound that is not a part of the film's world, e.g. musical score or voice-over narration.
>
> **Diegetic sound**
> Sound that is a part of the film's world, e.g. birds singing, traffic passing.

Task 2.8
Watch the opening sequence of *Rear Window*. How are diegetic and non-diegetic sounds used to create the atmosphere?

Slumdog Millionaire uses diegetic and non-diegetic music throughout. The musical score draws on traditional and modern Indian music. The music was written especially for the film by Indian composer A.R. Rahman, who said that he wanted the music not just to be about India but to create the atmosphere that the story could happen in 'any place at any time'. The songs, designed specifically for the film, work to create excitement and fun in some scenes and then a more dramatic or romantic ambience in other sequences.

'Got to let it go brother' (Slumdog Millionaire).

Quick Question 2.5
Watch the O Saya sequence from *Slumdog Millionaire* on YouTube and write notes on how the music works in this scene to reflect a sense of time and place. This is a good example of how a soundscape is created through a combination of diegetic and non-diegetic sound.

Soundtrack

The term soundtrack is used to describe:

dialogue   **music**

sound effects   **silence**

GCSE Film Studies

Dialogue

Dialogue is speech, the main way of communicating within the film. The dialogue might not be where most of the action happens, in fact it's possibly the opposite because action and dialogue move the narrative on in different ways. Dialogue allows us to learn more about the characters, and action shows us the events within the narrative that actually unfold. The cool one-liners of Bond, the romantic innocence of Jamal in *Slumdog* and even how little a character might speak, give us important knowledge of their place within the film's narrative.

Actions speak louder than words (*Tsotsi*).

Quick Question 2.6

Tsotsi doesn't speak for a significant amount of time in the first part of the film. What does this tell us about his character and his role within the gang?

Key terms

Sound effects
Diegetic sound that is created artificially to emphasise action, for example tyres screeching, punches and explosions.

Ambient sound
Sounds used to create a sense of place. For example, birds singing and trees rustling in a woodland.

Sound effects

Sound effects can be on-or off-screen but are still used to help create a particular ambience. **Ambient sound** refers to sound used to create the atmosphere in a sequence.

For example, *Rabbit-proof Fence* starts with a narrative voice-over spoken in Aborigine. The sound of a didgeridoo can be heard and then fades as we focus on the sound of the spirit bird and the otherwise silent desolation of the outback.

Silence can be just as important as sound in a film sequence, so should not be ignored in your analysis of film. A silence can be used to indicate the discomfort in a situation and also as a way to emphasise something dramatic or frightening that is about to happen.

Skyfall's opening, in contrast, contains a score with a heavy drumbeat and the dialogue is accompanied by lots of dramatic sound effects, emphasising the excitement of the chase on motorbikes, a car, a train and a JCB.

All these uses of sound create the right kind of ambience for this genre of film and for the moment in time. *Skyfall* is an action/espionage film and Bond films regularly begin with an action-packed sequence such as this to grip the audience straightaway, ensuring their expectations are met. *Rabbit-proof Fence* focuses on the importance of the natural world and the indigenous people of Australia, so this is therefore emphasised in the opening.

Music

Music is very important in creating our responses to narrative events and can scare us as much as the action does in genres such as horror films.

Most of you will be able to get your head around diegetic and non-diegetic sound but may find it difficult to describe how music works and are concerned about how to discuss the use of instruments and pace, etc. You could also describe music by referring to the:

musical style or genre   **instrument(s) making the sounds**

country it originates from   **purpose of the music**

A combination of these would be even better.

Try to comment on how sound increases in pace or volume. When does the music get louder? When does it become quiet and why?

You do not have to be a musical expert and may have a limited knowledge of orchestral music, but if you listen closely you should be able to distinguish between the use of string, brass and percussion instruments, and to think about the ways in which they can create atmosphere or add excitement or tension to the action we are watching on the screen.

You will also start to realise that different kinds of musical sounds tend to accompany particular genres, which will help you to discuss music with more confidence.

Full of sound and fury, signifying? (*Skyfall*).

Task 2.9

Watch (and, more importantly, listen to) the sequence where Bond arrives in Macau at the Casino and then fights Patrice in the skyscraper.

See if you can identify the musical instruments that are being used and then write about how the music adds to the atmosphere and mood in the sequence.

GCSE Film Studies

Key terms

Parallel sound
Music that matches the action on-screen.

Contrapuntal sound
Music that seems to 'clash' with the on-screen action, thereby creating a particular effect on the viewer.

Musical motif
A short repeated pattern of music.

Another interesting way to consider sound is by using the terms **parallel sound** and **contrapuntal sound**.

Parallel sound is basically when the sounds, music and effects that are used match the action on-screen, and are the sounds we would expect to hear. However, contrapuntal sound is the opposite. It is music that seems to work against the on-screen action and therefore creates new meanings for the audience.

Musical motifs

A film often repeats a section of the score, at various moments within the film, called a **musical motif** and this indicates to the audience that the action on-screen is particularly important to the overall narrative or central theme. Most of you will be aware of the use of the Bond theme tune and when this plays in the film the audience can be assured that something particularly cool and exciting is about to happen. But *Slumdog Millionaire* also has a repeated refrain of music, a softer, gentler section that is used in moments of calm, usually when Jamal sees or thinks about Latika, as the whole purpose of his actions throughout the film is to find her.

Task 2.10

Pick a sequence from one of your close study films where you have noticed lots of different kinds of sound. Then answer the following questions:

1. How is diegetic sound used to inform you about the narrative and to create atmosphere or emotion? You should use the key terms ambient sound, dialogue and sound effects in your answer.

2. Then consider the non-diegetic sound. Discuss the music and how it works alongside the diegetic sound to enhance it, or maybe to make the scene more emotional or dramatic. Where does the music become more important? What effect does it have on us when it speeds up or when it slows down or softens? Does it help to move the narrative on or covey important things about particular characters? Trace the music throughout the sequence and consider how it develops alongside the action.

'Let's have fun' (Whiplash, 2014, Damien Chazelle).

Part 2: Film form

Editing

Basically, editing is the process of cutting all of the different shots that have been filmed in order to make a package of shots that then create the narrative. Editing is the most important part of the filmmaking process because it is where the filmed material is put in order and meaning is made. Filmmakers do not film in sequential order, they may film all of one character's scenes at once because of other commitments the actor may have. And, of course, if the beginning and ending are set in New Zealand, and the remainder of the film is set in Europe, these sections will be filmed at the same time or it would cost a fortune in flights.

Of course, it is not as simple as sticking it all back together in order. You need to be able to discuss the different editing processes and the impact these choices have on the audience's reading of events.

Type of edit	Speed of edit	Style of edit
Straight cut	Fast paced	Continuity
Fade	Slow paced	Graphic match
Dissolve		Cross-cutting
Wipe		Montage
Jump cut		

Terminology toolkit

Types of edit

The most common transition in editing is the **straight cut**. The straight cut is designed not to be noticed. It doesn't draw our attention to the cut but usually takes us smoothly from one image to the next. The straight cut is one element used in what is referred to as **continuity editing**. Continuity editing became very popular during the Hollywood studio era and is the most common form of editing in film today. It allows the narrative to be read in a continuous way, without interruption, so it creates a feeling of realism, drawing the audience into the story. The use of the **shot-reverse-shot** is another technique used as a principle of continuity editing for similar reasons.

Key terms

Straight cut
A smooth cut between one shot and the next.

Continuity editing
Editing that appears 'seamless', producing a flow to the narrative.

Shot-reverse-shot
A convention for showing dialogue that gives the audience the feeling that they are watching the conversation in a 'real-life' way.

'Ouch' (E.T. the Extra-Terrestrial).

GCSE Film Studies

'Ouch' (E.T. the Extra-Terrestrial).

Key terms

Fade
Where a shot gradually turns black or white.

Dissolve
An editing technique that creates a gradual transition from one image to another. Often used to connect the images in some way.

A **fade** edit is when the screen fades to black, or sometimes white (more often used to signify a character is fading out of consciousness). This fade signifies an ending of some sort. Informing the audience that another part of the narrative is coming into play, or that a change of setting is about to occur. The **dissolve**, however, maintains a certain level of connection, as the shot blends into another shot.

A dissolve shows the Spirit bird watching over Molly (Rabbit-proof Fence).

Key terms

Wipe
A type of film transition where one shot replaces another by travelling from one side of the frame to another or with a special shape.

Jump cut
Is an abrupt transition, typically in a sequential clip that makes the subject appear to jump from one spot to the other, without continuity.

A **wipe** is used less frequently than other types of editing, as it feels so unnatural, so you are more likely to see it in a trailer or a film that is not worried about realism, such as a comedy.

A **jump cut** is a jerky transition that is quite abrupt and draws the audience's attention to the fact an edit is being used. It is therefore a little uncomfortable to watch and is often used for this purpose or within an action or violent sequence, as it shocks the audience. A jump cuts draw attention to what is otherwise supposed to go unnoticed so it can be used in strategic and creative ways.

**Part 2:
Film form**

Quick Question 2.7

When the bomb explodes at the beginning of *The Hurt Locker*, editing, including jump cuts, is used very effectively. See if you can identify where the jump cuts are and consider why this sequence was edited in this way.

Jump cut 'I can't get a shot' (*The Hurt Locker*, 2008, Kathryn Bigelow).

If you find there are not many different types of edits used in a sequence you are analysing, there will still be plenty for you to talk about.

The **speed of editing** generally correlates with the speed of the action and can often relate to genre. It is not by accident that *Skyfall* begins with such a fast pace, as that is the kind of action an audience for this film will be expecting. It won't be like this all the way through the film, as that would be exhausting and wouldn't allow for any narrative – which may suit other films similar to this, but is not what the Bond audience would expect.

Cross-cutting is an important technique used in editing to create dramatic tension. It shows two different things going on at the same time and this is a great technique for involving audiences in the action, as we know more than the characters on-screen – who cannot be in two places at once. The director of *Rabbit-proof Fence* frequently uses a sophisticated mix of editing, sound and mise-en-scène in order to make powerful points about the oppression of the Aboriginal children.

Key terms

Speed of editing
Refers to how many consecutive shots are used in a period of time. Fast cutting involves several consecutive shots of a brief duration (e.g. three seconds or less). It can be used to convey a lot of information very quickly, or to imply either energy or chaos. Slow cutting uses shots of longer duration (any shot longer than 15 seconds depending on context). This often has the effect of slowing down the action and allowing the audience to concentrate for longer on key events within the movie.

Cross-cutting
Moving from one sphere of action to another often for extended periods. For example, A.O. Neville in Brisbane directing the search for Molly and Molly's progress on her long walk home in *Rabbit-proof Fence*.

'As you know, every Aborigine in this state comes under my control' (*Rabbit-proof Fence*).

29

GCSE Film Studies

'Notice if you will the half-caste child' (Rabbit-proof Fence).

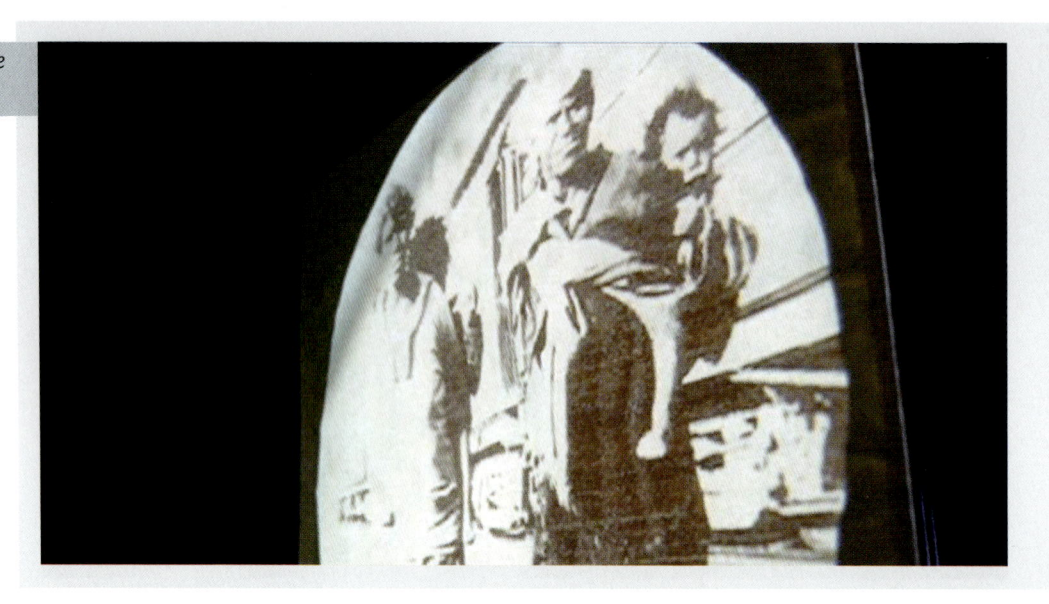

'Are we to allow the creation of an unwanted third race?' (Rabbit-proof Fence).

Key term

Sound bridge
Used to link two frames together, even if the setting has changed or the narrative action. They are often used to give a sense of continuity, to keep the connection in the audience's mind.

The shots above from *Rabbit-proof Fence* move us from one sphere of action to another – the Australian outback to the big city of Perth, yet the editing and a **sound bridge** that carries Mr Neville's words, 'As you know every Aboriginal in this state comes under my control', forces the audience to make connections between each place and its characters.

1. Look carefully at the three stills above. The sound bridge works with the edit to create a feeling of irony.

2. Use the sentence starters below to begin an analysis of the ways in which editing creates meaning and response in this very short sequence.

    (i) … cutting takes us from … to …

    (ii) By juxtaposing the image of the grieving women and Mr Neville, the audience is made to feel …

    (iii) Editing, sound and mise-en-scène work together in this sequence to create …

Task 2.11

Part 2:
Film form

'You are own your own Jamal' (*Slumdog Millionaire*).

Quick Question 2.8

Cross-cutting is used particularly effectively towards the end of *Slumdog Millionaire*, when Latika rushes to the television studio to find Jamal. What effect does this have on the audience?

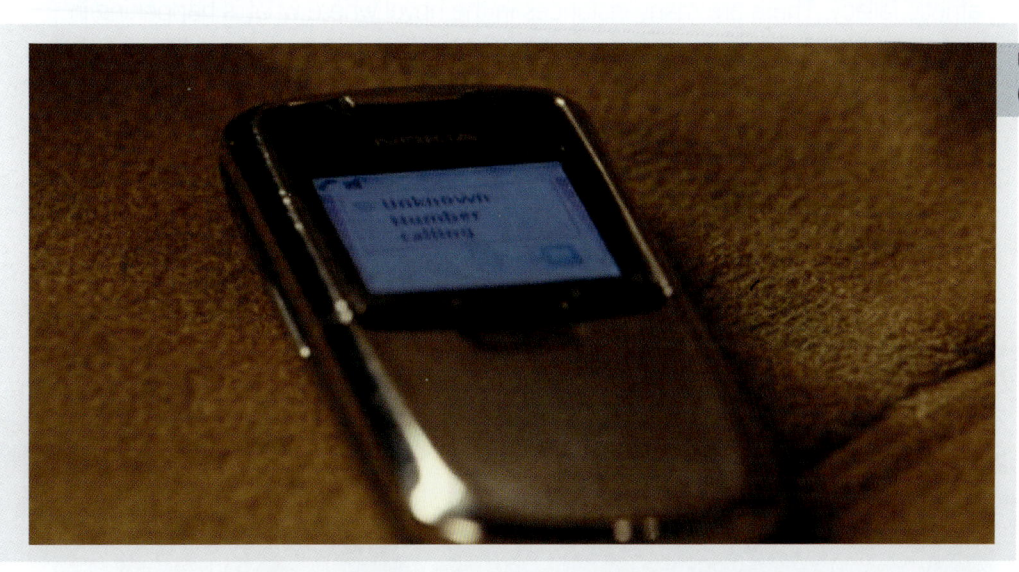

Unknown number calling (*Slumdog Millionaire*).

'Hello' (*Slumdog Millionaire*).

31

GCSE Film Studies

Mise-en-scène

Mise-en-scène is a French term originally used by theatre directors to describe the importance of everything that was put on the stage for the audience to see. In film it refers to everything that appears in the shot. So, it includes: lighting and colour, sets or location, props, costume and make-up, the positioning of characters within the frame and the characters' body language.

Although talking and writing about mise-en-scène can involve looking at each of the above elements separately, it is important to consider the ways in which they work together to create meaning. This means it can communicate in a similar way to the 'pathetic fallacy' in English literature. In books the term pathetic fallacy is used to describe the way in which an author can gives human emotions to inanimate objects of nature, for example referring to weather features reflecting a mood or an atmosphere. Emily Brontë's novel *Wuthering Heights* consistently makes use of the pathetic fallacy. There are many instances in the novel where what is happening in the natural world mirrors or draws our attention to what is happening in the narrative. For example, the 'violent thunderstorm' on the night Heathcliff leaves Wuthering Heights, and the stormy weather outside when Cathy makes a choice between Heathcliff and Edgar, indicate each character's emotions and their inner turmoil.

If you look at the following four frames, taken from the latter part of the opening sequence of *Rabbit-proof Fence,* you will clearly see how elements of mise-en-scène also create atmosphere and convey the emotional states of particular characters.

Quick Question 2.9

Look carefully at the two stills below. Describe the effect created by the separation of Molly from her mother by the car's back window.

Molly's mother chases the car (*Rabbit-proof Fence*).

Molly and the girls scream for help (*Rabbit-proof Fence*).

Part 2:
Film form

Molly's grandmother strikes her own head (*Rabbit-proof Fence*).

The mothers and grandmothers are left behind (*Rabbit-proof Fence*).

You may not have seen this film but a close analysis of the key elements of mise-en-scène will tell you much about the characters, their situation and the environment in which they live.

Setting

If we look at setting we see a dry, arid landscape where little seems to grow. It's a harsh landscape but the women seem part of it: their clothes are the colour of the dust. In the final shot they crouch into the earth like stones in the desert. Where they live and who they are will be important in terms of the narrative. The colour palette consists mainly of browns and dull yellow; even the trees look dry and leafless. As Molly's mother chases the car, we see the track stretching for miles beyond her. In three of the four frames we see a long fence that runs beside the track. The fence seems important; fences are used to keep people or animals in one space, or to keep them out of one. Is this going to be significant?

> 1. Write a few sentences analysing the meanings conveyed by the types of shots used in each frame.
> 2. Describe the emotional effect of the car's back window in the first and second frame.
> 3. Finish the following sentences:
>   (i) The low key lighting in the car creates dark shadows, this suggests …
>   (ii) The high key lighting outside creates a feeling of …
>   (iii) The repeated close-ups of Grace's mother's hand may be are important because …

Task 2.12

33

GCSE Film Studies

Mise-en-scène can also help to define a particular directorial style (way of presenting things). For example, Alfred Hitchcock often restricted the action in his films to a single room. This room would tell us a lot about the central character but it would also serve to restrict or contain them and increase tension (e.g. *Rear Window*, 1954).

Films such as *Slumdog Millionaire, Juno, Skyfall and The Hurt Locker* all have scenes that were shot on location. However, the filmmaker still wanted to be in control of the mise-en-scène and hence each of these films is quite different stylistically. The opening of *Slumdog Millionaire*, for example, with its high speed editing following Jamal's race from the police through the slums, intercut with bird's-eye views of the corrugated roofs and polluted river, is stylistically very different to the opening of *Rabbit-proof Fence* with its leisurely aerial sweep over the Australian outback. Both directors use real locations but the ways in which these are presented through film form are markedly different. The mise-en-scène in *Slumdog* suggests modern, overcrowded, fast, poverty-stricken, social conditions. The opening sequence of *Rabbit-proof Fence* still suggests poverty but also barrenness, isolation and a society that has changed little in centuries.

Often the setting of a film is established in the opening sequence but in a film such as *Skyfall* one of the audience's pleasures is the various cool or exotic locations that Bond travels to, and these are often presented to us in **establishing shots**. Set design and location are important in terms of the pleasures they can offer an audience. We may learn a lot about other cultures when we are shown the ways in which people live in other parts of the world. We may be transported to a different, fantastic universe or taken backwards or forwards in time. CGI can make this all the more possible and spectacular today. We may laugh at original versions of films such as *King Kong* (1933, Merian C. Cooper and Ernest B. Schoedsack), and think that *King Solomon's Mines* (1950, Compton Bennett and Andrew Marton) seems 'tame' when compared to *Raiders of the Lost Ark* (1981, Steven Spielberg) but it is important to remember that the effects used in early Hollywood films would have seemed as fresh, new and shocking to the audiences of that time.

> *Key term*
>
> **Establishing shot**
> A shot usually taken from a distance that typically shows where the film is set.

Quick Question 2.10

How is the setting established by the background details in this and the following image?

Exotic setting (*Skyfall*).

Part 2:
Film form

From the Souk to Shanghai (*Skyfall*).

Props, costume and make-up

Costume and make-up work alongside setting to establish time and place within a film's narrative. We may not have first-hand knowledge of what was worn in, for example, Ireland and New York during the 1950s (*Brooklyn*, 2015, John Crowley) but we expect the film to represent the characters and settings with a certain degree of accuracy. Odile Dicks-Mireaux, *Brooklyn*'s Emmy-winning designer, described the care required when designing costumes for Eilis (Saoirse Ronan), the young Irish immigrant who travels to New York.

> *Her journey is an emotional one … her looks helped to tell the story of a young lady who grows in confidence and embraces a new world. Her wardrobe had to reflect the very different worlds. New York was not touched by the Second World War, whereas Europe was. Therefore, when in America, I wanted her to look bolder and stronger.*

It's spring and Eilis blossoms into womanhood (*Brooklyn*).

> *By the time she got to spring, she was over the homesickness and met Tony. Therefore, I felt we could add some more color into her clothing. I used color to tell her story of growing up and becoming more of her own person. I tried to use it very carefully, not in a flashy way. I wanted the colors I used to be natural, what she would choose to go out and buy as she became more confident.* (Sharon Clott Kanter, '6 Georgeous '50s Outfits to Look for When You Watch the Movie *Brooklyn*', *InStyle*, 19 November 2015)

GCSE Film Studies

> **Top tip**
> Do not just identify a prop that you think may be important. Instead, explore what it might signify.

> **Key term**
> **Motif**
> A recurring idea or symbol in a film, e.g. dogs in *Tsotsi*, the spirit bird in *Rabbit-proof Fence*, water in *Submarine*, phones in *E.T. the extra-terrestrial*.

Costume, then, can work symbolically to give us clues about a character's narrative function or their mood. If we take Tsotsi, for example, his black leather jacket, worn during the opening part of the film, immediately signals 'gangster' and once this is signalled a whole set of expectations are set up about his character.

Props also give us more information about a character: Tsotsi carries a gun and could almost be mistaken for a young African-American gangster from 'the hood'. However, his necklace and bracelet signal the importance of ethnicity and the South African cultural influences on this character. He may initially be perceived as a gangster but there is more to him. He is not a one-dimensional character. Props and costume are important early on in *Tsotsi* in terms of establishing characters. Butcher has his knife and Teacher has his glasses and bottle – all giving the audience clear initial indicators to their personalities. In this opening sequence, several important themes are suggested by the repetition of certain **motifs**.

As the gang walk into the station, a high angle shot shows them dwarfed by a huge poster that states 'We are all affected by HIV or Aids'. In the foreground of the frame, which shows the gang on the football stand, Boston is being sick and top lighting picks out a similar poster to the one in the station spelling out the same message and another advertising the Lottery. These elements of mise-en-scène are important.

> **Top tip**
> Note down any recurring motifs that appear in your close study films and examine how these link with important ideas or themes within your films. Add these to your revision pack.

Tsotsi's shack (*Tsotsi*).

Quick Question 2.11

Contrast the interior of Miriam's home with this image of Tsotsi's shack. Mise-en-scène can tell us a lot about character as well as setting and narrative.
Look at all the different props you can see in the image of Miriam's house. What do they tell you about her and the way she lives?

Miriam's shack (*Tsotsi*).

Costume may be used symbolically, it may also remind us of the differences or similarities between characters. In *Tsotsi* Miriam wears traditional African dress, showing her pride in her appearance and her culture. Many students pick up on how Tsotsi's outfit changes from the beginning to the end as he wears dark colours at the beginning, then the warning colour of red and, finally, a clean, white shirt at the end, maybe symbolising his redemption. In *Submarine* (2010, Richard Ayoade), Oliver Tate looks and dresses more and more like his father as the narrative unfolds, highlighting the similarities between father and son, their personalities and life experiences.

Dad has been jilted (*Submarine*).

Oliver has been jilted (*Submarine*).

Costume is important in defining historical time, wealth and a character's situation. Bond's costume changes quite a lot in *Skyfall*, reflecting the different situations he is in, but his sharp suits are part of what we expect from this film franchise, so we will enjoy seeing his smartness resumed by the end of the film, even if he can't maintain it throughout.

GCSE Film Studies

When analysing make-up as part of mise-en-scène you may initially think about the way that it is used to make a female character more attractive. However, make-up can also make an actor look the exact opposite, by turning them into an alien or a zombie, or someone much older than their years. Make-up will work with costume to create a character in a particular situation. It can be important in terms of establishing time period – we all know how make-up and hair-styles can change according to the fashion of a particular time or place. If we think about G*rease* (1978, Randal Kleiser), for example (see stills below), make-up and hairstyle can serve a number of important narrative functions. It can signal changes in personality, innocence, sexuality and time period. It can also encourage certain moral judgements, albeit in a simplistic way, about characters and their situations.

Quick Question 2.12

How has make-up and costume been used for very different purposes in the images on the right?

'I'm losin' control' (Grease).

'Look at me I'm Sandra Dee' (Grease).

Framing and body language

Character positioning within the frame is also an important part of mise-en-scène. Their body language can inform us about relationships, emotions, responses to others and motivations. Every day, in social situations, we respond to other people's body language, the filmmaker uses our ability to do this by making sure we notice how facial expressions or gestures carry meaning. Often, key characters are foregrounded and/or shown centre frame. For example, we consistently see Oliver or Jordana in *Submarine* centre frame, in the foreground of the shot. Often they directly address the camera. This allows the audience an insight into their emotional world, what they are thinking and feeling, how they feel about each other and how they relate to other characters.

Body language and position within the frame can also show status. This may be more noticeable in genre films where hero, or arch villain, will have a strong stance and often occupy a large part of the frame. If you look back at the two frames on the previous page of Sandy in *Grease* you can see how body language works with costume and make-up in order to present two very different sides of the same character. In the stills below, Oliver and Juno are positioned at the side of the frame. Clearly, what is in each bedroom is important, the audience needs to see it, to associate it with the character, begin to understand aspects of their personality and their place in the film's world.

If you are asked to comment on mise-en-scène in a question you may be asked to break down your analysis into separate sections or you may need to look at all elements together.

'I think I'm pregnant' (Juno).

'My name's Oliver Tate' (Submarine).

Task 2.13

1. What do the different elements of mise-en-scène reveal about Juno's and Oliver's (*Submarine*) character in these stills?

2. Note down the similarities in terms of mise-en-scène between both stills. What might this tell us about each film?

GCSE Film Studies

Although elements of mise-en-scène are initially looked at separately, you must always consider how each area combines to create meaning and response. Ask yourself what is the overall effect of this scene or frame?

Mise-en-scène links closely to genre and its codes and conventions. Each of the pairings on offer for the comparative study focus on a different genre. So, for example, if you choose *Raiders of the Lost Ark* and *King Solomon's Mines* you will be expecting exotic settings, settings that trap the characters, stock characters such as the hero, villain (often identified as 'foreign' with some kind of scarring or deformity), damsel in distress and a quest that drives the narrative.

The best way to begin an analysis of mise-en-scène is to look closely! Consider everything you see but don't try to make meanings where there are none. Just break down all the micro aspects of film language and consider how they work, alongside the others, to create emotion, to reinforce genre, to reveal aspects of narrative and basically keep the target audience watching. But always remember, the films you are commenting on are films that may have been produced in different eras for different audiences. We may watch the *Invasion of the Body Snatchers* and fail to see what it was that frightened audiences or 'touched a nerve' in terms of what was happening in America in the early 1950s, but our study of context will help to shed light on common fears among the American people of 'invasion' by Communist Russia (see 'The paradox of 1950s America', *Invasion of the Body Snatchers* Case study, page 127).

> **Top tip**
> Always bring your knowledge and understanding of the film's context to your 'reading' of the images when considering mise-en-scène.

Invasion of the Body Snatchers: 1950s America and aliens are threatening the well-being of the American people.

Part 2: Film form

How film form is used: the structural elements of film form

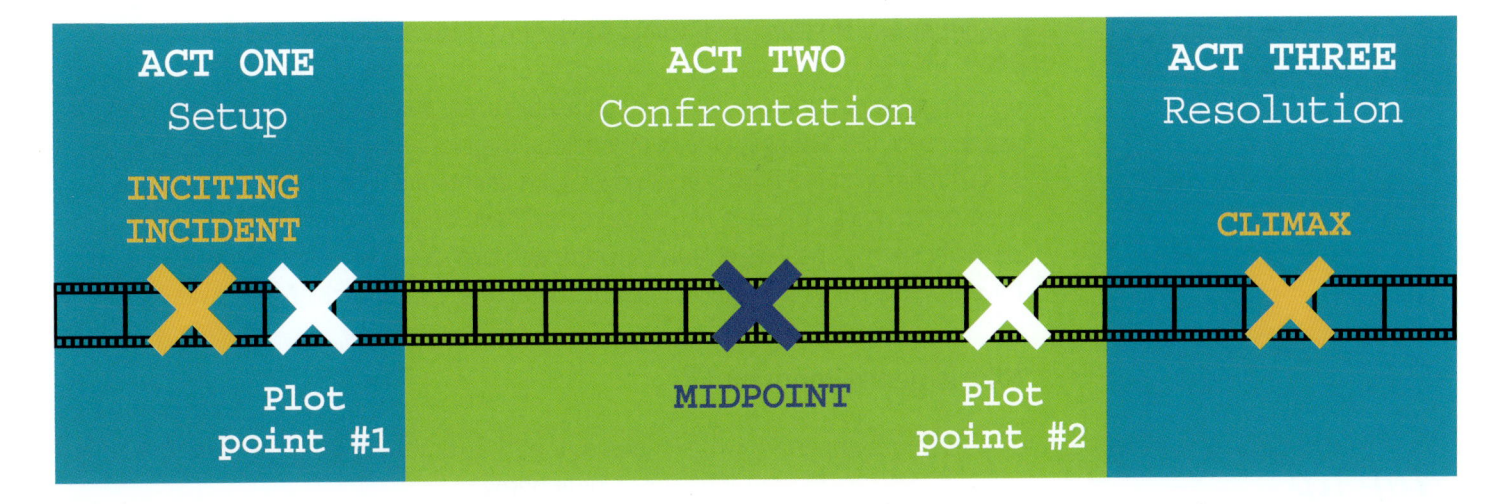

| ACT ONE
Setup
INCITING INCIDENT
Plot point #1 | ACT TWO
Confrontation
MIDPOINT — Plot point #2 | ACT THREE
Resolution
CLIMAX |

Once you have grasped the key elements of film form you will need to consider how they are organised into structures. This involves exploring and comparing similar or different kinds of films (genre) and thinking about the ways in which they tell their stories (narrative). You will also investigate the ways in which films may communicate ideas and issues (representation).

Often we remember films because of the distinctive ways in which a filmmaker has used film form. There may be particularly striking visuals created, evidencing a close relationship between cinematographer and director.

Jamal emerges from the depths (*Slumdog Millionaire*).

Sometimes the music (*Whiplash*) or editing (*Slumdog Millionaire*) leave an indelible mark on our memories. In this section we shall explore how film form can create a strong emotional response, how it is used artistically – its aesthetic qualities.

The films we watch or study are inevitably affected by the social, technological and institutional influences. In this section we will consider the ways in which time, place and technological advances may be reflected in the study films.

Finally, in this section we will explore ways of talking and writing about film by looking at a range of critical studies, and giving you the opportunity to develop your personal critical response to some of your study films.

GCSE Film Studies

Genre

Genre is a French word meaning type or category. In Film Studies, sorting films into categories or groups, and looking for similarities or differences, has become an important way of talking and writing about films, their audiences, and the ways in which they are produced and marketed. In English lessons you will have learnt that a certain genre of book will have a recognisable style, this will be conveyed through the words used, the settings, type of characters, the plot and perhaps even the colours or illustrations on the book's front cover. Film genres are signalled in a similar way; even before we go to see a film its genre will have been apparent from pre-production publicity such as posters or trailers. Once we have identified a specific genre we will have a whole set of expectations about characters, plot and cinematic style.

Why is genre important?

Genre is important when choosing the film we want to watch at the cinema or at home.

⬇

If it influences our choice of films it will also influence the kinds of films made. Producers need to know there is a market for their product.

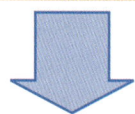

⬇

It has become a key way of looking/writing/analysing/critiquing films and how they are received by audiences. If films can be sorted into categories it becomes easier to make comparisons, observe what they have in common and where they differ or innovate.

⬇

It allows us to look more clearly at how films alter over time and to consider how those changes relate to social, technological and industrial changes.

> *Top tip*
> It can at times be difficult to 'slot' a film into a particular category, and it's useful to remember that all films are, to some extent, cross-generic.

> *Key terms*
> **Cross-generic**
> A cross-genre (or hybrid genre) is a genre in fiction that blends themes and elements from two or more different genres.
>
> **Codes and conventions**
> The detailed 'rules' of a genre – the elements of film form and structures we come to expect when we hear a genre name.

When we talk or write about genre we have to consider the areas that help us to identify a film. We 'test them' in order to assess whether they match our expectations of a particular category, or type, of film. These areas are known as its **codes and conventions** and most commonly include: setting or location, themes, characters, style, props or significant objects, narrative and plot.

Part 2: Film form

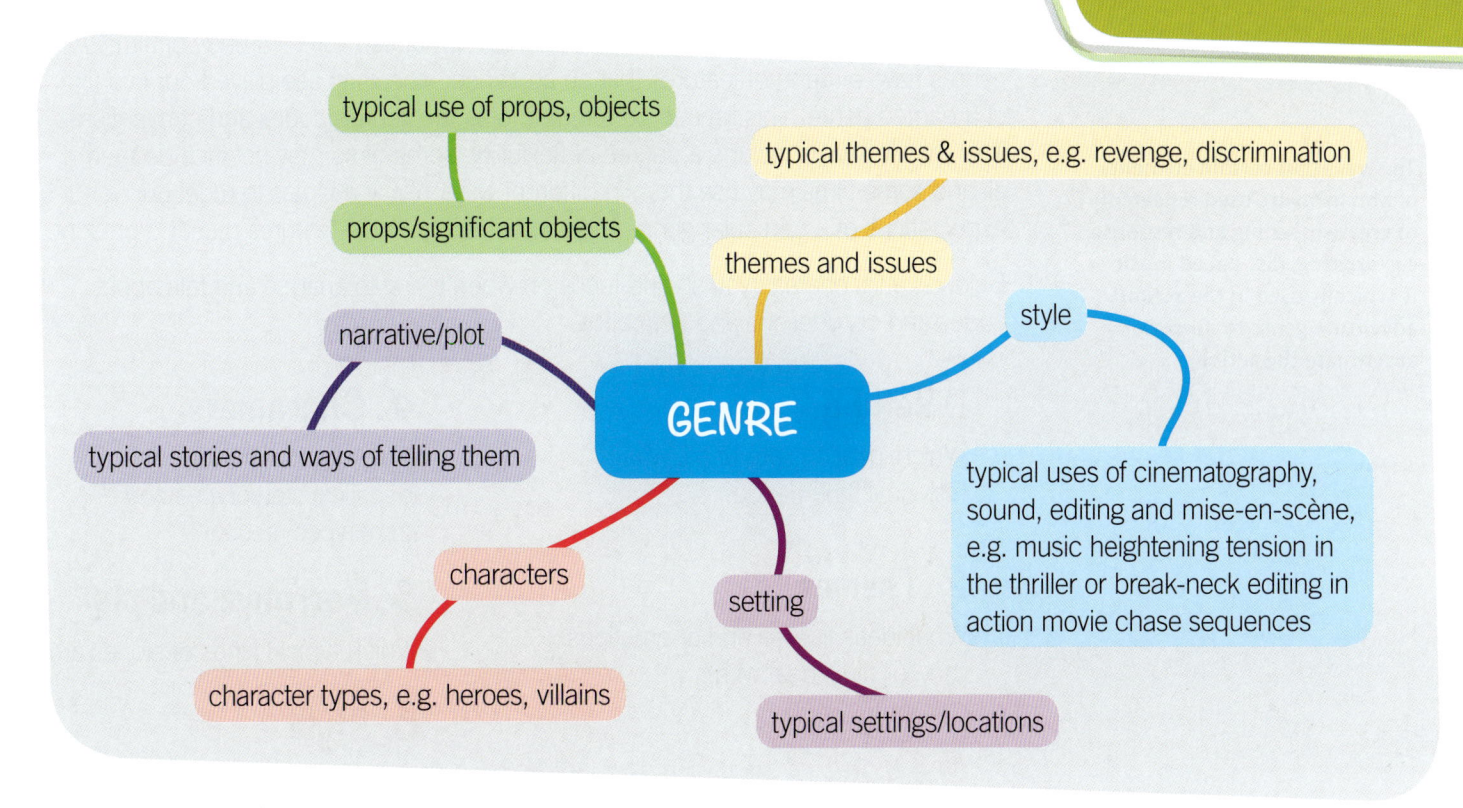

Genre mind map

- **typical use of props, objects** — props/significant objects
- **typical themes & issues, e.g. revenge, discrimination** — themes and issues
- **style** — typical uses of cinematography, sound, editing and mise-en-scène, e.g. music heightening tension in the thriller or break-neck editing in action movie chase sequences
- **narrative/plot** — typical stories and ways of telling them
- **characters** — character types, e.g. heroes, villains
- **setting** — typical settings/locations

Tracking typicality: investigating genre

The films you have chosen for your comparative study will enable you to focus on one film produced in Hollywood in the 1950s and one Hollywood film made in the 1970s or 1980s. This will give you the chance to think about and analyse the typical ingredients of the genre you are studying. It will also allow you to look at differences between these films and observe how genres can be seen to change over time, often reflecting changes within society.

Each pair of films for your comparative study deals with typical themes associated with their genre. Themes such as: the triumph of good over evil; love and how it can overcome any obstacle; crime and justice; teenage rebellion; and the fear of anything that appears 'alien' or different to us The pairings of films offered for the comparative study are as follows:

ACTION ADVENTURE
King Solomon's Mines and *Raiders of the Lost Ark*

CRIME THRILLER
Rear Window and *Witness*

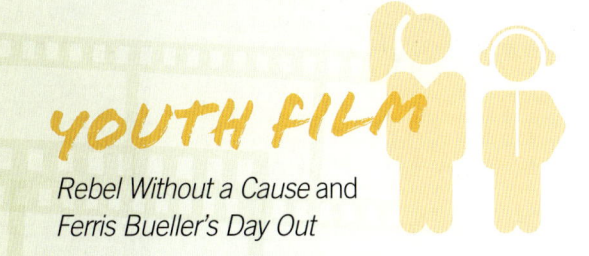

YOUTH FILM
Rebel Without a Cause and *Ferris Bueller's Day Out*

SCIENCE FICTION
Invasion of the Body Snatchers and *E.T. the Extra-Terrestrial*

Musical
Singin' in the Rain and *Grease*

43

GCSE Film Studies

> **Key term**
>
> **Typicality**
> The ways that certain elements of film form are used repeatedly to create meaning and response, e.g. exciting, fast-paced music is typically used in the action/adventure genre to mirror or accentuate the action.

When initially thinking about genre, we look for similarities across a body of films. All genres have a menu of features that an audience expects to see played out in a film of a named genre. This list can be referred to as the genre's codes and conventions. This list will always include a degree of flexibility. Some films may not include them all and some films may use them in different ways. Yet, if a film is to meet our expectations of a particular genre, then some recognisable features must be present.

Below is a list of areas you should focus on when trying to analyse and talk about codes and conventions and **typicality**:

1. Setting
Which locations are used, what historical time period?

2. Themes
What ideas, issues and/or emotions do your films deal with?

3. Props or significant objects
What kind of props or important objects might we expect in a film belonging to a particular genre category?

4. Characters
Which typical powers, secret identities, stereotypes and archetypes reoccur?

5. Narrative and plot
Which typical kinds of stories are told?

6. Style
How typical is the 'look' of the film? Here you should consider elements of film language such as mise-en-scène, editing, cinematography and the use of special effects/CGI.

Task 2.14

1. Look at the stills below. Write down the genre of each film.
2. Do either of the stills use typical characteristics associated with other genres? What might this tell you?
3. Note down the typical features that help you to identify genre in each image.

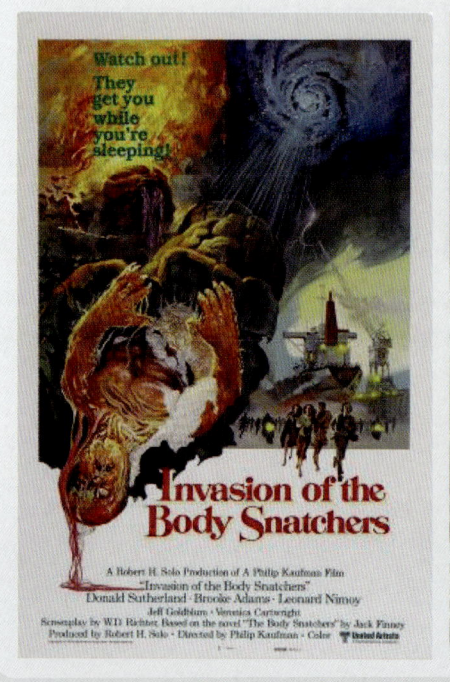

Part 2:
Film form

Typical settings

We commonly consider films in terms of their genre – the set of characteristics that distinguish, say, a science-fiction from a musical film (see posters on the previous page). We recognise genres by their narratives or their themes, their use of settings, and also by their **iconography**, characters and certain stylistic elements (e.g. lighting, camera style). As audiences, we enjoy the repetition of the familiar, but we also look for something new, a change from familiar forms. Often we can recognise the genre of a film very quickly; for example, the setting of a film often immediately establishes its genre.

Task 2.15

1. Look at the stills below. What genre is established?
2. Briefly outline what you think might have happened in the story up to this point?
3. What particular **narrative function** does each of the characters have?
4. Briefly outline what you think might happen in the story after each still?
5. If you can predict what has happened before and what may happen after, what pleasures will each film still be able to offer you?

Into the mines in search of treasure (King Solomon's Mines).

Into the mines in search of treasure over 30 years later (Raiders of the Lost Ark).

Key term

Iconography
A symbolic representation. It is used within film to describe the visual language of a film, particularly within specific genre. We expect to see certain objects on-screen when we see a particular genre; for example, in a horror film, we may expect monsters, haunted castles, gravestones and dark, scary woods.

Key term

Narrative function
The importance of, for example, a particular type of character to the ways in which the story is told and understood. The predictions we can make about their actions once we have identified what type of character they are.

45

GCSE Film Studies

The stills on the previous page highlight some key elements of the typical worlds created for the action adventure 'hero'. CGI and special effects are used to create settings that appear realistic but have a tenuous relationship with the 'real world' as we know it. Rugged, handsome Allan Quartermain in *King Solomon's Mines* and rugged, handsome Indiana Jones in *Raiders of the Lost Ark* are stereotypical adventurers inhabiting stereotypical worlds of the not too distant past; in this case the 1930s. Their exotic world is inhabited by 'savages', tribal witch doctors, devoted African guides and feisty females (who still need protection). These worlds have been influenced by storybook adventures of pirates and explorers. Audiences do not expect authenticity when they go to see an action adventure film; they expect other pleasures.

These exotic locations serve a variety of narrative functions:

- They give the central character the opportunity to demonstrate strength and ingenuity as they contend with the extremes of climate, as well as evil forces.
- They provide difficult obstacles to overcome before the 'hero' can succeed in his quest (usually for some kind of hidden treasure).

Jeff's neighbour leaves his apartment carrying a mysterious suitcase (*Rear Window*).

Quick Question 2.13

Look at the still opposite. Identify the genre of the film. Note down the elements of film form that help you to make this identification. What might you expect to happen in an environment such as this?

Task 2.16

1. Describe an important setting in one of your comparative study films.
2. Write a short paragraph exploring the ways in which the setting provides opportunities for you to find out more about the film's central character.

Characters

Certain character types recur across a range of genres. Typically in, for example, the action adventure or crime thriller our first impression of the main protagonist is that he's a fairly normal chap with a pretty good education and a fair amount of specialist knowledge. Indiana Jones is an archeologist and Allan Quartermain (*King Solomon's Mines*) in is an adventurer and elephant hunter (shame on him). Heroes in other genres, such as the superhero or science-fiction, may have more powerful, supernatural powers. However, these heroes have similar narrative functions – to save the world or solve the crime, save the girl, discover what needs discovering and to defeat the forces of evil.

Typical characters who battle against the 'forces of evil' take themselves and the twists and turns of the plot very seriously, even when faced with all manner of criminal masterminds, and strange creatures or machines. They also have helpers, frequently not too bright but invariably willing to aid the hero. These helpers often add humour and diffuse frightening situations. The heroine, meanwhile, can serve a number of different functions. She can be the love interest, the helper, the damsel in distress.

Task 2.17

1. Identify typical characters in both of your comparative study films.
2. Name the characters and sort them into pairs. For example:

   Hero – Allan Quartermain and Indiana Jones.
3. Create a PowerPoint presentation that explores the differences and similarities between the characters in each pairing. You should include comparisons in terms of costume, narrative function, dialogue, personalities and stars.

Style

In your study of genre it is important to consider our expectations in terms of the overall style of our focus films. This requires an analysis of typical ways in which elements of film form are used in particular genres. If we think about the action/adventure genre our expectations may include:

- fast-paced editing
- CGI and special effects
- music that recurs at key points in the action signalling a chase, a particular character or a climactic moment
- frequent close-ups of key characters or props
- high key lighting

The crime thriller typically uses:

- Close-ups of characters and props that give vital clues about a crime or criminal.
- Slow-paced editing, interspersed with short bursts of intensity often as the plot nears its climax.
- Music created to build suspense.
- Low key lighting creating shadows to create mystery about characters, their motivations and their environments.
- Cinematography that frames characters watching others from half-closed doorways, windows, alleyways, etc.

GCSE Film Studies

Characters watching from half-closed doorways. Samuel just keeps on witnessing things that he shouldn't (*Witness*, 1985, Peter Weir).

The crime thriller – Jeff is also obsessed with watching and it's going to get him into trouble (*Rear Window*).

Task 2.18

1 Research the following genres:
- science fiction
- youth film
- musical.

Create a bullet point list of stylistic conventions for each genre.

Genre narratives

Most early genre films followed the **Classic Hollywood three-act structure**. It is a very old method of organising a narrative, which is still widely used in storytelling today. It can also be found in plays, poetry, novels, comic books, short stories and video games. Hollywood has maintained its dominant position in the filmmaking world by using it. Audiences expect it (to a large extent). Of course there are alternatives to telling a story and increasingly cine-literate audiences like to be challenged, hence the popularity of films such as *Memento* (2000, Christopher Nolan) and *Inception* (2010, Christopher Nolan). So saying, the three-act structure is a highly accepted and greatly successful method of scriptwriting.

When looking for typical narratives within your genre films it is useful to 'test' if or how they 'fit' into the three act structure and then explore the ways that the filmmaker ensures they give new twists on old genres in order to maintain our interest.

Taking *Witness* and *Raiders of the Lost Ark* as examples, let's focus on **Act One** usually termed the **set-up**. The first act is where the main characters and the world they inhabit are introduced. There will also be some kind of conflict that drives the action forwards. At this point it's important to ensure the audience continues to watch, so a strong **hook** is needed. *Raiders of the Lost Ark* begins with an action-packed, attention-grabbing sequence that introduces Indiana Jones (Harrison Ford) performing acrobatic stunts whilst speeding through temples and underground tunnels in search of some kind of treasure.

Act Two is the **confrontation**. During the second act of *Witness*, John Book (Harrison Ford) and Amish widow Rachel Lapp (Kelly McGillis) engage in a brief courtship that fails to evolve into an affair. At this point in the narrative, Book also befriends many members of the Amish community – an event that **foreshadows** the resolution in **Act Three**, when the community comes to Book's rescue. As also shown in *Witness*, the second act may be a moment in which the hero leaves his comfort zone; this fuels the writer with another set of possibilities.

Act Three typically presents the final confrontation of the movie, followed by the **denouement**. This act is usually the shortest in length because the main character finally comes face-to-face with the villain or the problem. Some kind of showdown ensues and the action reaches its conclusion.

The third act is also when the writer ties up any loose ends and offers a resolution to the subplots. In *Witness*, the third act takes off when the corrupt cops find John Book hidden in the Amish community. The mandatory confrontation between the opposing forces takes place and Book and Rachel have to make decisions about their relationship.

> **Part 2: Film form**
>
> ### Key terms
>
> **Classic hollywood three-act structure**
> A narrative structure based on cause and effect. Occurrences are organised along a line of action and connected through a theme or themes.
>
> **Hook**
> An exciting scene early in the script that grabs the audience's interest.

Raiders of the Lost Ark: the final showdown.

> **Task 2.19**
>
> Test your two focus films against the three-act structure by writing three short paragraphs charting the main action in each section of the film. Begin each section with the following sub-headings: Act 1 The Set-up, Act 2 Confrontation, and Act 3 Final confrontation and resolution.

GCSE Film Studies

Key term

Dynamic paradigm
The word dynamic is used to describe something that is characterised by constant change, activity or progress. Paradigm comes from the greek *paradeiknyai* (to show side by side) and is used to identify a pattern or an example of something.

Genre – a dynamic paradigm

Here come the girls – singin', dancin' and lovin' in 1952 (*Singin' in the Rain*).

Here come the boys – singin', dancin' and lovin' in 1978 (*Grease*).

And now for something completely different (*Dancer in the Dark*, 2000, Lars Von Trier).

Although you begin your study of genre by exploring the typical 'ingredients' that help to define genre films, you should be aware that genre study involves so much more than a simple identification of the similarities between groups of films. We know that most films contain elements of a number of different genres.

Part 2:
Film form

We also know that two films we may have identified, for example as science fiction, may look and feel quite different from each other. Genres are constantly changing, adapting to and reflecting changes in society. Sometimes a genre film will offer us a completely 'new take' on an old genre (see *Dancer in the Dark*, opposite). Sometimes it may build on a nostalgia for a previous era and combine new ideas with conventional narratives (see *Grease*, opposite). Sometimes it can comment on changes in society and even changes in the film industry itself (see *Singin' in the Rain*, opposite). Whichever genre you choose to study, make sure you extend your study to include looking at these areas. Look for patterns within the films you are studying but also think of genre as 'dynamic', constantly changing and progressing.

Top tip

Below is a list of revision tips for your comparative study:
- Pick one or more key sequences from each of your films that feature important settings. Make notes on the importance of these settings in terms of narrative themes and issues. Compare the sequences from both films looking for differences and similarities.

- Collect a number of stills that include typical props or motifs. Label the stills.

- Create a character study for the key characters in each film. Again, note down similarities and/or differences.

- Devise a PowerPoint presentation, which explores the ways film form, especially cinematography and editing, is used to create a particular style for each film.

- Make sure you are clear about the context of each film:
  - when and where it was made and set
  - what it says about that particular period of time
  - how it reflects the differences in technology and society.

Raiders of the Lost Ark: typical props, setting and costumes.

GCSE Film Studies

Writing about genre

Film genre is an important concept for critics, academics, filmmakers and audiences. Films are categorised by their genre at every stage of their existence from pre-production (ideas, pitches and screenplay), production (funding and making the film), distribution and exhibition. Post-exhibition films are received and written about by audiences, critical reviewers and academics. Invariably, genre is an important consideration when responding to a film after its release or evaluating its importance decades later.

If you read through the short excerpts from the following critical reviews, you will notice the importance of genre in both reviews. Roger Ebert, who was one of the world's most influential critics, argues that *Witness* should not have been sold (billed) as a thriller as it was '*first and foremost an electrifying and poignant*' romance. He goes on to talk about narrative and the important central issues. Finally, he returns to genre, considering the body of Alfred Hitchcock's work underlining his importance as one of the world's most influential directors of crime thrillers.

His second review features Hitchcock's *Rear Window*. Again, the mixing of genres is discussed within the review. Hitchcock's directorial style is considered by focusing on how elements of film form combine to 'great beauty' in terms of visual story-telling. He also includes a consideration of narrative and audienc, acknowledging the ways in which Hitchcock challenged his audience by allowing them to '*piece things together visually*'.

Roger Ebert (1942–2013).

> *Witness comes billed as a thriller, but it's so much more than a thriller that I wish they hadn't even used the word 'murder' in the ads. This is, first of all, an electrifying and poignant love story. Then it is a movie about the choices we make in life and the choices that other people make for us. Only then is it a thriller – one that Alfred Hitchcock would have been proud to make.*
> (Roger Ebert, *Roger Ebert's Four-Star Reviews 1967–2007*, Andrews McMeel Publishing, 2007, page 861)

> *Within seconds after the credits, we know who James Stewart is, what he does for a living, and why he is confined to a cast and a wheelchair, all without a word of dialogue. It's extremely economical visual storytelling, and the great beauty of* Rear Window *is that you can notice such techniques while still simply being entertained. The film is so overflowing with suspense, romance, and comedy that it looks like it was the easiest, most effortless movie in the world to make. Hitchcock knew that audiences love to work – to piece things together visually, to understand relationships through editing, staging or camera movement, and that is why* Rear Window *is so captivating.*
> (Roger Ebert, www.rogerebert.com/reviews/great-movie-rear-window-1954)

Task 2.20

1. Download at least two reviews for each of the genre films you are studying. Highlight the parts that deal either with genre or elements of film form.
2. Write your own short review for each film, focusing upon genre and film form.

Part 2: Film form

Narrative

The way that the key elements of film form are organised into structures, genre and narrative, involves studying films as a whole. Although you will think about the ways in which narrative is organised and what it conveys in each of the films you study, your in-depth narrative investigation will be your Global English Language film (Component 2: Section A).

Below is a checklist of the main features you should be able to recognise in relation to your focus film:

- ✓ The distinction between plot and story.
- ✓ Cause and effect as a structural principle of narrative.
- ✓ Narrative conventions in screenwriting, including the three-act structure, plot points, inciting incident and climax (see 'Writing about genre', page 52).
- ✓ The role of character and character function (see 'Writing about genre', page 52).
- ✓ Themes and issues raised by narrative.
- ✓ How narrative generates spectator response.

Narrative refers both to the story of a film and the way that story is structured in its re-telling. A book is usually separated into chapters, but these can sometimes contain alternate characters' stories, or jump to a different time period. Film can do similar things through the use of editing and by using different narrative structures. Sometimes a voice-over can narrate parts of a story either from a first- or third-person perspective.

However, a film is perfectly capable of telling a story without a narrator: the combination of moving pictures, dialogue and music is powerful enough to convey complicated plot twists, establish background information and even provide insight into a character's innermost thoughts.

Top tip
When exploring narrative you should investigate the role of screenplays when producing a film. This knowledge and understanding will underpin your production work in Component 3.

Narrative terminology toolkit

Structure	Viewpoint	Theory
Linear	Voice-over	Binary oppositions
Circular	Restricted	Character types
Episodic	Omniscient/unrestricted	Enigma codes
Cause & effect		
Flashback/flash forward		

Story and plot

The narrative includes both story and plot. The story of a film includes the events within a film that are not shown but are still relevant to the events that we do see.
The plot of a film refers to how the key conflicts within the narrative are established and then resolved, so they are slightly different ways of analysing a film. Stories change but plot structures follow patterns.

GCSE Film Studies

Narrative structure

There are essentially three ways in which a narrative can be structured:

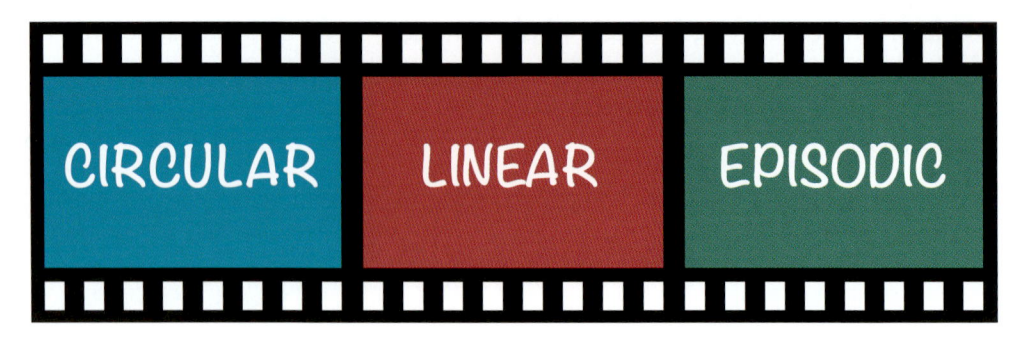

CIRCULAR   LINEAR   EPISODIC

> **Key term**
>
> **Circular narrative**
> A narrative that starts at the end then goes back in time to return to this point later on.

A **circular narrative** is a film that begins at the end. This might sound strange at first, but if you think about it there will be many films you can think of that start at the end and then use a series of flashbacks, or construct the whole narrative around one flashback; and then return to where the film began.

Slumdog Millionaire is a good example of a film that starts at the end, or almost. But it is not simply circular, the narrative does work its way through Jamal's life story from the end but it keeps coming back to the interrogation scene, so I would suggest it is both episodic and circular.

'I knew the answers' (Slumdog Millionaire).

'Catch it Jamal. Catch it' (Slumdog Millionaire).

54

Task 2.21

1. Scroll through the film of *Slumdog Millionaire* and look for the cut between present-day sequences and a story from the past.
2. Look at one of them in closer detail – why do you think the director chose this narrative structure and not a more simplistic one?
3. How does it affect the viewer's involvement in the narrative?

The **episodic narrative** structure is directly comparable to the ways in which fictional books break up a story into chapters. Often these chapters follow on sequentially but sometimes different viewpoints or aspects of the story are told in different chapters and these interrupt or disrupt the **chronological** flow.

Often, choosing an episodic structure can separate the audience from the film rather than bring the two closer, as it makes you more aware of the film as a construct. It can also be a stylistic choice to signify a director's mark on the film's storytelling. It can add pace or interest to a film that may otherwise be overemotional or simply too straightforward. It is up to you to consider why Danny Boyle (*Slumdog Millionaire*) chose this style for his film or why Phillip Noyce (*Rabbit-proof Fence*) chose a linear structure.

These films are quite similar; they both tell a story of childhood. Noyce could have chosen to show us Molly as an old lady looking back over incidents in her life, instead a brief voice-over, by what we assume is a very much older Molly, simply informs us that this is 'a true story'. The central focus is then on young Molly.

Directors choose different ways to ensure that the audience is gripped to the very end. We want to know if Jamal and Latika will be reunited and we don't find this out until the end. We want to know what happens to Molly and her sisters and it could be argued that if, for example, the 'real-life' footage of her as an old woman was shown at the opening of the film it would have ruined the central tension of it.

A **linear narrative** is the most simple and commonly used narrative structure, as it refers to a story that is told in the order that events happen: from beginning to end. These are sometimes referred to as **cause and effect** narratives, as the consequences of one event lead to an effect on something else and things move along in this linear fashion. *Song of the Sea* (2014, Tomm Moore) is a perfect example of this because of its 'quest'-based narrative. Ben has to follow all the clues, the songs, to help save his sister, and each forward step in the narrative leads him closer to the goal. The fear that she might not survive, that he may not succeed, drives the narrative forward.

Linear narratives make more sense to us, as it is most like 'real life', but within this structure there can still be flashbacks, interesting use of editing to compress and stretch time, and audiences may still be expected to work out complex plots.

Task 2.22

1. Take a well-known story, this could be from a film or just a simple story you know people will recognise, as long as it has a linear narrative structure.
2. Construct a new version of the story that is circular.
3. Try and create a version using an episodic structure.
4. Write these ideas as if you were going to pitch them to someone as an idea for a new film.

Key terms

Episodic narrative
A narrative that has clearly separated sections, often broken up by a title, date or by the cut back to a narrator.

Chronological
The arrangement of things following one after another in time.

Key terms

Linear narrative
A narrative told in chronological order.

Cause and effect
Something that triggers an event or action (cause) and the effect of the event or action.

GCSE Film Studies

Key term

Characters
The people who feature in the film's world.

Usually, the agents of cause and effect are **characters**. Characters – who may be flat or well-rounded – have particular traits (attitudes, skills, habits, tastes, psychological drives, etc.), which play causal roles in the story action and, as such, have a particular narrative function. It is usually a character or some characters that provide the causal drive in a film. For example, in *Rabbit-proof Fence* it is Mr A.O. Neville, when he orders that Molly should be removed from her home in Jigalong and separated from her mother and grandmother, who provides the causal drive. This then drives her need to escape from the River Moore settlement and begin the long journey home.

In some cases, for example disaster movies, the action is set in motion by particular events. Most of us try to connect events or actions in terms of cause and effect. We try to find out what causes a character to behave in a certain way. Sometimes, apparently minor details can, in fact, play major causal roles. For example, in the bar scene in *Tsotsi* we are initially surprised by his violent reaction to Boston, who simply wants to know his name. References to dogs also trigger violence and it isn't until later in the narrative we discover how these things relate to the powerful past experiences that had shaped his present. Filmmakers can choose when to hide causes and provoke curiosity in the audience. They often withhold effects to provoke suspense. Indeed, some films can deny us knowledge of causes or effects even at the end leading us to interpret the final scenes and what might come after them in our own way.

Task 2.23

1. Think about your focus films for Component 2.
2. Define the narrative structure for each one.
3. Write notes about the following as appropriate:

    (i) What difference would it make to the film if it had a circular narrative?

    (ii) Would it change my feelings about the film?

    (iii) How does the film manipulate time and space to keep me interested?

    (iv) Does the narrative voice in my film make it easier for more people to understand it? Would an episodic structure be too confusing or more exciting?

Narrative viewpoint

As well as considering how the narrative is to be 'read', it is also important to consider from whose viewpoint you are experiencing the story. A narrator can tell us which character we are meant to feel most connected to, the camera can also add to this by showing us relationships or events from their point-of-view, both within the narrative and literally through point-of-view shots.

Voice-over narration

Film is often talked of as predominantly a visual medium, but voice-overs can be an important narrative tool. For example, they can give the audience a much deeper understanding of characters, their motivations and their past or present experiences.

In *Slumdog Millionaire*, Jamal's voice-over explanations of the life experiences that have informed the answers to the *Who Wants to be a Millionaire* questions, work in tandem with flashbacks to narrate the story of his life.

Often, the addition of a narrator can give the impression of full disclosure or complete honesty. Sometimes it can create quite the opposite effect! For example, Oliver Tate narrates his own story in *Submarine* but humour is created by allowing the audience to see the contrast between his perception and what actually happens.

'Oliver Tate RIP – We Envy the Angels' (*Submarine*).

An omniscient narrator might give the film a literary feel, adding a sense of history and weight. Voice-over narration often makes the film seem more factually realistic, even though it's a device that distances the viewer one step further from their immediate understanding of the story.

Confessional first-person narration (as with Jamal in *Slumdog Millionaire*) pulls the viewer into the world of a character.

Often with first-person narration we only hear the character's voice at the beginning and end of their story so the narrative flow is not interrupted unnecessarily. Jenny, in *An Education* (2009, Lone Scherfig), closes the film by letting us know just enough about her future whilst holding on to some secrets:

> So, I went to read English books, and did my best to avoid the speccy, spotty fate that Helen had predicted for me. I probably looked as wide-eyed, fresh, and artless as any other student ... But I wasn't. One of the boys I went out with, and they really were boys, once asked me to go to Paris with him. And I told him I'd love to, I was dying to see Paris ... as if I'd never been.

Opening sequences frequently signal central narrative issues in films. *Rabbit-proof Fence* does this by giving us several seconds to read factual, contextual information.

> **Western Australia 1931**
>
> For 100 years the Aboriginal Peoples have resisted the invasion of their lands by white settlers.
>
> Now, a special law, the Aborigines Act, controls their lives in every detail.

The title sequence of *Rabbit-proof Fence*.

GCSE Film Studies

> Mr A. O. Neville, the Chief Protector of Aborigines, is the legal guardian of every Aborigine in the State of Western Australia.
>
> He has the power "to remove any half-caste child" from their family, from anywhere within the state.

What the audience needs to know about historical, social and political context.

The political, historical 'background' information is then followed by a sequence that gives us more contextual information about time and place. We are shown the nature and sheer size of the Australian outback via a long, sweeping aerial shot. A voice-over accompanies the shot, it is the voice of a much older Molly adding to the narrative information we have already been given:

> *This is a true story of my sister Daisy and my Cousin Grace and me. When we were little our people, the Jigalong mob, we were desert people then walking all over the land. About how white people came to our country. They made a storehouse here at Jigalong. Bought clothes and other things: flour, tobacco, tea. Gave them to us on ration day. We came to a camp nearby. They were building a long fence.*

Task 2.24

Read the information in the two frames from *Rabbit-proof Fence* and Molly's opening voice-over. How does the **intertitle** and voice-over combine to immediately evoke a sympathetic audience response to the Aborigines and their situation?

Key term

Intertitle
Printed text or narration shown between scenes.

The film ends with 'real footage' of a very old Molly who we are told was taken back to the Moore settlement many times, only to escape and begin her long walk home once more. There are several reasons why Phillip Noyce, the film's director, has chosen to include the footage. Firstly, the ending ties in effectively with the opening sequence. As the film opens we are given factual information, the written form gives it a certain weight. We are encouraged to read the narrative that is to follow in a certain way. Molly's voice-over emphasises that this is 'a true story'. The filmmaker is signalling that we should perhaps be shocked or surprised by what is to follow. The real-life footage at the end brings us back to the 'truth' of the story and the sight of the elderly Molly, who continued to battle against the unjust laws, evokes a powerful response.

Sometimes, in the most interesting cases, the world we are shown in a film, or the characters who inhabit it, can prove to be unreliable. *District 9* (2009, Neill Blomkamp), for example, begins as an after-the-fact documentary, confidently presented to camera using a style that appears to assume that the audience knows exactly where the story is heading. The narrative clues certainly don't hint at the fact that the nervous 'nerdy' character (Wikus van der Merwe), who is talking directly to the camera, will end up strapped into the cockpit of a striding cyberweapon, pulverising all who draw near! Independent films often subvert accepted or familiar narrative codes and conventions in order to create something new or challenging for an audience.

'Everything's fine. Right?' (District 9).

A director can choose to limit our knowledge of narrative events through a **restricted narrative viewpoint**. In a restricted narrative the audience only gets to know as much as the characters. This creates enigma and complexity, as we have to work out what is going to happen as the story goes along, just like the central character. This is a more common narrative viewpoint in horror or crime films.

Other films give audiences a god-like perspective. In these films we see much more than the main characters in the film. We see events that they don't and might be aware of others plotting against them. This is referred to as an **omniscient narrative**. Omniscient narratives create suspense rather than mystery because we know lots of aspects of the narrative; we are just left in suspense as to how the main characters will find out. **Unrestricted narrative viewpoints** are much more commonly used than restricted narrative viewpoints, particularly in mainstream cinema, as they are more satisfying for the audience.

> *Key terms*
>
> **Restricted narrative viewpoint**
> The audience only know as much as the main character.
>
> **Omniscient/unrestricted narrative viewpoint**
> The audience see aspects of the narrative that the main character does not.

Narrative time and space

What is drama but life with all the dull bits cut out? (Alfred Hitchcock)

Filmmaking could be seen as the representation of life but with the boring parts eliminated. Generally, if a film is to move, excite or surprise an audience it is important to remove all the 'dull bits' that could annoy them.

Read through the excerpt from the film script for the credit sequence of *An Education* below:

```
1 INT. SCHOOL. DAY

JANUARY 1962. MONTAGE

A nice girls' school in a south west
London suburb. We see girls doing what
girls did in a nice girls' school in
1962: walking with books on their heads,
practising their handwriting, making
cakes, playing lacrosse, dancing with
each other.
```

Now watch the opening sequence on YouTube (00:00:40–00:02:17).

Explain why you think the scriptwriter, Nick Hornby (who also wrote the screenplay for *Brooklyn*), has chosen to begin the film with a montage.

What do we learn about time and place in a very short amount of screen time?

Task 2.25

GCSE Film Studies

Micro-elements of film language, particularly editing, are closely linked with the manipulation of time and space within a narrative. Time can be compressed by creating a montage, for example, or stretched through the use of parallel editing, as in the final sequence of *Slumdog Millionaire*.

'It's my brother's number but ...' (Slumdog Millionaire).

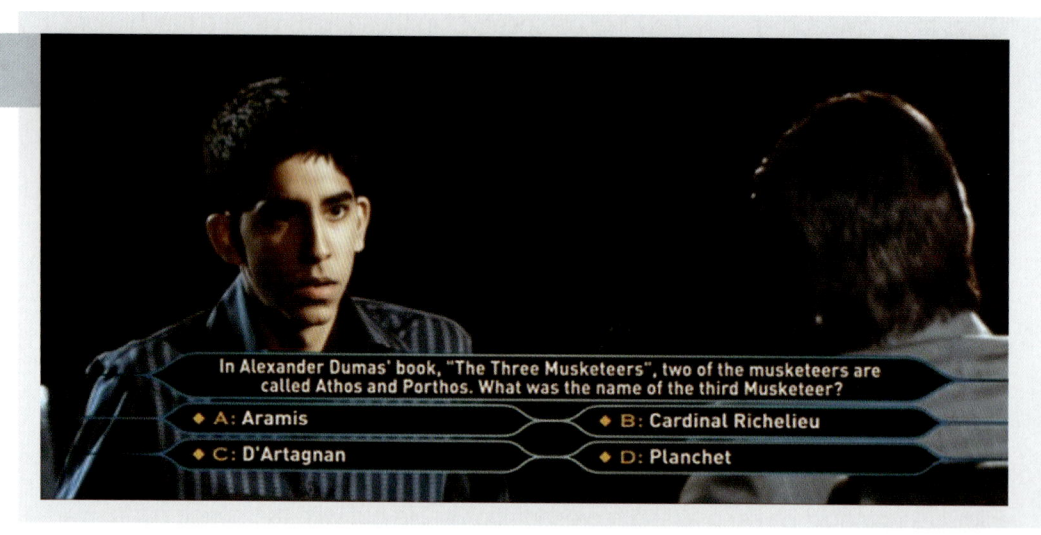

'It's my brother's number but ...' (Slumdog Millionaire).

Key term

Ellipsis
The most basic idea in filmmaking, it refers to the omission of a section of the story that is either obvious enough for the audience to fill in or concealed for a narrative purpose, such as suspense or mystery.

When we watch a film we accept that details are left out, we do not need to review the 'dull bits' as we are anxious to enjoy the ups and downs, the complexities and pleasures of the story that is unfolding. These gaps in irrelevant happenings and the moving on to a more exciting, relevant narrative time or space is referred to as **ellipsis**. Ellipsis is both a narrative device and the most basic idea in film editing. Ellipsis concerns the omission of a section of the story that is either obvious enough for the public to fill in or is concealed for a narrative purpose, such as suspense or mystery. It assumes we are an active audience. Producers tend to prefer a screenplay that doesn't include too much minute detail. In many cases they prefer a film that 'hits the ground running', such as *Slumdog Millionaire*.

> Watch the opening sequence of your global English Language focus film.
>
> 1. Write a brief analysis of the ways in which you are drawn into the narrative.
> 2. What have you learnt about the characters and their situation?
> 3. Are there any examples of ellipsis? If so what has been left out and why?

Task 2.26

Part 2: Film form

Narrative theory

There is a number of key theories that can be applied to the study of film narrative, although they may not have been designed for this purpose in the first place. You may find them useful in considering how narratives work, but it is important to only refer to theory when relevant rather than try and force it into your exam responses.

Propp

One of the most well-known of these theorists is Vladimir Propp. Although his theories were originally written in the 1920s and refer to Russian folk stories, they have since been used in reference to many modern films in Film Studies.

Propp referred to eight main character types, the:

- hero
- false hero
- princess
- father (of the princess)
- helper
- villain
- donor
- dispatcher

Each of these character types has a specific role within the narrative: the dispatcher sends the hero on their 'quest'; the princess is the reward for the hero's endeavours. Sometimes, one character may take on two character functions, such as the helper and the donor are similar as they both help the hero in some way, but the roles are slightly different. The donor gives the hero something to help them, whereas the helper helps them along the way.

GCSE Film Studies

Task 2.27

See if you can apply Propp's character types to the film you are studying.

Wadjda – a typical princess? (*Wadjda*, 2012, Haifaa al-Mansour).

Latika – a typical princess? (*Slumdog Millionaire*).

Vladimir Propp (1895–1970).

You must also remember that a narrative can have various versions of these character types: there can be more than one villain in a narrative. Also, the 'princess' in modern narratives doesn't have to be a woman, just someone that needs saving. Various narratives from different genres have central protagonists who must achieve a goal by the end of the film and characters serve to either help them, or prevent them, from reaching this goal.

Obviously, you can't simply take a theory from around 80 years ago about Russian stories and relate it directly to every film made; however, taking into account social change and the difference in form, it is surprising how accurately Propp's theories can be applied to many modern film narratives.

Knowledge of Propp's theories about character types and their narrative functions can be useful in terms of identifying characters and thinking about their role within a film's narrative. Some movie genres, such as the action/adventure (*King Solomon's Mines* and *Raiders of the Lost Ark*), are built on identical character types and their narrative quests, to the extent that we feel cheated if they don't appear. Undoubtedly, audiences often look for a strong hero character to engage with and a villain to provide conflict and tension. The ability to recognise a character's purpose in the story can allow a clearer understanding of the plot and characters.

However, be careful, identifying a character as hero or villain doesn't really tell us much about motivations or issues. Many of the films you are studying contain complex characters in challenging situations. They resist stereotypical identifications, they may change and grow, and defy our expectations. So do not try to force complex characters or narratives into a one-size-fits-all list of Propp's character types or narrative structure.

Todorov

Tzvetan Todorov, was a Bulgarian academic, identified three basic stages in a narrative.

1. The equilibrium – the state of balance in the narrative, where we get to know the characters and their situation.

2. The dis-equilibrium – where the disruption to this balance occurs that leads to the main action of the narrative.

3. The new equilibrium – the problem is solved and harmony is resolved; although things may have changed.

Tzvetan Todorov (1939–2017).

Task 2.28

1. Compare the opening sequence with the closing sequence in your chosen film.
2. Can you identify the disequilibrium and the central conflict?
3. Does the ending resolve these conflicts and establish a new equilibrium? How is this achieved?

Lévi-Strauss

Claude Lévi-Strauss devised a series of *binary oppositions*, which he suggested were the basis of conflict in narratives. He based his research around myths and legends, but again they are often used in studies of film narratives. These oppositions include:

Male v **Female**

Individual v **Community**

Peace v **WAR**

Barthes

Roland Barthes suggested five narrative codes that can be related to films, including the code of enigma and the action code.

Action codes are when the use of a prop suggests a particular action to the audience. So for example, if we see someone packing a suitcase – this action code suggests the character is leaving. If they are loading a gun, they are just going to threaten or kill someone.

Enigma codes are aspects of the narrative that create questions, puzzles for the viewer to solve – who is that? Why did that character react like that?

Key terms

Action codes
Significant events that move the narrative on in a particular direction, e.g. Mr Neville's phone call to the police in Jigalong to take Molly, Gracie and Daisy to the River Moore settlement.

Engima codes
Questions or puzzles posed that invite/encourage an audience to become involved with a film, curious as to what will happen next, they also help to move on the narrative.

GCSE Film Studies

Task 2.29

Many narratives employ action and enigma codes – enigma codes are more often seen in the opening – to keep you interested, and action codes are normally in a scene where something is about to happen.

With this in mind, analyse a scene in the middle and in the beginning of your chosen film and make notes on the action and enigma codes used.

Alternative narratives

There have been filmmakers throughout film history that have rejected the kinds of narrative structures discussed above. Rather than making films with *mainstream* narrative structures they have created films that have used new, alternative techniques, which mean stories are told in a totally different way.

Anti-narrative films, such as some of those created by the French director, Jean-Luc Goddard, provide audiences with films that have narratives with no sense of chronology and little sense of realism. Anti-narrative film makers suggest audiences of mainstream films are passive and absorb messages from films that uphold values that should be challenged.

Soviet montage cinema uses editing and camera work **symbolically**, so rather than images following each other in narrative order, they would be cut together to create meaning. Shots could even be repeated.

Surrealism and **expressionism** are other **movements** in film that have considered alternative ways of looking at narrative, but these are aspects of Film Studies that we do not need to cover in detail at this point. What is very important for you to know is that these different movements in film have influenced many films that audiences enjoy within mainstream cinema today. Film director, Terry Gilliam, for example, uses many ideas from surrealist films, and Tim Burton often uses techniques and images first seen in **German expressionism** back in the 1920s.

Planning a narrative analysis

Below is a list of key narrative areas to consider. As you study your focus film, create a bank of revision notes for each area. Make sure you also identify particular sequences that evidence/reinforce your ideas.

- Structure: how is the narrative organised and structured?
- Characters: how are characters delineated? What is their narrative function? How are heroes and villains created?
- Audience: where is the audience positioned in relation to the narrative?
- Themes: what are the major themes of the narrative? What values/**ideologies** does it embody?
- Film form: what is the role of such features as sound, cinematography, mise-en-scène and editing within the narrative.

Key term

Symbolically
A mark, sign or word that indicates, signifies or is understood as representing an idea, object or relationship, e.g. In *Rabbit-proof Fence* the hawk symbolises freedom and the spirit world.

German expressionism
A film movement originating in Germany just after World War I, using mise-en-scène to express the inner thoughts or emotions of particular characters or their situations.

Key term

Ideologies
A collection of beliefs held by an individual, group or society.

Part 2:
Film form

How is film form used?

This section looks at how films can be used as a way of communicating ideas and issues artistically (its **aesthetic** qualities). Each of the films you have studied, or are about to study on this course have been chosen because they present contrasting social and cultural film worlds. They offer a wide variety of representations of different people and places. The ways in which they present important ideas about, for example, gender, ethnicity, age or different cultures may reflect the social, cultural or political context in which they were made. They may challenge the audience to think about groups of people and their situation in a different way. They can reinforce our particular view of the world.

Key term

Aesthetic
Concerned with beauty or the appreciation of beauty. Designed to give pleasure through beauty. Of, or relating to, art or beauty.

Representation

STUDYING REPRESENTATION

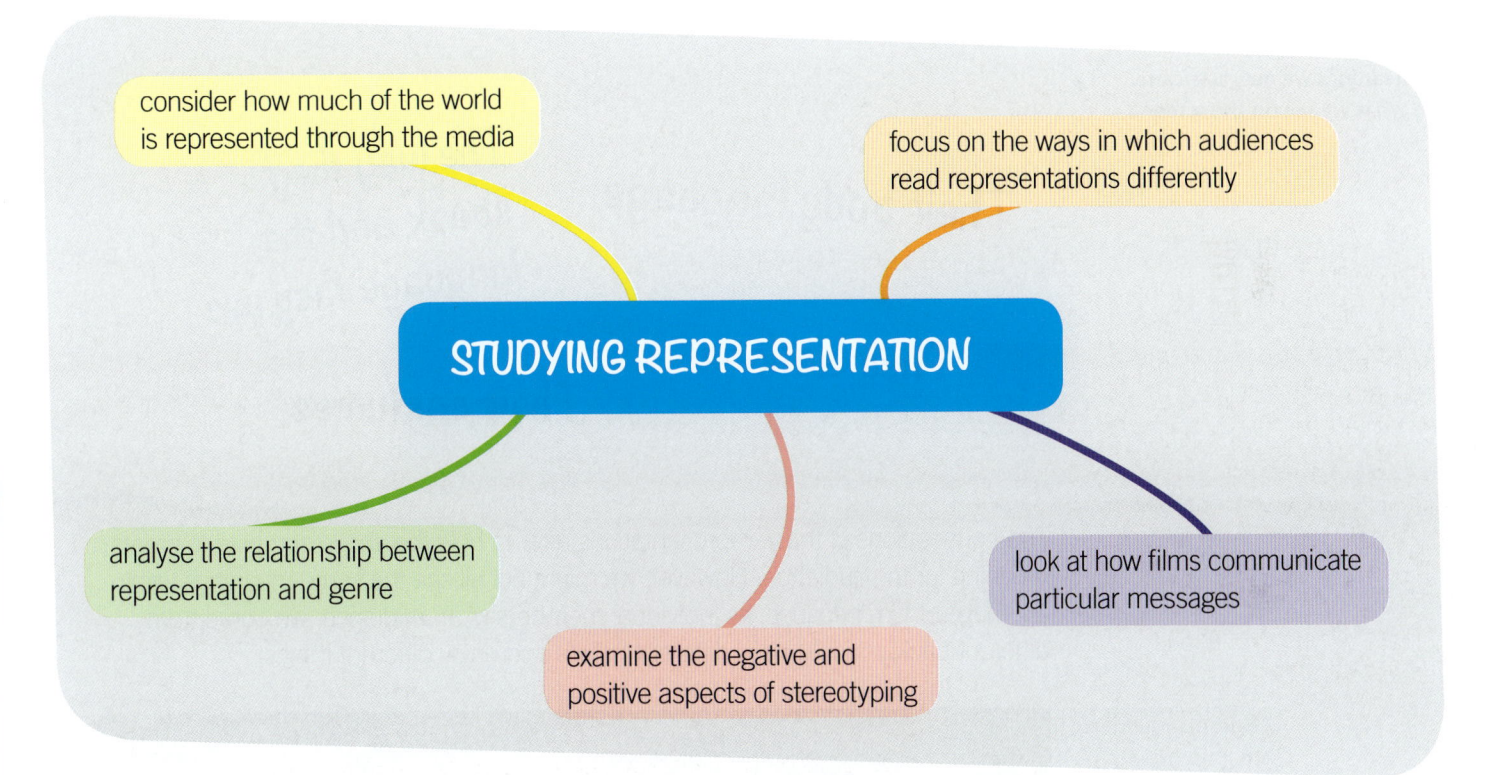

- consider how much of the world is represented through the media
- focus on the ways in which audiences read representations differently
- analyse the relationship between representation and genre
- examine the negative and positive aspects of stereotyping
- look at how films communicate particular messages

Representation refers to the way the world is represented to us in films – the images we are shown and the way we then interpret these images. Films communicate how characters in different situations behave and react, but they also carry messages relating to important social issues such as poverty, racism or sexism. In today's world, where we are bombarded by powerful media images, it is important for everyone to understand that so much of what know about our world has been presented through the 'eyes of the media'.

Representation is an important concept when considering how film can be used as a way of communicating ideas and issues. The images we view in any film are never simple 'pictures of reality', they always provide a point-of-view about what they portray. Probably, the first and most important thing to remember about representation is that everything we see and hear on the cinema screen has been created for our viewing and listening.

GCSE Film Studies

Key terms

Gender
What is expected of a man or woman in a particular society or culture.

Ethnicity
How people are identified in terms of their ancestry.

Culture
The customs, standards and beliefs of a particular community or civilisation.

Denotation
What we see on the screen.

Connotation
The meanings we may associate with what we see on the screen.

In this section we will explore the significance of different representations in a range of the films set for Components 1 and 2. We shall focus on the following areas:

- The ways in which different films offer varying representations of **gender**, **ethnicity**, age and **cultures**.
- How representations communicate particular ideas, values or messages about people and places.
- The ways in which audiences may read or respond to representations differently.

All films create meanings for audiences in different ways. Some of these meanings are directly expressed and others are implied. In Film Studies we refer to these two methods as **denotation** and **connotation**. In order to explore these areas in some depth you must initially focus on describing what you see on the screen at a certain point in the action.

Denotation refers to exactly what we see. The denotation of characters (see still of *Juno*, 2007, Jason Reitman, below) refers to:

Their body language

The way they speak and the language they use

Their actions

Their costumes

The connotations of these representations refer to how the above combine to create meaning for the audience. However, we might not all see the same meanings within an image or film because, as individual members of an audience, we come from different backgrounds, have different beliefs and enjoy different things.

Our introduction to Juno (*Juno*).

66

Part 2:
Film form

Task 2.30

1. In pairs, note down what is denoted in the frame from *Juno*.
2. Still in pairs, note down what you think is connoted.
3. Share your ideas with other pairs in the class.

Hopefully, you will find that there is little debate about what is denoted in the frame. However, we may 'read' the image, what is connoted, in different ways. Even if we have not seen *Juno*, our introduction to the central character, in the opening sequence, gives us many clues about her personality and her attitude towards the rest of the world. Her clothes suggest she dresses for comfort rather than style, the trousers, boots and anorak could be worn by males or females. Her body language suggests strength: she fills the chair, arms and legs spread out. She is smoking a pipe, she is quirky, alternative. Juno is not your typical teenage girl. She dresses in flannel shirts and baggy jeans and could not care less about make-up. Her body language conveys a sense of confidence – almost defiance. Juno defies the 'normal' behaviour for her gender.

The opening sequences of films can be very important when considering representation. They often introduce us to various characters and we may quickly identify specific character types. We may make a whole series of assumptions about central characters based on our first impressions of them – the gangster, the 'maverick' teacher, and the weak, vulnerable child who is lonely and isolated

Top tip
When analysing particular representations look carefully at what is denoted, describe it briefly, then discuss what is connoted. However, avoid looking for meaning where there is none. For example, the colour of Juno's jacket is not important, her prop (the pipe) is though.

Task 2.31

1. Watch the opening sequence of one of the following: *Tsotsi*, *Wadjda*, *Let the Right One In* (2008, Tomas Alfredson), *Spirited Away* (2001, Hayao Miyazaki) or *The Wave* (2008, Dennis Gansel).
2. In groups, note down the key elements of film form that help to create our first impressions. Once these key elements have been identified, discuss what might we expect from them as their stories unravel.

If you have already watched one of these films you may find that your first impression of the central character has been challenged, or changed, by the end. Rainer Wenger (*The Wave*) is seen as a charismatic teacher in the opening of the film and yet our sympathies towards him change several times during it. Likewise with David, the central character in *Tsotsi*, who is initially seen as a heartless thug, or Oskar in *Let the Right One In*, who is first seen as a weak vulnerable child. When representations are more complex, less stereotypical, they are likely to elicit different audience responses. We know what to expect when we go to see a James Bond film, or in many cases an animation. They typically feature **stereotypical** or **archetypal** characters. We are much more challenged by films such as *The Wave*, *Wadjda*, *Tsotsi* and *Let the Right One In*.

Films made outside Hollywood can often contain characters that are harder to 'read', they may challenge our assumptions about people or places. Films made in Hollywood are perhaps less likely to do this; certainly big budget genre films tend to contain stereotypical characters that are easier to identify and will act according to type.

Key terms
Stereotype
A simplified representation of a person, or group of people, repeatedly used so it becomes seen as the norm.

Archetype
An easily recognised representation of a character that has been used over a long period of time.

The representation of gender

Gender is a term that is often misunderstood. It is not about being male or female (our biological nature).

Pink for a girl and blue for a boy.

Baby boy   Baby   Baby girl

Gender actually refers to what a particular society, or culture, expects of a woman or a man. It is important because it can define: how individuals fit into different societies; how they are treated; what is expected of them in terms of how they look or behave; and what is considered to be normal or abnormal. It therefore links very closely with culture and ethnicity.

What is expected in terms of males or females changes over time in order to reflect changes in society. You will probably notice that the representations of gender in the films you are studying reflect these changes. Some of these representations could be seen to be stereotypical, while some are more complex.

As previously mentioned, you may notice a difference between many of the Hollywood films and the non-Hollywood films you study, especially in reference to representations of people from different cultures. You may also notice that independent films, or films made in other parts of the world, can offer less stereotypical representations of particular groups in society. In your work on denotation and connotation you will already have begun to explore what could be viewed as a less stereotypical 'heroine' in *Juno*. Even if you have not watched or studied the film you will already have made assumptions about this character along the lines of, 'She's strong, independent, challenging, does not try hard to fit into a stereotypical female role and in terms of the narrative this unwillingness to do what's expected of her may cause problems.'

When a particular way of representing a character has been used repeatedly over a long period of time it becomes what is known as an archetype. The Bond villain is one example of the use of archetypes.

Following is one critic's description of typical Bond villains:

> ### Top tip
> When studying representation it is important that you always consider when the film was made, the setting, who is making the film and what messages are being conveyed.

Part 2: Film form

Since the very first villain in Dr No, these antagonists have taken on many forms. There have been psychotics, megalomaniacs, monopolists, thugs, billionaires and master manipulators to name just a few. Usually with some elaborate plan ranging from world domination, global genocide, extortion, revenge or simply good old money and greed, it's always up to Bond to stop their villainous schemes. Sometimes adopting a very hands-on approach, stepping back and letting their henchmen do all the work, or full of deception and deceit, the villains are always adopting new and interesting ways to try and fulfil their master plan.

With super-human strength, menacing physical characteristics, lethal gadgets and evil geniuses to deal with, it's no wonder that some of the film's most memorable moments have been provided by the villains and their henchmen. (www.jamesbondmm.co.uk/bond-villains)

Sylva – the embodiment of criminality and immorality (*Skyfall*).

Bond, the physical embodiment of masculine charm – designer suit, immaculate hair and Aston Martin – what more could any girl want? (*Skyfall*).

69

When thinking about gender representations it can be useful to consider changes over time and/or to contrast alternative representations offered in contemporary films. For example, representations of men and women in *Skyfall* are markedly different to those presented in *Juno, Wadjia, Whiplash* or *My Brother the Devil* (2012, Sally El Hosaini).

Eve before 'the fall' (*Skyfall*).

Eve after 'the fall' (*Skyfall*).

Although it could be argued that the representation of women has changed over the decades, a 'Bond girl' is still very much just that. Audiences know what to expect when they see a Bond film, and even when a female character initially appears strong and self-reliant, she will ultimately need Bond (the alpha male) to protect, rescue and (providing she is young and beautiful enough) to make love to her.

If we look at Eve, for example, in *Skyfall,* she is initially shown as a highly physical, able agent. The opening sequence features her following Bond who is pursuing a villain. Eve's role is to protect Bond if possible. However, when under extreme pressure she crumbles, is unable to use her initiative and makes an error that could have cost Bond his life. This error means that she is given more 'appropriate' roles —initially as office secretary, then helping Bond to dress before he goes to the Casino, giving him a shave and fulfilling his (and her) sexual needs.

Part 2: Film form

Task 2.32

1. Compare the two stills opposite taken from *Skyfall*. How is costume used to convey Eve's changing role?
2. What signals Eve as a stereotypical Bond girl before her change in costume and role?
3. Look for an image from one of your study films that shows an alternative representation of a female character. Write a short paragraph describing how the character is shown (denotation) and exploring the connotations associated with the image.
4. Create a great revision guide by completing a chart similar to the following one for the key characters from each of the films you are studying in Component 2: Global film.

The representation of women in *Skyfall*

Character	Role	Costume	Narrative function
M	Head of British foreign intelligence, implied to be authoritarian, uncaring, untrusting and incompetent. Seen to make bad decisions throughout the film. By the end of the film, all the female characters have either died or moved down in their posts. All of the men have survived and moved up in their posts (except the villain, who basically doesn't count).	Well-fitting blue or grey suits (a little cleavage on display at times. Immaculate make-up and carefully groomed, short, grey hair. Shoes just high enough to signal 'femininity'. Towards end of narrative, wears heavy blue woollen coat, little make-up, flat shoes, signalling she is vulnerable, needs replacing and is in need of her protector (Bond).	Another weak or incompetent woman for Bond to finally rescue and put in her place. She is, as a result, suitably replaced at the film's end by the more reliable, old school ex-military man, Mallory. The only figure of female autonomy is gone, replaced with the powerful, magnanimous Mallory (Ralph Fiennes).
Clair Dower	A high-ranking government minister who is jointly responsible for monitoring the work of MI6. Educated and articulate but easily overshadowed by her male counterparts, e.g. Mallory.	Her representation seems to suggest she really has no place in a man's world. She may have reached a certain position by virtue of her age but is found to be lacking what is needed in order to control effectively. She may have been given a key government role but in the end the challenges facing society can only be tackled by strong.	Another woman who clearly is not competent enough to carry out an important/powerful role in society. Like M, she represents an overzealous incomprehension of the way that power really works and also needs Mallory (see above) to put her back in her place.
Eve	Initially a secret agent, she fails miserably in opening sequence and is relegated to office duty. Works her way 'up' to Bond's helper when staking out the Casino. Knows her place, helps him to maintain his appearance. Decides her talents are more fitting for a desk job.	As an agent, wears combat trousers and jacket over strategically unbuttoned dark shirt, desert boots. As an office worker, pencil skirt, high heels, strategically unbuttoned shirt. In Casino, expensive, tightly fitting long dress.	Demonstrates women should really leave all the action up to men. A love interest, attractive casino mate, barber, secretary and so on. Bond's end reward for being so strong, clever, sexy, etc., etc.

71

The representation of ethnicity and culture

An important way in which people are identified is in terms of their ancestry. For example, where their parents or grandparents were born and their shared social experiences – what they eat, their religion, dress and physical appearance. The term ethnicity can also be used to refer to a race, people or nation. Several of the films you will have a chance to study during this course deal specifically with issues of culture, gender, age and ethnicity. It is important to remember when watching and studying these films that the ways in which we were brought up, our own experiences and cultural beliefs will affect the ways in which we respond to these films.

So, for example, a young aboriginal girl may respond quite differently to the issues raised in *Rabbit-proof Fence*. She will probably have a clear understanding of the importance of the spirit world to her culture and recognise the symbols and sounds associated with it. These elements of her culture may seem quite strange or unusual to a young British viewer who may 'read' the film in a quite different way. Because of this unfamiliarity it is particularly important to consider how the key areas of age, gender, culture and ethnicity are represented. The consideration of different ways in which audiences may respond to a film is referred to as 'reading' in Film Studies.

'My father was a white man working on that fence. The white people call me half-caste' (Rabbit-proof Fence).

Opening sequences are often important in establishing ideas or issues about ethnicity and specific cultures. In *Rabbit-proof Fence* the representation of setting and characters conveys a strong sense of a culture that may be unfamiliar to a European audience.

There are two equally important elements in the film's opening sequence, the setting and Molly the central character:

The Aboriginal voices chanting over the credits, conveys a feeling of 'otherness'.

Part 2: Film form

The cinematography and sound work together to create an unfamiliar, mystical world, where nature is viewed as a sacred and powerful force. The aerial shot, which opens the film, travels over and looks down upon the vast, dry landscape of Western Australia. We see no houses or roads; simply mile after mile of bush land.

Eventually, the camera pans down to reveal a dirt track and a few small buildings, then cuts to a mid-shot of Molly. She is not shown as separate from her environment, an example of civilisation, she appears to be just one element of the natural world, framed by the trees and sky, her eyes shining as she smiles and watches an eagle circling above her. Later, her mother tells her the eagle is a 'spirit bird' that will protect her where-ever she goes.

> 1. Watch the opening sequence of either: *Tsotsi, The Wave, Wadjda, Spirited Away* or *Let the Right One In*.
> 2. Write a short analysis of how two of the key elements of film language combine to convey ideas about culture or ethnicity.

Task 2.33

Top tip

Whenever you are analysing representation, use the following questions as a guide for your answer:
1. Who or what is being represented?
2. What is happening? Is the activity presented as typical or atypical (not the kind of thing you would expect to see)?
3. Where are the characters? How are they framed? Are their surroundings natural or artificial? What is in the background and/or the **foreground**?
4. What do costume, make-up, dialogue and body language tell you about the character?
5. What do we see in the setting? What does it tell us about characters or their situation? Does it link to important themes or issues in the film?

The term culture is notoriously difficult to define. For example, many of us refer to ourselves as British, as being part of a British culture. Dig a little deeper though and you may find that we may all have very different ideas of what our culture is. We may have shared beliefs but we don't all act in the same way, have the same likes and dislikes, follow the same religion or have the same political views.

As mentioned earlier, because we are individuals, we all react slightly differently to the films we watch. If your reaction to a film is broadly similar to others who have seen it, and you understand or agree with the ideas that the filmmaker seems to be trying to convey, you are said to have a **preferred reading** of the film. If you agree with some of the filmmaker's points but not others, then you are giving a **negotiated reading**. If you really disagree with what the filmmaker seems to be saying then you have an **oppositional reading**.

Key terms

Foreground
The front of the frame.

Preferred reading
When the spectator understands and largely agrees with the messages and values evident in a film.

Negotiated reading
When a spectator agrees with some but not all messages and values in film.

Oppositional reading
When a spectator disagrees with or dislikes a film's messages or values.

GCSE Film Studies

Task 2.34 Read through the following three excerpts from critical reviews of *Skyfall*. Decide what kind of 'reading' the critic is giving in each review?

The 50th anniversary of the big-screen Bond was the right time to pull off something big. Skyfall *is a hugely enjoyable action spectacular, but more grounded and cogent than the previous and disappointing outing,* Quantum of Solace. *It finds the right position on the spectrum between extravagance and realism his is the seventh time Judi Dench has played the enigmatic spy-chief M. But it is only in this storming new Bond movie that her M has really been all that she could be. Under the stylish direction of Sam Mendes, Dench's M is quite simply the Bond girl to end all Bond girls.* (Peter Bradshaw, 'Skyfall – Review', 25 October 2012, *The Guardian*)

Deakins certainly makes it all look good: the smoke and sunlight, fall-grey London and mist-covered Scottish moors, and Craig's hardened face in all its increasingly craggy glory. But throughout Skyfall *there's also a feeling of Mendes trying too hard, no matter how effortlessly the end result appears on the surface. Bond's wry quips and British-bulldog toughness seem forced, and the constant attempts to pay homage to the 50-year-old film franchise's checkered past, with jokes about exploding pens and ejector seats, feel like pandering, winking distractions.* (Hammer & Thump film blog)

Skyfall is one of the most smoothly manufactured acts of purely forgettable filmmaking we are likely to see this or any year. I'm glad I took notes, because when I woke up the morning after seeing it, they were the only thing to remind me that I had seen a film at all. The storytelling, too, is locked away in antiquity. No Bond ritual goes unperformed. No obvious twist goes untwisted. No **cliché** *goes unspoken. Instead of going to this movie, stay home and ask yourself what a Bond film with Javier Bardem as the villain would look like.* (Stephen Marche, 8 November 2012, *Esquire*)

The representation of age

Generally, it is relatively simple to analyse the ways in which age is represented in a particular character. It's a little harder when looking at a specific age group. Words such as young or old can cover a range of ages so try to be specific when talking about the representation of age within a film. It always helps to consider the filmmaker's intentions.

Key term

Cliché
A stereotyped expression; a sentence or phrase, usually expressing a popular or common thought or idea, that has lost originality.

Top tip

Here are some useful questions to bear in mind when focusing on how age is represented in a range of films:
- If a group of teenagers is shown, do they look and behave in a stereotypical way?
- Alternatively, are they shown to be individuals with complex personalities and motivations?
- Do their experiences change them?
- Do group dynamics change and how is this shown?

Part 2:
Film form

Task 2.35

1. Look carefully at the stills from *Tsotsi* below. Note down the differences in the way Tsotsi is represented at the beginning of the film and at the end of the film.

2. In the first still he is shown with his 'gang'. What do we learn about his status and personality? Give evidence for your ideas.

3. Is it possible to make predictions about the other members of the gang just from analysing the still? If so what are they?

4. What changes do we see in Tsotsi in the second still? What is connoted by these changes? Why do you think he is alone at this point in the film?

5. Tsotsi is about 17 years old in the film, what issues are raised about this character at this age? How are we shown the importance of his childhood experiences in terms of how he acts and what he does as a teenager?

Leader of the gang (*Tsotsi*).

A soul in torment (*Tsotsi*).

Top tip
Download at least two stills of key characters from each of the Global films you are studying. Make notes on what these stills tell you about the age, gender, culture and/or ethnicity of these characters. Use these notes when revising for your final exam.

GCSE Film Studies

The aesthetic qualities of film

Images that stay in the memory (*Slumdog Millionaire*).

There is something that might be called cinematic beauty. It can only be expressed in a film, and it must be present for that film to be a moving work. When it is very well expressed, one experiences a particularly deep emotion while watching that film. I believe that it is this quality that draws people to come and see a film, and that it is the hope of attaining this quality that inspires the filmmaker to make his film in the first place. (Akira Kurosawa, 'On Cinema on General', 31 May 2006, http://akirakurosawa.info/akira-kurosawa-quotes/kurosawa-quotes-cinema/)

In the introduction to this book we talk about film as perhaps being the most important, or influential, art form in contemporary society. The study of a film's aesthetic qualities involves looking at how all aspects of film form combine artistically. In order to do this you should be aware of the artistic decisions made by the filmmakers and be able to explore the ways in which audiences respond to those decisions. When exploring the aesthetic qualities of film you may look at cinematography – how individual shots are composed – and mise-en-scène in general.

Our response to a film is often shaped by the ways in which a film appeals to our senses – how it makes us feel. Often a film stays in our memory via a series of particularly striking images. These images touch our emotions; they may be beautiful, sad, moving or uplifting. Films may be influenced by others that have gone before them. They may contain many stylistic features that stay in the memory.

When considering how a striking image is created, you could consider cinematography. Think carefully about the shot – framing, the colour palette, depth of focus and even the different types of film stock used. Also consider mise-en-scène – how does it work to create meanings or touch our emotions? Editing and sound can also contribute to a particular aesthetic effect, which may only be momentary or may create a distinct aesthetic style to the film.

Part 2:
Film form

Abdullah and Wadjda: a forbidden friendship (*Wadjda*).

Look at the still above, taken from the film *Wadjda*. You may not have seen the film but the image is striking, it tells you a lot about the characters and their situation; it may also make you smile.

1. What do the props and costumes tell you about each character?
2. How is humour created?
3. Just by analysing this image, what issues do you think might be raised in the film?

Task 2.36

Aesthetics and popular culture

Sometimes actors can achieve a kind of **iconic** status and their images become an important part of **popular cultures**. You may not have seen any of James Dean's films, for example, but chances are that you will be very familiar with his image. Dean only starred in three major films — *East of Eden* (1955, Elia Kazan), *Rebel Without a Cause* (1955, Nicholas Ray) and *Giant* (1956, George Stevens) – but his tragic death in a car crash cemented his bad boy persona as a permanent part of pop art and culture. He died in 1955, yet over 60 years later his legacy still endures: his image and persona continue to inspire famous artists such as Andy Warhol, poetry, films, cartoons and hit songs.

Key terms

Iconic
An image, emblem, idol or hero.

Popular cultures
Cultures based on the tastes of ordinary people rather than an educated elite.

And man existing alone seems himself an episode of little consequence (*Rebel Without a Cause*).

77

GCSE Film Studies

Famous pop artist Andy Warhol's 'James Dean'.

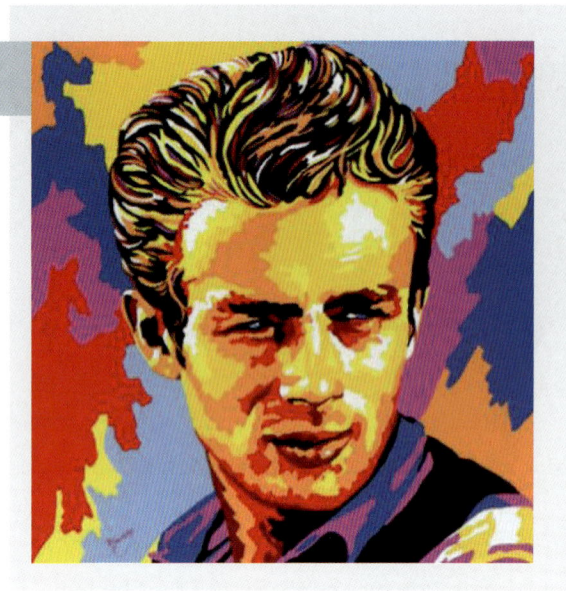

Quick Question 2.14

Note down as many actors as you can that may have influenced popular culture and/or have inspired other artists.

Popular culture also helps to keep particular sequences from films made throughout cinema history alive. John Travolta's 'bad boy' roles in *Saturday Night Fever* (1977, John Badham), *Grease* (1978, Randal Kleiser) and *Pulp Fiction* (1994, Quentin Tarantino) may have been influenced by James Dean's *Rebel Without a Cause*, but it was his iconic dance scenes in these three films that have struck a chord with audiences across the decades. You may have chosen to study *Singin' in the Rain* and *Grease* for your comparative mainstream USA study – both films contain well-known and well-loved sequences that have been handed down over the years through various forms of popular culture.

John Travolta 'strutting his stuff' and influencing audiences across at least three decades (left: *Saturday Night Fever*; middle: *Grease*; right: *Pulp Fiction*, 1994, Quentin Tarantino).

78

Task 2.37

1. Watch the advert for Volkswagen Golf GTI cars, which features *Singin' in the Rain* on YouTube.
2. The Volkswagen advert is designed to reach a wide audience. Which features target specific age groups?
3. What does the final slogan, 'The original updated', suggest?
4. In pairs, find two more examples of a film, film sequence or particular actor/character that has had an influence on popular art/culture. Give some possible reasons for their ability to affect our emotions and/or stay in our culture's **collective memory**.

Key term

Collective memory
The memory of a group of people, passed from one generation to the next.

You may not have seen the film but you'll know the image and the song! (*Singin' in the Rain*).

Undoubtedly, Volkswagen reached wide audiences with its rendition of Gene Kelly performing 'Singin' in the Rain', 21st-century style. The advert features the famous scene from the 1952 musical movie. Instead of tap dancing in the rain, Kelly break dances. This updated dance sequence, incorporating an original much loved sequence using the latest cinematic technology, is used to sell the new, updated Golf as a classic and iconic car.

Style and aesthetics

You will have begun your study of films by looking at separate elements that work together to create film form. Typically, particular directors and/or cinematographers will use these elements in different ways in order to create a specific 'look' to the film. Often audiences will come to expect a particular director to make films that they can identify as typical of his, or her, work. For example, a typical Hitchcock film e.g. (*Rear Window*) will use cinematography to create a sense of looking, or spying, on key characters.

GCSE Film Studies

Danny Boyle uses breakneck editing in *Slumdog Millionaire*. The film bombards the viewer with nearly 60 scenes and about 2,700 shots in under two hours. The overall effect created drives the audience through the full gamut of emotions at a whirlwind pace. *Slumdog Millionaire*, like Boyle's earlier *Trainspotting* (1996), has incredible energy; it takes off from the outset and never slows for an instant. Lively editing and thumping music keep the flow surging with incredible power. Boyle seems to bring this kind of energy to all his artistic work – think of the opening ceremony of the British Olympics.

If we view film as art then, we must focus on what makes a particular film aesthetically pleasing, what it has to say and how it has been received critically.

Task 2.38

Read carefully through the observations written by Bordwell and Thomas in the passage below. Then watch the opening sequence of *Slumdog Millionaire*.

1. In pairs, choose one particular image or scene that you feel has a particularly powerful emotional appeal (it may be unusual, beautiful or disgusting, and it may create a feeling of intense excitement).

2. Describe the part you have selected to your partner and explain how the effect is created.

3. Share your observations with the rest of the class.

Quick Question 2.15

What does the still below suggest about the childhoods of the young characters in *Tsotsi*? How does it affect you emotionally?

Tsotsi: working with the emotional beats of the story.

Then there's the film's slick technique. The whole thing is presented in a rapid-fire array, with nearly sixty scenes and about 2700 shots bombarding us in less than two hours. Critics both friendly and hostile have commented on the film's headlong pacing and flamboyant pictorial design. If some of Slumdog's storytelling strategies reach back to the earliest cinema, its look and feel seems tied to the 1990s and 2000s. We get harsh cuts, distended wide-angle compositions, hurtling camerawork, canted angles, dazzling montage sequences, faces split by the screen edge, zones of colored light, slow motion, fast motion, stepped motion, reverse motion (though seldom no motion). The pounding style, tinged with a certain cheekiness, is already there in most of Danny Boyle's previous work. Like Baz Luhrmann, he seems to think that we need to see even the simplest action from every conceivable angle. (David Bordwell, *Observations on Film Art,* blog, 'Slumdogged by the Past')

Lance Gewer, *Tsotsi*'s cinematographer, talked about the aesthetic that influenced his shooting style on the DVD's 'extras'. He underlined the importance of cinematography in establishing/communicating the emotional world of the characters in the film.

The cinematography of Tsotsi *lies in interiors, the emotional states of the characters. There isn't much camera movement, and when there is a move it's always dictated by the choreography of the characters and the story. Our work was more about keeping the camera quite still, exercising restraint, studying the characters and trying to get to know them quite intimately. We worked with the emotional beats of the story, trying to catch every nuance and implication.* (Rachael K. Bosley, 'An Angry Young Man', *American Cinematographer,* March 2006)

Gavin Hood also emphasised the importance of other artistic influences when making a film.

> *When people heard what* Tsotsi *was about, a number of them said, 'You should shoot it like* City of God,' *but stylistically our film is closer to* Central Station, *more of a one-on-one relationship movie. We needed to get the audience right into Tsotsi's mind, and he's initially somebody most viewers feel is very different from them. I didn't want to use handheld because I didn't want the audience to feel we were in the room, documenting; I didn't want to look at the character in a vérité way.* (Rachael K. Bosley, 'An Angry Young Man', *American Cinematographer*, March 2006)

Task 2.39

Write an analysis exploring the ways in which cinematography is used in a key sequence in order to deepen our understanding of a key character's emotional state in one of your study films.

Colour and lighting is also important in terms of creating beautiful images that carry important meanings.

The township in the morning (left) and the railway tracks at evening (right) (*Tsotsi*).

Quick Question 2.16

Look at these images and note down the effect of colour and lighting in each still.

Here are some of the stylistic features you should identify for *Tsotsi* in terms of considering the aesthetics:

- The colour palette – most scenes take place at night or in the rosy glow of early morning or early evening.
- The use of 35mm film enhances some scenes, creating a rich amber blue or deep palette. This highlights Miriam's bold patterned dresses, glass hanging mobiles, the deep red soil and the contrasting deep blue sky.
- Scenes are often framed by dust and much of the action takes place at night.
- Shot on location using local actors, local dialects and accents giving touches of realism.

Music invariably mirrors, or comments on, the action and heightens poignant moments. However, it does do so much more than this in *Tsotsi*: it comments on the action and evokes a vibrant, noisy, angry, energetic present and painful, spiritual, poignant past.

GCSE Film Studies

Let the Right One In cinematographer, Hoyte van Hoytema, also stressed the idea of film as art and the importance of the cinematographer when discussing the making of the film:

> *I see cinematography as a great blend of music, painting, poetry and technique, and I sometimes think my interest in filmmaking comes from the fact that I wanted to be a musician, painter or writer. As a cinematographer, I can combine those things into one language.* (Jim Hemphill, 'An Unusual Romance', *American Society of Cinematographers*, December 2008)

Van Hoytema also touched upon the director Tomas Alfredson's artistic influences:

> *He [Alfredson] wanted the visual language to be as pure and as unspoiled as possible, though we did turn to [painter] Hans Holbein as a reference point. Holbein's eyelines are quite unexpected – they can be deep in the bottom of the frame or very far off outside the frame, almost profile, and then again sometimes very close. In* Let the Right One In, *we tried to make Oskar meet Eli's eyes very gradually. In the beginning, Oskar hides himself not only from the people around him, but also from the camera. As the story evolves, we slowly meet his eyes as he tries to open up.* (Jim Hemphill, 'An Unusual Romance', *American Society of Cinematographers*, December 2008)

Oskar hides from the camera and the audience (*Let the Right One In*).

We slowly meet his eyes (*Let the Right One In*).

Quick Question 2.17

Compare these two stills. The first still is taken from the beginning of the film, the second from near the end. How does cinematography highlight changes in his personality?

Part 2:
Film form

Sound and aesthetics

There will be moments in all of the films you study during this course that tug on your emotions in some way. Danny Boyle, Tomas Alfredson and Gavin Hood underline the ways in which they use elements of cinematic form in order to create particular kinds of artistic or emotional effects. They discuss the ways in which they have been influenced by other artists who may have used different art forms, they collaborate with musicians, painters and choreographers, and they experiment with new cinematic techniques or incorporate iconic images into their work. In *E.T.* Steven Spielberg worked with the composer John Williams to create musical themes that dominate the more dramatic elements and serve to represent the powers that E.T. uses to both heal and fly, and to also convey a broader sense of magic and mystery. Music combines with cinematography in order to create a mood of wonder and amazement during the iconic scene when Elliot and E.T. fly past the moon.

> **Top tip**
> When researching your study films, print out any references made to other directors, artists, musicians or writers by critics describing the film's style.

How can we forget an image like this (*E.T. the Extra-Terrestrial*)?

Spielberg also takes more classical images as inspiration and creates a new 'take' on classical painting.

DID YOU KNOW THAT ET'S FAMOUS MOVIE POSTER WAS BASED ON MICHELANGELO'S CREATION OF ADAM ?
SKEPTICALARTIST.COM

> **Task 2.40**
> 1. Choose a moment, image or brief sequence from two of the six films you have studied. Download a still that illustrates your choice.
> 2. Create a PowerPoint presentation that outlines what makes each of your choices appeal to you emotionally. You may consider editing, cinematography (including colour and lighting), sound or mise-en-scène. Conclude your presentation with at least one critical review of each film that focuses on style or artistic influences.

GCSE Film Studies

How we make sense of film

Context

Any film is influenced by the various contexts in which it is produced. They may have been made at any point during the past 120 years or so but they will invariably reflect and respond to what was happening in the world at the particular time and place in which they were made and/or set.

Contexts as reflected in study films

SOCIETY AND CULTURE

Which aspects of society and/or culture (e.g. social issues, structures, and ways of living, beliefs and values) are reflected in the film you have studied?

POLITICS

Which political issues and events are evidenced in the film you have studied?

HISTORY

What was happening in the particular society and culture where the film is set and/or made?

INSTITUTIONS and TECHNOLOGY

Funding and production of film and how it has affected the kind of film made (production values). The effect of technologies, e.g. CGI or Steadicam, on cinematic style and in some cases how they may be reflected in the narrative, e.g. *Singin' in the Rain*.

Key terms

Context
The background, environment, framework, setting or situation surrounding an event or occurrence.

Framework
A supporting structure around which something can be built. A system of rules, ideas or beliefs that is used to plan or decide something.

Political
Of or relating to the government or public affairs of a country.

Social
The interaction of the individual and the group, or the welfare of human beings as members of society.

Institutional
The organisations created to pursue, promote or produce a particular type of endeavour, e.g. filmmaking.

When thinking or writing about each of your study films, it is important to consider its **context** both in terms of when the film was made and when and where it was set. You need to explore the background or **framework** of the film. This involves a consideration of **political**, **social**, cultural, historical and **institutional** issues together with the new technologies that may have influenced the making of the film, its narrative and how it was received by audiences across the world. This may sound like a daunting task but it's really not that difficult. Most obviously it is the film's narrative (the story and how it is told) that reflects the context in which it was made, and by the time you have completed this course you will, hopefully, know your study films really well.

Part 2:
Film form

Context – films made in the US

A good place to begin your contextual investigation is by finding out where and when the film was made, and then exploring what was happening in that society at that time. As you explore your chosen films you should look at each of the contextual areas shown in the diagram on page ooo. However, it is important to note that each of the groupings of films in both components requires a slightly different focus.

Section A (the comparative study) enables you to compare films made in Hollywood. Each pairing contains one genre film made in the 1950s with another of the same genre made in the late 1970s or 1980s. Each choice will give you the chance to see how genres develop and change over time. All comparisons in this section reflect US society at the time the films were made.

Rear Window and *Witness* are crime thrillers that deal with two very different kinds of society using different stylistic techniques.

The two central characters in *Rebel Without a Cause* and *Ferris Bueller's Day Off* are teenagers who are challenging different kinds of authority in contrasting ways, whilst *Invasion of the Body Snatchers* and *E.T.* underline changing social attitudes towards 'aliens' during the 30 years from the 1950s to the 1980s. *Invasion of the Body Snatchers* reflects anxieties about communism (see page 126) and *E.T.* advocates the acceptance of difference.

A teenager who challenges authority (*Rebel Without a Cause*).

Task 2.41

1. Watch the trailers for *Invasion of the Body Snatchers* and *E.T. the Extra-Terrestrial* on YouTube.

2. Note down key words or phrases that are used to 'sell' each film, e.g. 'They're not human', 'They're here already', as opposed to 'the wonderment, the enchantment', 'the connection has been made'.

3. Now read through the descriptions of US society in the 1950s and 1980s below.

   In America in the 1950's, the fear of the bomb and the pleasures of prosperity existed at the same time. The image of the ideal community was in fact a disguise for much nastier things happening beneath the surface. One was them was the racism that ran through American Society. Another was the fear of communism. Most American had very little idea of what communism or socialism was and it was possible for extremist politicians to stir up `witch hunts' against any body who might be a communist sympathiser. (Jackie Newman and Roy Stafford, *Representation, Realism and Fantasy: Key Concepts for Analysing Film and Television*, 2002)

   Changes appeared in many parts of American society. They affected popular culture, education, and politics. For example, one of the most popular television programs of that time was about serious social issues. It was called 'All in the Family'. It was about a factory worker who hates black people and opposes equal rights for women. His family slowly helps him to accept and value different kinds of people. ('The 1980s', history.com, www.history.com/topics/1980s)

4. Rewatch the two trailers. Discuss the ways each of these reflect some of the changes or issues mentioned above.

5. What differences are can also be observed in terms of the ways that the films are 'sold' to the audience'?

GCSE Film Studies

King Solomon's Mines and *Raiders of the Lost Ark* perhaps show less evidence of change in terms of genre conventions and representation over the 30-year period. However, they do underline the changes in terms of technology and special effects, and evidence the growing need for spectacle among audiences.

Heroes and heroines in action in the 1950s (*King Solomon's Mines*).

Not much change in the 1980s (*Raiders of the Lost Ark*).

Singin' in the Rain and *Grease* look back on earlier historical periods. *Grease* looks back nostalgically from the late 1970s to a 'simpler decade' (the 1950s) a time when musicals drew massive audiences, teenagers 'rocked around the clock' and many American families were enjoying post-war affluence (more money for cars, electrical goods, houses and leisure).

Singin' in the Rain – a movie made in the 1950s but set in 1927.

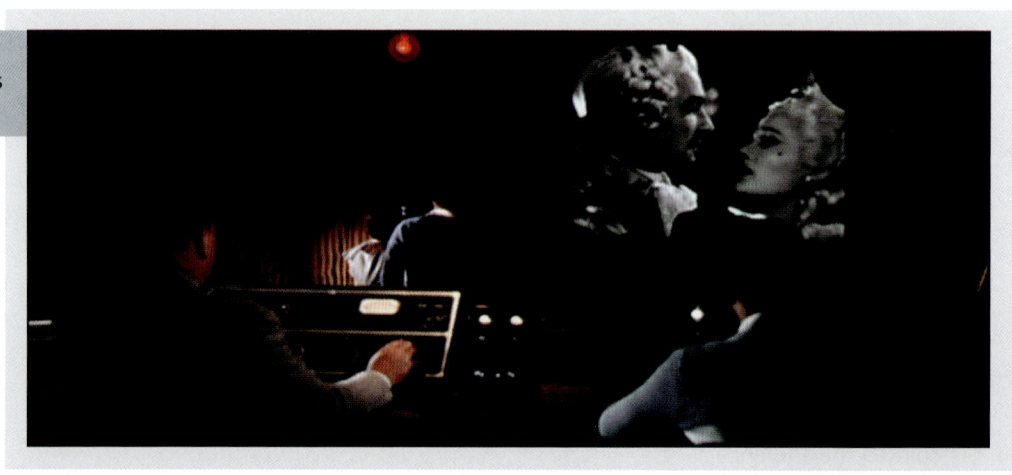

The previous still is set in 1927 and a musical is being completed using 'new' sound technology. Kathy and Don (the two central characters in *Singin' in the Rain*) are dubbing the duet sung by Lina (on the black and white screen).

Ironically, Kathy's (Debbie Reynolds) singing voice was dubbed by Betty Royce for all the scenes where Reynolds' character dubs Lina Lamont's singing voice. So in this scene, when Kathy Selden (Debbie Reynolds) is dubbing Lina Lamont (Jean Hagen), Betty Royce is actually dubbing Reynolds dubbing Hagen!

Singin' in the Rain provides a rich opportunity to learn about elements of the rise of Hollywood and development of sound. It's obviously a musical but it's also a film about making a movie in Hollywood at a crucial time in film history – the coming of sound. It raises questions about sound and image, and involves the audience in the creation of a work of art.

Sound presented Hollywood with exciting artistic possibilities; it also posed huge problems for filmmakers and stars. The central characters in *Singin' in the Rain* decide to make a movie, a 'talkie' and a musical – the problem is the female lead can't sing and her acting style/voice is terrible. The audience is presented with a multi-layered narrative – a musical, about making a musical and the need to develop/utilise new technologies in order to cope with new technologies (dubbing, sound and camerawork) at a key point in film history.

Because all the films in this section were produced in Hollywood, you need to know something about the studio system and other significant developments in the history of film. This will include the:

- **FIRST MOVING IMAGES**
- **RISE OF HOLLYWOOD AND THE DEVELOPMENT OF SOUND**
- **INTRODUCTION OF COLOUR FILM**
- **EMERGENCE OF WIDESCREEN TECHNOLOGY AND 3D FILM**
- **DEVELOPMENT OF PORTABLE CAMERAS AND STEADICAM TECHNOLOGY**
- **ROLE OF CGI IN FILM**

Your understanding of these areas will be enriched by your study films. In addition they are covered in some depth in the Case study (see page 110). You may not have chosen to study *Invasion of the Body Snatchers* and *Witness* but this section will provide you with a comprehensive view of American society, its history and politics leading up to and during the 1950s and 1970s–1980s. It contains timelines with key events, developments and dates.

GCSE Film Studies

> **Task 2.42**
>
> Create a diagram that shows the key elements of the social, political and historical context for each of your study films. Use these diagrams as a revision aid.

Whichever pairing of films you choose to study in Section A, you will need to have a clear knowledge and understanding of what was happening in American society during both time periods. Below is a list of questions that will help to guide your research:

- What important events or issues were happening socially, culturally, historically and politically in the US leading up to and during the 1950s?
- What was happening during the late 1970s and 1980s in the US?
- What important changes in US society can be noted when comparing society in the 1950s to society in the late 1970s and 1980s?
- Which aspects of US society are reflected in your films?

As mentioned earlier, although each pairing shares the same context, the ways in which these contexts are reflected within each film can be quite different. *Singin' in the Rain* may have been set in the past – it certainly employs many of the traditional musical genre conventions of the established Hollywood musical – but it also pushes the boundaries of the genre and allows a consideration of the ways in which movie-making adapts and changes institutionally and technologically.

Below are the areas you should consider when considering technological or institutional contexts in your focus films.

Which technological changes can be noted in the films productions?

What do they enable the filmmaker to do that had not be done before?

Do technological changes, for example the development of portable cameras, Steadicam cameras and CGI, become more apparent when comparing films made some 30 years apart? What effect do they have on audiences?

How were the films funded? What was the importance of genre in terms of production, distribution and exhibition?

Context – US independent films

Study of Hollywood film will move you on to a consideration of US independent films. Most of the contextual background information on indie cinema is covered in Part 3 Section B, pages 202–219. This section gives you an opportunity to study films produced in the 21st century that have been made, and at least in some part funded, outside the Hollywood system. It also allows a consideration of how institutional issues affect the kinds of films made.

Little Miss Sunshine (2006, Jonathan Dayton and Valerie Faris), *Me and Earl and the Dying Girl* (2015, Alfonso Gomez-Rejon), *Juno* and *Whiplash* all place younger people and their experiences centre stage. In contrast, *The Hurt Locker* (directed by a female, Kathryn Bigelow) explores male values and attitudes within the context of a war film.

There is considerable debate among academics, critics and filmmakers about just how independent Indie cinema is in the 21st century (see the two contrasting views following).

Part 2:
Film form

An Indie film can be whatever it wants, or indeed needs, to be. Indie films are not intended to break box office records, though many have surprised us. Divorced from the compulsive need to sell the movie as many people as possible, the directors, screenwriters, and actors have the freedom to make their choices for the sake of art rather than commerce. In doing this, they are often likely to shock, break from type, infuriate, or inspire; but they are truly free. (Ross Carey, 'The 30 Best Indie Moves of the Last 25 Years', tasteofcinema.com)

The 2000s was the best of times for indie, and it was the worst of times for indie. It was the dawn of cinema's second millenium, a clean slate for a new century of cinematic art. However, it was not all good news for indie cinema. On one hand, following the indie **renaissance** *of the 1990s, there was certainly more of a return to big studio films in the 2000s.* (Ross Carey, 'The 20 Best American Indie Movies of the 2000s', tasteofcinema.com)

Key term

Renaissance
A new growth of activity or interest in something, especially art, literature or music.

When exploring indie cinema you should be aware of these debates and think about the ways in which it may develop in the future. Look for similarities as well as differences between this film and the other US films you have studied. Most importantly, when thinking about context always come back to the film itself. What are its main concerns and how are they represented? What do they tell us about US society in the new millennium?

Task 2.43

1. Watch two of the following trailers on YouTube:
   - *Juno*
   - *Whiplash*
   - *Me and Earl and the Dying Girl*
   - *Little Miss Sunshine.*

2. Note down the social and cultural issues that are raised in each trailer.

3. Identify similarities in terms of settings, representation of characters, style and narratives.

4. What do your findings suggest about the concerns and lives of young people in the US today?

'I want to be one of the greats' (Whiplash).

'Why's everyone staring at me?' (Juno).

89

GCSE Film Studies

Context – global films

For Component 2 we move from the US to consider films made in the rest of the world. Obviously, a consideration of setting is going to be very important when exploring these films.

Section A contains films made in Australia, Great Britain, India and Ireland. Because each film is set in a different country and or time, your exploration of context will depend on your choice of focus film. Below is a brief outline of some of the contextual issues/facts for each film:

Rabbit-proof Fence: made in Australia in 2002. Set in 1936 in Western Australia. Opens in Jigalong, an Aboriginal settlement near the rabbit-proof fence that runs across the continent. Moves to the River Moore Native Settlement and then follows the three central characters on their journey across the outback following the rabbit-proof fence back to Jigalong. Deals with the despair experienced by Aborigine women and children caused by the enforcement of the 1931 Western Australian Aborigines Act, which allowed mixed-race children to be taken away in order *'to have the blackness bred out of them'*.

Rabbit-proof Fence: the social and historical context.

> For 100 years, the Aboriginal peoples have resisted the invasion of their land by white settlers. Now, a special law, The Western Aboriginal Aborigines Act (1931), controls their lives in every detail.
>
> Mr A.O. Neville, the Chief Protector of Aborigines, is the legal guardian of every Aborigine in the State of Western Australia. He has the power 'to remove any half-caste child' from their family anywhere within the State.

Rabbit-proof Fence: removing 'half-caste' children from their families.

Task 2.44

1. During the credits, even before we have seen the image of the Australian outback on the screen, we are given the information seen on the right. Why do you think the director Phillip Noyce has chosen to do this?

2. What impact does it have on the way the audience responds to the narrative that follows?

Part 2:
Film form

District 9: is a science-fiction film set in a slum on the fringes of Johannesburg – this film would go well with an exploration of the sci-fi genre (*Invasion of the Body Snatchers* and *E.T.*) and *Tsotsi* (Non-English Language section) as the setting says so much about narrative issues, such as being an outsider, poverty and discrimination. It has stunning special effects and focuses on the plight of one outsider who is hunted by aliens through the back alleys and derelict buildings of a shanty town.

Song of the Sea (2014, Tomm Moore): an Irish animated film that draws on **Celtic mythology** and fantasy to explore the loss of a mother during childbirth on a family living in a remote place on the West Coast of Ireland.

> Read through the excerpt from a newspaper review below:
>
> > The movie's Johannesburg setting (also Blomkamp's hometown) obviously makes *District 9* an apartheid **allegory**. Marooned aliens – dubbed with the epithet 'Prawns' for their crustacean appearance – were banished to District 9, which eroded into a junkyard ghetto. Humans nearby complained loud enough to force the government to relocate the aliens 200 miles away. Doing it legally requires each Prawn to sign a waiver. (Steve Persall, *Tampa Bay Times*)
>
> You may not have seen the film but just by reading the excerpt above, discuss, in pairs, what concerns about social and political issues in today's society may be represented allegorically in *District 9*?

Task 2.45

Key term
Allegory
A story, poem, picture or film narrative that can be interpreted to reveal a hidden meaning, typically a moral or political one.

Key term
Celtic mythology
The ancient Celts had a vibrant mythology made up of hundreds of tales featuring romance, magic and heroism. The Celts did not record their myths in writing but passed them down through the generations orally.

Song of the Sea was nominated for Best Animation Feature Oscar 2016 Award.

GCSE Film Studies

Created by Tomm Moore, an Irish animator, this film employs classical hand-drawn style in order to create a story inspired by a Celtic myth, incorporating magic and ancient rock drawings in order to create an extremely beautiful looking film. Its institutional context features the involvement of an Indie distributer – Gkids. It had a limited release and was reliant on success in high-profile film awards to achieve long-term financial gain. This film provides an interesting contrast to the Disney blockbusters that tend to be predominantly led by plot and character. In contrast, *Song of the Sea* delivers a much more aesthetic, poetic experience. Typical Disney fare tends to 'shoehorn' fairy tales or legends into a tried and tested formula. This film strives to create an appropriate style in order to communicate culturally specific narrative traditions.

Task 2.46

Watch the trailer for *Song of the Sea* and Disney's *Moana* (2016, Don Hall and Chris Williams) on YouTube. Answer the following questions:

1. Identify the differences in terms of the ways in which film is 'sold' to the audience.
2. Note down the similarities between each trailer.
3. Which film would you prefer to see and why?

Slumdog Millionaire: is set in India in the 2000s; the narrative focuses on an 18-year-old orphan from the slums of Mumbai and raises issues of poverty status and corruption.

> *The gap between rich and poor has become more marked, even in the most economically developed nations. This is a problem which the conscience of humanity cannot ignore, since the conditions in which a great number of people are living are an insult to their innate dignity and as a result are a threat to the authentic and harmonious progress of the world community.* (Pope John Paul II, World Youth Day 1993)

Quick Question 2.18

Note down the ways in which the gap between rich and poor talked about by Pope John Paul II are represented in *Slumdog Millionaire* (see opposite paragraph).

If we examine the opening sequence of *Slumdog Millionaire* it hits the ground running, we're plunged into a breathless, exciting world. We are given snapshots of the real India of different social levels. Although romance lies at the heart of the film, we are moved by the shots of people living in dire poverty, women crawling from cardboard boxes. Men bathing in fire hydrants. Sequence after sequence bridges the two Indias: that of the world's largest middle class, with expensive cars, education and luxury houses; and that of the poor whose only hope of escape lies in dreams of winning a million. Jamel is high spirited and defiant, and, like so many slum children, he is a survivor – he has to be because there seems liitle in terms of social or government support. The poverty of his environment is a sharp contrast to the sumptuous, opulent Taj Mahal where he tries to make a living.

Part 2:
Film form

Sorting through the sewage (*Slumdog Millionaire*).

'But the swimming pool, as you can see, was finished in top class fashion' (*Slumdog Millionaire*).

> **Task 2.47**
>
> 1. Analyse the ways in which mise-en-scène creates meaning in the previous two stills.
> 2. Which issues are signalled in these stills?
> 3. What do the contrasts in environment tell you about important social/cultural or historical issues dealt with in the film?

The pleasures of the film lie in a number of different areas; the story is both modern and traditional. We see the terrible poverty that so many have to endure in India today but we also experience the new technological 21st century with its media-based culture. A culture that peddles the dream that we can all be rich and famous if we want it enough.

Context: global non-English language films

This section of Component 2 focuses on global non-English language films and provides a choice of South African, Swedish, Saudi-Iranian and Japanese films. *Rabbit-proof Fence* is set in Australia in the 1930s and deals with the determination of three mixed-race Aborigine girls to return to their own families and community, thus rebelling against attempts to assimilate them into 'white' values.

Spirited Away is an animated fantasy adventure film produced by the famous Japanese studio Ghibli. It tells the story of Chihiro, a headstrong ten-year-old girl, unhappy that her family are moving and that she will have to make new friends.

Top tip
When considering the main issues dealt with in a film, collect a series of still images that illustrate how mise-en-scène conveys these issues.

GCSE Film Studies

The strongest theme in *Spirited Away* is that of childhood. Young girls as the main characters are a common form of story in anime. This is referred to as *Shojo* in Japan and uses the perspective and situation of a young girl to explore many themes and stories. *Spirited Away* features issues of cultural change, family values and growing up.

Tsotsi relates the story of a gangster from the shanty towns of Johannesburg who undergoes change as a result of finding a baby. The film asks questions about the relationship between criminality and social environment.

The Wave tells a disturbing story of the consequences of conformity as part of a school project into the roots of facism.

Let the Right One In, a Swedish horror film set in the early 1980s, uses the vampire genre to raise several issues about young people and the problems of integrating. Like *Attack the Block* (2011, Joe Cornish) it uses genre to explore social and political issues.

Wadjda is the story of a young Saudi girl whose burning desire for a bicycle leads her into bold defiance of her society's restrictive codes of gender and religion. Although her plans are continuously thwarted, she maintains her determination to fight for her dreams.

The two-point study plan

QUESTION: What is it?

ANSWER: A useful, manageble way of considering how your chosen films reflect the contexts in which they were made.

QUESTION: There seems to be so much to cover, where do I start?

ANSWER: Start with your film! There may have been some amazing, earth-shattering events happening in the period/culture when your film was made or set but if these are not reflected in your film you don't need to consider them. Below are the main steps in the study plan:

Carry out some brief initial research on the social, cultural, historical and political context of the film.

1. What was happening in the country in which the film was made during the time the narrative was set or the film was made?
2. After completing your research, pick two themes that reflect these contexts.
3. Rewatch two key sequences that relate to these themes.
4. Make notes on how aspects of society, culture, historical events or politics are evidenced in these sequences.
5. Go back to your film and, using your notes, make links between the two main themes and social, cultural, politics and/or historical events.
6. Find two interesting facts relating to the funding of the film and how it affected the kind of film made.
7. Find two key aspects of the history of film or film technology that are reflected in your film.

Part 2: Film form

Let's see how this works on a film from this section, for example, *Tsotsi*.

1. What was happening in the country in which the film was made during the time the narrative was set or the film was made?

Answer: Begin with listing what you think may be important points revealed by your research. See below a possible list, focusing upon South Africa, for *Tsotsi*.

- *Violent crime is a huge problem – the legacy of over a half a century of racism, neglect and discrimination.*
- *Over 25% of the population do not have work.*
- *20% of the adult population have been infected with HIV Aids, causing many children to grow up without family support.*
- *In spite of a big housing programme, much of the population is still living in shanty towns constructed from scrap.*
- *South Africa's population is made up of many nationalities and cultures.*
- *It is unique in terms of its history. Its population is made up of a large number of groups all speaking a variety of languages, which have come together over many centuries.*
- *Communities are highly segregated – white separated from blacks, rich from poor.*
- *Historical issues (see above) have influenced the ways in which the township culture developed in the 20th and 21st centuries. Originally, townships consisted mainly of men who had left their families in order to earn a living. These townships centred on bars and had high levels of crime.*

Not all films will have as much to say about social and historical context as *Tsotsi*, but all of the choices allow you to explore people, places and events that have helped to shape their narrative.

2. After completing your research pick **two** themes that reflect these contexts.

Answer: *Wealth inequality and crime.*

3. Re-watch **two** key sequences that relate to the themes.

For example, the opening sequence) 00:00:20–00:05:09 and sequence where Tsotsi and his gang return to Pumla's house (0:57:40–1:04:36).

> **Top tip**
> Group your research when you think that issues are linked, e.g. poverty, poor housing, unemployment.

Quick Question 2.19

What do you think has been the major historical reason for the segregation of black and white people in South Africa today?

Tsotsi inhabits the baby's nursery (*Tsotsi*).

95

GCSE Film Studies

4. Make notes on how aspects of society, culture, historical events or politics are evidenced in these sequences.

Answer: *Opening sequence:*

- Wealth inequality – Tsotsi's shack made from junk (things others have thrown away). Only one room, no basic facilities (long shot of people queuing up at the water pump). A bed but no 'home comforts', the place is dark and dirty. Poverty is shown by long shots of the makeshift homes, the sprawling, densely populated township.

- Crime – Tsotsi initially represented as a dark character (lighting in his shack). His name is not even a real name it means 'thug' or 'gangster'. The robbery and murder of a commuter in a tightly packed train. Differences in reactions between each of the gang members. Link between poverty and wealth inequality made through the poverty of his environment: there are clearly few opportunities and the gang turn to crime in order to survive. The murder shows how far they will go to get money, although Butcher is obviously more violent than the others, all have worked together to rob the murdered man.

Second sequence:

- Wealth inequality – begins outside Pumla's house in an **affluent** Johannesburg suburb – large, detached and gated (gates and front door locked and alarmed). Tsotsi, Aap and Butcher arrive on foot, huddle against a wall, John arrives in an expensive, large car. Immediately, huge contrasts established in terms of wealth and poverty. Contrasts continue as gang enters the house, camera tracks each character as they explore each room. Smart, modern, sophisticated and wealthy. Aap underlines gap between different life experiences and styles, asking questions about wine and food. The nursery is a turning point for Tsotsi, mise-en-scène underlines differences between his childhood and the baby's.

- Crime – the scene that precedes this sequence shows Tsotsi promising Boston he will make sure he can finally take his exams and become a teacher. This sequence highlights the differences between the gang members and how experiences have changed Tsotsi. Aap and Butcher believe they have come to Pumla and John's simply to rob it. Tsotsi's **motivations** are less clear. Certainly, he makes straight for the baby's room (see previous still). But he only takes things that are necessary for the baby, as he looks at the family photos and what the baby is offered in terms of life chances because of the family wealth (and love) a turning point is reached – he cannot condemn the baby to a life such as his, with no hope or real family. Aap chats to John as if he's an old friend; he continues to be the one who is led, who obeys orders and is loyal to his childhood friend. Each have a different motivation for committing the crime, but Butcher is the only one who seems to have no conscience and is so brutalised that there is no hope for any kind of change in his personality.

5. Go back to your film and, using your notes, make links between the two main themes and social, cultural, political and/or historical events.

Answer: At this point you have all the information you could possibly need! Highlighted in **green** are two important links between modern-day South Africa (when *Tsotsi* was set) and wealth inequality as represented in two key sequences.

Top tip
Watch key sequences that highlight contextual issues in your study films several times. Make sure you have made detailed notes on the ways film form is used to communicate these issues.

Key term
Affluent
Having a great deal of money or other material goods.

Key term
Motivation
A reason or reasons for acting or behaving in a particular way. For example, the reasons (motivations) for Tsotsi's criminal behaviour is his poverty and/or because he is unemployed.

Part 2:
Film form

- *Economic wealth contrasts with terrible poverty. Half of the population live on the poverty line – many exist on just a dollar a day. Communities are highly segregated – white separated from blacks, rich from poor. In spite of a big housing programme, much of the population is still living in shanty towns constructed from scrap.*
- Historical issues have influenced the ways in which the township culture developed in the 20th and 21st century. Originally, townships consisted mainly of men who had left their families in order to earn a living. These townships centred on bars and had high levels of crime. Violent crime is a huge problem – the legacy of over a half a century of racism, neglect and discrimination. Over 25% of the population do not have work.

Go back to your research and your notes on key sequences. It should be clear from your research and your study of the film, that *Tsotsi* makes strong links between the issues of wealth inequality and crime, as represented cinematically.

Crime and wealth inequality often go hand-in-hand, so hopefully you will have already explored the links between them as represented in the film. Wealth inequality (poverty) and crime are social issues but bear in mind that these may have the historical, cultural or political roots. For example, the townships that developed during the 1900s were formed when men from all over South Africa began to gravitate to the big cities for work.

Tsotsi has been set in modern, post-apartheid South Africa. Today, South Africa is governed by those who represent the majority of its people. It has abundant natural wealth, together with a rich, vibrant culture, and yet a huge majority of its people live in poverty. The film *Tsotsi* reflects these contrasts in contemporary South African society. These huge differences between rich and poor lie at the heart of the film's narrative. The contrast between the gated communities of the wealthy and the shanty towns of the poor are repeatedly underlined by the cinematography. In the opening sequence of the film we see how the people have to live and the conditions that force some young people into crime. Today, there is political freedom and optimism but South Africa is still blighted by political corruption, poverty, crime, disease and drug addiction.

6. Find **two** interesting facts relating to the funding of the film and how these affected the kind of film made.

Answer:

- *During apartheid years the South African government only funded Afrikaan films so effectively very few 'black voices' in South African cinema. In the 1990s, Hollywood made films set in South Africa with American stars. Following the success of* Tsotsi *the South African government has started to fund the film industry, looking to encourage the making of films that more closely mirror the rich cultute of the country.*
- *In the late 1990s, Hollywood chose to ignore the diversity of languages and dialects spoken in South Africa.* Tsotsi *is an important film that has been credited for bringing a uniquely South African voice to the 'big screen' and raising the global profile of its film industry.* Tsotsi *won the Oscar for Best Foreign Film in May 2006. This is often seen as a turning point for the South African film industry. It has attracted both black and white audiences.*

Quick Question 2.20

Debate the following statement in class, 'Poverty and crime always go hand in hand'. Give arguments for and against the statement.

Top tip

Always relate your research on context to what you have seen in the film. So the wide social issues of poverty and crime in South Africa are relevant to your `reading' of *Tsotsi* but more personal issues about changing attitudes regarding relationships and adolescence are dealt with in *Juno*.

GCSE Film Studies

Unusually Tsotsi *did very well at the box office in South Africa. Oscar success also allowed it to attract a large global audience. Note – even today the gap between rich and poor is apparent in audiences. Most cinemas are in shopping malls with very unaffordable ticket prices.*

7. Find **two** key aspects of the history of film or film technology that are reflected in your film.

Answer:

- *Unaffordable ticket prices led to a huge demand for 'bootleg' DVDs all over South Africa. Poorer audiences, while not being able to enjoy the 'big screen' experience, were able to watch it on other media platforms.*

- *The soundtrack headlines the musical voice of young, black, urban South Africa – a mixture of all the music that 1990s South African youth grew up on: rap, disco, hip hop, rhythm and blues, and American and British house music. Again, popularity of the film in South Africa was partly due to the importance/appeal of music made in the townships, which is shared through a variety of different media platforms.*

Task 2.48

In pairs, create a short PowerPoint presentation that explores how film history, technology and *funding* has helped to shape your focus film.

Context – contemporary UK films

The UK films offer a selection of films made in Great Britain during the past six years.

Submarine has many of the hallmarks of an indie comedy. It plays with the typical codes and conventions of mainstream film and refers back to groundbreaking filmmakers of the 20th century in order to explore the inner turmoil of Oliver Tate, an eccentric, self-conscious 15-year-old, intent on losing his virginity and saving his parents' marriage.

Attack the Block draws attention to the social problems of urban London, using comedy and science fiction to suggest political parallels with the threats posed by 'aliens' (as seen in *Invasion of the Body Snatchers* and *District 9*).

Skyfall is in many ways a typical Bond film, with high production values, big stars and sophisticated cinematography. However, it gives a new accent to the action thriller by exploring the relationship between controller and controlled – between M and James Bond.

Life in Ireland is contrasted with Brooklyn, New York. *Brooklyn*, begins in Ireland and is a coming-of-age story, done on a modest scale, about a small-town Irish girl, Eilis Lacey, who emigrates from Ireland to America in the 1950s. Like so many emigrants, she is torn between her longing for her homeland and a future that offers new and exciting possibilities. Although the narrative is set in the 1950s, the film's style harks back to 1930's and 1940's Hollywood when 'women's films' (or **melodramas**) starring actressess such as Bette Davis, Joan Crawford and Barbara Stanwyck were popular.

Key term

Melodrama
A film or literary work in which the plot is typically sensational and designed to appeal strongly to the emotions.

Part 2: Film form

'I'd forgotten how much I'd missed these places' (Brooklyn).

'For the first time since I've been in America I can say I'm truly happy' (Brooklyn).

My Brother the Devil (2012) is writer-director Sally El Hosaini's debut feature film. It is a coming-of-age movie set in multi-ethnic East London. In this case the sons of a hardworking Egyptian-born bus driver on a Hackney estate make the usual mistakes of joining rival gangs, carrying knives, buying guns and dealing drugs.

Using the two-point plan create a revision resource for your UK focus film.

Task 2.49

GCSE Film Studies

Specialist writing on film, including film criticism

Thinking, talking and writing about film

In order to develop and extend your knowledge and understanding you are required to study specialist writing on film. Although researching and reading film criticisms, reviews or magazine articles on all your study films may have helped you to find out more about all of your focus films, Section C of Component 1 (US Independent Film) of your exam will ask you to consider specialist writing covering three areas of film form as follows:

- one source on cinematography
- one source on US Independent film
- one magazine or online review of the film you have studied or this section

A consideration of genre often features heavily in film writing, as does the reference to artistic influences, for example the work of other influential directors past or present.

You may have written film reviews during this course. There are many writers all over the world whose job it is to review films, especially immediately after their release. These reviews may be communicated via a range of different platforms, e.g. newspapers, magazines, online blogs or websites. Almost anyone with a strong opinion can write a review; sometimes we may disagree with those opinions, sometimes they echo our own responses to a film. We may have a favourite reviewer, one whose opinion we trust, so that when they recommend a film we are more inclined to watch it.

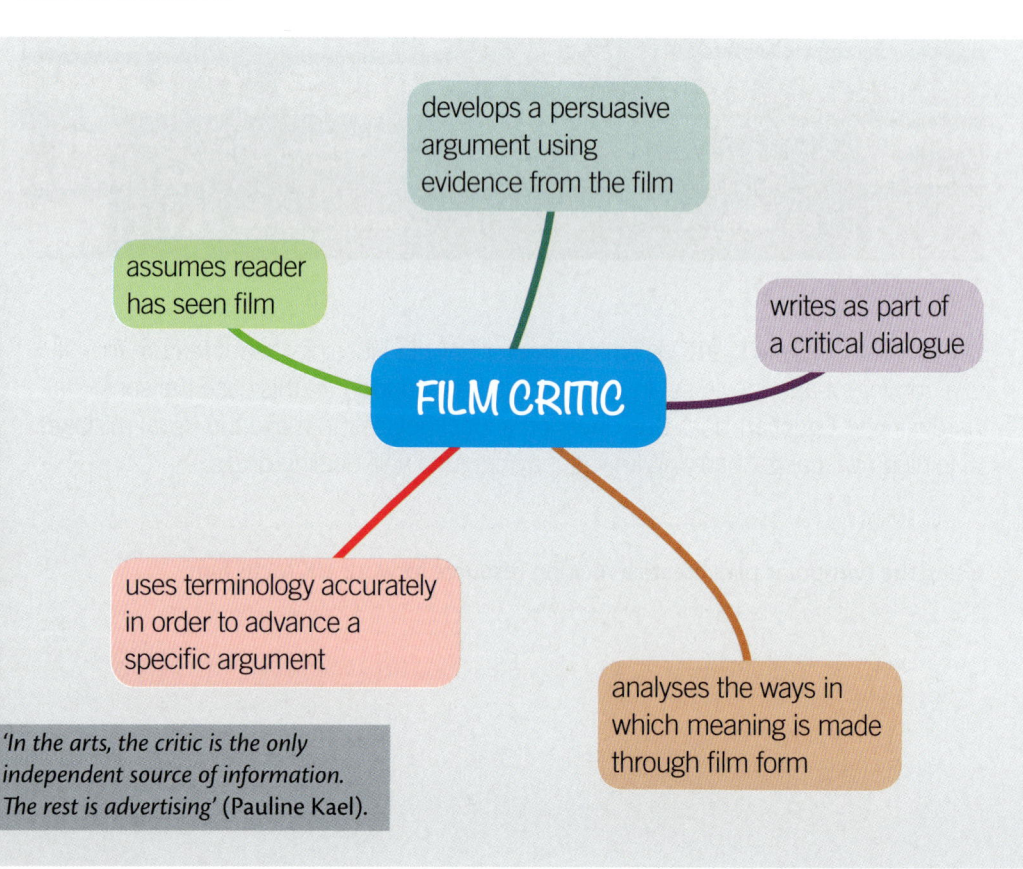

> **Top tip**
> A list of these sources will be published on the WJEC's secure website from 2017, so take a significant amount of time to read and study them and to consider the ways in which they enrich, inform or deepen your understanding of independent cinema. They will also demonstrate how ideas and persuasive arguments are communicated using evidence based on the ways that the key elements of film form and structure are used to create meaning and response in the film.

> **Top tip**
> We've said before that in order to write and talk about film it is really important to consider how film form creates meaning and response and to be able to use the correct terminology.

FILM CRITIC
- develops a persuasive argument using evidence from the film
- assumes reader has seen film
- writes as part of a critical dialogue
- uses terminology accurately in order to advance a specific argument
- analyses the ways in which meaning is made through film form

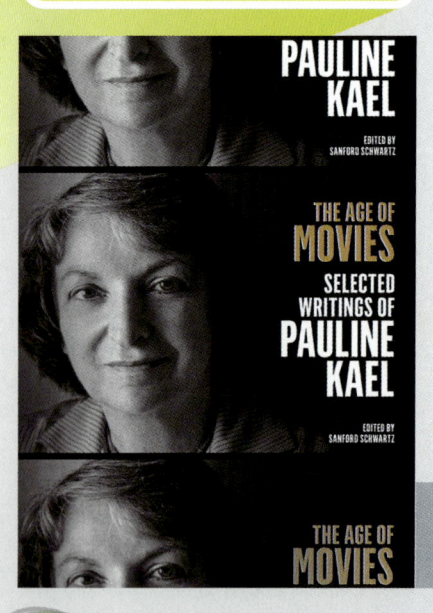

'In the arts, the critic is the only independent source of information. The rest is advertising' (Pauline Kael).

Part 2:
Film form

FILM REVIEWER

- usually writes for those who haven't seen the film
- often gives the film star ratings
- creates a 'consumer guide' containing value judgements/personal response
- uses terminology accurately but meanings are not always fully analysed
- designs review to encourage or deter prospective viewers

A film critic's role is different from the reviewer's role in that the critic usually writes for those people who have seen the film and the reviewer writes for a possible future audience. However, the lines between critic and reviewer are becoming increasingly blurred as, over the years, the definition of what is a critic and what is a reviewer have come to be almost identical. Even the majority of modern English language usage dictionaries reflect this opinion by using one to define the other, 'a critic is someone who write reviews, and a review is something written by a critic'. While it's true that more and more often there is little distinction to be made between the two in the way they are applied, in most instances (newspapers, online blogs, magazines, television and other venues of pop media), it does not mean there is no distinction. Indeed, it could be argued that it's only because of the need to supply a mass market of filmgoers with easily understood opinions (good/not good; one star/five stars, predictable/original, shocking/tame) that the concept of what we call a review has even come about.

Star ratings provide easily understood critical opinions.

101

GCSE Film Studies

Film form and specialist writing

Thomas Mann and Olivia Cooke in *Me and Earl and the Dying Girl*.

Top tip
If there are words that you don't understand in the critical reviews you read, note them down and then look up their meanings in your revision notes. If they are useful words you may want to use them in your exam answers to impress the examiners!

Key terms

Self-effacing
Being modest about what you have done. Not encouraging praise and not trying to get the attention of other people.

Art house classics
An art house film is a film that is intended to be a serious artistic work rather than a piece of popular entertainment aimed at a mass market. Art house classics are the most highly regarded of these, often made during the 20th century.

Precociousness
Being very clever, mature or especially good at something, often in a way that is usually only expected in someone much older.

Below are three different examples of specialist writing. The first two sources refer directly to *Me and Earl and the Dying Girl*. The final source focuses on independent cinema.

Cinematography source: Me and Earl and the Dying Girl

Me and Earl and the Dying Girl is funny, highly original and very moving too, even if it becomes a little gloopy in its final reel.

*It is also a cinephile's delight. The film comes littered with references to and in jokes about other movies. Its **self-effacing** young hero, Greg (Thomas Mann), has posters of* Mean Streets *and* The 400 Blows *on his wall. He and his 'co-worker' Earl (Cyler) spend their spare time at high school making very ingenious spoofs of **art house classics** (Seven Seals, Death In Tennis and the like.) They are avowed admirers of Powell and Pressburger, Stanley Kubrick and Werner Herzog, whose Germanic pomposity they love to mock.*

*Me and Earl is shot in dynamic and inventive fashion, with swooping camerawork and stylised mise en scène. It uses voice-over, animation and intertitles as well as including frequent scenes from Greg and Earl's home movies. There is never a sense that the filmmakers are patronising their audience or trying to be too clever. The story takes its tone from its own lead character. Very engagingly played by Mann, Greg's charm lies in his mix of diffidence and extreme **precociousness**. He goes to extreme lengths to fit in at high school. That means being pleasant to everyone and suppressing his real feelings. The film, based on Jesse Andrews' 'young adult' novel, covers familiar territory – young love, illness, the perils of a germ-filled, rebellious adolescence at a tough American high school – but it has a zest and wit that leaves other, similar films like* The Fault in Our Stars *flailing in its wake.*

(Geoffrey Macnab, 'Me and Earl and the Dying Girl', 3 September 2015, *The Independent*)

The above review above focuses on style and genre.

The opening paragraph praises the film's originality whilst also referring to it as 'a cinephiles delight'. If given this extract as source material for the exam after the initial reading you should go back and examine each stage of the critique/review. Firstly making sure you understand what phrases or words mean.

So what is a **cinephile**? Well, hopefully by the end of this course you'll be one! It's a term used for someone who is passionate about movies and knows a lot about them. A cinephile is typically seen as an educated film consumer with the toolkit to distinguish average films from outstanding ones. Up to this point in the study of the film you may barely have noticed the posters and the movies that feature on Greg's wall. This article could prompt you to re-visit sequences and ask yourself what these references to other iconic films tell you about both the hero and the director of the film. If you go on to choose *Submarine* as your UK focus film, you may note that Oliver Tate also has iconic posters on his bedroom wall and is also into filmmaking. Some of you may even go on to consider if a film can be influenced, or refer to other films, and still be truly original, at that point I'd say your 'toolkit' is a becoming a really sophisticated one.

> *Key term*
>
> **Cinephile**
> A devoted moviegoer, especially one knowledgeable about the cinema.

1. The *Independent* review on the previous page talks about 'dynamic and inventive camera work' and a 'stylised mise-en-scène'. Pick a short sequence from your study film that features the use of dynamic or inventive camerawork and/or stylised mise-en-scène. Describe the effect that is created in terms of creating meaning and response.

2. Much of the first paragraph focuses on references to other films. Why does the writer think the references are important?

3. Does your focus film contain any references other films or directors? If so, what references are there and what do they tell you about characters, cinematic style or narrative?

Task 2.50

Film review source

The next source has been written by Sheila O'Malley.

Read through the following review:

> If you grew up, as I did, watching old black-and-white movies on a local television channel, then you know the experience of learning young that there is a whole world of movies outside the ones shown at the multiplex. 'Me and Earl and the Dying Girl,' the baffling Sundance hit (it won both the Audience Award and the Grand Jury Prize), directed by Alfonso Gomez-Rejon, with a script by Jesse Andrews, based on his best-selling novel, features two teenage characters obsessed with the Great Movies. Other than that acquisitive movie-mad mindset, it is a pandering, self-flattering mess, featuring unearned **catharsis**, lazy clichés and characters presented in broad, sometimes-offensive stereotypes. The worst part is that 'Me and Earl' believes it is aware of all of this. Every cliché arrives with a wink of self-knowing commentary before it, to say, 'Yes, we know this is a cliche, but we are making a comment about the cliché!' Saying it don't make it so. Besides, such commentary has been done before, and it's been done much better.
>
> *(continued)*

Task 2.51

> *Key term*
>
> **Catharsis**
> The process of releasing strong emotions through a particular activity or experience, e.g. watching a moving film or listening to sad music.

GCSE Film Studies

Key term

Cultural tropes
When a character holds up one culture or element of that culture (often but not necessarily their own) as a shining example of development and progression. The evidence for their assertions is invariably flawed or fictitious (think Donald Trump).

There's a laziness at work in 'Me and Earl,' a reliance on well-trod ground and over-chewed **cultural tropes**, and perhaps it is supposed to be that way (these are kids who see everything through the lens of their movie-watching), but it still doesn't work. The winks about the clichés, including the one in the title, only serve to point up how tired those clichés are. Earl is another problem. Earl is black. For no other reason, apparently, he lives in squalor on a terrifying-looking street of derelict houses, overrun by weeds, and has a scary aggressive brother with a pit bull. Earl speaks with profanity-laced language, and constantly asks Greg about Rachel's 'titties.' Has Greg seen/touched the 'titties' yet? Earl's language is completely unmotivated, coming from nowhere, and therefore represents a failure of the imagination when it comes to the character. Who is Earl? I'd actually like to know. How does he feel about the films they watch? What's his take? Later, when Greg has hurt Rachel's feelings, Earl steps up in a big way, showing that he has more common sense and more of an understanding of what is at stake for Rachel than Greg does. (This is also a cliché: the black sidekick understanding more about matters of the heart than the white lead.) (Sheila O'Malley, 12 June 2015, RogerEbert.com)

Sheila O'Malley clearly did not like this movie! One of her initial criticisms is that it features numerous cliches.

1. Which cliches appear to upset her the most?

2. She also accuses the filmmaker of featuring *'unearned catharsis'*. What evidence is given to back-up this statement?

3. Find a negative or positive review of your study film. Write your own review putting forward an opposite point-of-view. Make sure you back-up all your criticisms – positive or negative – with evidence from the film.

Indie cinema source

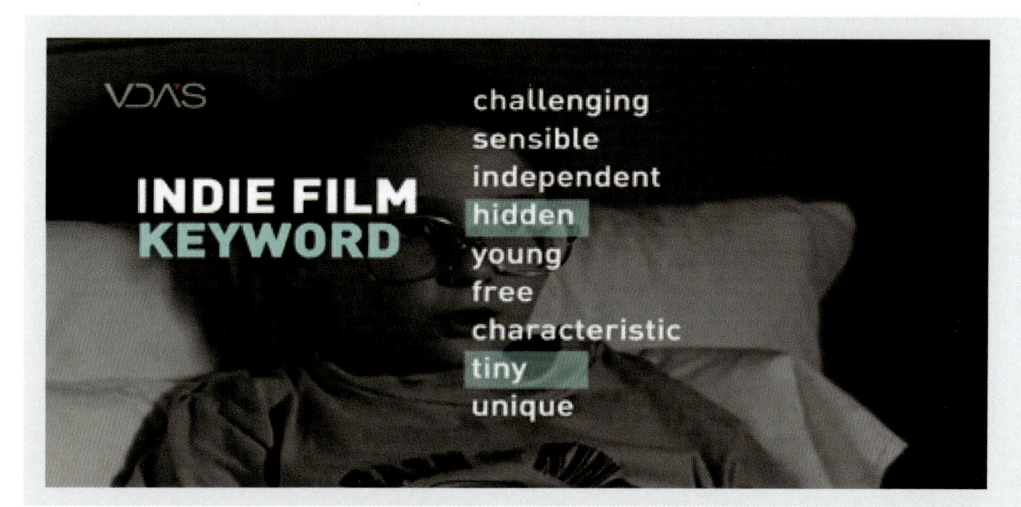

Task 2.52

Create an Indie Film Key Term poster for your film (see above for *Little Miss Sunshine* as an example).

Part 2:
Film form

The third source is from an article that focuses upon what we understand by the term 'indie cinema' by asking filmmakers and actors who have made or featured in independent films to offer their own definitions.

Tilda Swinton (pictured right): 'Independent in my mind means free. Independent films have changed so much over the past years. For example, when I started making films with Derek Jarman in the 1980s, that was really independent film-making, going around with a Super 8 camera to make The Last of England. That was before the studios started making what I would describe co-dependent films, films that were on a leash but given the impression that they were studio-light.

'Independent means you are free to say what you want. It does not necessarily say you will be able to do it very easily and anyone is going to give you any money to do it. It might mean it is very uncomfortable, it might mean you work with chaos on a daily basis, though it does mean that you don't have someone breathing down your neck … So that is what indie means to me.'

Michael Winterbottom (pictured right): 'I think from the point of view of making films, I just want to make the films I want to make. In a sense that is the best definition of independent, people making the films they want to make rather than working within the studio system and making a film for the studio.'

Paul Andrews Williams (pictured right): 'Indie means to me not very much money to make the film. London to Brighton cost £85,000 and was shot over three weeks … It's much freer and not full of stars. It's about the film. When I saw Reservoir Dogs, I thought, wow, someone who has never directed a film before. It was edgy, it has got things in it that a studio would be too afraid to put it. (Richard Vine, 'What is Indie Cinema?', *The Guardian*, 4 November 2008)

Task 2.53

1. Which of the definitions in the extract above do you find most useful?
2. Each of the filmmakers/actors talks about the freedom or independence offered by independent filmmaking. What do they say are the advantages of making or acting in an independent film rather than a mainstream film? What seems to be the main disadvantages?
3. How important do you think the idea of freedom is to the independent filmmaker or actor?
4. What are the main differences between indie films and mainstream Hollywood films?
5. Has the article helped to deepen your understanding of independent cinema?

Part 3
Component 1: Films made in the USA

Sections A & B
The comparative study and key developments in film and film technology

Content

You will study two out of the three US films for this component of this section. These will be a pair of mainstream films for comparison (from a choice of four pairs). Each pair of films includes one film produced between 1930 and 1960 and one film produced between 1961 and 1990. The pairs are:

- *King Solomon's Mines* (Bennett and Martoon, USA, 1950) and *Raiders of the Lost Ark* (1981, Spielberg, USA)
- *Singin' in the Rain* (19778, Donen and Kelly, USA) and *Grease* (1978, Kleiser, USA)
- *Rear Window* (1954, Hitchcock, USA) and *Witness* (1985, Weir, USA)
- *Rebel Without a Cause* (1955, Ray, USA) and *Ferris Bueller's Day Off* (1986, Hughes, USA)
- *Invasion of the Body Snatchers* (1956, Siegel, USA) and *E.T. the Extra-Terrestrial* (1982, Spielberg, USA).

Part 3: Component 1: Films made in the USA

Why study mainstream American film?

Comparing the two films will allow you to discover how genres develop and change. The comparisons will reflect on US society at the time in which the films were made – the 1950s and the late 1970s and 1980s. In the example of our case study, *Invasion of the Body Snatchers* and *E.T. the Extra-Terrestrial*, both films show strikingly different attitudes towards 'aliens'. *Invasion of the Body Snatchers* reflects anxieties about communism whilst *E.T. the Extra-Terrestrial* advocates the acceptance of difference. This comparison will involve the following areas of study:

- Contexts of each film's production (social, cultural, historical, political, technological and institutional), including key aspects of the history of film and film technology.
- Key elements of film form (cinematography, mise-en-scène, editing and sound).
- Structural elements of film form (genre and narrative, including screenplays).
- Representation of people and ideas.
- Aesthetic qualities of the films.

Not only will this give you a much keener insight into the films and their genre but will also help you chart Hollywood and mainstream filmmaking's journey through the development of film and film technology.

Who would want to miss out on that?

Quick Question 3.1

Find out who produced the films you are studying and how much **box office** they took.

Key term

Box office
The financial success or failure of a movie measured by the total value of ticket sales.

Los Angeles, downtown Hollywood.

GCSE Film Studies

Introduction – mainstream Hollywood

To say that the film industry took its first tentative steps in the Hollywood land of Los Angeles, which has been successful, is, in most ways, an understatement. Not only is it unrelenting in its commercial drive but also in its insatiable appetite for creativity and talent. This hunger for dollars has driven it to create an industry that has dominated the world of mainstream movie-making. Not only has one country's movie-making (the US) become the world's movie-making but one town's approach (Hollywood) to filmmaking has rarely found a corner of the globe it could not colonise.

There has always been a tension at the heart of Hollywood, in whatever form it has morphed, to keep the box office receipts flowing. This tension was best summed up by screenwriter and director Garson Kanin:

> So it can be seen that the trouble with the motion-picture art was (and is) that it is too much an industry; and the trouble with the motion picture industry is that it is too much an art. It is out of this basic contradiction that most of the ills of the form arise. (AZ Quotes)

Kanin describes the tension between the need to make money and the desire to make art as a contradiction, and in many ways it is. Yet out of this contradiction have come films that exemplify both ends of the spectrum, be it critically praised **auteur blockbusters** such as the Godfather films, or critically reviled franchises such as the Transformers films. Hollywood has produced both types, and in any discussion of the system, in its various incarnations, we have to accept that one cannot exist without the other. Without income no movies can be made but without constant creative renewal even the blockbuster will fail to engage its audience.

If nothing else, Hollywood has proved itself to be the most adaptable of industries. From its golden era of the **integrated studio system**, through its struggles with the challenge from TV into the era of deal making, and the summer blockbuster and modern **globalised conglomerates**, it has always seemed to find a form to keep feeding the huge market of people that will pay to be entertained by its particular brand of big screen magic. Perhaps the last word in this introduction should be left to an expert in the Hollywood screen writing art, William Goldman, who now infamously observed in his book *Adventures in the Screen Trade: A Personal View of Hollywood* (1983):

> Nobody knows anything ... Not one person in the entire motion picture field knows for a certainty what's going to work. Every time out it's a guess and, if you're lucky, an educated one.

This often misunderstood quote is not a judgement on studios or the producers' ability but is another way of looking at the tension that pushes the mainstream movie-making business forwards. Despite what often appears to be Hollywood's pursuit of a magic formula of ingredients (genre or otherwise), for bankable commercial success they can never know for sure how successful any given project will be.

Key terms

Auteur
A filmmaker whose individual style and complete control over all elements of production give a film its personal and unique stamp.

Blockbuster
Any film that takes over 100 million dollars at the American box office. Usually created with both huge production and marketing budgets.

Quick Question 3.2

Give an example of a critically acclaimed auteur film made in Hollywood. Give an example of a formulaic franchise film. Why does Hollywood need to produce both kinds of films?

Key terms

Integrated studio system
The system of organisation where studios controlled production, distribution and exhibition. This enabled the studios to apply assembly-line manufacturing and cost control methods to film production.

Globalised conglomerate
A large business made up of many smaller businesses and brands that are large enough to trade on a worldwide basis.

Part 3: Component 1:
Films made in the USA

Movie-making is a financially risky business and you can reduce that risk by working within secure **pre-sold properties** such as a *Harry Potter* franchise but you cannot be complacent about their success. Creative people need to deploy their skills to keep audiences coming back. In an industry with such an appetite for product (100s of films are released every year) there are only so many *Harry Potter* franchises to be had. In a worst-case scenario of Goldman's observation, we find an example in 2013s *The Lone Ranger* (Gore Verbinski). All the ingredients seem to be there – a producer and director with a long record of commercial success; one of the world's biggest stars (Johnny Depp); a major studio (Walt Disney Pictures) with the resources to back both major production and marketing costs – only to result in a rumoured loss of between $160–$190 million. Who would have guessed? There may be many theories but most of it boils down to a simple truth – the audience just did not like it. This underlines how difficult it is to predict how such a large group of people will react: most times predictably but never enough to be sure.

Perhaps it is this unpredictability that keeps both Hollywood and us moviegoers on our toes and always hoping for a surprise?

Key terms

Pre-sold property
A basis for a film that the producers have paid exclusivity to use. Pre-sold as it comes with its own audience. For example, the Harry Potter books film rights were sold to Warner Brothers and had sold millions of copies before the movies were made.

Harry Potter: a secure investment?

Task 3.1

Use the internet to create a project about a Hollywood film that was considered to be a financial failure or 'flop'. You could include:

- the financial facts and figures
- the reasons that have been given to explain its failure
- your ideas why people did not go to see it
- posters and images to enhance your project.

'All this time, money and effort and the audience still doesn't like us!' (*The Lone Ranger*).

GCSE Film Studies

Introducing the industry and its context

Film timeline – Part 1

The first moving images and silent film 1850s–1950s.

1880s	Lengths of celluloid photographic film and the invention of motion picture cameras, which could photograph an indefinitely long rapid sequence of images using only one lens, allowed several minutes of action to be captured and stored on a single compact reel of film.
1895	First movie was shown in theatres, but it was black and white with no sound, American Woodville Latham and his sons, French brothers Auguste and Louis Lumière are among the first. The first attempts at colour, hand-tinted movies such was *Annabelle Serpentine Dance* (1895, William Kennedy Dickson and William Heise) from Edison Studios.
Turn of the 20th century	Films started stringing several scenes together to tell a story. The scenes were later broken up into multiple shots photographed from different distances and angles.

The rise of Hollywood

1895–1927	The era of silent cinema, the movies had no sound during this time period.
1907	Movie-makers begin to move to the sleepy town on the west coast of America called Hollywood. In the first film explosion, the population of Hollywood grows from under 5,000 to 130,000 by 1925.

The introduction of colour film

1917	Technicolour: Technicolor Motion Picture Corp. was the first company to make a film using technicolour – *The Gulf Between* (1917, Wray Bartlett Physioc).

Grace Darmond photographed for *The Gulf Between* (1917, Wray Bartlett Physioc).

Part 3: Component 1:
Films made in the USA

	The development of sound
1927	*The Jazz Singer* is released. This became known as the first talkie although only 354 words were spoken in it. Within three years most feature films became talkies – a case of silent movies going silently!

The Jazz Singer (1927, Alan Crosland and Gordon Hollingshead) movie poster.

1935	The Bolex camera was introduced using half-width 16mm film stock. These smaller cameras satisfied the demand from both the growing newsreel and documentary fields, as well as the emerging amateur market. The Bolex also saw limited use in professional filmmaking.
1935	The first full-length technicolour film arrives. *Becky Sharp* (Rouben Mamoulian; an historical drama based on Thackeray's book *Vanity Fair*) is not a complete success. One critic describes the actors as looking like 'boiled salmon dipped in mayonnaise'.

	The emergence of widescreen technology and 3D film
1952	Cinerama is unveiled by film bosses who decide that size really does matter. Unfortunately, they soon find that huge pictures mean huge costs. Eventually, Cinerama becomes obsolete.
Late 1952	The 'golden era' of 3D began with the release of the first colour stereoscopic feature, *Bwana Devil*, produced, written and directed by Arch Oboler.

GCSE Film Studies

1953	20th Century Fox develops anamorphic CinemaScope; one of the first successful widescreen processes.
1953	Columbia Pictures was the first major studio to release a 3D movie – the black and white *Man in the Dark* (Lew Landers), it was also the first 3D feature ever released by a major American studio.
1953	Warner Bros' first 3D film, the horror classic *House of Wax* (Andre de Toth), was the first full-length colour 3D film produced and released by a major US studio – it was also the first 3D film with a stereo soundtrack.
1954	Paramount Studio's first VistaVision widescreen production was director Michael Curtiz' hit film *White Christmas*, an Irving Berlin musical.
1955	The Todd-AO widescreen process (with 65mm (or 70mm) wide film) was successfully introduced with director Fred Zinnemann's landmark musical *Oklahoma!*
1956	Two science-fiction classics: *Forbidden Planet* (Fred M. Wilcox) and *Invasion of the Body Snatchers* were released.
1957	The Academy of Motion Pictures Arts and Sciences' bylaws denied eligibility for Oscar nominations or consideration to anyone who admitted Communist Party membership or refused to testify before the House on Un-American Activities Committee (HUAC) – in other words, artists who had been blacklisted.
1959	The Academy of Motion Pictures Arts and Sciences modified its bylaws from 1957, and abandoned its practice of denying eligibility for Oscar nominations or consideration to anyone who had been blacklisted.

(Source: Filmsite.org)

Oklahoma! was filmed using the Todd-AO widescreen process.

Part 3: Component 1:
Films made in the USA

Film in the 1950s

> **BOX OFFICE TOP TEN AMERICAN FILMS OF THE 1950S:**
>
> 1. *The Ten Commandments* (1956, Cecil B. DeMille)
> 2. *Lady and the Tramp* (1955, Clyde Geronimi, Wilfred Jackson and Hamilton Luske)
> 3. *Peter Pan* (1953, Clyde Geronimi, Wilfred Jackson and Hamilton Luske)
> 4. *Cinderella* (1950, Clyde Geronimi, Hamilton Luske and Wilfred Jackson)
> 5. *Ben-Hur* (1959, William Wyler)
> 6. *Sleeping Beauty* (1959, Clyde Geronimi)
> 7. *The Bridge on the River Kwai* (1957, David Lean)
> 8. *Around the World in 80 Days* (1956, Michael Anderson) (tie)
> 9. *This is Cinerama* (1952, Merian C. Cooper, Ernest B. Schoedsack, Mike Todd, Jr and Gunther von Fritsch) (tie)
> 9. *Seven Wonders of the World* (1956, Tony Garnett, Paul Mantz, Andrew Marton, Ted Tetzlaff, Walter A. Thompson)
> 10. *The Greatest Show on Earth* (1952, Cecil B. DeMille) (tie)
> 10. *Quo Vadis* (1951, Sam Zimbalist)

(Source: Filmsite.org)

We begin our look at the film context of the 1950s by considering the most popular films of the decade and observing some wider trends in Hollywood film production. The 12 films in the list above seem to break down into three main types. The top two and two others are family-centric Disney animations. A further four belong to the historical epic genre, in some ways the ancestors of the modern blockbuster, and the remaining four are large-scale widescreen adventure-based films. In many ways the last two groups can be viewed as Hollywood's response to the growing threat from its small-screen rival television, particularly the Cinerama productions. Taken as a whole, we can see the films as a last flourish of the fading studio system. Whereas Disney would continue on to the present day as its own entity separate from conglomeration, the studios responsible for the rest would be absorbed by larger media concerns as the decades progressed towards the present day.

Quick Question 3.3

Search the internet for images of James Dean in *Rebel Without a Cause* and Marlon Brando in *The Wild One* (1954, László Benedek). What do these images have in common? How is the idea of youthful rebellion represented?

Cinerama, *How the West Was Won* (1962, John Ford, Henry Hathaway, George Marshall and Richard Thorpe) starring James Stewart.

GCSE Film Studies

> **Key terms**
>
> **Cold War**
> The non-violent conflict between the US and the former USSR after 1945 that would last until 1990.
>
> **Vertical integration**
> The ownership of the chain of production by one business. In the case of filmmaking this involved the studios producing, distributing and exhibiting their films.
>
> **Brand recognition**
> How easily a consumer can correctly identify a particular product or service just by viewing the product's or service's logo tag line, packaging or advertising campaign. How famous a business is.

In the wider world of American cinema, outside of the box office charts the 1950s films very much reflected the times in which they were made. As teenagers emerged as a distinct group with their own money to spend, the movies reflecting this market emerged. Marlon Brando and James Dean were the movie symbols of adolescent, anti-authoritarian rebellion in *The Wild One* and *Rebel Without a Cause*, respectively. More commercially, and linked to the rising popular music phenomena (rock 'n' roll), Elvis Presley also began his film career in the 1950s.

Reflecting a darker aspect to the 1950s were science-fiction films that were influenced by the heightening **Cold War** era. There were many, notable among them being *The Day the Earth Stood Still* (1951, Robert Wise), *The War of the Worlds* (1953, Byron Haskin), *The Thing* (*From Another World*) (1951, Howard Hawks and Christian Nyby), *Invasion of the Body Snatchers* and *Forbidden Planet* (1956, Fred M. Wilcox). Linked to this were the science-fiction films that reflected anxiety at the atomic threat that accompanied the Cold War – *Them!* (1954, Gordon Douglas) and *Godzilla – King of the Monsters* (1954, Terry Morse and Ishiró Honda) among them.

Other popular genres maintained their appeal: musicals, *Singin' in the Rain* being a prime example; romantic adventure with films such as *King Solomon's Mines*; and the Hitchcock thrillers *Rear Window*, *Vertigo* (1958) and *North by Northwest* (1959).

In 1948 Paramount Decrees ruled that much of the way Hollywood organised its business was anti-competitive and illegal. This brought to an end their **vertical integration** of production, distribution and exhibition. This meant virtually all of the major Hollywood studios would be subject to reorganisation and change in the 1950s. Ultimately, this lead to them all being sold off to larger business entities (some more than once) over the coming decades. The strength of their **brand recognition** built up over their golden age (1930s–1950s) is what preserves their names up to the present day.

Quick Question 3.4

Which film trend or genre do you think was the most important in the 1950s?

Film after the 1950s

Film timeline – Part 2

1960–1990: major changes for Hollywood.

1960	The talented scriptwriter Dalton Trumbo, one of the **Hollywood Ten**, received full credit for writing the screenplays for Otto Preminger's *Exodus* and Kubrick's *Spartacus* thus becoming the first blacklisted writer to receive screen credit.
1963	The worst year for US film production in 50 years (there were only 121 feature releases). The largest number of foreign films released in the US in any one year was in 1964 (there were 361 foreign releases in the US v 141 US releases).
1963	The first theatre originally designed as a **multiplex** (a multi-screen movie theatre) opened in the Ward Parkway shopping centre in Kansas City. *Cleopatra* (Joseph L. Mankiewicz), the most expensive film ever made at that time, opened. It was one of the biggest flops in film history (cost-overruns made the $2 million budget become $44 million). It finally turned a profit in the 1980s.

> **Key terms**
>
> **Hollywood Ten**
> Of the 41 screenwriters, directors and producers called to testify by the US government about Communists working in Hollywood ten refused to cooperate. They were 'blacklisted' by Hollywood and not allowed to work in movies due to their stand on free speech.
>
> **Multiplex**
> A cinema with several separate screens.

Part 3: Component 1:
Films made in the USA

1964	Theatre admission numbers had dropped dramatically to below 1 billion. However, the trend started to reverse itself with the arrival of blockbusters and multiplexes, but Hollywood would never get back to its glory days of the 1940s and 1950s.
1966	Paramount's purchase by Gulf & Western marked the beginning of a trend towards studio ownership by diversified, multi-national conglomerates. It was the first instance of a Hollywood studio being acquired by a corporate conglomerate.
1975	Steven Spielberg's *Jaws* was the first modern blockbuster film to top the $100 million record in box-office business in North America.

The development of portable cameras and Steadicam technology:

1975	Steadicam, a brand of camera stabiliser mounts for movie cameras, was invented by Garrett Brown.
1976	The Steadicam was used for the first time in director Hal Ashby's *Bound for Glory*. Director of photography Haskell Wexler won the Oscar for Best Cinematography. John Schlesinger's *Marathon Man* was the first commercially-released film using the Steadicam.

The first use of the Steadicam, Garrett Brown (left) and Haskell Wexler (right) (*Bound for Glory*, 1976, Ashby).

GCSE Film Studies

		The role of computer-generated imagery in film:
	1982	A film featuring a character who looked like a cross between Albert Einstein and a new-born baby becomes a huge hit, *E.T. the Extra-Terrestrial* takes $700 million worldwide.
	1982	Jim Clark founded Silicon Graphics, a cutting-edge company that contributed to the growth of computer imaging and animation in films. *Star Trek II: The Wrath of Khan* (Nicholas Meyer) just beat *Tron* (Steven Lisberger) into release, to attain the honour of being the first film to use computer-generated images (CGI) to any extent.

Early CGI, taken from *Star Trek II: The Wrath of Khan*.

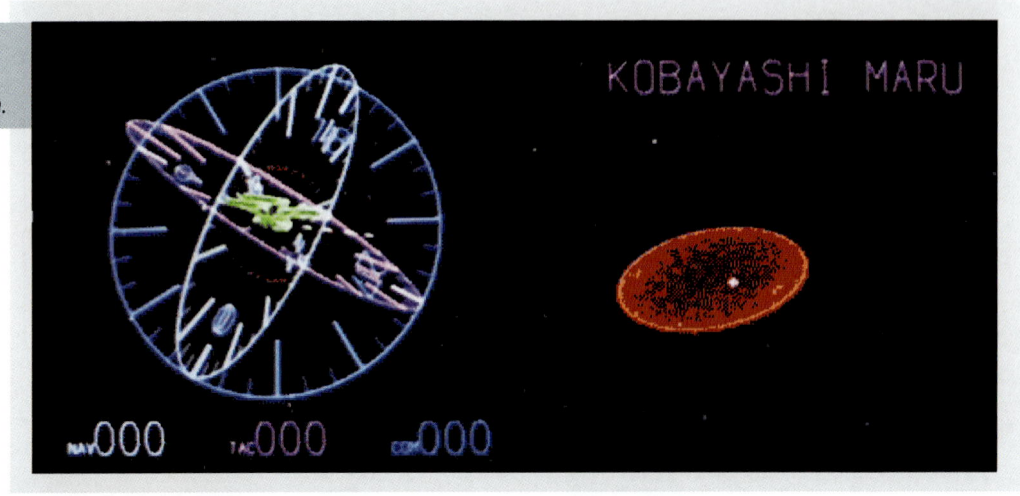

	1985	Disney's PG-rated film *The Black Cauldron* (Richard Rich and Ted Berman) was the first animated feature film to contain 3D CGI elements (digital fire and a boat), and was the first Disney animated feature to use 3D computer graphics technology.
	1986	Steve Jobs established the independent company Pixar, also called Pixar Animated Studios.
	1988	Pixar's five-minute *Tin Toy* (John Lasseter), the inspiration for *Toy Story* (1995, John Lasseter), was the first computer animation to win an Academy Award. Billy, the baby character in the short film, marked the first time that a computer-generated (CG) character had realistic human qualities. Digital morphing (the seamless change from one character or image to another) of several animals was first introduced by ILM and debuted in director Ron Howard's live-action fantasy-adventure film *Willow*.
	1989	A new generation of expensive CGI and graphics in the 1990s was heralded by the slinky, translucent water creature in James Cameron's big-budget *The Abyss*.

(Source: Filmsite.org)

Part 3: Component 1:
Films made in the USA

Film in the 1980s

BOX OFFICE TOP TEN US FILMS OF THE 1980S:

1. *E.T. the Extra-Terrestrial* (1982, Steven Spielberg)
2. *Star Wars: Episode VI – Return of the Jedi* (1983, Richard Marquand)
3. *Star Wars: Episode V – The Empire Strikes Back* (1980, Irvin Kershner)
4. *Batman* (1989, Tim Burton)
5. *Raiders of the Lost Ark* (1981, Steven Spielberg)
6. *Ghostbusters* (1984, Ivan Reltman)
7. *Beverly Hills Cop* (1984, Martin Brest)
8. *Back to the Future* (1985, Robert Zemeckis)
9. *Indiana Jones and the Last Crusade* (1989, Steven Spielberg)
10. *Indiana Jones and the Temple of Doom* (1984, Steven Spielberg)

(Source: Filmsite.org)

We can observe some wider trends in Hollywood in the 1980s by looking at popular films of the time. The 1980s can be viewed as the decade in which Hollywood built on the blockbuster foundations laid by movies such as *Jaws* (1975, Steven Spielberg) and *Star Wars* (1977, George Lucas) in the 1970s. Of the top ten, seven were part of multi-film franchises, much as we see today – *Star Wars*, *Batman*, *Indiana Jones* and *Back to the Future*. Of those remaining, *Ghostbusters* would spawn a sequel and a 2016 **re-boot** and *Beverly Hills Cop* would have two sequels and be an indicator of the enduring popularity of the comedy genre.

E.T. the Extra-Terrestrial stands alone at the top of the chart without a sequel and as a template for the blockbuster that became the favoured Hollywood production model especially for children's animation films that were to follow: *Toy Story* (1995, John Lasseter) and *Shrek* (2001, Vicky Jenson and Andrew Adamson). In other ways its success would be difficult for Hollywood to replicate as, although sci-fi is a strong element in its mainstream make-up, its family oriented nostalgic treatment would not be the direction this ingredient would be taken; the future for blockbuster sci-fi would include far more explosions than this gentle tale of alien visitation.

In the wider world of American cinema, outside of the charts the 1980s films reflected the times in which they were made. The America of the 1980s was a time of rising economic confidence (if not reality) and the true emergence of the Hollywood blockbuster was a reflection of this trend. It became the era of the **high-concept films**.

Key term

Re-boot
To discard all continuity in an established series in order to recreate its characters, timeline and back-story from the beginning.

Key term

High-concept films
Movies with simple ideas at their heart that could be pitched in one or two sentences making them easily marketable and understandable to the mainstream audience.

GCSE Film Studies

Alongside of this was George Lucas with *Star Wars: Episode V – The Empire Strikes Back* (1980) and *Star Wars: Episode VI – Return of the Jedi* (1983), Steven Spielberg with *E.T. the Extra-Terrestrial* (1982) and collaboratively with the Indiana Jones trilogy (*Raiders of the Lost Ark*, 1981, *Indiana Jones and the Temple of Doom*, 1984, and *Indiana Jones and the Last Crusade*, 1989).

Traditional franchises were not neglected either, with James Bond appearing in six films, as Roger Moore handed the licence to kill over to Timothy Dalton. New action heroes also emerged to share the stage with James Bond although rather than being a character-based franchise they were franchises based around the films' stars. The two 'titans' of the box office in the 1980s were Stallone and Schwarzenegger, who between them starred in 23 films across the decade. It was also the beginning of a lower **film budget** but still lucrative trend of the horror film sequel; there were eight *Friday the 13th,* five *Nightmare on Elm Street* and four *Halloween* films produced in the 1980s.

> **Key term**
>
> **Film budget**
> The money made available to make a film.

So, mainstream movies had become big business once again, the emergence of the blockbuster model finally allowing Hollywood to escape from the shadow of the studio system's collapse decades previously. Big business required big money to fund rapidly increasing budgets. The move from **major film studios** towards global media business structures continued with a number of takeovers, Warner Communications merged with Time to become Time-Warner, Inc., a component of the media empire AOL-Time Warner.

It wasn't all big business in the world of Hollywood though; other notable trends embraced a range of genres. *Ferris Bueller's Day Off* (1986, John Hughes) was one notable example of the wave of 1980's teen movies most associated with the group of young actors who became known as the 'Brat Pack' starring in many of the films of director John Hughes. Other examples were *Sixteen Candles* (1984, John Hughes), *The Breakfast Club* (1985, John Hughes) and *Pretty in Pink* (1986, Howard Deutch). It was *Ferris Bueller's Day Off* that defined the teenage rebel of the 1980s, much as Marlon Brando and James Dean had in the 1950s.

> **Key term**
>
> **Major film studio**
> A production and film distributor that releases a substantial number of films annually, and consistently commands a significant share of box office revenue in many markets. The current big six are considered to be: Warner Brothers, 20th Century Fox, Paramount Pictures, Universal Pictures, Sony Pictures Entertainment (earlier known as Columbia-Tristar Pictures) and Walt Disney Studios.

Science fiction continued to be popular: John Carpenter's *The Thing* (1982) channelled a late Cold War feeling of paranoia in its 'one could be the enemy' narrative. While Ridley Scott's *Blade Runner* (1982) looked towards a darkened future of renegade artificial life forms and the potential challenge of a technological future. Lighter entries to the science-fiction canon had a major box office impact. Prime among them being Robert Zemeckis' *Back to the Future* (1985)*, Back to the Future Part II* (1989) and *Back to the Future Part III* (1990).

The musical following on from late 1970's successes *Saturday Night Fever* and *Grease* continued to make an impression in the form of dance-centric musical films. Popular entries to this genre being *Flashdance* (1983, Adrian Lynne), *Footloose* (1984, Herbert Ross) and the perennially popular *Dirty Dancing* (1987, Emile Ardolino).

Traditional films and modern-day dramas were also steadily popular with both critics and audiences. Examples being *On Golden Pond* (1981, Mark Rydell), *An Officer and a Gentleman* (Taylor Hackford, 1982), *Rain Man* (1988, Barry Levinson) and Peter Weir's *Witness* (1985). *Witness* had a flavour of Hitchcock as we accompany Harrison Ford on his journey to protect a young witness who had the misfortune to be in the wrong place at the wrong time. Director Weir, an Australian, brought an outsider's eye

Part 3: Component 1:
Films made in the USA

and a vaguely indie sensibility to the film: territory soon to be explored by an emerging indie scene:

> ... *in his best work he brings a unique quality of cerebral, outsidery oddness that we want to see more of.* (Indiewire.com)

The 1980s saw the continued rise of independent filmmaking outside of the creative constraints of the new Hollywood system. Director David Lynch made a lasting impact with his brilliant but disturbing *Blue Velvet* (1986). Other memorable non-Hollywood productions include Wim Wenders' *Paris, Texas* (1984) and Steven Soderbergh's *Sex, Lies and Videotape* (1989). A huge presence in independent film also emerged in the 1980s with the first film from Ethan Coen (producer) and Joel Coen (director), *Blood Simple* (1984), followed by *Raising Arizona* (1987).

Joel and Ethan Coen on the set of *Raising Arizona*.

Task 3.2

1. Talk to older relatives and friends about the films of the 1980s. Ask them what they remember. What were the highs and lows from their point-of-view? How does this compare with what you think of the films from the 1980s you have seen?
2. Share your findings with the class.

GCSE Film Studies

Film after the 1980s

Film timeline – Part 3

1990s–21st century – new frontiers for Hollywood

1991	The first truly believable, naturally-moving computer-generated character was the morphing, liquid molten metal, T-1000 cyborg in James Cameron's *Terminator 2: Judgment Day*. It was the first instance of a computer-generated main character.
1992	*The Lawnmower Man* (Brett Leonard), a breakthrough film with eight minutes of ground-breaking special effects introduced virtual reality to films. It was one of the first films to record a human actor's movements in a sensor-covered body suit – a technique called Body Motion Capture.
1993	Steven Spielberg's influential blockbuster *Jurassic Park* is released. It was noted for its full-motion, computer-generated (CGI) dinosaurs created at George Lucas' ILM facility. The dinosaurs were very realistically-rendered and seamlessly integrated within live-action sequences. DTS Digital Sound also made its theatrical debut in the film.
1993	James Cameron launched an innovative, state of the art, visual effects digital production studio, called Digital Domain, with partners IBM, character creator Stan Winston, and former ILM chief Scott Ross.
1994	Best Picture winner *Forrest Gump* used revolutionary digital photo tricks to insert the film's main character into archival historical footage with past Presidents (John F. Kennedy and LBJ) and other situations
1995	The cutting-edge *Toy Story* (John Lasseter) was the first totally-digital (or computer-generated) feature-length animated film.
1995	IMAX 3D was introduced with the 40-minute movie *Wings of Courage* (Jean-Jacques Annaud) which cost $15 million to make. It was viewed through high-tech goggles with liquid crystal lenses.
1995	The first feature film with a digitally-created, CG character that took a leading role (almost 40 minutes of film time) was *Casper* derived from the Harvey Comics character.
1996	CARIcature software was first used by Industrial Light & Magic (ILM) for the state-of-the-art digital animation in the 10th century fantasy fable *Dragonheart* (Rob Cohen).
1997	*Marvin the Martian in the Third Dimension* was the first computer-animated CG film that was to be viewed with 3D glasses.

Tom Hanks as Forrest Gump (*Forrest Gump*, 1994, Robert Zemeckis).

120

Part 3: Component 1:
Films made in the USA

1997	James Cameron's *Titanic*, the most expensive film of all time at the time, it was the first film with a budget of $200 million. When adjusted for inflation *Cleopatra* (1963, Joseph L. Mankiewicz, Rouben Mamoulian and Darryl F. Zanuck) still had the highest budget of any film release. *Titanic* (James Cameron) was the first movie to gross over $1 billion worldwide, $1.8 billion in total, but when adjusted for inflation *Gone with the Wind* (1939, Victor Fleming, George Cukor and Sam Wood) remained the highest grossing.
1999	*Star Wars: Episode I – The Phantom Menace* (George Lucas) was released and contained more computer animation and special effects than any previous film – over 90%. It also featured a completely CGI-generated (all digital), fully-articulated main humanoid character named Jar Jar Binks.
1999	*Tarzan* (Walt Disney) was the first film to use a 3D painting and rendering technique dubbed 'Deep Canvas', which allowed 2-D hand-drawn characters to exist in a 3-D environment.
1999	*The Matrix* (Lana Wachowski and Lilly Wachowski) included bullet-dodging (digital effects dubbed 'flow-mo' and 'bullet time' virtual backgrounds.
2000	The first live-action feature film to be entirely colour-corrected by digital means, giving the film a sepia-tinted tone, was the Coen Brothers' *O Brother, Where Art Thou?*
2000	The first major business deal of the 20th century was the America Online (AOL) purchase of Time Warner Inc.
2001	*Final Fantasy: The Spirits Within* (Hironobu Sakaguchi and Motonori Sakakibara) the first photo-realistic, fully computer-generated feature film, was premiered.
2001	Director Pitof's dark 19th century crime fantasy *Vidocq* was the world's first-completed theatrical feature film shot entirely on Hi-Def digital video using a Sony HD-CAM 24P1 (1080p, 24fps) high-definition digital camera. It was released a year before George Lucas' and Hollywood's first big-budget all-digital production of *Star Wars – Episode II: Attack of the Clones*.
2002	In the second part of the trilogy, *The Lord of the Rings: The Two Towers* CGI-imagery was combined with 'motion capturing' (of the movements and expressions of actor Andy Serkis, who also served as the voice).
2003	Disney announced that it would no longer be producing traditionally-hand-drawn animated feature films, but switching to the 3D, full-CGI style originally popularized by Pixar.
2003	Walt Disney Pictures' *Ghosts of the Abyss* a James Cameron documentary and Disney's first 3D picture, was the first full-length 3D IMAX feature.

Jar Jar Binks from *Star Wars*.

Andy Serkis as Gollum in *The Lord of the Rings* (2002, Peter Jackson).

GCSE Film Studies

2003	The last in *The Lord of the Rings* trilogy of Tolkein's literary fantasy, *The Return of the King* (Peter Jackson) is released. In the trilogy of films, the large battle sequences involved more than 200,000 characters, created digitally by MASSIVE software (Multiple Agent Simulation System in Virtual Environment) developed by New Zealand's Weta Digital, a visual effects company.
2004	The *Polar Express* (Robert Zemeckis) was the first film to entirely use the 3D Performance Capture technique, whereby the physical movements of the actors were digitally recorded and then translated into a computer animation. It was also the first feature-length mainstream film to be released in both 35 mm and IMAX 3D.
2004	*Able Edwards* (Graham Robertson) was the first publicly-released feature film shot entirely without physical sets against a green screen.
2004	Pixar's *The Incredibles* (Brad Bird) was the first computer-generated animation to successfully show believable human figures or characters, instead of the traditional animal, toy, and creature characters of previous animations.
2006	Walt Disney Co. announced the purchase of long time partner Pixar Animation Studios, Inc.
2007	*Look* (Adam Rifkin) was the first US mainstream movie to depict events solely through the "eyes" and point-of-view of surveillance devices and video cameras (including ATM cameras and robot security cameras) found in shopping malls, dressing rooms, school parking lots, ATM machines, grocery stores, police cars, elevators, offices, storage rooms and on cell phones.
2009	DreamWorks sci-fi spoof of 50s monster movies, *Monsters vs. Aliens* (Rob Letterman and Conrad Vernon) was the first computer-animated feature film to be shot directly in stereoscopic 3D.
2009	D-Box, a vibrating movie theatre chair, invented by a Montreal-based company is used in the first major theatrical release Universal's *Fast & Furious* (Vin Diesel, Justin Lin, James Wan, F. Gary Gray, Rob Cohen, John Singleton and Philip Atwell), with the Motion-Code technology written into it.
2011	The year was noted as having the most releases of film sequels ever in a single year – 28 in total.
2011	*The Artist* (Michel Hazanavicius) was the first near-silent film in 83 years to be nominated (and win) an Oscar.
2011	The number of 3D releases jumped from 20 in 2009 to 45 in 2011, usually with an average of $3.50 more per ticket.

Mr Incredible (*The Incredibles*, 2004, Brad Bird).

Watching a film in 3D.

2012	*The Hobbit* (Peter Jackson), was filmed with new technology that used 48 images (or frames) for every second of footage rather than the traditional 24 frames per second rate, thereby enhancing clarity and smoothness for 3D viewing (reducing eye strain).
2012	The number of American 3D screens increased to almost 15,000, more than four times the count in 2009.
2013	Paramount Pictures has become the first major studio to stop releasing movies on film in the US – its Will Ferrell comedy *Anchorman 2: The Legend Continues* (Adam McKay) was their last film released on 35mm film.
2013	*Gravity* (Alfonso Cuaròn) involved the most extensive lighting ever on a movie set. 'Zero-gravity' footage was filmed within a custom-built light box containing 1.8 million high-powered LEDs.
2013	The golden age or craze for 3D films had hit some lows with fewer and fewer 3D ticket sales. Many reasons were given to assess the problem, including fatigue with inferior 3D products, and unnecessary post-conversions of films to 3D. Despite these troubling numbers, Hollywood remained committed to at least five dozen 3D movies through 2016.
2013	*Ender's Game* (Gavin Hood) contained 950 special-effects shots (mostly from the special F/X studio Digital Domain). For the final battle sequence, the studio created 333,443 individual spaceships, all of which appeared simultaneously in shots comprising more than 27 billion polygons. This was the most extensive digital object ever created.
2014	A multi-platform release strategy for films, meaning that new films were simultaneously available in theatres and also online, proved in some cases that there were no damaging effects on profits. Examples of films that did well in both venues were Margin Call, Arbitrage and Bachelorette.
2015	Mass audiences seem not to be supporting movies that were not sequels, remakes, re-imaginings, spin-offs or an adaptation of a young adult novel. With multiplexes crowded with major franchise films, smaller, indie movies were being edged out – and were appearing in other places, such as on Netflix and other VOD services (without a theatrical release).
2015	Director Sean Baker's comedy/drama *Tangerine* (2015) was filmed exclusively on three iPhone 5s smartphones.
2016	Start-up *Screening Room* (developed by entrepreneur and tech mogul Sean Parker) offered consumers the ability to watch new Hollywood releases in their own homes the same day that they were released to movie theatres. The cost was $150 for a set-top box, and a $50 per film rental fee (for a 48-hour viewing window).

(Source: Filmsite.org)

Watching Netflix on a laptop.

GCSE Film Studies

Task 3.3

Research a timeline of your own. Choose a period of recent time, a year perhaps. You could include:

- The films that have been important to you.
- Stars and film people that have caught your attention.
- Other important events that link to changes in the film world.

You could present it as a PowerPoint presentation or project booklet.

Two decades and beyond Hollywood in the 21st century

Hollywood's future? A six-metre tall Optimus Prime figure stands along Tsim Sha Tsui at the world premiere of Hollywood movie *Transformers 4* in Hong Kong, China.

We conclude our look at the mainstream Hollywood movie landscape with a brief comparison and an attempt to see how the influences of both decades persist to this day. As we look at the top 10s of both decades it is a similar kind of film that tends to dominate; although very different in genre it is the four quadrant family friendly film that continues to be the mainstay of large-scale mainstream success.

In the 1950s; it was the Disney animation in the 1980s, films and franchises such as *E.T.* and *Indiana Jones*. This pattern remains strong; in 2015 the number 1 film was *Star Wars: The Force Awakens* (J.J. Abrams): a big budget sci-fi. At number 2 *Jurassic World* (Colin Trevorrow) a Spielberg legacy. At number 3 *Avengers: Age of Ultron* (Joss Whedon) continuing the love affair with the superhero, *Batman* (1989, Tim Burton) was number 4 for the 1980s. *Inside Out* (2015, Pete Docter and Ronnie del Carmen) maintained Disney's perennial presence. Perhaps the only new presence being *The Hunger Games: Mockingjay – Part 2* (2015, Francis Lawrence) as a representative of a girl-friendly mainstream film aimed squarely at the key demographic; a particular kind of teen movie that has taken elements of the genre pioneered in the 1950s by Brando and Dean continued through the John Hughes' 1980s to find 21st-century success by adding a sci-fi/fantasy gloss (see also *Harry Potter*).

The Hunger Games: a girl-friendly mainstream film.

Both in the 1980s and today we see the reliance on franchise and sequel over genre; in the 1950s it seemed to be much more about attacking TV through the widescreen appeal of historical epic and adventure resulting in one-offs rather than sequels.

Many of the studio and distributor credits remain the same from the 1950s through the 1980s until now. Those names provide the finance for the independent producer approach that became dominant out of the 1970s. Whereas a film such as *Ben Hur* is known as a MGM movie, the names Lucas and Spielberg dominate over Paramount when it comes to *Indiana Jones* – we associate the new *Star Wars* films with J.J. Abrams as much as we do their new owners Disney.

Hollywood's block-buster movies still provide an escape for the mainstream audience today much as they did in the 1950s and 1980s. The 1950s may have been a 'last fling' for the old studio system before the collapse and uncertainty of the 1960s, but the 1980s were definitely a confident commercial resurgence building on the 1970s' discovery of new formulas and approaches – primarily the all conquering summer (more recently Christmas as well) blockbuster. In the 21st century there are many who say this model is now creaking under the strain, as the old studio system did in the 1950s, but its dominance remains as yet unchallenged. Indeed, the obituary for cinema going has been prepped and ready to go in many decades but the habit still persists. Box office numbers still remain significant despite the challenges mainstream Hollywood has faced; in the 1950s it was television, in the 1980s home video and today streaming (and piracy), but Hollywood, like a line about love from one of its own movies, '*still finds a way*'.

Quick Question 3.5
What are the major difference outlined in terms of the types of films produced in the 1950s and those produced in the 1980s?

Task 3.4
What do you think will happen to Hollywood movies in your lifetime? Try to use both research and your imagination to come up with an answer. You could write a letter to your future self who would be able to judge the accuracy of your predictions. You could also make notes to use in a class discussion of what the future may hold.

The wider social, political and economic context

An American dream – suburban America of the 1950s.

America in the 1950s

The US became a world **superpower** after World War II. Before the war, the US was the biggest economic power, but the pre-war government concentrated on problems at home and tried not to get too involved overseas. However, after the war, they became far more involved across the world in order, as they saw it, to stop the Soviet Union (Russia) spreading its influence and 'communist ideals'.

The basic premise of communism is shared ownership – everyone in a community sharing its resources, lands, businesses and wealth. It is a philosophy/ideology with a long tradition. However, in the 20th century it became almost solely associated with a particularly repressive form of government in the Soviet Union. In some countries communist governments were elected; in others the communists took control after a violent revolution.

The fear of communism was strongest in America, which had a long tradition of individualism and opposition to any form of collective ownership. In the 1950s, a suspected communist in the US was treated with the same fear and distrust as a supporter of Al Qa'ida is today. The problem was that everyone who expressed ideas that could be seen to question the establishment or government of the time was labelled as a communist and therefore an 'enemy of the state'.

Key term

Superpower
A country with a dominant position in international relations that has the power to exert influence on a global scale. This is done through the combined means of technological, cultural, military (conventional and nuclear) and economic strength, as well as diplomatic influence.

Part 3: Component 1:
Films made in the USA

The shadow of the bomb

At the end of World War II another conflict known as the 'Cold War' began between Russia and America, it was to last for over 40 years. Each state saw the other as an 'arch enemy' and they built more and more nuclear weapons in order to 'defend' themselves and deter the other from launching an attack. Young people growing up in the 1950s lived in fear of nuclear war – you might want to ask you grandparents what it was like to live in fear of 'the bomb'.

Politically the decade was dominated by the **Republican** president Dwight D. Eisenhower, in office 1953–1961.

> *During his presidency, Eisenhower managed Cold War-era tensions with the Soviet Union under the looming threat of nuclear weapons, ended the war in Korea in 1953 and authorised a number of covert anti-communist operations by the CIA around the world. On the home front, where America was enjoying a period of relative prosperity, Eisenhower strengthened Social Security, created the massive new Interstate Highway System and manoeuvred behind the scenes to discredit the rabid anti-Communist Senator Joseph McCarthy. Though popular throughout his administration, he faltered in the protection of civil rights for African Americans by failing to fully enforce the Supreme Court's mandate for the desegregation of schools in* Brown v. Board of Education *(1954).* (www.history.com)

> **Key term**
>
> **Republican Party**
> One of the two main US political parties (the other being the Democratic Party), favouring a right-wing stance, limited central government, and tough, interventionist foreign policy (en.oxforddictionaries.com).

The paradox of 1950s America

In America during the 1950s, the fear of the bomb, communism and invasion, and the pleasures of prosperity existed at the same time. The image of an ideal community with neat houses and white picket fences could be seen to disguise much nastier things happening below the surface. One of them was racism – black people were still segregated, they did not have equality before the law. Another was a fear of communism – artists and others who expressed anti-establishment views were put on trial and either lost their jobs or were forced into exile. During the 1950s, a number of writers, actors and directors who protested against the hardship and unemployment caused by the capitalist system at the time, found themselves hunted out and exposed by a political campaign led by Senator McCarthy. Many American citizens had more in terms of material wealth than ever before, the more they had the more frightened they became of losing it. They looked for 'reds under the bed' each night or someone or something that would 'invade' their comfortable lives and 'snatch' away their new-found wealth.

Quick Question 3.6

Using the internet, create a quiz about the 1950s. You can choose what to include, you may want to include more about things other than films, for example popular culture and sport.

127

GCSE Film Studies

America in the 1980s

Impressions of the 1980s.

Key term

Paradox
A situation where two contradictory ideas exist at the same time.

An enduring, more open, more complex paradox persists and multiplies

If the 1950s were the true beginning of the Cold War, the 1980s was the last full decade of this superpower confrontation, as the Berlin Wall came down and the Soviet system fell apart. At the start of the decade the Cold War showed no signs of warming with the election of President Reagan who believed that the spread of communism anywhere threatened America and freedom everywhere. This resulted in an American government more intent on opposing what Reagan dubbed 'the evil empire'. The 'Reagan Doctrine' meant financial and military aid to anticommunist governments and insurgencies around the world. The nuclear confrontation was intensified with the Strategic Defence Initiative (SDI) film referenced as 'Star Wars' that promised to render the Soviet Union's missiles obsolete; it proved to be as much a technological fantasy as George Lucas' movies. This continued, probably at a desensitised lower level, the 1950s' constant fear of potential global conflict and destruction. There was some late 1980s' relief from the shadow of mutually assured destruction when Reagan and Gorbachev eventually concluded the landmark Intermediate-Range Nuclear Forces (INF) agreement and established the foundation for the Strategic Arms Reduction Treaty (START), which was concluded in 1991.

The Reagan 1980s: social and economic change

The 1980s was the decade that seemed to be about rewarding success and allowing people with money to keep more of it. It built on the theory that higher earnings would encourage people to buy more goods and invest in businesses, and that the resulting economic growth would 'trickle down' to everyone, but it didn't. As we have seen more recently, the reality has been acceleration in the growth of the gap between rich and poor and a shrinking American middle class.

Part 3: Component 1:
Films made in the USA

For many people a symbol of the decade's approach to wealth and economics was the 'yuppie': a **baby boomer** with a college education, a well-paying job and expensive tastes. Many people criticised yuppies for being self-centred and materialistic, and surveys of young urban professionals across America showed that they were, indeed, more concerned with making money and buying consumer goods than their parents and grandparents had been.

Socially the 1980s was a time when family dynamics and societal views changed to allow men and women to share the financial and domestic responsibilities within their family. While the overall number of families grew between 1980–1999, the greatest change occurred in the lone-parent family, rising by 74%. Alongside this, the 1980s saw a huge rise in divorce rates. So, since the 'white picket fence **nuclear family** era' of the 1950s' marriage had experienced a sustained decline. The 1950s 'culture of marriage' had perhaps become a 'culture of divorce'.

So, returning to the idea of a paradox, the image of an ideal community with neat houses and white picket fences had become tarnished by social change. Something much nastier was happening underneath the 'American dream' and it was coming ever closer into view. Problems of race and racism persisted; the 1980s experienced several minor race riots along the road to the 1992 major riots in Los Angeles. Paradoxically there was the general feeling of prosperity abroad in the America of the 1980s. When Ronald Reagan left office in 1989, he had the highest approval rating of any president since Franklin Roosevelt. When we look back to that decade we can see clearly a new division emerging in American society, as the value of an average person's wage began to reduce and credit became a much more necessary part of people's lives. To quote Reagan's predecessor Jimmy Carter in a televised speech to America:

> *In a nation that was proud of hard work, strong families, close-knit communities, and our faith in God, too many of us now tend to worship self-indulgence and consumption. Human identity is no longer defined by what one does, but by what one owns. But we've discovered that owning things and consuming things does not satisfy our longing for meaning. We've learned that piling up material goods cannot fill the emptiness of lives which have no confidence or purpose.*

The America of the 1980s seemed to be a decade-long attempt to prove Carter's prophetic assertion wrong, perhaps in the 21st century these (in many ways 1950s) ideals that have remained below the surface of American culture may start to re-emerge. Perhaps it is fitting that we leave this decade with a quote from one of its most iconic film characters, Gordon Gekko from Oliver Stone's *Wall Street* (1987):

> *The point is, ladies and gentlemen, that greed, for lack of a better word, is good. Greed is right. Greed works. Greed clarifies, cuts through, and captures the essence of the evolutionary spirit.*

Not only did this seem to capture the spirit of economic **zeitgeist** but, as Michael Douglas often recalls, it became a call to arms in 1980s' America, inspiring many to attempt to emulate Gekko rather than consider these words as the warning they were intended to be.

Key terms

Baby boomer
A person who was born between 1946 and 1964.

Nuclear family
A family unit that includes two married parents of opposite genders and their children living in the same residence.

Quick Question 3.7

Using the internet, create a quiz about the 1980s. You should include some political and social context questions but you can also include other things, for example popular culture and sport.

Key term

Zeitgeist
The spirit of the time; general trend of thought or feeling characteristic of a particular period of time.

GCSE Film Studies

Context – a brief comparison

When studying the films set in the 1950s and 1980s we must try to find both similarities and differences that help us to understand the films themselves.

Similarities and differences in 1950s and 1980s America.	1950s	1980s
	Influenced by the Cold War, at the start	Still influenced by the Cold War, at the end
	Economically prosperous, enjoying genuine post-war growth	Economically prosperous, mainly due to working class Americans' reliance on credit
	Politically dominated by Republican presidents, although their approach was more what in the 1980s would be considered a **Democratic** approach	Politically dominated by Republican presidents, with a modern Republican approach
	Socially, projected an idea of the perfect nuclear family – the original father, mother and 2.4 children	Socially, saw the breakdown of the family unit, with rising divorce rates and number of single-parent households

Key term

Democratic Party
One of the two main US political parties (the other being the Republican Party), which follows a broadly liberal programme, tending to support social reform and minority rights (en.oxforddictionaries.com).

So, overall two very different decades; this difference being clearly reflected in the approach to science-fiction aliens that we see in *Invasion of the Body Snatchers* and *E.T. the Extra-Terrestrial*. As the Cold War began, America looked for an enemy that seemed impossible to track down; as it ended it sought after a reluctant friend.

Task 3.5

Having looked at the 1950s and 1980s, what is it like to live in your decade? Write an essay that describes your zeitgeist and compares it with the two other decades. Discussing it with your friends, teachers and adults should help.

What is likely to happen in future decades?

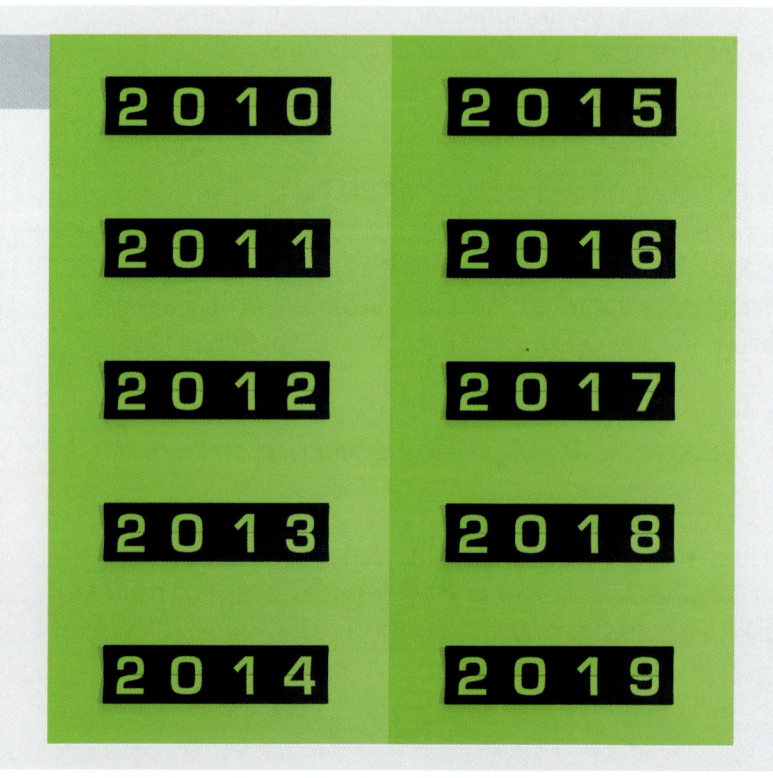

2010 2015
2011 2016
2012 2017
2013 2018
2014 2019

130

Case study: Invasion of the Body Snatchers and E.T. the Extra-Terrestrial

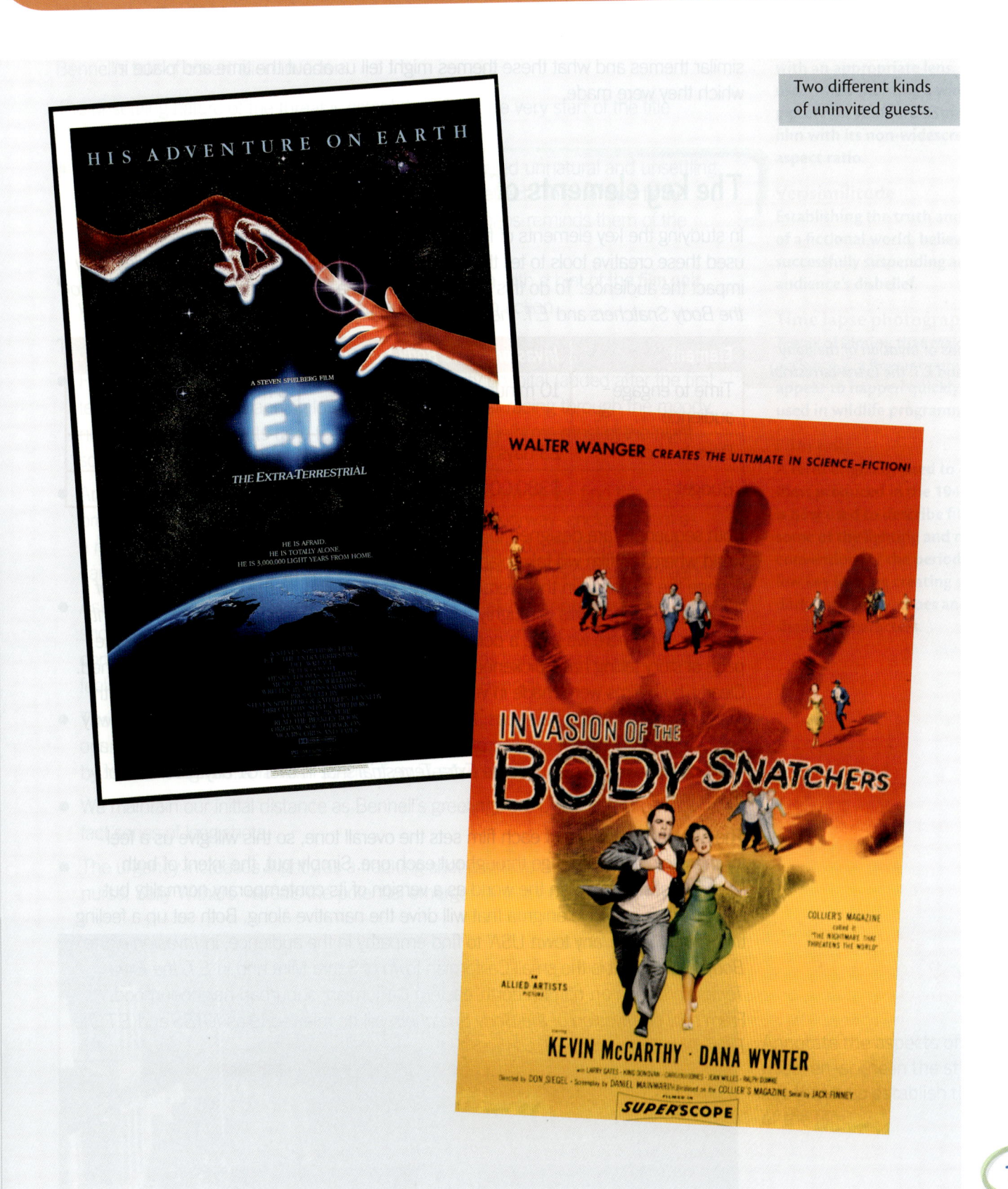

Two different kinds of uninvited guests.

GCSE Film Studies

> **Key term**
>
> **Back projected**
> Sometimes called rear projection. Way of projecting images onto a translucent screen so that they are viewed from the opposite side. Used to create the illusion that the characters in the foreground are moving. It was widely used for many years in driving scenes, e.g. *Psycho* (1960, Alfred Hitchcock) or to show other forms of distant background motion, e.g. *King Solomon's Mines*.

- Inside the car we watch a standard **back projected** two-shot close-up conversation as Sally Withers brings the doctor up to speed with the situation and recent town gossip: Becky Driscoll's (an employee at the San Francisco Health Department) name being a pointed reference.
- This is interrupted by a long shot as Jimmy Grimaldi darts into the road and the audience experiences the jolt of a near collision.
- So far the conventional framing has not drawn attention to itself; it is the exposition in the conversation and the action in the road that has held our attention.
- As the depiction of the journey draws to a close we share in long shot the scene of Grimaldi's abandoned vegetable stall, which foreshadows the rising threat to Santa Mira.
- The next scene is in Dr Bennell's office; the first shot is a close-up of Bennell framed to include the reflection of main street to the left-hand side, further reinforcing the apparent normality of Santa Mira.
- Into the office arrives the aforementioned Becky Driscoll, she is clearly top lit to emphasise her attractive features and this helps to reveal Bennell's feelings for her.
- They catch up and Becky begins her story of how her Aunt Wilma is insisting that her Uncle Ira is not him. This shot-reverse-shot conversation is shot from two different angles: Bennell from a low angle and Becky from a high angle. This not only reflects their relative position on-screen but perhaps also the 1950s respective gender roles of power and authority.
- As the characters move to leave the office the camera movement continues its steady fluid motion, helping to establish the sequence's immersive immediacy.
- The two protagonists descend the office staircase and they are prophetically silhouetted against the harsh exterior light as a potentially ideal couple.
- On main street, natural Californian sunshine lights the scene as the camera tracks them across this typical small town American scene: a clear contrast to the dark city where we first met Bennell at the end of both his tether and narrative trajectory.
- The opening sequence comes to a close with a second visit to the doctor's office. It starts with a close-up of the exterior to show the passage of time as the clock now stands at 4.45pm. The working day is nearly done and the lower light level begins to cast the shadows of oncoming evening … and Bennell's first real encounter with the hysteria. He has finally caught up with Jimmy Grimaldi who of his mother exclaims, 'Don't let her get me'.

Throughout this opening sequence the conventional and unobtrusive framing and movement has smoothly established the world of Santa Mira. It has drawn us into, alongside Dr Bennell, the mysterious goings on both discussed and finally witnessed; the scene is set.

Cinematography in E.T. the Extra-Terrestrial

E.T. is a colour film shot in **35mm** using **Panavision** cameras with an **aspect ratio** of 1.85:1. Both then and now the variously lit colour photography lends it a feel of verisimilitude, with a combination of both childhood innocence and an adult nostalgia for such. This fantasy-tinged reality helps to immerse us in a world seen through both Elliott's and E.T.'s eyes.

- In the opening sequence both aspects of the cinematography, lighting and camera set-up, establish a pattern that is used throughout the rest of the film. This evokes a sense of wonder and innocence that has an almost nostalgic fairy-tale feel.
- Spielberg's use of the camera is tailored to a child's eye or, in this case, aliens-eye view of the world. The film is predominantly shot from lower camera angles, mimicking a child's point-of-view. This creates an effect where younger viewers can identify with the characters; adults appear overwhelming and intimidating as we see them from the waist or knees down. It also means that adult viewers are reminded of how the world looked when they were younger and to some extent they spend a short time reliving their own childhood.
- Specific examples of this framing can be seen in two introductions: one of the spaceship and another of the men. We first get close to the ship in a mid-point-of-view shot of the boarding ramp; it is shot looking through the trees at a low level that suggests we are seeing it through somebody's or something's eyes. This is quickly confirmed as the camera does a low angle track around the ship from E.T.'s POV; the POV being confirmed with a close up of his long, bony fingers touching the tree branches.
- When the men arrive to shatter what has been a wonder-filled exploration of the woods by E.T., the low angle of the camera is further cemented.
- Spielberg starts with a brief whip pan from E.T. to a low angle shot of a rapidly arriving truck, which dominates the screen. This is made even more intimidating by an extreme close-up of the truck's radiator grill and headlights, a long shot then reveals the relentless arrival of even more trucks.
- Additional low angle close-ups of an exhaust pipe polluting the forest, a man revealed as a pair of legs and an emphatic boot splashing through a puddle further illustrate E.T.'s point-of-view.
- The audience now shares his feelings of dread at what this arrival means. This brief interlude of tranquil exploration has been broken by this intimidating adult transgression.

In terms of lighting, Spielberg evokes much of the magic and mist of nostalgia by the manipulation of this aspect of film form. In the opening sequence light sources are carefully placed to evoke many emotional responses from the audience. The diffuse light, often back lit, that surrounds the ship and the forest glade it sits in creates a magical grotto effect (both inside and out). Our first view of the alien ship makes it look like a Christmas tree bauble placed incongruously in the woods with the harsh glow of the suburban backdrop in the far distance.

Part 3: Component 1: Films made in the USA

Key terms

35mm
The film gauge or width most commonly used for motion pictures and chemical still photography. It is significantly more expensive than 16mm film but is seen as the cost-effective option for mainstream films producing a good trade-off between price and quality of image.

Panavision
Company that produced a camera with a type of widescreen lens, the word is formed from elements of panorama and vision.

Aspect ratio
The ratio of the width to the height of an image or screen.

Quick Question 3.9

Describe the ways in which a camera can be used in order to give a child's-eye's view of a film world.

GCSE Film Studies

E.T. the Extra-Terrestrial – a scene is set.

Quick Question 3.10

Annotate the aspects of mise-en-scène in the still on the right that help to establish the world of the film.

There are many clear examples in this opening sequence of how Spielberg uses light.

- In the establishing shot of the forest glade, the light pall of the suburb encroaches on the scene and serves to give softness to the illumination.
- In the glade the ship is the main light source, its eerie glow acting as a backlight to give us our first glimpse of E.T.'s silhouette.
- Inside the ship are low level diffused light sources. As the camera tracks around the interior, lending it a 'grotto' feel as we see its strange glowing cargo of alien wonders, the low key lighting creates shadows that give the effect of face-like features on some of the plants.
- Later, more harshly, headlights act as searchlights and, as more trucks arrive, **lense flare** emphasises their 'rude interruption' and transgression of the scene.
- During the chase the light of the ship's glow intensifies to signal the imminence of it departure.
- The chase itself heads for the ship's single spotlight presence in the trees, in mid-shot its interior acts as backlight and silhouettes dramatically E.T.'s companion, who is waiting for his return.
- Finally, after the ship leaves E.T. behind, he descends towards the light of the suburb as the camera tilts up to fully reveal his destination.
- Throughout this opening sequence the unconventional framing and movement and subtly intimate lighting has clearly established a point-of-view on events that is literally alien in its vision. Drawing us into this perspective and what is now E.T.'s very daunting predicament.

Key term

Lense flare
The effect created when light is scattered or flared in a lens system, often in response to a bright light. It usually produces an undesirable effect on the image but has increasingly been used by filmmakers to create an aesthetic effect, e.g. Oliver Tate's '2 Weeks of Lovemaking' video in *Submarine*.

Task 3.6

Having read the two sections on cinematography and re-watched the opening sequences of both *IOTBS* and *E.T.*, compare the similarities and differences in approach of the two films.

Mise-en-scène in Invasion of the Body Snatchers

The opening sequence of *IOTBS* has a basic matter-of-fact mise-en-scène that is significant in underpinning its realistic feel. Several locations are used:

- a clouded sky,
- an urban back street hospital,
- a rural train station hemmed in by hills,
- a country road with its abandoned stall,
- a modest doctor's office and
- a small town main street.

These unremarkable settings not only establish the film's reality but serve to suggest that the invasion could be happening where you are right now.

The costumes, such as suits and ties, suggest a comfortable prosperity. Although Becky on her first appearance, in what could be a prom dress complete with formal looking gloves, appears over-dressed for a day at the hardware store, perhaps she had other motives in mind when dressing that morning?

The props, x-rays and other medical trappings – serve much like the locations do in grounding the opening in a familiar reality. We are immersed in the 1950s perfect white picket fence world familiar to the audience, either first hand or through TV. Suggesting, perhaps, that this is the greatest treasure that could be threatened or more subversively that this bland community is a symptom of the conformity that eases the way for the invasion itself.

Main street small town America (*Invasion of the Body Snatchers*).

Quick Question 3.11

Annotate the aspects of mise-en-scène in the still on the left that help establish the world of the film.

GCSE Film Studies

Mise-en-scène in E.T. the Extra-Terrestrial

The opening sequence of *E.T.* employs a mise-en-scène that **imbues** the film with a sense of wonder, innocence and magic. It is focused on one main setting: that of an isolated forest glade. Within this we experience an alien spaceship both inside and out. We also never loose the feeling of how close the brightly lit suburb is where the main story will take place. It is not just the alien ship that helps create the magical air to the film but the way Spielberg films the more prosaic forest and suburb that starts the film with an almost fairy-tale feel.

The costumes, such as they are, do not give a clear indication of who E.T.'s pursuers are. They carry a clearly masculine threat but do not establish their later identities as scientists in the employ of an impersonal government agency. They are an indication of how the costumes throughout the rest of the film will reflect both character and a 1980s reality; their initial **ambiguity** is perhaps a reflection of how ultimately at least one of these government 'agents' will side with Elliott in his mission to get E.T. home.

> **Key terms**
>
> **Imbues**
> Fills someone or something with a particular feeling or idea.
>
> **Ambiguity**
> Something that is unclear or confusing, or can be understood in more than one way.

Strange cargo (*E.T. the Extra-Terrestrial*).

Quick Question 3.12

Annotate the still on the right to highlight the use of light inside the space ship.

We have two sets of props to consider: the alien's and the humans'. The alien props firmly underpin the science-fiction element to the film. Yet they do this with a non-threatening air of magic and curiosity. The ship is a friendly bauble twinkling in the forest night. Its contents, being strange and alluring, are glowing conical space fungi and stunted tree-like plants that may or may not have faces. The human props seem more out of place in the forest than the alien ones. The trucks speak of threat and trespass and the men with their probing torches and custodial belt-hung keys are intimidating to both alien and audience alike. Should we consider E.T. himself as a prop? At this early stage the puppet is viewed with curiosity and a growing feeling of empathy that will mature along with his relationship with Elliott. Nevertheless, E.T. is a puppet and works well in evoking innocence and vulnerability, particularly in long shot, but in some of the closer shots, like when we see his attempting to 'bounce' back to his ship, is something the audience is still becoming accustomed to.

Ultimately, the use of mise-en-scène is successful in establishing two worlds of wonder for the audience: E.T.'s world for us and our world for him.

> Having read the two sections on mise-en-scène and re-watched the opening sequences:
> 1. Find and annotate film stills that illustrate the uses of mise-en-scène in both films.
> 2. Compare the similarities and differences in approach of the two films.

Task 3.7

Editing in Invasion of the Body Snatchers

- IOTBS is constructed in the classic conventional Hollywood style of **continuity editing**. It is put together at a mostly even pace (perhaps slow by today's standards) that never draws attention to itself. Nor does it at any point threaten to break the audience's immersion in this representation of a familiar 1950s America. The audience, even city dwellers, would recognise and understand this world, even if was from the experience of other movies and increasing amounts of television drama and situation comedies.
- The style largely employs the straight cut, except for major shifts in time and space. Here it employs the standard dissolves as we are transported into the flashback, from car journey to office x-rays, a daytime hardware store exterior, to the evening and an office exterior and the final office shot to cousin Wilma's home.
- When we first encounter Dr Miles Bennell, a series of even paced straight cuts in a shot-reverse-shot conversation construct the initial conversation with the police doctor. The even pace during Bennell's increasingly hysterical outburst give the scene a dispassionate feel, where we seem to be invited to judge his sanity for ourselves. This scene ends with a typical 'watery ripple' dissolve for the start of the extended flashback that would tell us his full story.
- The opening sequence continues as a long series of unobtrusive straight cuts that are even paced until Jimmy Grimaldi runs out in front of Bennell's car, then the driver's shock is emphasised with a slight increase in editing pace.
- Overall, the editing feels slow by modern standards, an almost dogged pace in its mission to establish this world and the enigma at its heart. The use of this seamless style of continuity editing is perfectly suited to effectively and quickly immerse the audience in the mundane normality of this world. A world, however, that has something going on just below the surface and the audience, such as Miles Bennell, wants to find out more.

Key term

Continuity editing
A style of editing that gives the viewer the impression that the action unfolds consistently in space and time. In most films, logical coherence is achieved by cutting to continuity, which emphasises the smooth transition of time and space.

Top tip

Always make sure you use the correct terminology when analysing the speed or types of edit used in a sequence.

A white picket fence world (*Invasion of the Body Snatchers*).

GCSE Film Studies

Quick Question 3.13

What kinds of editing are used in the opening sequence? What effect do these have on the audience?

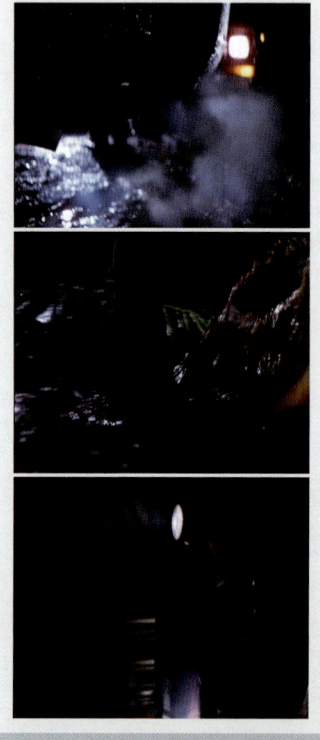

Cut to ... (E.T. the Extra-Terrestrial).

Editing in E.T. the Extra-Terrestrial

The editing style in *E.T.* is a fine-tuned use of continuity editing; there is a relatively unobtrusive variation in the concentrated use of the dissolve transition.

- A series of barely perceptible dissolves match the shifting light to maintain the smooth travel of the tracking shot and act to draw us into the scene. After the straight cut to the ship's landing site there is a series of at least six consecutive dissolves that help the scene to entrance the audience; this culminates with a final dissolve to a spot-lit alien finger in close-up that mirrors a shot resembling both the film poster and an iconic shot from later in the film.

- The pace of editing is quite deliberate as E.T. explores this new world and we get to absorb the wonder of the sequence. The editing picks up pace with the speed of chase. Both camera movement and editing pace continue to increase as the chase accelerates in a series of straight cuts that position the audience firmly in the role of pursued rather than pursuer. It slows down for a long shot pause in the chase only to re-commence at a frantic pace anew as E.T. becomes more desperate to reach his ship. When he fails in this it slows down and returns to a more even pace reflecting E.T.'s weary resignation as he begins his trudge towards the bright lights of the Californian suburb.

- Overall the editing of the opening sequence has been carefully constructed so as not to disturb the fragile sense of wonder and magic that Spielberg wants to imbue this most benign of alien 'invasions'. The use of this seamless style of dissolve enhanced continuity editing is perfectly suited to seduce and immerse the audience into this 'fairy tale'. The pattern is only disturbed when the human men arrive as unwanted trespassers pressing an urgent search. The quickening of pace appropriately reflects this disturbance both on-screen and in the attention of the audience. The world of the magical forest 'grotto' is now gone with the departing ship; E.T. must seek out new wonders as we wonder as to his fate.

Task 3.8

Having read the two sections on editing and re-watched the opening sequences, analyse the closing sequences of each film comparing the similarities and differences in approach to editing of the two films.

Quick Question 3.14

The still on the right is from the framing device at the start of *IOTBS*. Look at the framing device at the end of the film and answer the following:
1. Do you think the framing device was necessary in *IOTBS*?
2. Explain your answer.

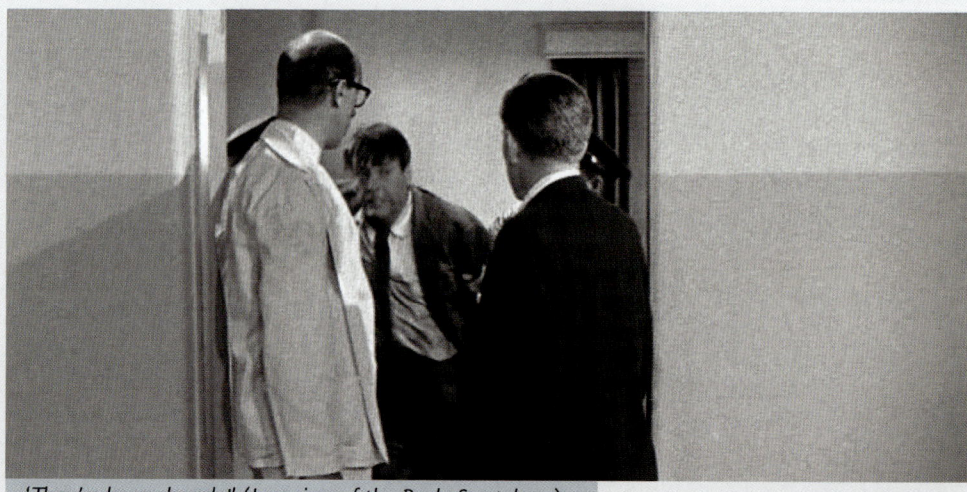

'They're here already!' (Invasion of the Body Snatchers).

Sound in Invasion of the Body Snatchers

The mix of diegetic and non-diegetic sound is fairly standard in *IOTBS*, with the bulk of the opening sequence being orchestrally scored. The score has a strong emotional impact, it helps to plant the seeds of doubt and mystery in the audience, the diegetic sound has an equally important role to play. The diegetic sound we hear from the matter-of-fact delivery of natural sounding dialogue, to the sounds of everyday life is essential to establishing the verisimilitude of the on-screen Santa Mira.

- Key examples of the non-diegetic musical score occur at frequent intervals throughout the opening sequence. From the very start of the title sequence, dramatic strident brass and rising strings invoke a sense of impending melodrama – that something big is behind that sky – the titles climaxing in a foreboding fanfare.

- The orchestral score continues its work by emphasising the strength of feeling behind Miles' initial outburst, as a thriller- or horror-style tension builds. At this point the second non-diegetic sound element is introduced in the form of the voice-over, guiding us towards and into the central narrative; the haggard Bennell dramatically intones: 'Something evil had taken over the town.' The score is applied in a variety of ways throughout the opening sequence, from slightly mournful strings to underscore the forebodingly abandoned Grimaldi's vegetable stall; through the romantic flourish of strings to herald Becky Driscoll's 'love interest' entrance; to the final scenes and the pensive notes under the 4.45pm clock – nothing's happened, no patients have come and we begin to realise that's the point.

- The first diegetic sound does not let up on the drama, as a police siren splits the night to introduce the framing device and perhaps sound a warning alarm for the audience that echoes Bennell's final warning shouted directly into camera at the film's end: 'They're here already! You're next! You're next, You're next …!' As we move through the opening sequence, the diegetic sound is that of the everyday noise of small town America; from a solitary tolling railroad bell through to the hustle and bustle of the emblematic main street. The only truly strident diegetic sound is that of the sharp shock of the loud car horn warning Jimmy Grimaldi and temporarily startling the already absorbed audience.

So, as we can see in this special-effects free, science-fiction opening, the combination of the dramatic music and realistic sounds of normality are vital to establishing both the believability of the world and the unseen menace that will come to increasingly threaten our main protagonists, Santa Mira, America and the whole world. The fact and feeling that something is wrong in this idyllic community is almost exclusively evoked by Carmen Dragon's poundingly ominous score.

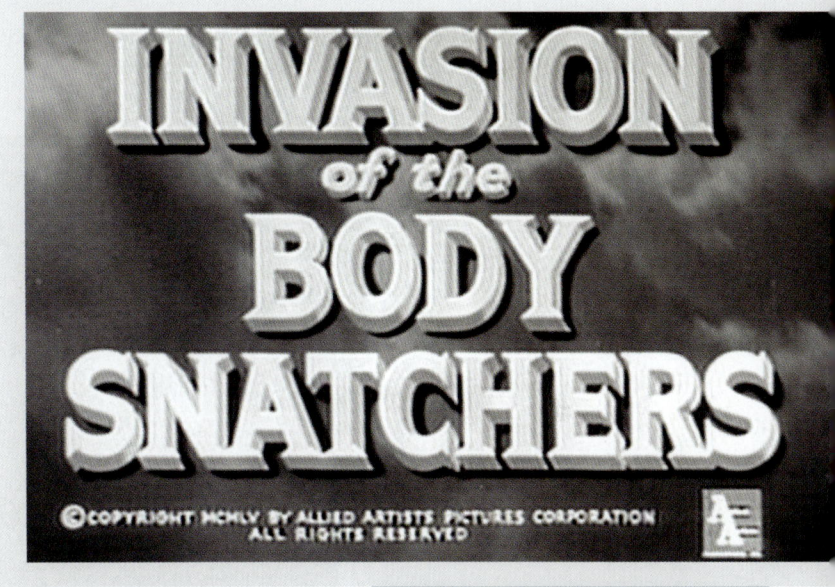

Duumm derrr! Carmen Dragon's soundtrack introduces the film with unmistakable drama.

Top tip
When describing sounds make sure you have a 'bank' of words that can be used to describe the soundtrack and the effects created (see opposite).

Sound in E.T. the Extra-Terrestrial

The mix of diegetic and non-diegetic sound is both effective and at times subtle in the opening sequence of *E.T.*

- The non-diegetic score is a mix of typically science-fiction sounding themes combined with light orchestral sounds to evoke wonder, only changing to a more traditionally dramatic feel when the humans appear on the scene. The diegetic sound uses elements typical of science fiction to underscore the spaceship and its occupants; it also provides a contrast between evoking a feeling of nature's gentle wonder to the shattering of this by man's sudden incursion into this innocent scene.

John William's score rises to a crescendo then descends to a few pensive notes as E.T. is left behind (*E.T. the Extra-Terrestrial*).

- Non-diegetic sound is deployed immediately over the opening titles to establish *E.T.* as a science-fiction film. Creepy, otherworldly Theremin-style, electronic moaning sounds evoke both previous science-fiction films and the ominous depths of space that set the tone for the rest of the film. The remaining non-diegetic score is largely conventional in approach. John Williams employs piping flutes as we enter the scene proper. The music has a gentle sense of playful mystery lending the atmosphere a kind of daybreak expectancy. There are typically strange fiction-style strings, with a xylophone ripple, to evoke the alien feel for the ship's interior. Williams moves to lower register notes of the music to signal the ominous arrival of men and their trucks, this increases in tempo with an urgent foreboding. As the scene crashes into action the pace of the music mirrors the chase in tempo using loud pulsing horns and racing strings. We move towards the sequence's climax with a fanfare heralding the spaceships' take-off. Finally, the music dies down with E.T.'s worried gulp to more gentle horns, strings and piping flute to re-emphasise our empathy with the stranded creature's predicament.

Part 3: Component 1:
Films made in the USA

- Diegetically the sound is used as we would expect. There is a range of slightly strange non-threatening sci-fi sounds like the gentle ringing of the alarmed E.T.s, their gulping and grunting speech and the whirring of the ship itself as it powers up to leave. The earthly sounds are set in contrast to one another. Nature is evoked with crickets chirping and owls hooting; these gentle, calming night noises are brutally disturbed by the harsh sound of the men and their machines, rumbling exhausts, loud splashing and the sparse dialogue cries of 'This way!' and 'I think I see him!' The sequence ends with the sounds of a different kind of night as a police siren and distant dog bark signify the potential hazards of the suburbs and humanity E.T. must now face.

- One of the more successful elements is how the non-diegetic and diegetic sounds are subtly mixed on frequent occasions to enhance the mood of the sequence. As we review the landing site, a mix of strings, chirping crickets, mysterious sounding chords, hooting owls, the gently barking aliens and sci-fi beeping sounds all blend together to build the drama, and to underscore a feeling of discovery, exploration and intrigue that are central to the sequence.

So, as we can see, or more correctly hear, just as in *IOTBS*, the soundtrack is integral to establishing both genre and mood at the start of the film. The clever and subtle mix of diegetic and non-diegetic sounds create a feeling of innocent wonder.

> Having read the two sections on sound and re-watched the closing sequences, analyse the use of sound in each film and answer the following questions:
>
> 1. What are the key elements of sound in both sequences?
> 2. What effect do you think these key elements were designed to achieve?
> 3. What are the main similarities and differences between the approaches of each film?

Task 3.9

An adventure begins (*E.T. the Extra-Terrestrial*).

Key term

Chiaroscuro

An Italian term originally used in art to refer to the high contrast light and darkness in Renaissance paintings. Later used in in cinema to describe the use of high and low key lighting in, for example, film noir films.

Concluding aesthetics

In defining film aesthetics, for our purposes we have to consider how all aspects of film form are combined artistically to create a distinctive 'look' or style; where the 'spectacle' of a film engages spectators more than a film's narrative. This idea about the collective impact of the use of film form certainly applies to both films. The idea of aesthetics can be hard to pin down at first. If we step back from the detailed analysis for a moment we should remember that it is not just individual films that may or may not have an overall guiding aesthetic. It is not uncommon to associate a particular look, style or feel to genres, directors, studios and film movements. This is not true of all examples in each of those categories; in some an aesthetic is more fundamental to its artistry than others. For example, in the case of the German expressionist film movement the use of **chiaroscuro** lighting, highly expressive acting and highly subjective sets and camera angles are essential in their attempts to convey meaning and create their art.

IOTBS and *E.T.* are generally considered to be science-fiction films and this genre is often associated with a cold, antiseptic, bright and shiny future aesthetic style. Neither of our films employs much of this kind of look or style, although clear examples of science-fiction style can be found in both films. In *IOTBS* the alien pods, and in *E.T.* the creature itself, are clear visual references to the science-fiction genre. In the case of our comparative study we are considering an aesthetic determined by the individual filmmakers rather than wholesale use of genre iconography and style.

When we consider the combined use of film language in both opening sequences of the films, they are both engaged in building a version of a normal world.

Don Siegel (1912–1991).

Siegel intends the aesthetic of *IOTBS* to reflect an unremarkable and ordinary version of 1950s small town America, much as Spielberg's guiding aesthetic is that of an unremarkable and ordinary version of 1980s suburban America. It is the use of film form to infuse these similar worlds with a different nuance that brings their respective aesthetics into focus.

In *IOTBS* normality is coloured with a flavour of film noir and paranoid threat; in *E.T.* a similar normality is instead imbued with a sense of innocence and nostalgia. These 'styles' or 'looks' are not just limited to the opening sequences but run throughout the films. One only has to consider the first home we visit in *IOTBS*, as a perfect lawn is mowed by a unnervingly happy drone-like Uncle Ira or the consumerist clutter that colonises Elliott's 1980s bedroom to realise that these aesthetic flavours of meaning run throughout both films.

Steven Spielberg (1946–).

Task 3.10

1. Research a short biography of each director, you might include:
   - their background
   - their films
   - any other interesting things you find out about them.
2. Write a short paragraph about any similarities you find, anything they have in common.
3. Write a short paragraph about any differences you find; how different are they as directors?

The structural elements of film form

Genre and science fiction

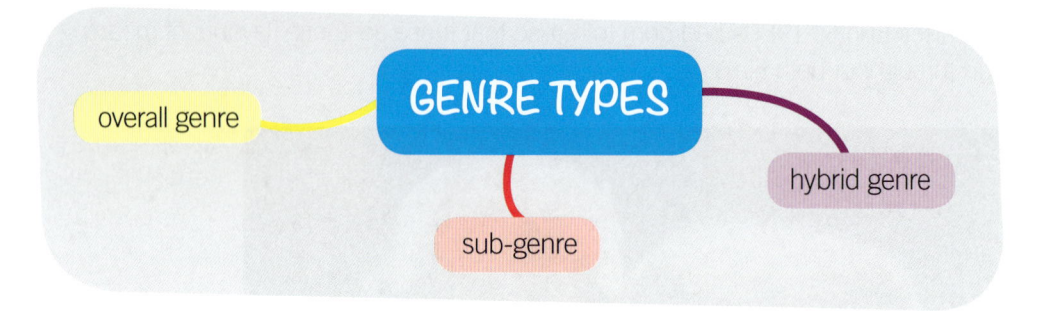

GENRE TYPES: overall genre, sub-genre, hybrid genre

Key terms

Genre
A type or category. The characteristics that distinguish, for example, a science fiction from a romance.

Sub-genre
A sub-category within a particular genre: they are identifiable sub-categories of the larger category of main film genres, with their own distinctive subject matter, style, formulas and iconography.

Hybrid genre
A film that combines two or more distinct genre types. It cannot be easily categorised by a single genre or sub-genre type.

In deciding what the **genre** of a film is we must look to three possible categories: overall genre, **sub-genre** and **hybrid genre**. Genre itself can be defined as categories of film based on frequently recurring patterns of form, style and, particularly, subject matter. So, as we consider science fiction as the genre for our two comparative films, we start to think about what kind of things allow us to recognise a science-fiction film? What are the frequently recurring patterns of form and style? A typical list begins to emerge in which are things such as spaceships, the future, robots, time travel and so on. The more we think, the longer this list will become. With just a brief glance at this list it is enough to show us that these kinds of things do not really describe our films. So we need a much more focused definition to help us. One definition of science fiction was coined by author Theodore Sturgeon:

A good science-fiction story is a story about human beings, with a human problem, and a human solution, which would not have happened at all without its science content. (Quoted in William Atheling Jr, *More Issues at Hand,* page 12)

This gets us closer to a sci-fi definition as invasion and threat is a human problem and the alien can perhaps be considered as the 'science content', if only speculatively so. The important element within this initial definition is the human. If we look at nearly all science-fiction films what engages us in them is how the humans, who we can identify with, react to the challenges they face. Perhaps we all ask ourselves, 'What would I do if faced with an alien invader?' Perhaps a tighter definition for science-fiction films may read:

A film that uses speculative or fictional science or technology as the basis for a story of how people might deal with its discovery.

This should provide a solid basis on which to judge whether our choices are science-fiction films or not. Visitation by aliens, friendly or not, is certainly speculative science, and in both of these cases the films are very much about how the people involved deal with this. A potential sub-text that involves a clever choice of fictional science or technology can also make possible that other important aspect of science fiction – film as mirror or metaphor. In the best science fiction the themes and issues of the film are about us and now. The fictional context allows the filmmaker to deal with themes in an interesting and engaging way. In *IOTBS* we perhaps get to think about the dangers of conformity and paranoia, while in *E.T.* the value(s) of home and family are considered.

Part 3: Component 1:
Films made in the USA

'Someone's not happy with my definition of science fiction ...'
(*Terminator 2*, 1991, James Cameron).

As a class:

- Each think of at least one film that you consider to be science fiction.
- Compile all the films into a list.
- Test whether they fit the definition.
- How could we change the definition?

Task 3.11

This still leaves us with a problem, although the definition works it defines the boundaries of the category in a very wide way. How does this help us sort out the massive list of films, many of which seem very different from each other, that fall under its terms? This is where the use of sub-genres will help. Even ignoring our definition of the science-fiction genre, it is a huge genre within which we can list 1,000s of films. When a genre becomes so large, groups of films with more specific typicalities and similarities emerge. The sub-genre our films could be said to belong to might be called alien invasion or alien visitation. Here, the overall defining feature for membership would be an alien or aliens arriving on Earth and people's reaction to this event.

Now we have decided what category our films fit into, we have to go back to what we need to consider in more detail when studying genre. The commonality of genre conventions based on iconography, including mise-en-scène, characters, narratives and themes, is what we use. These aspects will often act to define genre and sub-genre in different ways with a different emphasis depending on the specific category. In the case of alien visitation it is the characters, narratives and themes that are the most important. In both our films we have characters that know and do not know about the aliens, and of course the alien itself. Narratively the stories are about how we cope with the new arrival. Theme is perhaps the key; how do we react to the 'other' or the 'stranger'? What are their motives? Here the films perhaps reflect on how we as both individuals and groups deal with outsiders of a less alien kind.

GCSE Film Studies

More 1950s visitors to Earth (*The Day the Earth Stood Still*, 1951, Robert Wise).

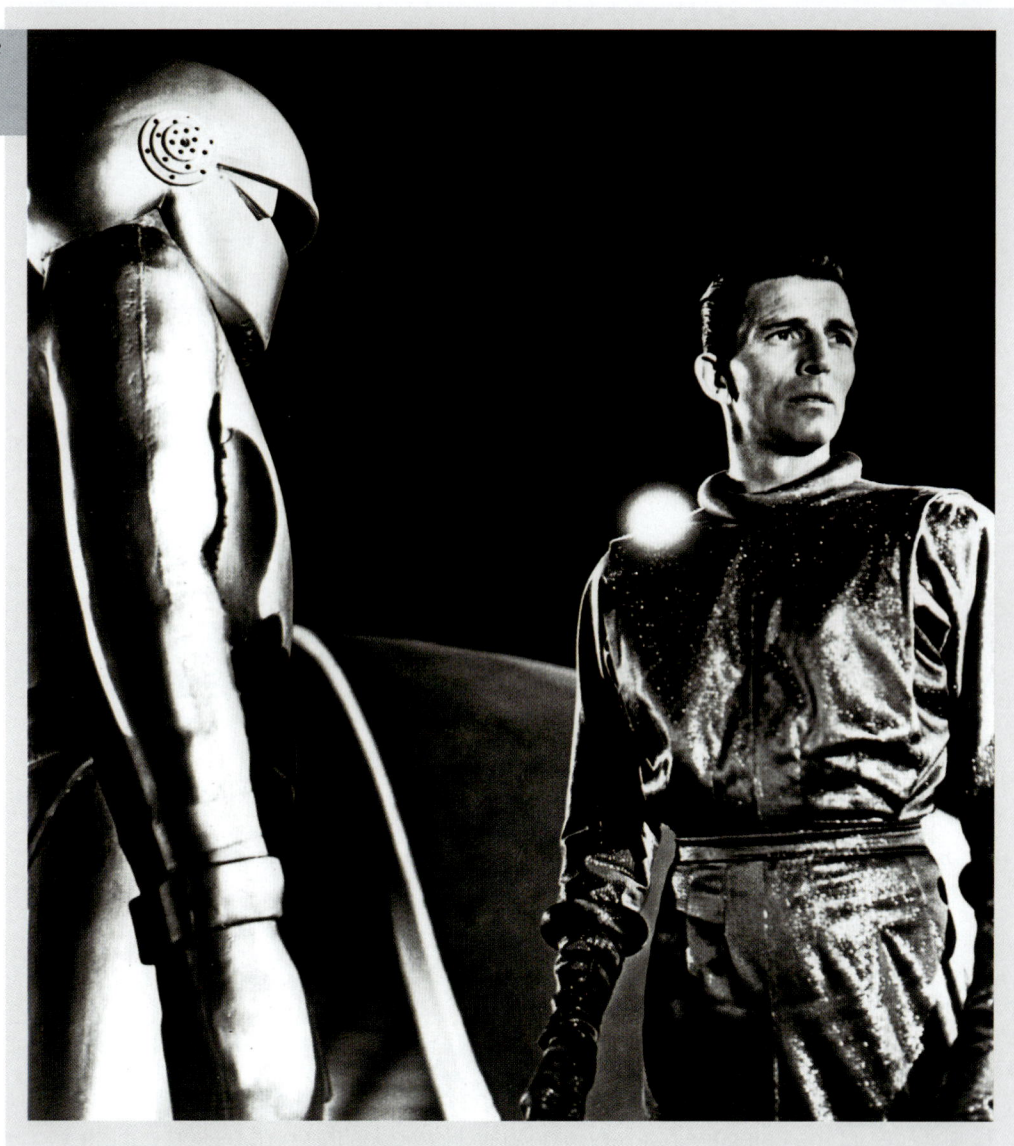

In other sub-genres of science-fiction films, iconography and mise-en-scène may be more important in defining the category. In the space opera sub-genre it is the futuristic technology, spaceships and space travel that are the characteristics we look for. These are less obvious in our films but we can say that the iconography and mise-en-scène should at the very least draw us a picture of a familiar world we can identify with as it is disrupted by the alien arrival.

Task 3.12

Choose a big genre, for example science fiction or horror, then:
- list as many sub-genres you can think of
- state what the defining characteristics of each are.

Now we may have found a way of grouping films that seems to be able to manage the 1,000s of films in the overall genre; but there will always be films that still seem not to fit. This may be because they have some strong characteristics that are not really science fiction in nature. If a film has two or more genres within it this is known as a hybrid genre. In some discussions *IOTBS* is an example of this. Many commentators refer to it as a horror–science-fiction hybrid. The terror of the pods experienced by people probably leads them to this conclusion. However, we do know that the pods come from outer space not some dark Earth-bound place of horror and by today's standards the horror would be considered very mild indeed. Much better examples of horror–science-fiction hybrids would be *Alien* (1979, Ridley Scott) and John Carpenter's *The Thing* (1982). Interestingly, *The Thing* came out in the same year as *E.T.* as a re-make of a 1951 film *The Thing from Another World* and is more similar in story to *IOTBS*. The alien visitor in this film has no intention of making friends – only in surviving – much to the cost of any creature that crosses its path. It was far less successful than *E.T.* at the box office; perhaps the audience in 1982 felt the need for a friend rather than another enemy? If you would like to read a more detailed discussion of *IOTBS* and *The Thing* check out:

https://popsmut.wordpress.com/2011/04/19/two-eras-of-terror-comparing-the-invasion-of-the-body-snatchers-and-the-thing/

E.T. wasn't our only visitor in 1982 (*The Thing*).

We always have to be careful when trying to figure out a film's genre. We need to be flexible and be ready to justify our analysis through argument and evidence. Take the example below; would we be wrong to put this film into the western genre?

> *Set in the past, on the frontier, with good guys encountering bad, featuring a trade dispute and shoot-outs as an evil organisation attempts to swallow up individual settlers and traders.*

Perhaps, but if we consider it more closely, it is in fact a logline for the *Star Wars* films. Now there is an interesting genre discussion – are the *Star Wars* films science fiction or westerns? We can add even further 'confusion' by throwing the hybrid of the science fiction–western into the mix, for example *Cowboys & Aliens* (2011, Jon Favreau). It might be a fun debate to sort out in class!

GCSE Film Studies

Science fiction – ever popular with producers and audiences.

One final question we should ask is why is genre so important, particularly in the US film mainstream? In answering this we should remember that genre is significant to both film producers and film audiences. Some of the reasons are set out in the boxes below.

Producers and filmmakers

A simple and effective way of selling their films to a specific target audience.

It can help reduce the risk of financial failure.

It can be a formula for simplifying filmmaking.

The conventions can help, or provide a short cut to, the making of meaning(s).

Subverting the conventions can provide a creative approach to making a film.

Audience

It is an easy way to spot the kinds of film they like or dislike.

It is a way of comparing one film with another.

We enjoy subconsciously responding to the short cuts and clues within its film language.

Genres offer comforting reassurance and a closing down of the complexities of life.

Meeting audience expectations equals pleasure.

Of these various reasons, many, if not all, will apply to individual films. Overall, the producers of mainstream films are usually looking to repeat the success that a genre has already enjoyed, whereas the audience is usually looking for a kind of film they know they will enjoy.

Task 3.13

Using the films chosen for your comparative study, write an essay that discusses why their genre is important to both producers and audiences. Use the reasons in the boxes above as well as any ideas of your own.

Representation

When considering representation in our comparative study, or any film, we need to consider the points-of-view or perspectives that provide a context to help us understand what we are looking at. There are two key perspectives to be aware of: our perspective as a contemporary audience and the perspective of the filmmakers and audience in the era of the film's production.

What do we mean by perspective? Context is the key term in understanding this. At the start of this study we looked at the political, economic and social aspects of each decade that influenced the audience of the time. We have to try and form some feeling or idea of what people's attitudes were back then. This is where it is important to remember our point-of-view and the influences on it, and try to take this into account when drawing conclusions about the representations we see. We need to remember that attitudes and ideas can be very different within just one person's life time. For example, people's attitude towards sexuality has changed a lot in my life time. Before 1967 you could go to prison for being a homosexual; very different from our modern acceptance of this particular human difference.

So, we must take into account the context of the time the film was made to help us interpret the representations we see. That should not be confused with excusing something we now may find offensive, but should be more to help us understand why people were more accepting of it at that time.

Why consider representation in the films we are studying? Just like the key and structural elements of film form we have studied so far, it should help us understand not just the films themselves but the times and people that shaped them, which is central to the appreciation of any film or work of art.

Quick Question 3.15

What do you understand by the term 'perspective'? What are the two key perspectives to consider when analysing representation in your focus films?

Task 3.14

Find someone you know, a friend or relative, and chat about what life was like for them in the 1950s and 1980s. This may have to be two different people. Did they go the cinema to see either of the films? If they did what did they think?

Invasion of the Body Snatchers and E.T. the Extra-Terrestrial

It may seem out of step with the rest of this section of the book to discuss both films together for this topic, as so far each has been considered separately topic by topic. This is to emphasise straight-away how similar both films are in a key approach to the representation we see. In discussing representation in *IOTBS* and *E.T.* what is absent from the screen is as important as what is present. What we are presented with in both cases is virtually an all-white middle class world. In *IOTBS* we see no African-American people in this small town, white American world; both of our central figures are prosperous and college-educated white people. The only hint of an ethnic minority is in the working-class Grimaldi family, an echo of a previous generation's immigration, as no trace of an accent can be detected in either Jimmy or his mother. Likewise, the world of *E.T.* is the insular white American suburb. This time we do see an African-American but in the briefest of cameos towards the end of the film, in the form of a police detective who questions Mike about why he's in the van.

GCSE Film Studies

This is significant for us to consider because as we have seen race is an important ongoing social issue throughout both decades. Even allowing for how both narratives deliberately narrow their focus for reasons of dramatic **claustrophobia** and/or intimacy, this 'whitewash' of both films illuminates, at least partly, the cultural attitudes of mainstream US film at the time. It is perhaps not racism, but it is certainly a form of 'colour blindness' that illustrates in some way cultural attitudes current at the time.

1950s (left) and 1980s (right) America – members only?

Key terms

Claustrophobia
A fear of being in closed or small spaces or an unsettling, uncomfortable feeling caused by being in a situation that limits or restricts you.

Key demographic
A term used by government agencies, political parties and manufacturers of consumer goods to describe particular groups in society. Films are often aimed at a 'key demographic', e.g. a particular age group or gender grouping.

As we should consider perspectives on gender, ethnicity, age and different cultures, this leaves us only two areas where there are things to look at. In terms of gender both are typical of their times. In *IOTBS* we see men in all the positions of authority with women taking on a secondary role (even among the aliens). Even Becky, who, for a time at least, seems as determined and as strong as Miles, reverts to being the damsel in distress by the film's end. This 1950s attitude towards women's dependence on men is clearly stated in Becky and Miles' first conversation about their divorces. The word divorce not being mentioned so as to not offend 1950s family values; the reference to Reno (a centre for 'quickie' divorces) would have been understood by the 1950s American audience. In this conversation Miles jokes about legal divorce settlements by saying, 'Except that I'm paying dues while you collect them.' Clearly commenting on how men pay alimony to their dependent ex-wives. Age in *IOTBS* is fairly unremarkable in its representation, except perhaps that even though our protagonists are relatively young their roles in modern **key-demographic**-focused films might be filled with actors closer to teenagers rather than the '30 somethings' we see here.

In *E.T.* things have moved on in terms of attitudes to divorce, as it is a key element of the family's back story. The mother is depicted as capable of raising the family herself. She is a much stronger female character than those in *IOTBS*, apart from calling the police when Elliot is missing, she does not feel the need to be rescued by a man. Nevertheless, despite the presence of a mother and a sister in Elliott's life, the rest of the cast is still largely male dominated. It is the boys that rescue E.T. from the scientists, who are led by men reflecting that in 1980's America equality of gender roles still had some way to go – it still has, both in front of and behind the camera of US mainstream film. Age representation is, by the nature of the narrative, a rich area of discussion. Through the staging of the film from the alien's or child's point-of-view, adults and their world are cast in a villainous light. The children and the alien are the vulnerable heroes we all root for. Elliot's mother, who is shot openly, and Keys, who is only shot openly when we realise he is an ally, being 'bridges' between the two age groups.

Perhaps in the final analysis, the representation open to most interesting discussion is that of the alien. As an audience we can decide for ourselves who or what the alien represents in each of the films. In *IOTBS* at one end of the spectrum it could be the communists and their desire to subvert the American way of life. Equally, at the other end of the spectrum the pods could be the American way of life itself and how rising materialism and social conformity are turning people into unthinking drones. In *E.T.* he could be a friendly immigrant with much to offer who is pursued as dangerous by a suspicious government. He could also be part of our innocence and wonder that we somehow thoughtlessly 'send away' in our rush to grow up. Whoever, or whatever, you decide the alien is standing in for, it is something interesting to discuss.

Quick Question 3.16

What do you think about how young people are depicted in the film? Write your response in bullet point form. Share with the class to see who agrees or disagrees.

'Who would you like me to be?' (*E.T. the Extra-Terrestrial*).

'It's humanoid!' (*Earth vs the Flying Saucers*, 1956, Fred F. Sears).

This has been a brief look at some of the key representation in each film. What is important to remember when we look at any film or character in them, is that we should ask ourselves: What do they say about the people who made the film and the times in which they lived?

Task 3.15

1. Discuss how people are represented in your chosen films.
2. Refer to at least one sequence from each film, commenting on the roles that cinematography, mise-en-scène, editing or sound play in their representation.

GCSE Film Studies

'Keep watching the skies' (Earth vs the Flying Saucers).

Further reading

- 'E.T. the Extra-Terrestrial', 1982, www.filmsite.org/etth.html
- *E.T. the Extra-Terrestrial from Concept to Classic: The Illustrated Story of the Film and the Filmmakers*, 30th Anniversary Edition (Pictorial Moviebook), Steven Spielberg and Melissa Mathison, Newmarket Press, 2012.
- *Invasion of the Body Snatchers* (BFI Film Classics), Professor Barry Keith Grant, British Film Institute; 2010.
- 'The Greatest Sci-fi Movies of the 1950s', www.denofgeek.com/movies/16511/the-greatest-sci-fi-movies-of-the-1950s

Section C — US independent films

Part 3: Component 1: Films made in the USA

Introduction

You can study one of the following five options:

Juno (2007, Reitman), *The Hurt Locker* (2008, Kathryn Bigelow), *Whiplash* (2014, Damien Chazelle), *Little Miss Sunshine* (2006, Jonathan Dayton and Valerie Faris) and *Me and Earl and the Dying Girl* (2015, Alfonso Gomez-Rejon).

Little Miss Sunshine, *Me and Earl and the Dying Girl*, *Juno* and *Whiplash* place younger people and their experiences centre stage, whereas *The* **Hurt Locker** explores male values and attitudes within the context of a war film. All films reflect aspects of US society in the first two decades of the 21st century; while *The Hurt Locker*, in addition, raises issues about the US involvement in the 2003–2011 Iraq war. As with all film options, the films offered for study are cinematic in contrasting ways and will allow learners to explore how the films are shot and constructed.

Why study American independent film?

The perfect answer to this question is another question: 'Why would you want to miss out?' Cinema is all about story-telling and, as we all know, there are many different kinds of story out there told in many different ways. All too often we miss out on some really great films, or, if we are lucky, catch them online or on DVD. These 'great films' quite often are **independent (or indie) films** that escape our attention as they don't have the massive (and expensive) publicity that comes with a mainstream movie. To quote *Empire* film magazine's '50 Greatest American Independent Movies' article:

> As much as blockbusters can thrill us, beyond the well-tended flowerbeds and spacious corner offices of Hollywood there's a world bubbling with creativity, free spirits and up-and-coming talent.

Who would want to miss out on that?

In this section of the book we will be looking at one of the films from the list, *The Hurt Locker*. In the case study we will examine what areas you should study for whichever choice you make. Discussing further what an 'indie' film is, the context/times the film was created in, a look at a sample of how the key elements of film form were used and some specialist writing about the film itself.

Key term

Hurt locker

The term 'hurt locker', according to the writer-producer Mark Boal, is military slang that means 'a bad and painful place'. The online Urban Dictionary defines it as 'a period of immense, inescapable physical or emotional pain', citing usage examples: 'This recession has been a real hurt locker.' 'She did not foresee her actions as contributing to the hurt locker she would soon be in.' 'That last track meet – Man, what a hurt locker!'

Key terms

Independent film
One that received less than 50% of its funding from one of the 'big six' major film studios; typically, with a relatively small budget, where the filmmaker gets to tell the story they want to tell in the way they want to tell it.

Film production budget
The money allowed to be spent on making the film project.

Task 3.16

1. What do I know already? Chose an indie film. You will probably have seen one or more of the listed films; if not, then a film like them that counts as an 'indie' – check with your teacher.

2. Using your experience of watching both indie and mainstream movies, construct a table that compares what you expect from each type of movie. For example, a low **film production budget** for indie compared to a high one for mainstream.

3. Discuss with a partner or the whole class the points you can use to compare them before you start.

155

GCSE Film Studies

Applying this to The Hurt Locker

Financially *The Hurt Locker*, both in terms of its production and distribution, had a relatively small budget and received no support from any of the big studios. Artistically it is very much Kathryn Bigelow's film – her vision being key in its creation. It is very centred on the story of Sergeant First Class William James and was considered by many a challenging depiction of a military figure and how his role impacts his life. So, all in all, *The Hurt Locker* is very much a clear example of an American independent film.

Timeline of American independent films.

1960s
- *Night of the Living Dead* (1968), Director: George Romero

1970s
- *THX-1138* (1971), Director: George Lucas

1980s
- *Evil Dead* (1981), Director: Sam Raimi
- *Blood Simple* (1984), Directors: Ethan Coen, Joel Coen
- *The Terminator* (1984), Director: James Cameron
- *She's Gotta Have It* (1986), Director: Spike Lee

1990s
- *Slacker* (1991), Director: Richard Linklater
- *Reservoir Dogs* (1992), Director: Quentin Tarantino
- *Clerks* (1994), Director: Kevin Smith
- *The Blair Witch Project* (1999), Directors: Daniel Myrick, Eduardo Sánchez

2000s
- *Memento* (2000), Director: Christopher Nolan
- *Donnie Darko* (2001), Director: Richard Kelly
- *Little Miss Sunshine* (2006), Directors: Jonathan Dayton, Valerie Faris
- *Juno* (2007), Director: Jason Reitman

2010s
- *Winter's Bone* (2010), Director: Deborah Granik

Task 3.18

1. Look at the above timeline of examples of American independent film and discuss as a class the following questions:
   (a) What do you notice about the genre of the films listed?
   (b) Do any appear to be very different from the rest?
   (c) Which of them have you seen?
   (d) What do you think of them?

2. Look at each film and:
   (a) Find out what possible important contribution to film each one made?
   (b) Choose one to prepare a PowerPoint presentation covering:
   - cast and crew
   - financial data
   - narrative
   - who went on to become famous and for what
   - influence on the wider film world and what this was.

Context

Iraq

The Hurt Locker was first screened at the Venice Film Festival in September 2008 and continued what was almost a tour of **film festivals** until its release 'proper' in June of 2009. This means that throughout both its production and release the war, or **insurgency** as it became known, in Iraq continued. So the realities that the film dramatised were still going on as the film audience watched on.

The film's events were inspired by the writing of a freelance journalist (Mark Boal). Boal tracked an American bomb squad in the 2004 Iraq war and later published an account of his (and the 'squaddie's') experiences during that period. Throughout the time he was in Iraq, Boal was in touch with Kathryn Bigelow, they shared ideas and the film began to take shape. In 2005 Bigelow and Boal began to work on the script. Bigelow drafted some early storyboards with the intention of producing as authentic a film as possible, telling Nick Dawson of *The Times* in 2009 that she wanted to 'put the audience into the Humvee – into a boots-on-the-ground experience'; the film was shot during 2007 in Jordan and Kuwait. Throughout this pre-production and production period, the conflict in Iraq continued despite the then president, George W. Bush's 2003 'mission accomplished' declaration on 'Operation Iraqi Freedom'. During 2003, events in Iraq transformed from an out and out military conflict to the much more chaotic events of an insurgency.

The term insurgency refers to what has in differing historical conflicts been described as a guerrilla-, partisan- or resistance-based conflict. Where a group, or groups, uses various 'terrorist'-style tactics over a medium- to long-term time period to 'convince' an occupying force their presence is costing more than it is worth. In Iraq there were many groups, and continue to be so, involved, including a changing mix of militias, foreign fighters (such as Al Qaeda, later being replaced by Islamic State in the headlines), some former Iraqi military forces and parts of the former government. They variously used tactics such as the **improvised explosive devices (IEDs)** that feature so strongly in the film, as well as mortar bombing, missiles, suicide attacks, snipers, car bombs, small arms fire (usually with assault rifles) and rocket propelled grenades (RPGs), and many other acts of sabotage designed to cause chaos for both the occupiers and the population.

The period of 2008–2009 did mark a significant period of change in policy towards the conflict in Iraq. In November 2008 George W. Bush was succeeded by Barack Obama, when he won the election to become America's first black president on a platform taglined with the slogan of 'yes we can' in regard to change. Obama's election emphasised how much people had taken to heart his overall message of 'hope' for the future. The emphasis in American military strategy was about to experience some of this 'change'. In January 2009 Obama announced the proposed closure of the Guantánamo Bay detention facility in Cuba, and the withdrawal of most of the American forces in Iraq by August 2010. The remaining 35,000–50,000 troops were to leave by the previous government's deadline of December 2011. So the endgame in terms of large-scale American occupation of Iraq had begun; indeed, between January and June of 2009, 150 military bases shut down or handed over control to the new Iraqi authorities.

Key terms

Film festivals
Organised, extended presentations of films in one or more cinemas or screening venues, usually in a single city or region.

Insurgency
A movement within a country dedicated to overthrowing the government. An insurgency is a rebellion.

Key term

Improvised explosive device (IED)
A homemade or makeshift bomb.

GCSE Film Studies

> **Key term**
>
> **Post-traumatic stress disorder (PTSD)**
> A mental health condition that is a result of a terrifying event – either experienced or witnessed. Symptoms may include flashbacks, nightmares and severe anxiety.

It is against this backdrop of changing circumstances for the conflict that the audience members would view the film. As the film ends, William James returns for another year's tour of duty in Iraq to 'escape' his **post-traumatic stress disorder (PTSD)** damaged home life – the supply of his 'war drug' in Iraq is in reality coming to a close. Indeed, *The Hurt Locker* can be seen as a culmination of the sub-genre of Iraq war films. Its critical and awards success had largely eluded its predecessor films on the subject. It received nine nominations and six wins at the 2010 Academy Awards. In Martin Barker's book, *A 'Toxic Genre': The Iraq War Films* (2007) he comments:

> *In several senses, Kathryn Bigelow's* The Hurt Locker *closes my cycle of films. I believed this before the film won its six Oscars at the 2010 Academy awards. That merely became another dimension to the closure, which is mainly the result of how it differs from the others.*

A difference we will also consider when we look at key and structural elements of film form.

What else was going on?

As is the case with any film, the world into which it comes is also the world in which it was created and, perhaps more importantly, viewed. So a brief rundown of some other events happening in 2008–2009 would be useful. Some of these events are highlighted by the *Guardian* newspaper at: https://www.theguardian.com/world/2009/oct/17/decade-timeline-what-happened-when

Task 3.19

1. Look at the *Guardian* website (see above link). Pick out between six–ten key events for 2008 and 2009.
2. Some of these events may mean very little to many of you; ask your teacher and other adults to talk about those that they remember. Their memories are important to think about because most of them may have affected our lives as well the life of the film to a greater or lesser extent.
3. Produce your own timeline of the UK and world events that you think are important to the film and your life now.

Film in 2009

In one way, within the world of film production and distribution, *The Hurt Locker* found itself as one of absolute contrast because one of its main competitors at the 82nd Academy Awards was James Cameron's *Avatar*, matching *The Hurt Locker*'s number of nominations with nine, but only managing half the number of wins with three. If *The Hurt Locker* is a good example of an independent film, *Avatar* is the very definition of a mainstream blockbuster.

Like most industries, Hollywood was trying to tackle the aftermath of the 2008 financial crisis in the form of a global recession and falling demand.

Part 3: Component 1: Films made in the USA

Rank	Title	Distributor	Worldwide gross
1.	*Avatar*	Fox	$2,749,064,328
2.	*Harry Potter and the Half-Blood Prince*	Warner Bros	$934,416,487
3.	*Ice Age: Dawn of the Dinosaurs*	Fox	$886,686,817
4.	*Transformers: Revenge of the Fallen*	Paramount	$836,303,693
5.	*2012*	Columbia	$769,679,473
6.	*Up*	Disney	$735,099,082
7.	*The Twilight Saga: New Moon*	Summit	$709,711,008
8.	*Sherlock Holmes*	Warner Bros	$524,028,679
9.	*Angels & Demons*	Columbia	$485,930,816
10.	*The Hangover*	Warner Bros	$467,483,912

Highest-grossing films of 2009

(Source: '2009 in Film', https://en.wikipedia.org/wiki/2009_in_film)

Task 3.20

1. What do you notice about the top ten films of 2009? Think about:
   - genre
   - studio
   - box-office
   - stars.
2. How does *The Hurt Locker* compare?

When we look at what was successful in 2009 we see that Hollywood continued to rely on the tried and tested to tempt an audience that had less spending power to the cinema. Half of the ten highest-grossing films are sequels and franchises, of the other half we have:

- two big budget spectaculars, *Avatar* (James Cameron) and *2012* (Roland Emmerich)
- *Up* (Pete Docter and Bob Peterson) a family-friendly Disney film
- *Sherlock Holmes* (Guy Ritchie) a star vehicle for the increasingly popular (again) star Robert Downey Junior
- the perennial Hollywood staple of a franchise beginning comedy in the form of *The Hangover* (Todd Phillips).

So it is into a very 'safe' and 'conservative' market that the ultra real, edgy and potentially controversial Iraq war film was launched. This kind of competition, partnered with its limited release, goes some way to explain that despite its six Oscar wins *The Hurt Locker* only just managed to scrape into the top 100 worldwide grossing films at number 96 (source: Boxoffice mojo.com). Compare this to the previous year's semi-independent winner (eight wins, ten nominations) *Slumdog Millionaire* with an identical $15 million budget and a global box office of $377.9 million (16th highest overall) and we can see how hard it is to sell Iraq war films to the cinema-going audience – 'a toxic genre' indeed.

Kathryn Bigelow receiving her Oscar for Best Achievement in Directing, for *The Hurt Locker*.

161

GCSE Film Studies

Studying the key elements of film form

Introduction

Key terms

Meaning
What the director intends you to think and feel while watching the film.

Documentary
A non-fictional film intended to document some aspect of reality, for the purpose of maintaining a historical record. To be real.

Aestheticised
To depict as being pleasing or artistically beautiful; represent in an idealised or refined manner.

Cinematic
Does it feel like we are watching a film? Having qualities characteristic of films – big screen, big sound, big drama, a feeling of created or designed intensity. Adding additional layers of meaning, making the viewer involved and the ability to create a story in a viewer's mind.

Authenticity
Real or genuine: not copied or false, true and accurate, made to be or look just like an original.

16mm film
A frequently used, economical gauge of film. 16mm refers to the width of the film. It is not generally used for mainstream films unless the filmmaker wants to create a gritty or grainy look for the film.

As with all the films you are studying on this course, an important, if not the most important, aspects of this study is the key elements of film form: cinematography, mise-en-scène, editing and sound. We need to understand how these are used to create **meaning** in the film overall; we can especially gain much from considering how they are used in the opening sequence, as this sets the tone for much of the rest of the film. Although we will discuss them separately, we must never lose sight of the fact that they are all working together to achieve the filmmaker's overall objective. Kathryn Bigelow is known for her ability to direct action well, which is a very strong feature of *The Hurt Locker*, together with a desire for a **documentary** feel of authenticity. In an interview with Nick Dawson for *Filmmaker* magazine she explained:

> *Okay, you want to make it as real and as authentic as possible, to put the audience into the Humvee, into a boots-on-the-ground experience. How do you do that? You do it by finding a look, a feel and a texture that is very immediate, raw and vital, and yet also is not* **aestheticized.** *I wanted, as a filmmaker, to sort of step aside and let just the rawness and integrity of the subject be as pronounced as possible and not have it feel sort of* **'cinematic'**.

So as we consider how the key elements of film form are used throughout the film, this explanation is a very important guide for our analysis; we should ask ourselves the question 'does it feel authentic, does it feel like we are "there"?'

Cinematography and lighting

> *She wanted to use four cameras running simultaneously. We chose to shoot on Super 16mm, which might seem unusual for a Kathryn Bigelow film, but she was very happy to go with that choice. It offered financial freedom and liberated the cameras a bit. So we showed up with Aaton cameras and a crew from all over the world, and we wound up shooting quite a lot of Fuji film – over a million feet.* (Scott Macaulay, 'Cinematographer Barry Ackroyd talks *The Hurt Locker*', *Filmmaker*)

> *We got camera's everywhere, we call them ninja cameras …* (Jeremy Renner interviewed during 'The Making of', DVD extra)

> *Literally no place you could turn where you wouldn't see a camera.* (Kathryn Bigelow, interviewed during 'The Making of' DVD extra)

The quotations above underline Bigelow's overall goal of **authenticity**. It was a major influence on how the filming took place: the multiple cameras give great flexibility of choice when it comes to editing and the use of **16mm film** rather than the standard 35mm film helped with the documentary feel. This documentary approach was

Part 3: Component 1:
Films made in the USA

further enhanced by unconventional framing camera shaking, loose and at times changing focus, snap or crash zooms, and an overall hand-held camera style that evoked filmmaking 'on the run', at times almost creating a found footage aesthetic. Nevertheless, there was some use of the camera vocabulary of action/war films Bigelow is so well versed in, for example overhead shots of many of the dramatic set pieces, which would be less common if the footage was solely news crew type filming where the camera is embedded with the soldiers and follows them at a more consistently ground level.

Much of this is clearly in evidence during the opening sequence where we see a bomb disposal team dealing with an IED for the first time in the film.

A robot's eye view (*The Hurt Locker*).

The opening shot from the bomb disposal robot's camera is ultra-authentic as its **CCTV** style picture breaks up on its journey to the IED. We then cut to an extreme close-up tracking shot of the robot that barely allows us to take in what we are seeing, the first instance of using the camera to instil a feeling of 'immediate, raw and vital' chaos in the situation.

We then cut to a series of four shots of the local people being evacuated that takes us away from the close-up danger of the IED into the wider feeling of disruption and panic of the scene.

Key term

CCTV
Closed-circuit television is a TV system in which signals are not publicly distributed but are monitored, primarily for surveillance and security purposes.

163

GCSE Film Studies

Baghdad: panic in the streets (*The Hurt Locker*).

Key term

180-degree rule
A general rule used in cinematography and editing that aims to ensure that the camera is kept on one side of the action and the audience does not feel disorientated. For example, when two characters are having an on-screen conversation and we only see one character as he/she speaks, this rule ensures that the on-screen character keeps looking towards where the other (off-screen) character is standing or sitting.

Notice how the location is established in a very matter of fact, almost casual way, with the simple single word caption **'Baghdad'** again utilising the simple typewriter Courier-style font. The relaxed approach to camera framing that the hand-held zooming effect creates heightens the feeling of disorder; as does the gently breaking of the **180-degree rule** between the third and fourth shots.

This is quickly followed by an example of a snap or crash zoom, where the camera acts to speed up the action and increases the drama by moving from an extreme high angle long shot of the scene, without pause for focusing, into a lower angled more familiar style long shot of the robot's progress to the IED.

A crash zoom into the action (*The Hurt Locker*).

Part 3: Component 1:
Films made in the USA

Notice again how the two out of focus elements in the crash zoom use the 'rawness' referred to by Kathryn Bigelow to draw the audience further into the tension of the scene.

Next, we see a clear example of the four-camera set-up as the soldiers disembark from their Humvee, note how the editor is able to cut to at least four different angles of the event all happening at the same time.

Four cameras – one arrival (*The Hurt Locker*).

Notice also the **Dutch angle** effect in the shots as well as the seemingly non-conventional framing that adds to the immediacy of the documentary feel.

A vital component in establishing the real feel to the action in *The Hurt Locker* is the use of crash zooms to an almost dizzying extent and the very free use of hand-held cameras in the filming to create a very real sense of motion. Kathryn Bigelow explains this in terms of trying to get a feel more like the actual experience of 'seeing':

> *That's how we experience reality, by looking at the microcosm and the macrocosm simultaneously. The eye sees differently than the lens, but with multiple focal lengths and a muscular editorial style, the lens can give you that microcosm/macrocosm perspective, and that contributes to the feeling of total immersion.* (Patricia Thomson, (July 2009), 'Risk and Valor: *The Hurt Locker*', *American Cinematographer*, 90(7): 44–50)

Our final example for the camera is another example of an unconventional use of framing as we are introduced to two of the three main characters of this opening scene.

Key term

Dutch angle
A tilted camera angle that causes the horizon in the shot to be diagonal to the bottom of the frame. It can be used to express a character's drunken state (as in *Rebel Without a Cause*), mental state, disorientation and anxiety.

GCSE Film Studies

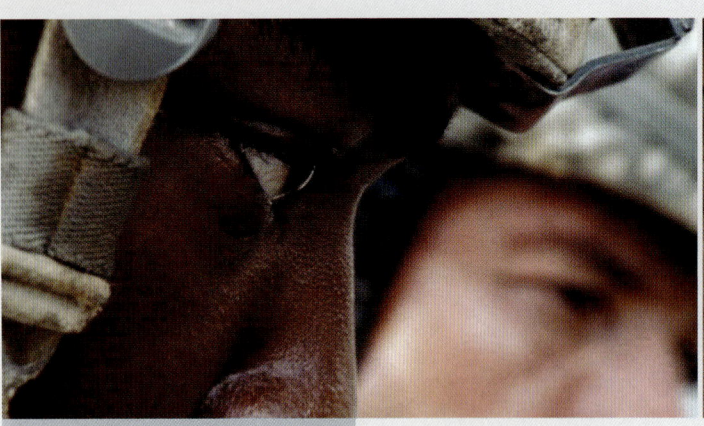

Extreme concentration and close-up (*The Hurt Locker*).

We see each soldier for the first time in extreme close-up, with barely a glimpse at who they are, but it does heighten both the intimacy and claustrophobic feeling of this high-pressure situation. It is interesting to note that the third of the three protagonists (Eldridge) is framed differently at this point:

Eldridge framed as an outsider (*The Hurt Locker*).

Almost 30 seconds later we see him stand up and look into the action from its edge, which sets up an aspect of his character for later in the film, as he is in some ways the outsider on the periphery of the relationship between the main characters.

Part 3: Component 1:
Films made in the USA

1. Examine the two shots below from *The Hurt Locker* and answer the following questions:

   Task 3.21

   (a) How would you describe these shots?
   (b) What is this type of framing called?
   (c) What does the framing and composition suggest to the audience?
   (d) What meaning is the director trying to create by framing these shots in this way?

2. Examine the next two shots from *The Hurt Locker* and then answer the following questions:

   (a) How would you describe these shots?
   (b) What type of framing is being used?
   (c) How are they different from the previous two shots?
   (d) What does the framing and composition suggest to the audience?

Slow motion

The sequences' climactic uses of super slow motion shots utilises cameras that can shoot up to 50,000 frames per second – 1,000 images per second. This allows for shots of much longer duration to hold the spectator in the moment of the explosive action taking in the extent of its power and destruction.

167

GCSE Film Studies

Detonation sequence (*The Hurt Locker*).

This final section of the opening sequence is constructed once again using multiple angles and distances. It is the use of slow motion that impacts the audience the most, especially given its contrast to the fast paced and frenetic editing immediately prior to it as the soldiers try to stop the man with the mobile phone from detonating the IED.

What would be an incident that would be over in a fraction of a second is given a full 35 seconds to unfold. When the scene cuts from slow motion to real-time action this acts in a similar way to the crash zooms earlier in the sequence, as it gives us a jolt, further increasing the impact of the explosion. The way that the explosion is filmed leaves the audience with a very clear and visceral impression of what the bomb disposal technicians will be up against throughout the rest of the film.

Task 3.22

In pairs:

1. Think of and list three examples of uses of slow motion from any other film.
2. What are the similarities and differences in the meaning created in each example?
3. Share your findings with the class – see if, as a group, you can compile a list of the typical meanings created by the use of slow motion in film.

Lighting

The Hurt Locker is a good example of a film shot with lighting designed to create a feeling of no formal lighting or with the use of natural light. This effect is key to underpinning the documentary feel Kathryn Bigelow was trying to achieve. Given its setting, the audience experiences high or even harsh levels of lighting that evoke reality within the desert setting.

Part 3: Component 1:
Films made in the USA

Cinematography (*The Hurt Locker*).

In the still above left, we see the use of the sun as the principal light source, the overall picture being clear and bright with clearly defined shadows created by the surrounding buildings. Again, in the still above right the audience is exposed (as far as is possible) to the harshness of the sun. The audience shares the experience with Staff Sergeant Matt Thompson of having to squint though his helmet's visor under the sun's harsh glare, when a passing helicopter attracts his attention.

Paired with this naturalistic approach to the use of daylight is the use of night shots of contrasting levels of low light, to suggest on-screen light sources, and the use of night vision effects of US military equipment. This provides the very foundations of Kathryn Bigelow's aim to produce '*a look, a feel and a texture that is very immediate, raw and vital*'. This is explained in further detail by the cinematographer Barry Ackroyd:

> *On daylight scenes I avoided lighting if I could. When it came to night, I would try and use a practical light as a source. I tried to avoid bringing too much technical equipment into a room. I used* **Chinese lanterns** *and* **Kino Flo tubes** *inserted into drainpipes. I cut out the central section and then you can diffuse the tube itself and stand them in corners. I like to disguise lights in that way. I'm always thinking about how to bring light into a scene without having to see it or have it interfere with the acting. [My approach] is about simplifying, not thinking too big and trusting the stock will carry.* (Scott Macaulay, 'Cinematographer Barry Ackroyd Talks *The Hurt Locker*', 14 November 2011, *Filmmaker*)

Key terms

Chinese lanterns
A great low-budget method for creating soft, diffused light in a number of directions.

Kino Flo tube
An LED and fluorescent lighting system.

Task 3.23

1. Watch the night sequence set in the aftermath of the tanker explosion (1:33:35–1:38:48), analysing the use of the lighting to create meaning. Consider:

   (a) What kind of lighting scheme is being used.
   (b) What is the overall effect created by the atmosphere of the sequence?
   (c) On-screen light sources and their effect.
   (d) Off-screen light sources and their effect.
   (e) What feeling does the silhouette effect create?
   (f) How far do you think we are watching action lit by natural light sources?
   (g) How is this important in the context of the director's overall aim for the film?

2. Experiment by filming at night with different levels of light to see for yourself how much film lighting may have been used in this sequence. Clue – torches usually give off beams of light; why don't they seem to have them here?

Mise-en-scène

Setting

Of the elements of mise-en-scène, perhaps key to realising Kathryn Bigelow's vision for an authentic feel is the setting. The film is shot in Jordan relatively close to the film setting of Iraq, which does not just afford the film the 'look' it needs to emulate Baghdad but also 'helps' the performance of the actors in reaching for the required realism, as Jeremy Renner (Sergeant William James) commented in the 'Making of' documentary – *'that sweat's real sweat!'*

The long walk (*The Hurt Locker*).

The Souk (*The Hurt Locker*).

We view the typical backdrop for the action in the above stills from the opening sequence. The civilian areas are either fully ruined or partially destroyed to reflect the aftermath of US's 'mission accomplished'. In the first image we see a typically basic and ramshackle open air Middle Eastern marketplace or Souk. In the second we get a wider view of what appears to be post-conflict temporary dwellings and burnt-out cars that help establish the combat-worn post-'mission accomplished' Baghdad.

The base (*The Hurt Locker*).

Removing the shutters (*The Hurt Locker*).

Another key setting, which doesn't feature in the opening sequence, is the US base, which is sparse and functionally military, with a vaguely temporary and faceless feel. This is illustrated in the stills above; on the left we see the base with its mix of concrete and basic steel shuttering and portacabin-style buildings that hold clean lines in stark contrast to the battle-worn Baghdad surroundings we have seen already. On the right still we see Sergeant J.T. Sanborn helping Sergeant First Class

William James removing the safety boards from the windows of his already sparse accommodation. Sandborn advises against it, to no avail, which clearly foreshadows James' attitude towards risk.

> Consider the following still (1:12:42); Sergeant James is *'enjoying some downtime'*:
>
> Isolation (*The Hurt Locker*).
>
> 1. Identify and explain the key elements of the setting.
> 2. How are these key elements being used to reflect Sergeant James' state of mind?

Performance

Much of the central characters' performances are **internalised** for a greater part of the film. We see a depiction of men in combat struggling to find their own ways of dealing with their situation. This builds up to emotional outbursts or 'explosions' that parallel the detonation of the IEDs.

The central performance is that of Jeremy Renner in the role of Sergeant First Class William James, who was nominated for the Best Performance by an Actor in a Leading Role Oscar. Renner's portrayal is very much that of a man dealing with inner turmoil and a struggle to reconcile what he is feeling and experiencing with the expectations of military men in combat situations. We see on the next page a typical moment of **introspection** from later on in the film.

Key terms

Internalised/inner turmoil
If you internalise your emotions or feelings, you do not allow them to show although you think about them while experiencing a state of confusion, disturbance and agitation.

Introspection
Observation or examination of one's own mental and emotional state, mental processes; the act of looking within oneself.

GCSE Film Studies

Heavy metal processing (*The Hurt Locker*).

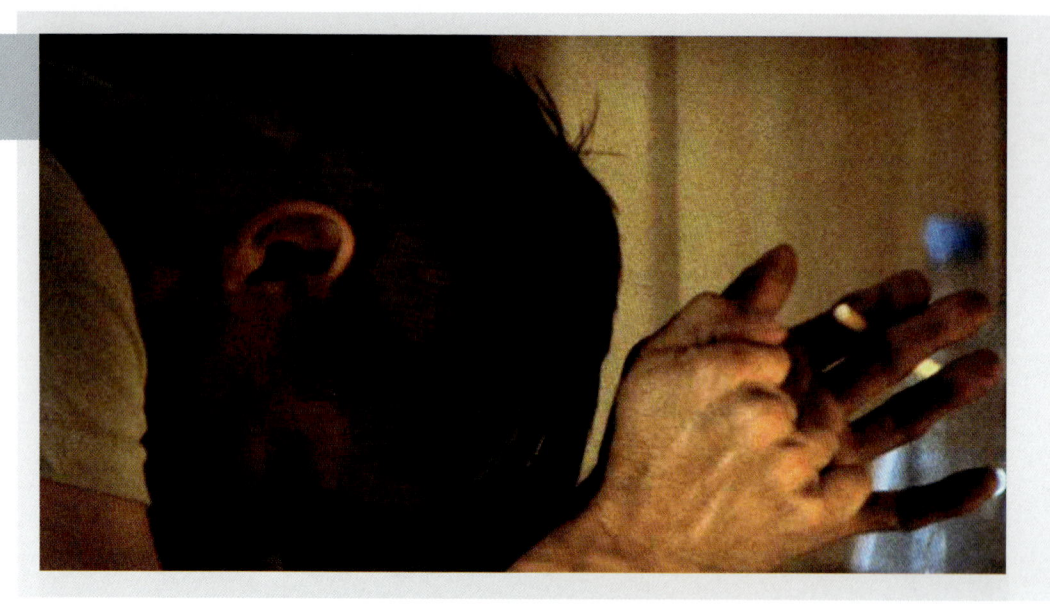

This performance as the 'brooding outsider' is one that Renner excels at, even to the extent of importing elements of it into his performance as Clint Barton in the mainstream blockbuster Marvel movies.

Other important elements within the performances are the relaxed relationships between the central characters for much of the time. Dialogue is 'banter' in style with suitably male posturing body language. There are at least two examples of this in the opening scene: the 'dick' exchange whilst manipulating the robot and the reference to the American version of *Steptoe and Son* – *Sanford & Son* in the vaguely racist conversation regarding the idea for a grass business.

Task 3.25

Complete the tasks below, considering the three main characters, Sergeant James, Sergeant Sanborn and Specialist Owen Eldridge:

1. Write a brief character description for each character.
2. Find a sequence that includes a performance element that demonstrates each one's character.
3. Explain why you think this is so.

Key terms

Blocked or blocking
Originally a theatre term referring to the positioning and movement of the actors on the stage. In cinema, blocking a scene entails working out the details of an actor's moves in relation to the camera and lighting.

Staged or staging
The process of selecting, designing, adapting to, or modifying the performance space for a film.

Positioning of characters and objects

Despite the, on occasion, unconventional approach to camera framing and movement, much of the chaos of authenticity is achieved through the ways in which the shots showing the relationship between James, Sanborn and Eldridge are edited together. There is a feeling of things happening spontaneously in front of the cameras, created, rather than being **blocked** and **staged**, in the style of a more conventional movie. If we look at the following still we see activity at various distances in the frame.

Part 3: Component 1:
Films made in the USA

'He's not gonna make it' (*The Hurt Locker*).

From the minaret in the far distance we have the Iraqi police moving into the focus of the scene with the partially framed officer and his men, with, finally, the barrel of another soldier's gun encroaching on the frame immediately in front of the camera. This multi-layered **composition** feels 'untidy' and once again helps towards fulfilling Kathryn Bigelow's overall ambition for rawness and authenticity.

Costume, hair and make-up

Much as we would expect, the most significant elements are the Americans on the one hand and the Iraqi population on the other. The still below, again from later on in the film, serves to illustrate this.

> **Key term**
>
> **Composition**
> How the elements of a shot are arranged, including sets, props, actors, costumes and lighting.

'It's not too safe here – I think we should move' (*The Hurt Locker*).

The American is seen in his clean and efficient-feeling desert camouflage uniform, which makes an officious contrast with the Iraqi's mix of time-worn old and new native garb. These are very much the costume images we have come to expect from news coverage of the ongoing conflict.

GCSE Film Studies

One key costume is the bomb suit: how its appearance seems to change the man inside into some kind of lumbering robot. This superficial appearance of power, however, is revealed as illusory in the opening scene as we see how little true protection it affords Staff Sergeant Matt Thompson once the IED explodes.

Thompson's death (*The Hurt Locker*).

We also see the use of make-up that indicates swiftly to the audience that he is badly injured or dead. Indeed, after this opening sequence, whenever the bomb suit comes out it is a signifier that something is about to happen or Sergeant First Class William James is about to venture once again into the very heart of the 'hurt locker'.

Props

The most significant props are the bomb disposal equipment, particularly the suit, the weapons and the IEDs. We also see the importance of the mobile phone as the means of detonation, the cutaway (below) of one from the opening sequence underlines early on this important tool of the insurgency and indicator of possible **jeopardy** in the film's narrative.

> ### Key term
> **Jeopardy**
> Hazard or risk of or exposure to loss, harm, death or injury; peril or danger.

'Put it down!' (*The Hurt Locker*).

174

Overall, the props become increasingly unobtrusive after a while, as the audience is immersed in this military environment and the authenticity of look and feel that gradually increases our acceptance of these accoutrements as part and parcel of the every day.

Task 3.26

Study the following still taken from the sequence where Sergeant James is confronted with dealing with a reluctant human bomb (1:48:24):

'Put his hands behind his head or I will happily shoot him' (*The Hurt Locker*).

1. Discuss as a group how the elements of costume, hair and make-up, and props contribute towards this scene.
2. Write a paragraph on how they add to the jeopardy of the situation we see here.
3. What other elements of film language contribute to what the audience is feeling?
4. Which narrative device common to mainstream action movies is used here?

Editing

Due to the nature of the sequence, we have partly discussed editing throughout the previous elements of film form. The guiding idea behind the editing choices again falls very squarely in line with Kathryn Bigelow's policy of 'raw, immediate and visceral'. The editor, Chris Innis, reflects this when he stated that they '*really wanted the film to retain that* **newsreel** *documentary quality ...*' This results in multiple uses of straight cuts that feel random in places, which tend to break traditional rules of the typical Hollywood **continuity editing** style. The editing plays fast and loose with the 180° rule and matching on motion and framing to evoke a feeling of documenting the chaos of a real panic. Slightly more conventional is the cross-cutting between the main protagonists to heighten the emotional drama and fear, particularly in the IED disposal situations.

Key terms

Newsreel
A short film of news and current affairs, formerly made for showing as part of the programme in a cinema.

Parallel editing
An editing technique of alternating two or more scenes that happen simultaneously but in different locations. If the scenes are simultaneous, they occasionally culminate in a single place, where the relevant parties confront each other.

Part 3: Component 1:
Films made in the USA

GCSE Film Studies

Similarly conventional is the **parallel editing** between the main protagonists and the unseen insurgents POV to build tension as Staff Sergeant Matt Thompson approaches the IED's disposal. As important as the style of cutting is the variation in shot length and pace to create drama and tension. The best example of this being how the length of shot shrinks to increase the pace of the action significantly, as the sequence builds up to the traditional action movie moment of will or won't Sergeant Matt Thompson escape the blast. Unlike a more clichéd Hollywood outcome, he does not survive.

Task 3.27

1. Watch the sequences 'How long you guys out here?' (51:51) and 'We need ammo!' (56:29) and then:

   (a) Explain the transition(s) used, why do you think this choice was made?

   (b) Discuss the impact the pace of editing has on the audience.

   (c) What impact does the use of cross-cutting have?

2. Time some of the shots to see how long they actually last; this may be useful if you have to edit your own film.

Sound

Last, but far from the least, we must consider the use of sound; or perhaps a more accurate description would be the construction of the film's **soundscape**. There is an unmistakeable emphasis on the use of diegetic sound, as we would expect in its role in supporting Kathryn Bigelow's overall goal of authenticity.

Despite this, the film is subtly scored, subtle to the extent that the first sound we hear is music, but only of a sort, it is an electronic tone that could almost be a sound being heard inside a stressed participant in the sequence. This tone acts as a sound bridge between the black of the opening caption as it morphs into the panicked Arabic shouting, which parallels the feel of the opening sequence. The **film score** is also used more conventionally, where often regional flavoured music is used to evoke an authentic Middle Eastern feel.

As the sequence progresses, multiple on-screen and off-screen sounds are layered, and collide to evoke what is now familiar in this depiction of a distrusted military occupation facing an immediate crisis. The disembodied loudspeaker Arabic voice, often the call to prayer but in this instance the IED warning, the insistent whirring of the bomb disposal robot, crowd noise, and the sound of jets and helicopters overhead are all a constant reminder of the intrusion of US military They might all combine to immerse the audience in the 'immediate, raw and vital' experience of the situation.

This build-up of intensity enhanced by the use of sound in the sequence culminates in the dramatic 'release' of the explosion. This large diegetic sound contrasts dramatically with the more intimate sound of Staff Sergeant Matt Thompson's increasingly laboured breathing as he tries to escape the explosion. The sequence ends in a silence that allows the audience to breathe once again and to take in and absorb what they have just seen and felt.

Key terms

Soundscape
A sound or combination of sounds that forms or arises from an immersive environment.

Film score
Original music written specifically to accompany a film.

Part 3: Component 1:
Films made in the USA

Task 3.28

Watch the sequence 'Ishmil' (1:23:17–1:25:09) a surprise attack. Now, complete the following tasks:

1. Identify the different sound elements used.
2. Which are diegetic and non-diegetic?
3. Which are on-screen and which are off-screen?
4. How are these individual elements used to support meaning and create atmosphere?
5. How do they work collectively to create meaning and atmosphere?
6. What meaning(s) does the sound bridge and the end possibly convey to the audience?

Task 3.29

Consider the following still from the closing shot of the film (2:00:48).

The final shot (*The Hurt Locker*).

Discuss:
(a) The thoughts and feelings of the audience created by this image?
(b) Watch the actual sequence and comment on the contribution of the sound and editing elements.
(c) What message are you left with?

177

GCSE Film Studies

Talking and writing about films

Here we will consider how other people have thought and written about *The Hurt Locker*. It is useful to deepen our understanding of the film by considering a range of responses. We will look at two reviews from publications aimed at different audiences and an extract from a more **academic study** of the film.

> **Key term**
>
> **Academic study**
> Usually used to describe work carried out in schools, colleges, and universities, especially work that involves studying and reasoning skills rather than practical skills.

Reviews

Let's consider the final 150–200 words of two reviews of the film when it was first released.

Mainstream media: *Empire* – Ian Nathan

The Hurt Locker, such a bruising, brilliant experience, can be viewed as the culmination, to date, of Bigelow's heightened MO. Amongst her snorting satire of macho posturing that was Point Break *crops up a pumped and tattoo-splattered surf-warrior derisively dubbed War Child. Now, heartbreakingly, she has found a true war child, a soul that can only function in country. Without the breast-beating of the Sarandon-Robbins crew, without much Bush-bashing at all, it's a tragic picture of men defined by conflict.*

If it lacks the grand breadth of the great war movies, the mythical elevation of an Apocalypse Now, *say, Bigelow has envisioned a stunning microcosm of hell that asks the most nakedly important question of all: will they make it?*

The most literally exciting film you will see this year. Forget the off-putting banner of another Iraq movie – go, watch, marvel, endure and book in the palliative of a stiff drink afterwards. ('*The Hurt Locker* Review', 29 July 2009, *Empire*)

About Ian Nathan

Ian Nathan, who lives and works in London, is one of the UK's best-known film writers. A former editor and executive editor of the world's biggest film magazine, *Empire*, he remains a contributing editor. Nathan has written several books on film including a filmography of the Coen Brothers, and a *Masters of Cinema* book dedicated to them. He is also author of *Terminator Vault* and *Alien Vault*, the definitive history of James Cameron's *Terminator* movies. He is a contributor to numerous publications including *The Times* and the *Independent*.

Task 3.30

1. Look up the whole review online at:
   http://www.empireonline.com/movies/hurt-locker/review/ and:

   (a) Read the review and make notes of any words or phrases you do not understand.

   (b) Look up their meanings or discuss them with your teacher or class.

   (c) What new information about the film did the review give you?

   (d) What did you agree with?

   (e) What did you disagree with?

   (f) What was your overall opinion on the review?

2. Look up another review from a mainstream source, for example *Total Film*. How does it compare with the *Empire* review?

BFI: *Sight & Sound* – Guy Westwell

The Hurt Locker is a powerful action movie in its own right, but it also offers a different take on the war in Iraq. Avoiding the high moral tone of Redacted or the plaintive soul-searching of In the Valley of Elah (also co-written by Boal), it confronts the fact that men often take great pleasure in war. While one sensitive character longs to leave the fighting behind and return to America to start a family, the film sides with Renner's character, inveterate risk-taker and adrenaline junkie Staff Sergeant Will James. James confesses to his infant son that he loves just one thing and in the very next shot he's back in Iraq and striding towards an unexploded bomb. In the context of the war in Iraq (where many reservists and stop-lossed veterans are not exactly volunteers) this unapologetic celebration of a testosterone-fuelled lust for war may gall. Yet there is something original and distinctive about the film's willingness to admit that for some men (and many moviegoers) war carries an intrinsic dramatic charge.
('Film Review: *The Hurt Locker*', 2008, *Sight & Sound*)

About Guy Westwell

Guy Westwell is Senior Lecturer in Film Studies and Chair of Department of Film Studies at Queen Mary University of London. A graduate of Keele University (BA Hons) and the University of Glasgow (MPhil, PhD), his main areas of research have focused upon the war film and antiwar film, film and politics, film and cultural memory, 9/11 and film, and iconic photographs and film. He occasionally writes film reviews for *Sight & Sound* and *The Conversation*. He was the recipient of the Drapers' Award for excellence in teaching in 2009. Publications include: *Parallel Lines: Post-9/11 American Cinema* (2014, Wallflower Press) and *War Cinema: Hollywood on the Front Line* (2006, Wallflower Press).

Task 3.31

1. Look up the whole review online at:
   http://old.bfi.org.uk/sightandsound/review/5082 and:

   (a) Read the review and make a note of any words or phrases you do not understand.
   (b) Look up their meanings or discuss them with your teacher or class.
   (c) What new information about the film did the review give you?
   (d) What did you agree with?
   (e) What did you disagree with?
   (f) How did this review compare with the *Empire* review?
   (g) What was your overall opinion on the review?

2. Look up another review from a cinephile source, for example *Film Comment*. How does it compare with the *Sight & Sound* review?

Task 3.32

1. Go back to the two original reviews and:

   (a) Note down the main features of each, for example the use of a star rating or a synopsis.
   (b) Which review included the most difficult language?
   (c) Why do you think that is?
   (d) In your opinion, which was the most effective review?

GCSE Film Studies

Task 3.33 — Using what you have learned about writing a review, write one of your own. Once you have finished, include a short explanation of why you have done it in the way that you have.

Academic study

Now let us look at an extract from academic study of the film taken from the *Journal of War & Culture Studies*, 'Embodiment in the War Film: *Paradise Now* and *The Hurt Locker*', by Robert Burgoyne.

> *The Hurt Locker* foregrounds the body in an equally explicit manner. Encasing its protagonist in a 100-pound Kevlar 'bomb suit', the film isolates the main character, Sergeant William James, as dramatically as the suicide vest isolates the human bomb in *Paradise Now*. Opposites or antitheses of each other, the suicide bomber and the leader of the bomb deactivation squad both bring into focus the problem of bodies in war, their destructive potency and their vulnerability. By underscoring the body at risk, *The Hurt Locker* also presents an implicit critique of the distance – moral and physical – of remote targeting and weaponry. The reality of war as embodied activity and embodied violence asserts itself here in a visceral way. (2002, Vol. 5, No. 3)

About Robert Burgoyne

Robert Burgoyne is a Professor of Film Studies at the University of St Andrews in Scotland. He completed his undergraduate degree at the University of Minnesota and a doctorate at New York University. His work has centred on the historiography of film, with a special emphasis on American cinema, history and national identity, and the counter-narratives of nation that have emerged in many films. His recent publications include *Film Nation: Hollywood Looks at US History* (2010, University of Minnesota Press) and *The Epic Film in World Culture* (2010, Routledge).

Task 3.34

1. Read the extract from Robert Burgoyne's article above and:

    (a) Write a short summary about what you think he is saying. Look up or ask about any difficult language or words.

    (b) Discuss with a partner or your group what you think Robert Burgoyne is saying.

    (c) Now write a short summary about what you think he is saying.

    (d) Write a short evaluation once you have finished explaining how and why your understanding changed.

2. You could now try to take on the whole article at:
   https://core.ac.uk/download/pdf/9821980.pdf

Part 3: Component 1:
Films made in the USA

Task 3.35

1. Use the internet to find your own examples of specialist writing about *The Hurt Locker*.

   A good place to start may with be with a specific issue, for example the area of gender, from the *Guardian* newspaper's headline (Matthew Weaver, 8 March 2010):

   # KATHRYN BIGELOW MAKES HISTORY AS FIRST WOMAN TO WIN BEST DIRECTOR OSCAR

   Once you have found a piece of writing that you find interesting create a critique of it to include:

   (a) A brief summary of the article.
   (b) The main ideas in the writing you think are most interesting.
   (c) List where you agree with it.
   (d) List where you disagree with it.
   (e) Any other thoughts or information you have as a result of this piece of writing.

2. Present your critique to the rest of your class.

Part 4
Component 2: Global film

Posters for global non-English language film *Let the Right One In* (2008, Tomas Alfredson, Sweden).

Part 4: Component 2:
Global film

Introduction

In Component 2 you will study films made outside the US. This will allow you to explore, respond to and understand films that are perhaps quite different from the ones you would normally watch. They will feature countries and cultures that you may be unfamiliar with, and they will invite you to learn about how the people in these countries live – the challenges they face, their beliefs and values, and their past, present and futures. Although some of the films may look dissimilar to the ones you are used to, they will share common social concerns.

The paper will assess:

- Assessment objective one (AO1): your ability to demonstrate knowledge and understanding of elements of film
- Assessment objective two (AO2): your ability to apply knowledge and understanding of elements of film, including analysing films

You will have studied elements of film in Component 1 and your work in Component 2 will further add to this.

Section A contains one stepped question on one global English language film.

Section B contains one stepped question on one recent global **non-English** language film.

Section C contains one stepped question on one contemporary UK film.

This part of the book contains three case studies. Each case study will focus on one film from sections A, B and C. They will explore each of the areas that you will need to cover for Component 2. Below is a list of the films offered in each section. You must study **one** film from each section.

A. One of the following five **global English language films**:

- *Rabbit-proof Fence* (2002, Phillip Noyce, Australia), PG
- *Slumdog Millionaire* (2008, Danny Boyle, UK), 15
- *District 9* (2009, Neill Blomkamp, South Africa), 15
- *An Education* (2009, Lone Scherfig, UK), 12A
- *Song of the Sea* (2014, Tomm Moore, Eire), PG

B. One of the following five **global non-English language films**:

- *Tsotsi* (2005, Gavin Hood, South Africa), 15
- *Let the Right One In* (2008, Tomas Alfredson, Sweden), 15
- *The Wave* (2008, Dennis Gansel, Germany), 15
- *Spirited Away* (2001, Hayao Miyazaki, Japan), 12
- *Wadjda* (2012, Haifaa Al-Mansour, Saudi Arabia), PG

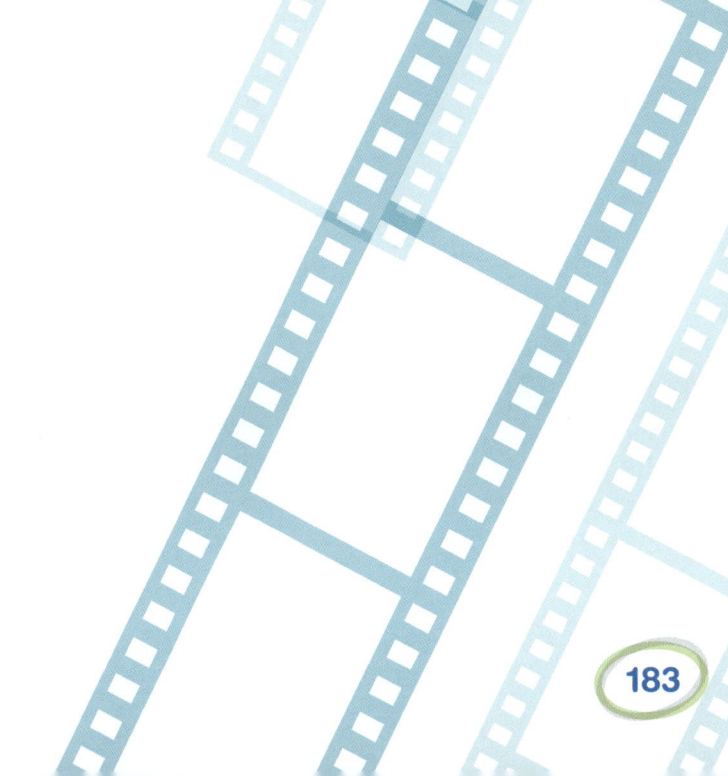

C. One of the following five **contemporary UK films (produced since 2010)**:

- *Attack the Block* (2011, Joe Cornish, UK), 15
- *Submarine* (2010, Richard Ayoade, UK), 15
- *Skyfall* (2012, Sam Mendes, UK), 12
- *Brooklyn* (2015, John Crowley, UK), 12A
- *My Brother the Devil* (2012, Sherif El Hosaini, UK), 15

Suggested approach

This book contains one case study from each of the above sections: A, B and C. Whether you choose to study the films used in these examples or opt for another of the available films listed, the assessment brief for, and suggested approach to, each section of Component 2 will remain the same.

In order to meet the assessment objectives for this component, you must explore each of your chosen three films in terms of:

- The key elements of film form: how the film communicates to its audiences through film language such as cinematography, lighting, mise-en-scène, editing and sound.
- Key contexts: how the film has been influenced by the contexts in which it was produced such as when and where the film was made and set, what it tells us about particular people and places (e.g. their culture, history or political systems) and any technological or institutional contexts that may have affected the production (including technological advancements, problems during the shooting and available budgets).

Furthermore, you will explore your films in terms of one additional area of study that is different for each section:

- **Section A: global English language films – narrative**: the way key elements of film form are organised into larger structures (see page 54). This should include the way and order in which the film is 'told', the function of characters, locations and settings, as well as our expectations of and responses to the film.
- **Section B: global non-English films – representation**: how films communicate particular messages and the ways in which these messages can be 'read' differently by audiences (see page 66).
- **Section C: contemporary UK film – the aesthetic qualities of film**: the 'look' or 'feel' of the film and its consideration as a work of art/how elements of film form have been used in an artistic way (see page 76). This should include any strong sense of style, emotional appeal and use of colour.

An example of how to approach each of these areas of study can be seen in the following case studies, but as a basic method for study it is recommended that you work through each of the required areas of study as listed above.

Global English language films

Section A

Case study: District 9

Country: South Africa

Production year: 2009

Director: Neill Blomkamp

Certificate: 15

Release date:
4 September 2009

Running time:
112 minutes

Introduction

District 9 is a science-fiction thriller based on Neill Blomkamp's 2005 short film *Alive in Joburg,* which sees aliens stranded in Johannesburg only to be exiled to slums. After adapting the story into a feature-length screenplay with Terri Tatchell, Blomkamp directed the 2009 film that follows one man as he becomes trapped in the alien territory.

GCSE Film Studies

Key contexts

As you will have covered in your former learning and in earlier sections of this book, the context in which a film is produced is very important. Films reflect and respond to the social, cultural, political, technological and institutional contexts in which they are made. Science-fiction films are particularly known for commenting on society at the time, often serving a political function (exposing corrupt industries and governments, for example). Over time, and thanks to great advances in technology and special effects, the genre has transformed into more of a money-maker and profit generator rather than tackling social issues. However, with *District 9* it appears to be harking back to its original form in many ways. It certainly suggests that the government and corporations are working together at the detriment of the people. For example, the government has hired MNU (the second biggest weapons manufacturer in the world) to deal with the aliens. The two are working together under the guise of helping the aliens to gain access to and learn from the alien weaponry. In fact, the people and the aliens are expendable and the end target is profit and global economic dominance.

At first glance the film is quite obviously a generic sci-fi film – aliens that are different from us, and that are to be feared, 'invade'. It is the classic 'them versus us'. But the fact that this very western type genre has been put into the third-world setting of a Johannesburg slum immediately makes the apartheid spring to mind. The segregation of the aliens from the humans can quite easily be read as the segregation of the blacks from the whites. The viral marketing campaign that helped promote the film's release also played on this idea, with posters being put up around the world suggesting certain areas were for humans only – reminiscent of posters and signs of a different era that suggested areas were only for whites or blacks. There was a subtle link on the marketing posters to the film's website, which was also separated into areas for humans and non-humans. Much of the advertising of the film (as well as themes within the film itself) link to the segregation of the blacks and whites during the apartheid, and Blomkamp admits that the film exists entirely because of this history.

Quick Question 4.1

As well as corruption and greed, what other themes and issues do you think the film comments on?

Marketing campaign posters for *District 9*.

Part 4: Component 2:
Global film

> **Task 4.1**
> Think about how you would feel if you were excluded from certain places or activities just because of who you were? How would this make you feel?

Blomkamp grew up in South Africa during the apartheid era. Although he was sheltered from its many inequalities and horrors, it is clear his exposure to this segregation influenced his work. But it is not just the history of the country that plays a part in shaping this film. It is also its present.

One of the designers on *District 9*, Greg Broadmore, said at the time of the film that social tensions were brewing in the city.

> *It's not just the whites and blacks … you have the Nigerians and Zimbabweans coming in as refugees, you have tribal fractions within that. It's massively broken up and stratified. It's an incredibly tense environment.*

The mass immigration, as refugees fled violence to find a better life, caused conflict. Nigerian and Zimbabwean refugees found themselves discriminated against and segregated (much like the aliens). Blomkamp's short film *Alive in Joburg*, which later would transform into *District 9*, was based on the same subject – unwanted aliens landing in Johannesburg and becoming segregated. To get a realistic feel to his documentary-style film, Blomkamp interviewed normal civilians about the influx of immigrants in real-life Johannesburg, and their honest and frank answers about real-life illegal aliens were perfectly transformed into a commentary about fictitious aliens, showing the tensions that were rising.

> **Task 4.2**
> 1. Watch Blomkamp's short film *Alive in Joburg*.
> 2. Now you know that the interview footage is about real people does this change the way it affects you? Was what the interviewees said more acceptable when the words were about aliens rather than human beings?

This discrimination against other cultures, particularly the Nigerians, is represented in *District 9* with the Nigerians being portrayed in a negative light.

> **Task 4.3**
> After watching *District 9* discuss the following points.
> 1. How do you think the Nigerians are represented? Make a list of words you would use to describe the characters.
> 2. The head Nigerian in the film shares his name with the former Nigerian president and Head of Military, Obasanjo. What does this suggest?
> 3. Nigerian-born, Brooklyn writer, Teju Cole, says:
>
>   *It is a fact that Nigerian immigrants in South Africa are often persecuted, stereotyped as drug dealers and prostitutes, and denied housing and jobs.* (Comment: *District 9* and the Nigerians, 11 September 2009, africaisacountry.com)
>
>   Do you think Blomkamp is merely holding a mirror up to society and how others see the Nigerian refugees or do you think this controversial representation shows an inherent prejudice?
> 4. Does it surprise you that the film is banned in Nigeria?

GCSE Film Studies

Negative portrayal of Nigerians in *District 9*.

More negative portrayals (*District 9*).

As well as portraying the different relationships between real-life groups of people, the film appears to be based on other real-life events as well. The aliens in the film arrive in Johannesburg in the 1980s, only a few years after the real-life massacre in Soweto. The 1980s in South Africa was a time of fear and unrest. The apartheid government declared a state of emergency and thousands were detained without trial, murdered or forcibly removed. This led to slums forming to house the displaced. Even the title of the film is a reference to real events in 1966 in which District 6 was declared whites only, and black South Africans were forcibly removed and put into townships. We can clearly see that these issues are reflected in the film. The aliens are put into townships and when they refuse to be evicted they are detained or killed without trial (Christopher Johnson's friend, for example).

In an even more life-imitating-art twist, a few weeks into the actual filming of *District 9*, the **xenophobic** attacks in South Africa that killed 62 people and displaced thousands took place. The fictional news footage at the start of the film is very like the footage of the 2008 attacks seen on South African television at the time. Blomkamp states that he had to be careful with the film after these attacks, as the issues had suddenly become much more sensitive.

Key term

Xenophobia
A dislike of or prejudice against people from other countries or places.

Part 4: Component 2:
Global film

Fictitious *District 9* news footage.

Real news footage from May 2008.

The key elements of film form

The above ideas not only set the context for the story but are a constant visual reminder throughout the film as well. The context of the film and the issues surrounding it are continued through the clever use of the elements of film form.

GCSE Film Studies

Cinematography and mise-en-scène

The cinematography used in the film was a clever way of showing the divide between the aliens and the humans. Apart from the CCTV and aerial footage, *District 9* was almost entirely shot using **RED One cameras** and was one of the first feature films to use this advanced equipment. The hand-held stressed, jerky footage used when around the aliens gives a sense of danger and threat. In contrast, the much more still talking head footage captured for the interview sections gives the audience a sense of security when around the humans.

Additionally, the settings used helped to illustrate the divide and inequality. The film was shot mainly on location in South Africa and a real township was used as the slum that the aliens lived in. The only shack that was created for the film was Christopher Johnson's shack. All the others were real. The residents of the real-life township had just been moved to new housing elsewhere, so using this location not only gave the audience a very real sense of what living in such situations would be like, but it was also very good for the small budget. Again, this location also clearly echoes the storyline of the film (the aliens being forcibly removed from the township) giving a real sense of art imitating life; however, it also created problems.

Everything in the slum was real, including all the props from the animal carcasses to the barbed wire and rubbish. This gave the film a gritty edge and added to the realism of the mise-en-scène. It would have been difficult to replicate such detailed imagery, especially within the small budget, but it also proved problematic for the filmmakers as they would often arrive in the morning to find items had been taken overnight. Despite such set-backs, the squalid slum location set against the sleek skyscrapers of Johannesburg worked well to illustrate the segregation and inequality in the area.

> **Key term**
>
> **RED One camera**
> A new camera used in a number of Oscar winning films, which is able to capture sharp, high quality images.

Real-life township used as D9 slum (*District 9*).

Another issue the filmmakers faced was that because Blomkamp wanted the slum to look like a war zone, he took the decision to film the real location in the harsh winter months when residents would burn things such as tyres to provide warmth. The dust and smoke created added to the atmosphere (with Blomkamp describing the slum at one point as looking like the Gaza strip); however, it also made the atmosphere very dirty and unhygienic for the cast and crew, not to mention the equipment, which stood up well to the windy and gritty conditions. To diffuse the harsh sunlight a huge silk sail was flown from a crane. The lighting in the journalists' material was unaltered to give a realistic feel.

Part 4: Component 2: Global film

So, the look of the film was very realistic and everything about the film seems to point to two opposing sides – the humans and the aliens. But, in some ways, there is also the suggestion that the two sides have a lot in common as well. The look of the aliens themselves is a key part of this.

The design of the creatures went through many changes during the making of the film. Blomkamp was adamant the aliens should resemble insects from the start but originally they were designed as 'great hulking creatures with leathery skin and tentacled faces' and were to be played by men in suits (possibly due to the limited budget).

However, it was decided that the aliens should look more human so that the audience could empathise with them. As Blomkamp explains in the 'Director's Commentry' on the DVD Special Features:

> *Our psychology doesn't allow us to really empathize with something unless it has a face and a (human) shape ... I felt like I had to give in to this Hollywood cliché. But that's just the way it goes. If you make a film about an alien force, which is the oppressor or aggressor, and you don't want to empathize with them, you can go to town. So creatively that's what I wanted to do but story-wise, I just couldn't.*

Dirty conditions during filming of *District 9*.

Task 4.4

Consider the three aliens in the images below, they all have quite human figures, they all have some kind of face (the latter two have very human faces). What is it about the design of the *District 9* aliens that make us empathise with them, yet we feel apathy towards the other two?

Alien creatures from (left to right) *Alien*, *Predator* (1987, John McTieman) and *District 9*.

GCSE Film Studies

Task 4.5

1. What do you like or dislike about the alien creatures in *District 9*?

2. What else, apart from their human-like form and face, makes them more acceptable to us than aliens in other films?

3. Blomkamp describes the aliens as worker bees with a hive mentality. Does this remind you of many immigrants to the UK who come here to work? Do you think this is another comment on society?

4. The aliens were all played by one actor in a trackball suit and every other alien in the film (apart from those on the medical lab tables) were CGI. Why do you think it was decided that the aliens would be realised in CGI rather than the bodysuits originally planned?

5. The prop of the cat food (the aliens' favourite food) was based on Blomkamp's memories from his childhood when he would see people selling cheese snacks out of huge sacks to the impoverished. He wanted the aliens to have a similar cheap food. But what does the choice of cat food make you think about the aliens?

Acting the alien (*District 9*).

Baby calls for his father (*District 9*).

Sound

The sound design for the film is very interesting and is another way Blomkamp suggests that the aliens are both different from us but at the same time similar.

To compliment the look of the aliens, their noises do have sounds that mimic insects, almost like the clicking of a cricket. The alien sound (made by rubbing a pumpkin) does, however, have similarities to many of the real tribal languages of South Africa, such as Zulu and Xhosa, which use clicking sounds in their vocabulary. The clicks in the alien language add to the other sounds in their speech, making them seem futuristic and giving it an almost technological sound; however, it also acts to show a similarity between the aliens and the humans. They are not that dissimilar to us.

Task 4.6

Watch the climactic fight scene between Wikus and Koobus, when Wikus wears the alien armour suit.

1. Describe the noises used to represent Wikus.
2. How do the sounds used suggest that Wikus is not dissimilar to the aliens?

Wikus in the alien armour suit (*District 9*).

The music in the film, by Clinton Shorter, is also a mix of two styles – African and technological. Of course, the latter represents the sci-fi genre, whilst the former reflects the setting well, but they also act to represent the humans and the aliens, whilst again suggesting a similarity between the two.

Quick Question 4.2

Discuss the two types of music. When do you think each style of music is used? Are there times when the two are merged?

GCSE Film Studies

Editing

Apart from the third-world setting, the film does follow in many of the conventions of sci-fi movies. The cinematography, mise-en-scène and sound we have come to recognise from such films are all there. We have the long shots of the imposing spaceship, the close-ups of the body horror, there are lasers and spaceships, aliens and soldiers, the sound is technological and exaggerated. However, in one way the film appears quite different from the norm – the special effects.

Blomkamp was a visual effects prodigy and was already working at the age of 14, so it is not surprising that special effects are in abundance. However, Blomkamp explained he did not want to put the effects on a pedestal and, unlike some Hollywood films that tend to be all singing and dancing, he wanted the effects here to be more subtle.

Special effects used in *District 9*.

Quick Question 4.3

Look at the two screenshots on the right. Pay attention to the positioning and lighting of the spaceship. What effect does this have on the scene? Where is your attention drawn? Why have the special effects been framed like this?

194

Narrative

As with many genres, when the audience is told that the film is a science-fiction movie then there are certain expectations on what the narrative will be about and what will happen.

Of course, *District 9* follows many of the narrative conventions of sci-fi films and there are many recognisable characters and images. It even has the expected **dystopian** view of the world but one thing that is a little different to the norm is that it is not set in the distant future but basically set in the present. By doing this it comments on society today, and makes the events unfolding seem more gritty and realistic. It gets people thinking. In many ways, it is a post-modern film utilising many different styles (documentary and naturalistic), crossing a hybrid of genres (sci-fi, thriller, perhaps even war) and it pays homage to many other films with its cinéma vérité, body horror and recognisable storylines.

The way in which the story is told to us is different. And it is important. The way the story is structured and revealed to us is one of the key ways it can position us as an audience. Films aren't always told in the order that events happened. They can move backwards and forwards in time. They can show us different people's viewpoints. They can manipulate the way we feel towards different characters and events. *District 9* is an excellent example of this.

Act one of the film sets up the world of the film and introduces the main characters and main problem. *District 9* uses a mix of **talking heads**, interviews and news footage to give us the backstory about the aliens, how they got here, what has happened to them so far and the fact that they are to be forcibly removed from D9. It also introduces us to some of the key groups of people – MNU (the Multi-National United Security Force, represented to us through Wikus) and the aliens (represented to us through Christopher Johnson).

When we are first introduced to the aliens they are portrayed in a negative light and as a threat. The fact that the film opens with professionals in suits, with impressive job titles and surrounded by books, discussing the aliens makes us believe these people are telling us the truth and we are immediately positioned with them. They are providing us with real footage of the aliens. They are discussing real events. Why would we not believe them?

It is this **pseudo-documentary** style that acts to **dehumanise** the aliens. We only see the aliens at the start through the media reports, news footage and interview commentaries. They are all negative and show the aliens to be hostile, violent and dangerous. Seeing the aliens only through the **gaze of the medium** removes us from them. We do not feel empathy towards them and are positioned with those who are behind the media reports and the local people who want them out.

Key term

Dystopian
A fictional world or place in which everything is unpleasant or bad and people are oppressed, unhappy and afraid.

Quick Question 4.4

Discuss in small groups what you expect from a sci-fi movie? What kinds of characters will there be? What will be the basic storyline? What kinds of images will you expect to see?

Key term

Talking head
When a person addresses the camera directly, viewed in a close-up.

Quick Question 4.5

In groups discuss what a three act structure is and what each act should do/reveal?

Key terms

Pseudo-documentary
Having the appearance of but is not actually a real documentary.

Dehumanise
Make less human.

Gaze of the medium
Seeing the world through the eyes of the camera.

GCSE Film Studies

Professionals discussing aliens in *District 9* opening.

Part 4: Component 2:
Global film

This negative reporting on immigrants is very similar to the way refugees are often portrayed in the media today. Think about the news reports of the migrants in the Calais Jungle, for example. They are often depicted as violent law breakers who riot and cause damage.

1. Discuss any news footage you have seen about the Calais Jungle. Is it negative or positive? You may wish to look up past news reports in groups.
2. What similarities are there in the way the aliens are being represented in *District 9* and the way the immigrants are being presented in the UK press?

Task 4.7

The edge of the slum in District 9 (*District 9*).

Quick Question 4.6

Watch the opening of *District 9* up until we meet Christopher Johnson. Make a list of the images you see and the sounds you hear that suggest the aliens are a threat.

Look at the image below of our first close interaction with an alien.

1. How does the over-the-shoulder shot help position us?
2. How do the length and angle of the shot affect how we see the alien?
3. The camera here is hand-held and jerks, reacting to the sudden movements of the alien. How does this make the audience feel?
4. Look at the different costumes used in this shot. What does each connote?
5. Who do you position yourself with here?

Task 4.8

Our first interaction with an alien (*District 9*).

197

GCSE Film Studies

So, the initial impression of the aliens is very negative because of the way the story is being told to us through news reports and talking heads. It is only when we look closer at the opening that we can start to see that the image of the aliens being presented to us may not be a completely true one.

Task 4.9

Look at this image of the spaceship over Johannesburg.

The alien spaceship hovers over Johannesburg (*District 9*).

1. Do you see any similarities between the city below and the spaceship in terms of colour and shapes?
2. Do you think the spaceship looks like an inverted city of its own?
3. What could this suggest about its occupants inside?
4. Do you think this image could show the aliens as a group in need of help rather than an imposing threat?

Re-watching the opening with closer attention to detail, we could also pick out other times at which aliens are seen less as a threat and more as the weaker species. MNU, which appears to want to help the aliens, is quite biased and even racist. Wikus refers to the aliens as prawns: a derogatory term that the professionals themselves suggest refers to them as 'bottom feeders that scavenge the leftovers'. The news footage that purports to show the aliens as dangerous and the cause of the riots actually shows the aliens doing nothing. In fact, the humans are the ones pulling the aliens and trying to forcibly move them. The humans are also the ones with the weapons, forming gangs and looking intimidating as they start riots. The spaceship itself is seen only as a shadow in the background, suggesting that the aliens are not there to cause trouble. The aliens can also be found searching through bins and trying to obtain food. They are doing what any human would do – they are trying to survive.

This is further highlighted when we meet Christopher Johnson. Up until this point act one has been seen mainly via Wikus' point-of-view (POV). When we meet Christopher Johnson the POV shifts to that of the aliens, and the representation of the species therefore changes too.

Part 4: Component 2:
Global film

"Good, little one."

Quick Question 4.7

Look at the still on the left, which shows the first time we meet Christopher Johnson. Discuss how the representation of the aliens now changes.

Christopher Johnson praises his son (*District 9*).

Christopher Johnson has many human characteristics. He appears civilised and intelligent. He has feelings, and seems to demonstrate loss and frustration when his friend is killed by Koobus. With the introduction of Christopher Johnson we start to see the aliens in a more human light. They have faces, which, as discussed earlier, helps audiences identify and empathise with them. Christopher particularly seems to have large, sad, almost puppy-dog eyes when he watches his friend die.

In contrast, Koobus, who represents the military, appears to have no feelings. He is presented early on as the villain of the film. He runs after the alien who is wounded and crawling on the floor, and speaks to it like a dog. He laughs at it, before pulling his gun and shooting it like an animal.

Look at the below stills taken from when Koobus chases and kills Christopher Johnson's friend.

1. Identify the shots used in the images. What does it say about the characters?
2. How are the two characters positioned within the frame of the first shot? What does this suggest?
3. This is the first time the aliens have been seen as the inferior and weaker species. What does this do to the audience? How does it make you feel?
4. Who are you positioned with here? The aliens or the humans?

Task 4.10

Left: Koobus targets Christopher Johnson's friend; right: *It will give me great pleasure to kill you, you bastard*' (*District 9*).

"No. No."

199

GCSE Film Studies

When we meet Christopher Johnson the aliens are shown to be more human than at first perceived, and it could be said that the humans (in particular Koobus) are seen to be more alien. This idea can be supported when we look at how Wikus van der Merwe is introduced to us.

Natives to South Africa would recognise his surname, van der Merwe, as the common name used in jokes about stupid, bumbling and incompetent people, and this is certainly a good portrayal of Wikus at the start of the film. He is a stupid, bumbling bureaucrat. A rule follower. He is likeable enough (he dotes on his wife and seems pleased to get attention from the cameras) and he is amusing (getting his mic caught in his lanyard and stumbling over his words), but he is ignorant and racist.

Although he means well, it is clear that he has no empathy for the aliens. He has, through his work at MNU and his family ties to its director, been conditioned to see past the horror of what he is doing to the aliens. He is almost like a programmed worker, in his tan pullover and his slicked hair, who has been dehumanised by the company. He refers to the aliens as prawns and it doesn't occur to him that this might be offensive. When they burn the shack containing the alien eggs, he says it sounds like 'popcorn', which again demonstrates his incapability of seeing the horror of what is actually happening – 1,000s of babies being killed.

> **Task 4.11**
>
> How true do you think the following statement is?
>
> Wikus starts the film being more alien to us than the creatures from outer space and must become an alien in order to become more human.

Quick Question 4.8

Can you think of any parallels with these evictions in today's society?

The fact that Wikus is more alien at the start of the film than Christopher Johnson, is what sets him up for a true hero's journey. When he discovers the fluid, a liquid that seems to fuel the alien Prawn's weapons and ships, and accidentally triggers it, this is the turning point. The sequence ends when Christopher Johnson refuses to sign the eviction papers, which had been served on all the illegal aliens (Prawns) living in District 9.

At the end of act one we are still largely viewing the film from Wikus' POV; however, we do empathise with the aliens and their longing to get home. We recognise their human characteristics and the inhumane actions of the humans, so act one remains open to several interpretations, which is interesting for a sci-fi film. As well as setting up the added conflict of the Nigerian gangsters, act one has also set up enigma codes surrounding Wikus and 'the investigation'.

This withholding of information and the use of an ellipsis makes the audience eager to watch more in order to discover what really happened.

Act two follows Wikus' deterioration as he starts to transform physically into an alien. He is probed and prodded by MNU and sees for himself the inhumane way that aliens are treated. He realises that he is expendable, as are the aliens, and his eyes are opened for the first time to the racist and corrupt corporation he works for. He flees, becoming a fugitive and is increasingly able to empathise with the aliens. The mid-point of the film is also his low point, when everyone seems against him and even his wife rejects him.

Part 4: Component 2:
Global film

After taking refuge in Christopher Johnson's shack, he realises he must now work with him in order to return to his human form. The second half of act two sees Wikus working with Christopher Johnson. They must approach the inner-most cave (the place most dangerous for them) by returning to MNU headquarters to get the fluid back. Act two also sees Wikus gain allies (Christopher and his son) and enemies (he is tortured and nearly killed by Obesanjo). When Christopher's son manages to re-activate the mothership, it acts as a second reward (seizing the sword in the hero's journey) and signals the start of act three.

In act three we see Wikus is now becoming more human (despite his appearance being quite the contrary). This is shown the most when he protects Christopher and saves him from being killed. The ultimate battle between Wikus and Koobus brings good and evil together with good prevailing.

Task 4.12

Look at the still below taken from Wikus and Koobus' final battle.

1. How does this image mirror the still you looked at earlier when Koobus kills Christopher Johnson's friend? Think about camera shots and positioning.

2. What does this suggest about Wikus and how he has changed? Think about his character arc?

3. What does this say about Koobus' character?

Koobus v. Wikus (*District 9*).

Task 4.13

At the end of the film, captions explain that D9 was demolished after the alien resettlement operation was completed. It continues:

District 10 now houses 2.5 million aliens and continues to grow …

What message do you think this sends to viewers?

Section B / Global non-English language films

Case study: Let the Right One In

Country: Sweden

Production year: 2008

Director: Tomas Alfredson

Certificate: 15

Release date: 10 April 2008

Running time: 114 minutes

Introduction

Let the Right One In (*Låt den rätte komma in*) was originally a novel written in 2004 by John Ajvide Lindqvist, who also wrote the screenplay. This 2008 romantic-horror was directed by Tomas Alfredson. It tells the story of a bullied 12-year-old boy who develops a friendship with a vampire child in Blackeberg, a suburb of Stockholm, in the early 1980s.

Key contexts

Let the Right One In was made at a time in which vampire films were very popular. Whilst this may account for its international success, it is important to note that this trend was not one that was adopted in the filmmaker's native Sweden. In fact, Ajvide Lindqvist claimed, on completing the novel in 2004, that it was the first Swedish vampire book since the 1800s, so whilst vampire narratives were (and had been for some time) a staple of popular culture in the English-speaking world, in Sweden they were a novelty. This perhaps explains why, although the film did well in the Swedish box office, it did not perform spectacularly and did far better with international audiences. Nevertheless, critics both at home and away praised the film but another movie (*Everlasting Moments*, 2008, Jan Troell) was chosen by the Swedish Film Institute as the country's submission for the Academy Awards.

Perhaps it was the film's distance from the norm that served to draw international praise, but at the same time it alienated some native audiences. Of course, the film was not a completely new take on original vampire ideas and it did employ several codes and conventions familiar in vampire horror movies (the pale skin, the fact that Eli cannot enter a room without being invited, an aversion to daylight). However, the filmmakers tended to mix these with conventions from other genres as well, such as drama, romance and coming-of-age. The result of this **hybridity** is a beautiful mix of dark and light, and good and bad. **Binary oppositions** are brought together and used to explore universal ideas of isolation, loneliness and exclusion from a wider social network. The two protagonists are separated from the world around them. The fact that one of them is a vampire is a mere detail.

So why is the film based around such morose and mournful themes? To get a better understanding we must look at what was happening in Sweden at the time the film was set.

The film is set in Backeberg, a small suburb of Stockholm, in the early 1980s. This is where the writer grew up and we get a real sense of this area thanks to the high production values – the dark winter nights, tall, grey buildings and thick, heavy snow. In the 1950s, as part of Sweden's modernisation into an industrial nation, the government built many suburban housing projects (much like the one seen in the film) in order to house the influx of immigrant workers who travelled to the country. Although they were well intentioned, social systems designed to provide workers with everything they needed (food, shelter, etc.) they were often seen as oppressive and controlling and separated immigrant workers from society.

The 1980s saw the second wave of immigration. Eli herself in some ways represents these immigrants – her dark hair and features and boyish looks are a far cry from the more Nordic look of the pale and blonde Oskar. She represents the 'foreigner'. Her 'otherness' to the rest of the characters (who all are native Swedes except one) singles her out as different from the rest and separates her from the common society around her. So the film could be said to be expressing the feelings of the time. In order to consider why Eli's representation of a vampire is different from the norm and what this may say, we must consider the context in which the film was made.

> *Key terms*
>
> **Hybridity**
> Concepts that can be evidenced in a film, making it difficult to fit easily into a particular genre category.
>
> **Binary oppositions**
> Characters or ideas that represent sets of opposite values, e.g. good and evil, light and dark.

> *Top tip*
> Download two stills of Oskar and Eli. Label the stills to highlight important binary oppositions and other key representational features. Keep these stills in your revision bank.

Task 4.14

Consider Eli's character.

1. What do you think of her? Do you like her?
2. Does your opinion of her change during the film?
3. If her existence can be compared to immigrants in Sweden at the time, do you think she is representing them in a positive or negative light?
4. If the film is said to be expressing the feelings of the time – is it expressing the views of native Swedes towards the immigrants or is it expressing the emotions of the immigrants themselves?

GCSE Film Studies

> *Key term*
>
> **Cultural norms**
> The accepted behaviour that an individual is expected to conform to in a particular group, community or culture.

Academic Rochelle Wright suggests:

> *… the visual association of vampires with dark-haired immigrants does not demonize the latter. Instead it reinforces a sympathetic view … [portraying] 'new Swedes' and second-generation immigrants with sensitivity and insight, focusing on the difficulties of adjusting to a foreign culture or negotiating between conflicting* **cultural norms**. ('Vampire in the Stockholm Suburbs: *Let the Right One In* and Genre Hybridity', www.public.asu.edu/~srbeatty/466/Let%20the%20Right%20One%20In%20Essay.pdf)

This is certainly the case with Eli, who, although not in completely the same situation, is a newcomer to Oskar's community and she faces obstacles when trying to develop a friendship with him.

The key elements of film form

Just as in your previous areas of study, the elements of film form used in *Let the Right One In* combine to communicate not only the story, but also important ideas to the audience. They work together to appeal to our emotions, create meanings and generate responses. The opening of the film, for example, tells us a lot about the upcoming narrative and the characters within it just from the way it has been constructed.

> *Top tip*
>
> It should be noted that it is only when the elements of film form combine that such complex information and meaning is generated. The best exam answers will always try to do this by analysing sequences in terms of several film elements at once, showing how they work together to communicate to audiences.

Cinematography and mise-en-scène

Mise-en-scène in the opening sequence contrasts the falling white snow with a silent, jet black sky. This immediately sets up ideas of binary opposition (black and white, dark and light), it also introduces the bigger themes and issues the film will deal with such as emptiness, isolation and loneliness. These ideas are strengthened when the morose, drawn-out strings of the Slovak National Symphony Orchestra begin. The fact that this orchestral score starts when we meet Oskar hints that this music (as well as the visuals) may reflect his feelings, or state of mind. The opening image is **visceral** and acts as a visualisation of what Oskar feels. As the camera cuts to the first establishing shot of the film – an empty courtyard covered in snow with a lone tree standing in the middle – the thematic ideas of loneliness and isolation are repeated. The fact that we are viewing this arena from behind a window pane suggests that the person behind the glass (Oskar) is separated from society. He is an outcast.

> *Key term*
>
> **Visceral**
> Affecting internal feelings.

Our first image of Oskar (*Let the Right One In*).

We first see Oskar via his blurred reflection in the glass. His body (extremely pale and pasty skin and almost white, blonde wispy hair) seem to blend with the snow outside making him appear translucent and almost invisible. This, coupled with the fact that he is positioned slightly to the right of the frame rather than the centre, could reflect how he feels – that he is insignificant, unimportant and invisible to others. His thin frame and lack of clothing (he appears almost naked in the opening, wearing only white underpants) suggest his youth and also a vulnerability. The fact that he reaches out and touches his reflection connotes that he yearns for physical contact; however, his undressed frame leaves him very exposed and this could suggest that he is about to be exposed to something new and perhaps even dangerous.

The resulting combination of all these film elements is that we see Oskar as a weak, vulnerable child who is lonely and isolated. He is alienated from the outside world – an outcast and an outsider.

Quick Question 4.9

Think about how Eli is first introduced to us when she is travelling in the car and subsequently arrives at the apartment building. What does the use of cinematography, lighting and mise-en-scène suggest about this character?

Task 4.15

Look at the still below taken from Oskar and Eli's first meeting. It is the first time we see Eli properly.

1. Identify the camera shot used here and suggest what it says about the two characters? How are the characters positioned in the frame and why?
2. What aspects of mise-en-scène are used to show that Eli is different from Oskar?
3. Are there any aspects of film form used here to suggest the two characters are similar?

Oskar and Eli's first meeting (*Let the Right One In*).

Quick Question 4.10

Re-watch the first meeting between Oskar and Eli (00:11:39–00:11:45). How does the camera movement and editing add to your understanding of Eli's and Oskar's characters?

One thing that you may notice about these two characters is that in the beginning Oskar is introduced as representing light whereas Eli is often shown as being quite dark (both physically and metaphorically). However, as the film progresses these opposing representations become more blurred and unclear. One way this is achieved is through the use of lighting and colour, and these are very important elements in the film.

The film's director Alfredson and his cinematographer Hoyte van Hoytema manipulated the lighting to create a highly **stylised** look. Filters were used to neutralise colours and street lights had their bulbs replaced with white bulbs to create a very pure and neutral look. The resulting effect of this lighting is not as dark or shadowy

Key term

Stylised
Has a particular 'look' or style.

GCSE Film Studies

as we might expect from a vampire or horror film. Neither is it predominantly well-lit (which you may associate with romances) but something that is stuck in-between the two. This not only suggests the complexities of the two main characters and the idea that they each contain both goodness and darkness, but also communicates an idea of hope as well as danger. Van Hoytema, the cinemaphotographer, explains

> … *the danger in this film isn't hidden in the darkness. It exists in everyday situations … Light means vulnerability for both Eli and Oskar, who try to live life as unnoticed as possible.* ('An Unusual Romance', *The American Society of Cinematographers*, December 2008)

Task 4.16

1. The connotations of light and dark sphere to have been **subverted** in this film. Discuss what this decision suggests about our vampire character Eli?

2. If light means unwanted attention and danger for our characters then it is no surprise that the climactic scene in which Oskar is attacked at the swimming pool is one of, if not the, brightest scene in the film. It is the most dangerous scene for Oskar. Discuss what effect the brightness of this scene has on the audience. How does it help position viewers with the characters?

Key term

Subverted
Undermine the usual way of doing something.

Alfredson and van Hoytema not only turned the usual meanings of light and dark on their head for this film, they also created their own type of lighting that they coined 'spray light'. Describing the result of this technique they said *'it is as if you have a spray can of light that you have sprayed around the room'* The light produced is diffused and appears softer and is used in more intimate scenes containing the two protagonists, such as when Oskar visits Eli's apartment for the first time.

Task 4.17

Watch the scene where Oskar first visits Eli's apartment (01:16:2–01:18:18).

1. What does the use of 'spray light' say about the relationship between the two characters? What atmosphere is created?

2. Choose one or two other sequences in the movie and describe the colour palette and lighting used. How do these aspects of film form support the ideas of isolation and loneliness?

Sound

The sound in the film has also been designed with a great deal of consideration and subtlety. Like many other horror genre films, certain sounds have been heightened or exaggerated. For example, animal sounds are used when Eli feeds to exaggerate the gore and horror of what she is doing. This is also the case with tiny, more everyday ambient sounds – the twisting of the Rubik's cube, the footsteps in the snow. Even the snow has a distinct sound of its own created by using a mix of air bubbles in water and sugar being poured onto marble.

Task 4.18

Choose a scene from the film where everyday sounds have been heightened.

1. Make a list of the sounds you hear.
2. Consider which of these sounds you would normally be able to hear in such a scene and which have been exaggerated.
3. Consider the effect created by exaggerating the sounds. Why has the director chosen to do this?

Key terms

Aural
Relating to the ear and hearing.

Interior monologue
Expressing a character's inner thoughts.

In addition to the distinctive sound effects, the film relies heavily on silence to help with the realism of the piece. This also adds to the themes of isolation and loneliness. Contrapuntal sound, sound that works against what we are seeing on-screen, is also used to challenge the ways in which we read certain images. The score, created by Swedish composer Johan Söderqvist, meets the director's requirements in that it sounds 'hopeful and romantic in contrast to the events on screen'. This contrapuntal sound is both melancholy and beautiful with its long, drawn-out notes pierced by more hopeful, higher-pitched strings. Once more the film elements used here seem to perfectly reflect the two sides of the main characters and express their thoughts and feelings through this **aural interior monologue**. Söderqvist has described the outcome as 'consisting of both darkness and light' – again symbolic of our characters.

The soundtrack itself contains very few actual songs – only seven different songs are played or part-played in the film. Alfredson explains that the decision to limit the amount of music was a purposeful one to make the film seem more realistic and bleak. Music is often diegetic in this film to add to the realism, and non-diegetic sound was often cut from scenes altogether. For example, when Oskar fails to invite Eli into his apartment (beginning 01:24:01) music was originally a large part of the scene, but was removed altogether after Alfredson said the scene did not work.

Because there are few songs in the film, when they are used they are very noticeable and effective. For example, after the above scene where Eli has shared part of herself with Oskar, Oskar shares something of himself with Eli. He plays her his favourite song, *Kvar I min bil* by Per Gessle. This is a brave act for Oskar who has never revealed himself to anyone before. It also helps to portray Eli in a light we have rarely seen her in – an innocent child, bopping her head naively to the beat. As well as allowing Oskar to become closer to Eli, the choice of song helps us to further understand the characters and their functions. The song references being alone and lost, not knowing where to go, and the influence of someone (presumably female) on the singer. This reflects both Oskar and Eli. The repeated lyrics 'you said you must get going' signify how Eli is helping Oskar to grow and also links to the end of the film when the two leave.

Another sequence where music is used to communicate ideas to the audience is the resolution of the film.

Quick Question 4.11

Consider the scene talked about in the paragraph opposite (01:24:01). Imagine how music could have changed your response to the scene. How do you think this would have changed it? Would it been more, or less effective, with music? What is the result of having no music at all?

Quick Question 4.12

In the final sequence in the swimming pool, one of the only recognisable songs plays – *Flash in the Night*, the biggest hit for Swedish band, Secret Service. The synth-pop single has obvious connotations of vampires due to its name and lyrics but how do the sounds of synthesisers and the upbeat tempo help increase tension and suspense in the scene? What kind of atmosphere does the song create?

GCSE Film Studies

Quick Question 4.13

One important scene that utilises the window or glass motif is the one studied in Task 4.17, when Oskar first visits Eli's home. Look at the stills below from this scene. What function does the glass play here? What are we learning about the characters as they mimic each other's hand movements?

Editing

The way that sounds are manipulated in the film is definitely one of the most interesting aspects of the post-production but another noteworthy element in the editing is the use of visual motifs.

The use of windows or glass is introduced to us right from the outset. As we discussed earlier, our first visual is seen from behind a window pane and Oskar is introduced via his reflection. Eli is also first seen looking out at the world from behind glass, as she views the world from inside Håkan's car. We understand this to mean that they are cut off from the real world and are outsiders. This is furthered by the fact that all the windows in Eli's apartment are covered. Although this is for her protection (to keep out the sunlight that could hurt her) it also separates her from others.

Windows and glass used as motifs (*Let the Right One In*).

Part 4: Component 2:
Global film

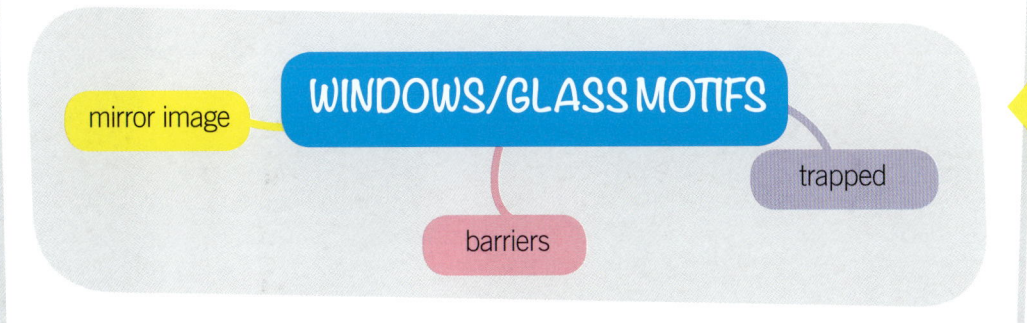

Task 4.19

```
            WINDOWS/GLASS MOTIFS
mirror image  ─┤                    │
                                     ├─ trapped
               └── barriers
```

Think about the use of windows and glass throughout the film.

1. Copy and complete the above spider diagram above. Is there anything else you think these motifs could represent?

2. Choose a scene where windows or glass features prominently. Analyse its use within the scene. What does it add to the narrative? Does it reveal anything new about the characters?

Just as the window/glass motif helps us to learn about the characters, so does the motif of eyes. Alfredson was inspired by Dutch painter Hans Holbein, whose work depicted people looking slightly out of frame. Alfredson decided to make Oskar and Eli also look out of or under the frame at the beginning of the film.

Eyes look out of the frames at the start of the film (*Let the Right One In*).

As the film progresses the characters stop averting their eyes and begin looking more and more into the frame, until they are looking directly at the camera.

209

GCSE Film Studies

Eyes look directly at the camera towards the end of the film (*Let the Right One In*).

Quick Question 4.14

Why do you think eyes are a visual motif in the movie? What could they represent? Why do the characters go from looking outside the frame to looking directly at the camera? What does this say about them?

It is not just recurring imagery and motifs that have an impact on the editing of *Let the Right One In*. The rhythm and pace of the film is also significant.

Unlike many horror films the pace is very slow. There is a stillness and calmness in the shots that is partly achieved through the use of frequent static extreme long shots, which are lengthy in duration and often do not contain any characters or life at all. This distance between the camera and the characters, as well as the empty snow-covered backdrops, not only slows the pace of the film but adds to the feelings of isolation and loneliness.

Isolation and loneliness in *Let the Right One In*.

Part 4: Component 2:
Global film

By allowing these shots to linger it helps to show the inner workings and mental landscapes of the characters. One of the longest duration shots in the movie is that of Oskar crying at the window just after Eli has killed Lacke and left. Alfredson held this shot for 40 seconds and describes it as being held 'for too long on purpose'.

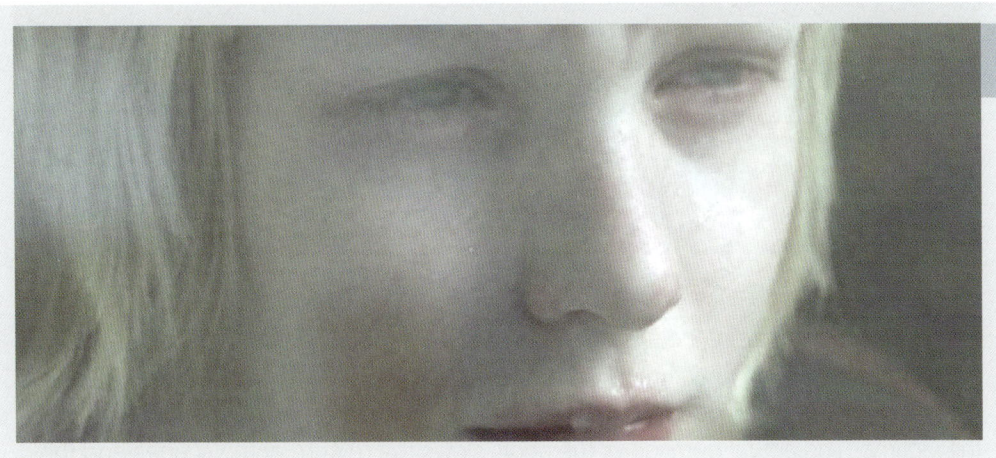

Oskar is heartbroken when Eli leaves (*Let the Right One In*).

Quick Question 4.15

Why has the director held this particular shot for so long? What is it suggesting? What does it do for the audience? This is also one of the closest shots of Oskar. Why has the director chosen to show this scene in an extreme close-up? Why have we not been this close to Oskar before?

Most of the filming used a single, fixed camera. Alfredson and Hoytema also opted for almost no hand-held shots, and few cuts and tracking shots, which were on a track-mounted dolly rather than Steadicam. These creative decisions combined to create calm, predictable camera movements that allow the viewer to forget about the presence of the camera and become immersed in the story. Take a look at Håkan's first murder for example.

The selection of his victim and the initial attack itself are filmed in a static, extreme long shot, whilst the remainder of the murder scene is revealed to us through a slow pan from left to right.

Håkan attacks his victim (*Let the Right One In*).

The distance between the camera and the violence is perhaps effective in reducing the horror of what is happening. After all, Håkan is carrying out this deed so that Eli can survive rather than because of some overwhelming evil nature.

This is the same when Eli attacks and kills Jocke in the underpass. The static long shot captures the attack and, although there are a few more cuts involved in this scene (perhaps as it results in a death when the previous attack did not), we are still always kept at a distance from the violence.

GCSE Film Studies

Eli takes matters into her own hands (*Let the Right One In*).

The physical distance of the shots removes us from the action and keeps us literally at a distance from the characters, so while we may not fully understand the motives and actions of the attackers at this point, we also do not feel overly sympathetic towards the victims. The actual duration of the shots slows the rhythm of the scenes and the slow pace makes them feel less violent and almost more acceptable – again, these actions are taken out of need and necessity, not desire.

The number of shots in each attack grows until the final end sequence in the swimming pool, at which point the cuts are frequent, the shots closer and the pace altogether faster (although still slow in relative terms to other horror actions sequences).

Task 4.20

Watch the final sequence where Oskar is lured to the swimming pool and attacked, starting with the phone call at 01:38:50 and ending with the final moments of the narrative.

The climax (*Let the Right One In*).

1. What effect do the slow zooms and tracking shots at the start of the sequence have? What impact do they have on the mood of the sequence?

2. Once the coach has left the pool area the number of cuts increases dramatically. Much of the threat towards Oskar comes from cross-cutting and shot-reverse-shots. How does this affect the pace of the scene? How does it help position the audience?

3. Many of the shots now are close-ups. Up until this point, close-ups have predominantly been used to denote intimacy between Oskar and Eli. How are they used now?

4. When the final battle commences and Oskar is held underwater, instead of becoming faster, as in the majority of horror films or action sequences, the camera and editing are still. We see Oskar in a medium shot and the violence taking place off-screen is heard in a series of muffled sounds. Why do you think the director chose not to show the violence?

5. Do you think that the different pace and editing of this attack, compared to the attacks carried out by Håkan and Eli discussed above, suggest that these normal schoolboys are more evil than Håkan and Eli ever were?

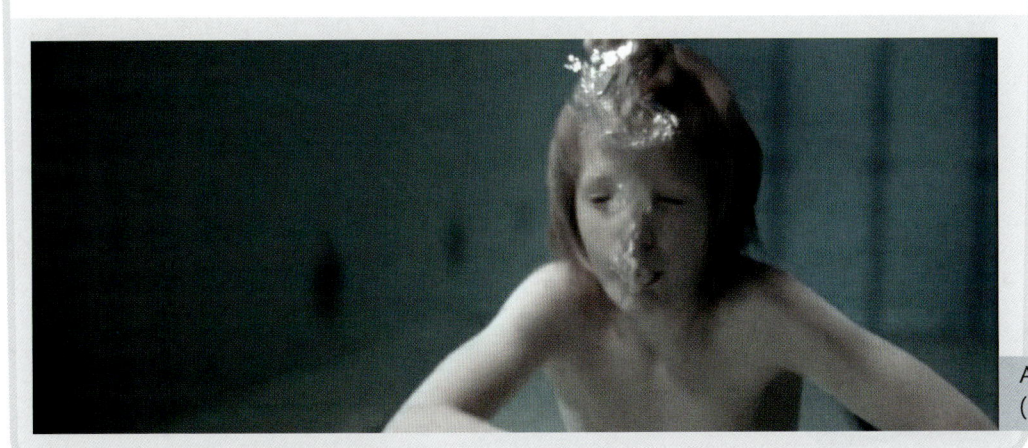

An off-screen attack (*Let the Right One In*).

Representation

The way people are presented to us as an audience is important to our reading of the film and these representations can inform and change our perceptions and expectations. Typically, we might expect the male character in a horror movie to be the stronger character, perhaps the hero, perhaps the bad guy and the female character would be the weak damsel in distress or victim. These gender stereotypes are almost reversed from the start in *Let the Right One In*.

Gender

As we discussed earlier, Oskar is introduced to us a weak and vulnerable child. Seen through his blurred reflection and heard via his high-pitched feminine voice, it is not even clear at the start whether he is a boy at all or just an undeveloped girl. His porcelain pale skin and long blonde hair also add to his femininity and it is only when he pulls out the knife prop that we get any sense of masculinity from him.

Eli, as we have discussed, comes across as very confident and strong. Her dark features and hair contrast with Oskar and make her look quite boyish. She appears more masculine when we first meet her and definitely holds the control. She even appears to be wearing a man's shirt in the first meeting between the two and is hardly ever seen wearing feminine clothing.

Both characters are quite **androgynous**. This was a conscious decision by the director and played a large part in the casting process even to point that Lina Leandersson (who plays Eli) was considered to have a voice that was too high-pitched and feminine; therefore, it was dubbed with another actress' voice in post-production.

Key term

Androgynous
Having both masculine and feminine qualities.

GCSE Film Studies

In the original novel Eli is a castrated boy and this is hinted at in the scene when Oskar spies on Eli getting changed and when Oskar asks Eli to be his girlfriend. She says 'I'm not a girl' – perhaps hinting not only at her vampire form but also her gender.

Often described as a horror-romance, it is true that the two characters form a relationship in the film and that they do love each other (they even share a blood-soaked kiss in one scene) but this love is presented to us more in a mutual respect and understanding way.

This representation of gender is different from the norm of both horror and romance genre films. Eli and Oscar do not appear to have a set, or defined, gender, or, if they do, it is inconsequential and irrelevant. They are presented more as two similar souls or two halves of one person. As Alfredson puts it, they are 'two sides of the same coin'. Oskar and Eli are represented as both the same and different. On one hand they are opposites. Oskar is male, blonde, weak, afraid and represents the light or good. Eli appears to be female; she is dark, strong, brave and represents the dark or evil side. However, on the other hand they are also the same. They are pale, young, vulnerable children with no-one to turn to. They feel alone and isolated. They are outsiders and social outcasts.

Task 4.21

Similarities	pale, young, vulnerable, children, no-one to turn to, alone, isolated, outsiders, social outcasts
Differences	male and female, blonde and dark, weak and strong, afraid and brave, represents light and dark, represents good and bad

Copy the above chart, which lists the similarities and differences between the two main characters. Are there any other ways in which the two are similar or dissimilar? Work as a class to add to the list.

Quick Question 4.16

Look at the still on the right from the beginning of the film. Analyse the aspects of cinematography, lighting and mise-en-scène, which highlight the similarities and differences between the two characters.

Oskar and Eli – the same but different (*Let the Right One In*).

Part 4: Component 2:
Global film

Task 4.22

Re-watch the scene just after Oskar has tested Eli by not inviting her into his apartment (01:25:54–01:27:11).

1. Just after Eli admits to being a vampire, she tells Oskar that she is 'just like him' – what does she mean by this?

2. This scene cross-cuts between the two with Eli getting closer to Oskar (and the camera) throughout. To what extent does this help symbolise Oskar's growing understanding of Eli and therefore the increasing closeness of their relationship?

3. Eli points out that she kills because she has to, whereas Oskar wants to kill for revenge. How does this subvert the good and bad connotations previously made in the film? How could this suggest that they are two halves of the same person?

4. At the end of the scene Eli says 'be me for a little while' and an extreme close-up of Oskar shows him closing his eyes. What does she mean by this?

5. As Oskar closes his eyes it is suggested that he is getting a glimpse into Eli's life and perhaps seeing through her eyes. What does the sound and the glimpse of an aged version of Eli suggest about her character? How does this moment impact their relationship and understanding of each other?

'Be me for a little while' (*Let the Right One In*).

GCSE Film Studies

Task 4.23

The representations of the two characters have all had a tendency to portray the two as opposing halves of the same person. One reading of the film (although it should be noted that it is one the director and writer do not agree with) is that Eli does not exist; that she is a figment of Oskar's imagination, a fantasy he has created in order to help deal with the bullies in his life. If Eli is just the darker side of Oskar this really would mean they are two halves of one person.

1. We have already noted the unconventional use of a still mid-shot of Oskar underwater during the final battle. Do you think this could have been chosen to suggest that the events happening above the water were just in Oskar's mind?

2. Some critics suggest that Oskar died in the pool and the final scene on the train is him going to heaven and finally escaping his bullies. How far would you agree with this?

3. When the final battle is over, we are given a close-up shot of Oskar emerging from the water. Do you think this, together with the extremely high-key lighting and heightened rasping sound of his first breath, suggests he is being reborn? How does the extreme close-up of his eyes, followed by the same shot of Eli's eyes suggest that they are now the same?

Quick Question 4.17

What are the differences between a person's sex and their gender?

Age

Through the representations of their gender (or lack of definite gender) Oskar and Eli are shown as both masculine and feminine, strong and weak, and brave and vulnerable. They are also shown as both young and old.

This is particularly the case for Eli who is portrayed physically as a young child but we get fleeting glimpses of her as an adult with tired, weary eyes and wrinkled skin.

This more negative depiction of adulthood runs throughout the film from the collective group of middle-aged drunks who have nothing better to do than hang out at the local Chinese restaurant, to those in a position of authority or responsibility (such as Oskar's parents, Håkan and the coach) who are shown as inadequate or incompetent. Oskar's mum is too pre-occupied with herself to notice the turmoil and torture her son is facing, his dad is an alcoholic and Håkan's incompetency as a killer leaves Eli looking more like an abused and neglected child in her baggy, dirty clothes and waif-thin frame. Even the coach seems to turn a blind eye to any bullying taking place.

A negative representation of age (*Let the Right One In*).

Part 4: Component 2:
Global film

Eli as both old and young (*Let the Right One In*).

The children are forced to look after themselves and take matters into their own hands – Eli must become the predator she needed Håkan to be and Oskar seems to live his life without his parents, before completing disowning them at the end of the film.

With a lack of a clear and supportive family structure or any real responsible adults, Oskar and Eli often become the parental figure for each other. Eli helps to give Oskar confidence and encourages him to fight back. She helps nurture Oskar and gives him protection and comfort just as a mother would.

However, whilst adulthood is represented negatively in the film, so is childhood. Eli has the burden of being undead, but Oskar has the burden of childhood. These two very different things are presented to us in the same way. School children are bullies and playgrounds are shown devoid of children and play. There is a real absence of childhood and the innocence of youth amongst the characters.

Empty playgrounds representing a lack of childhood (*Let the Right One In*).

GCSE Film Studies

Childhood represented as a frozen wasteland (*Let the Right One In*).

The ability to just be a child is something that both Oskar and Eli need and something that they find in each other. Oskar allows Eli to be a child again – bobbing to music and playing with Rubik's cubes.

Vampires

So far we have seen that Eli is not overtly male or female, young or old, but one thing we can be sure of is that Eli is a vampire; however, even this representation is different to the norm. She is not the usual vampire we have come to expect from horror films, but instead someone that 'lives off blood' (01:17:30).

Alfredson himself admits he was unconcerned with the horror and vampire conventions when making this film and decided to tone down many of these elements so that the main focus was the relationship between the two main characters.

Vampires in film over time. Max Schreck as the vampire Count Orlok in *Nosferatu* (1922, F.W. Murnau).

Part 4: Component 2:
Global film

Christpher Lee as Count Dracula in *Dracula* (1958, Terence Fisher).

Keifer Sutherland as the vampire David in *The Lost Boys* (1987, Joel Schumacher).

Eli does have certain traits that conform to vampire folklore and horror conventions.

1. Discuss in groups what you would normally expect from a vampire movie. What would you expect to see? What would the vampire be like? Are there any rules vampires must adhere to? Make a list.

2. Does Eli meet any of these codes and conventions? In what ways is she different?

3. Consider more modern vampire films such as *Twilight* (2008, Catherine Hardwicke), made in the same year as *Let the Right One In*. The two films appear to have more in common from the humanisation of vampires and the introduction of a human/vampire love story. What other similarities and differences are there between these two films?

4. How does the comparison of *Let the Right One In* to other vampire films suggest that in our film the evil is situated more in the everyday than the supernatural?

Task 4.24

GCSE Film Studies

Section C — Global films: Contemporary UK films

Contemporary British cinema: an introduction

– think what our view of film would be like if all we saw were British movies, with occasional touring productions of foreign work. No Hollywood blockbusters, no Korean ultra-violence, no Iranian minimalism. Nothing old, either – no Italian neorealism, or Czech new wave, or French poetic realism. Imagine what life for the British filmgoer would have been like, say, in 1978 – the highlight of your year would probably have been Death on the Nile, *or* Watership Down. *And let's not forget the dark days of 1999 and 2000, when this paper felt compelled to trash the jaw-dropping wave of terrible British films in the wake of the lottery-fund bonanza.* (Andrew Pulver, 'British Cinema's Golden Age is Now', The Guardian, 13 October 2011)

Whilst Hollywood has maintained its dominance of the film industry throughout the past seven or eight decades, many national cinema industries have struggled to compete for a variety of different reasons. Sometimes their demise has been caused by the quality of films produced, lack of funding or the power that Hollywood has in terms of control over production, distribution and exhibition.

Sometimes political factors intervene when governments censor or control the work of filmmakers in their country, for example in Iran. Economic factors may also hinder the growth of national industries or force filmmakers to produce their films in other countries using foreign funding. It's tempting to think that political or economic control does not affect the British Film industry – it does. For example, Ken Loach, one of our greatest filmmakers, struggled to find work in the 1980s. At that point in time he had abandoned drama, preferring instead to make social documentaries that criticised British politics. This brought him into conflict with Prime Minister Margaret Thatcher and the broadcasting establishment. His work was pilloried or banned, and he finally had to resort to making commercials for the likes of Nestlé and McDonald's. Even today, this director, who almost annually receives prestigious film awards, has to rely heavily on funding from Europe (mainly France) where his films achieve greater box office success than in England.

2009–2017: a golden age?

It's probably too early to talk about a 'golden age' but certainly the past decade has seen numerous British films achieving significant amounts of success in terms of awards, box office and reputation. Several of the highest grossing films of the past five years have been UK/US co-productions. These include *Skyfall* (2012, Sam Mendes), *Harry Potter and the Deathly Hallows* (2010, David Yates), *Fantastic Beasts and Where to Find Them* (2016, David Yates) and *Rogue One: A Star Wars Story* (2016, Gareth Edwards). Increasingly prestigious directors such as Tomas Alfredson (*Let the Right One In*), Fernando Meirelles (*City of God*, 2003) and David Cronenberg (*A History of Violence*, 2005, and *The Fly*, 1987) are making films in the UK. British auteur directors such as Ken Loach, Lyn Ramsey, Terence Davies and Andrea Arnold continue to make highly regarded films in the UK.

The future is very, very bright. There are a huge number of very talented young film makers out there and technology has empowered them to get out there and do it.

Young people can get their hands on equipment …, there is talent emerging everywhere and I think that the future of cinema is very rich. (Mike Leigh, Interviewed at the University of Warwick after receiving an Honourary Doctor of Letters, https://www2.warwick.ac.uk/newsandevents/pressreleases/mike_leigh_interviewed/)

Part 4: Component 2: **Global film**

Case study: Submarine

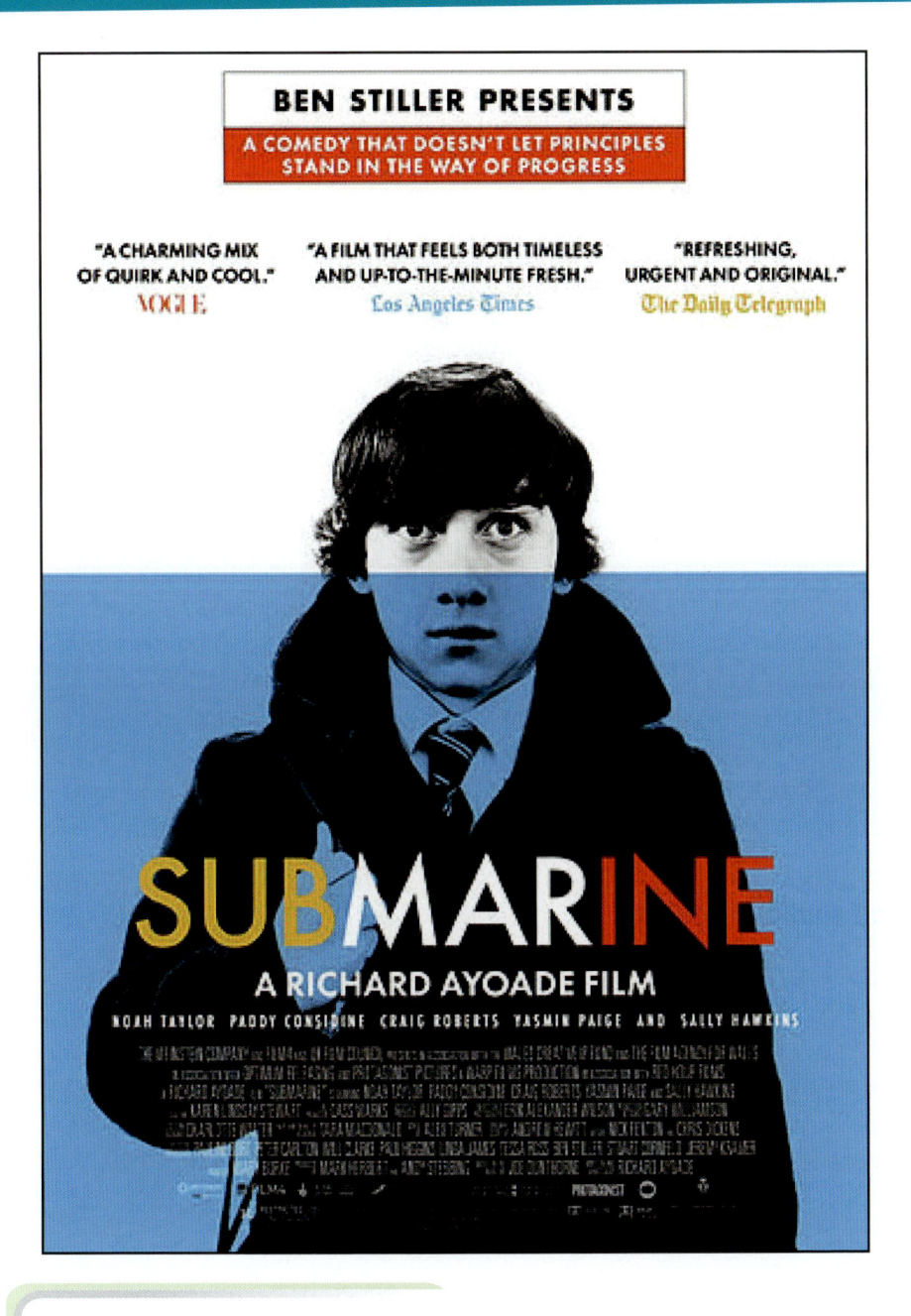

Directed by Richard Ayoade

Produced by Warp Films

Certificate: 15

Running time: 97 mins

Release date: 18 March 2011

Introduction

This case study has been designed to allow you to explore and analyse aspects of contemporary UK film and filmmaking. It is organised in a similar way to the other five case studies, using the framework contained in the WJEC Eduqas specification. The focus film is *Submarine*, a British film set in Wales that follows the story of Oliver Tate (Craig Roberts). Oliver is a teenager struggling with typical adolescent anxieties about age, sex, school, family and love. *Submarine* has been adapted from a novel by Joe Dunthorne and is director Richard Ayoade's first feature film.

GCSE Film Studies

Key contexts

Historical and political context

Although *Submarine* is set in the 1980s – a time of intense political upheaval, conflict and change, there is little evidence within the film of references to that decade. Oliver is certainly a descendent of Sue Townsend's Adrian Mole. Her first book featuring Adrian was published in 1990 but was set in 1981 and 1982. The book was written in diary style and focused on the worries and regrets of a teenager who believed himself to be an intellectual. However, Adrian refers to some historical events of the time such as the Falkland's war and the wedding of Prince Charles to Lady Diana. Mole was also a fierce critic of Prime Minister Margaret Thatcher, listing her as one of his worst enemies.

Oliver Tate is far more absorbed by personal problems rather than political ones (perhaps an indication of changes in society in 21st-century Britain when *Submarine* was made). So saying, the humour in *Submarine* and the humour in *Adrian Mole* originates from their unreliable narrators and the ways in which they confidently, yet naively, misinterpret the world around them. Rather than comment on the 1980s, Ayoade creates a world in *Submarine* that incorporates the spirit of a number of different time periods, especially in terms of art, that has had a lasting effect on our culture. References to influential art movements of the 1950s and 1960s abound in terms of style (Jean-Luc Godard's *Breathless* (1960) jump cuts) and memorabilia (posters of famous French films including *The Passion of Joan of Arc* (1928, Carl Theodor Dreyer) appear on walls in several different locations). Lloyd and Jill (Oliver's father and mother) both look back to the 1960s, a time when they were younger and had hopes and ambitions (Lloyd was to be an eminent marine biologist and Jill with her long, flowing locks was pursued by competing suitors – Lloyd and Graham).

Social and cultural context

Perhaps it is Ayoade's way of 'mixing' elements of several different time periods that has created a wide audience appeal. Today duffle coats are back in fashion as are vinyl records! Posters from the 1960s pop up with amazing regularity, Jill pines for her long 1960's hairstyle, whilst wearing blouses and skirts only worn by women of 'a certain age' in the 1980s. Musical accompaniment also plays along with the spirit of timelessness or the mixing of different times – especially songs written by Alex Turner (front man of the Arctic Monkeys), which work alongside the 1963 hit by the Japanese singer Kyu Sakamoto, 'Sukiyaki'.

The tendency towards creating a timeless world is continued by the representation of environment. Teenagers are seen playing in the school playground or running around in the woods. They wander along empty sea shores, they don't sit at computers to read and write. This is not a film simply about teenage angst, it is about innocence. Diaries, cassette covers, handwritten love notes combine to create a nostalgic vision of childhood in times gone by. Oliver recommends *The Catcher in the Rye* for Jordana to read (a 1951 novel by J.D. Salinger). The book, originally published for adults, has since become popular with teenagers, its protagonist Holden Caulfield has become an icon for teenage rebellion. It deals with complex issues of innocence, identity, belonging, loss and connection – themes also integral to *Submarine*'s narrative.

Quick Question 4.18

Why might mixing elements of different time periods create a wider audience appeal?

Quick Question 4.19

Is it important for British audiences to recognise their own experiences of life in Britain in a film?

Making the ordinary seem extraordinary (*Submarine*).

> One of the most romantic sequences in the film takes place in a very industrial landscape.
>
> 1. What features of the landscape are we shown?
> 2. How is cinematography used to make these ordinary features appear extraordinary?
> 3. How are Jordan and Oliver 'romanticised' in the still above?

Task 4.25

Submarine contains many of the features we have come to expect from a British film: from landscape to sense of humour. Joe Dunthorne set his novel in the 1990s, Richard Ayoade moves the novel back in time to the 1980s to a time when notes are passed in class and communication was more direct and perhaps more directly painful (no mobiles). Typewriters, polaroid cameras, super-8 footage and other technologies that are seldom used today, carry vital narrative importance as do handwritten notes, letters and diaries. Given the repeated references to, or use of, old technologies, it is perhaps surprising that the only other obvious period details are references to *Crocodile Dundee* (1986, Peter Faiman) being shown in the cinemas, Graham Purvis' (an old boyfriend of Oliver's mother) mullet hairstyle and his 'promo' video.

Technological and institutional context

Submarine was produced by Warp Films based in Sheffield. The film was adapted from Joe Dunthorne's first novel. Dunthorne was a friend of Ally Gibbs, currently Head of Development at Warp Films. Warp Films began life in 1989 as Warp Records, a Sheffield music label that made a significant impact on British culture with its experimental electronic music. Since then the name Warp has become linked with low budgets and a commitment to talented, innovative British artists. Warp Films was established in 2002, since when it has played an essential role in energising and rejuvenating the resurgence of an *'increasingly vibrant and successful British Cinema. Its films, like its music, have brought what was once considered underground into the mainstream'* (bfi.org.uk).

Top tip
When you rewatch *Submarine* note down the narrative importance of the different technologies used by Oliver or the other characters. Add these notes to your revision bank.

GCSE Film Studies

Warp Films expanded in 2006, setting up Warp X, a sister company producing creative, independent, digital low-budget films (six in the first three years).

Task 4.26

1. Research Warp Films and make a list of the films it has produced since 2006.
2. Note down what these films seem to have in common.

Quick Question 4.20

Why do you think Warp Films were keen to produce *Submarine*?

The production of *Submarine* clearly highlights the importance of Warp Films with its commitment to encouraging new, young talent. The extract below describes the ways in which the film was conceived and how quickly the project was actioned. The article also highlights the ways in which established artists such as the Beastie Boys and actor Ben Stiller are becoming increasingly involved in nurturing new talent and the rise of independent cinema across the globe.

> Producers Warp Films came across the book thanks to their then-intern Ally Gipps, 28 – a job he largely credits getting to Dunthorne, his university housemate.
>
> *Submarine*, in which a Welsh teenager plots to transform both his and his parents' troubled love lives, began as Dunthorne's 10,000-word dissertation for a creative writing MA, and hadn't even been published when Gipps presented it to his Warp colleagues; they loved it and hired the movie director Richard Ayoade.
>
> Dunthorne, a script consultant, describes visiting the set as 'totally mad – this real-time version of my imagination played out in front of me.' Then there was the successful Toronto Film Festival premiere. '[Executive producer] Ben Stiller flew up and brought one of the Beastie Boys with him; it was insane,' says Gipps, now credited as an associate producer on the film. One of the best weekends ever,' confirms Dunthorne. (Leigh Singer, 'Dunthorne Has Housemate to Thank for "Submarine" Launch', 25 March 2011, *The Independent*)

Submarine was well received at the 2010 Sundance film festival and secured a good distribution in the USA. Even though the film does not offer the iconic British landmarks or aristocratic country manors that make many British films attractive to American audiences, it has still managed to be relatively successful there perhaps because of its distinct 'indie' vibe and its similarity to other quirky coming-of-age films such as *Juno*, *Me and Earl and the Dying Girl* or Wes Craven's *Moonrise Kingdom* (2012).

However, *Submarine* bears all the hallmarks of a British teen movie. It combines romance, comedy and even some elements of the melodrama but it does not contain the 'glossy' look of *Juno* or *Me and Earl and the Dying Girl*. Colours are muted, scenery is shot using natural light, film stock creates a 'grainy' look in places and continuity is disrupted by jump cuts, caption cards, Oliver's imaginations and hand-held camera techniques. It does, however, share the high school setting, central teen romance and teenage protagonists. Oliver is the typical 'geek', Jordana is the misfit. Teen themes such as peer pressure, bullying, relationships, isolation and sexuality are also present. It incorporates the codes and conventions of the romance, comedy and melodrama (heightened use of mise-en-scène and symbolic use of colour with music used to emphasise moods and emotions).

Part 4: Component 2:
Global film

> **Task 4.27**
> 1. Note down the differences between *Submarine* and a typical American 'teen' movie.
> 2. What identifies *Submarine* as being uniquely 'British'?

Like many of the films produced by Warp Films, *Submarine* provides a glimpse of parts of Britain that are often overlooked on the screen

Richard Ayoade is best known as an actor and comedian in the TV series *The I.T. Crowd* and *The Mighty Boosh*. He had worked with Warp Films before, directing pop videos for the Artic Monkeys. The style of *Submarine* employs the techniques of 21st-century television – MTV (think montage sequence of Oliver and Jordana – see pages 241–242) and Oliver's imagined televised obituary (which fuses vox-pops, police news conferences, National TV outside broadcasts and interviews). Ayoade also plays with the form of the now outdated self-promotional videos in Graham Purvis' New Age Promo (which can also be seen in its entirety on the DVD extras). Graham Purvis' 'Mystic Bullshit' light show involves 1980s effects also played with in Ayoade's music video work.

Quick Question 4.21
Do you think it is important that British films should show real landscapes and cityscapes of everyday British life?

> **Task 4.28**
> 1. Watch *Fluorescent Adolescent* (2007) on YouTube (Arctic Monkeys, directed by Richard Ayoade).
> 2. Although the narrative of this short music video seems very different to that of *Submarine*, look for the similarities in terms of cinematography. Note down as many similarities as you can identify.

Awards

- Six BAFTA Cymru Awards: including Best Actor (Craig Roberts) and Best Feature.
- British Independent Film Award: Best Screenplay.
- Nominations for:
  - BAFTA: Outstanding Debut by British writer
  - Best Independent Film Award: Best Supporting Actress, Most Promising Newcomer (Craig Roberts and Yasmin Paige)
  - Douglas Hickox Award.

> **Task 4.29**
> Create a bank of research that focuses on *Submarine* and the British film industry. Use the following questions as a guideline for your research:
> 1. What other films has Warp Films produced in the past three years?
> 2. Do they seem to focus on a specific genre?
> 3. Do they have links with other companies?
> 4. What was the budget for *Submarine*?
> 5. How much did it achieve at the box office?
> 6. What is the purpose of Film Cymru (the Film Agency for Wales)?

GCSE Film Studies

Submarine and the key elements of film form

It's worth repeating that when talking and writing about film form you should consider how each element of form creates meaning and response, and use the correct terminology to describe it. However, at this point it will really help to strengthen your analyses if you consider them together. So, although the tasks in this case study may have one element of film form as their main focus, they will also encourage a consideration of how elements can combine to produce quite complex meanings and elicit a variety of different audience responses.

In Part 2 of this book (see page 11) you will have studied the ways in which elements of film form and film structure create meaning and response. The tasks below are designed to allow an analysis of the ways they work together in *Submarine* to drive, expand or illuminate the film's narrative and to allow a deeper understanding of how key ideas are expressed. The aim is to encourage an understanding about how every element of the visual image can carry meaning and create response.

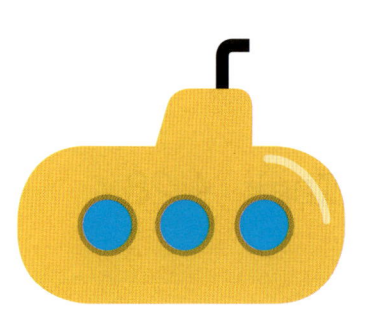

> **Submarine** (noun)
> 1. *Nautical* – A vessel that is capable of operating submerged.
> 2. A large sandwich consisting of a long roll split lengthwise and filled with layers of meat, cheese, tomatoes, lettuce and condiments.
> 3. A debut feature film from Richard Ayoade (black rimmed glasses from *The IT Crowd*, also of *Mighty Boosh* and *Nathan Barley* fame) (Adapted from '*Submarine*: Vessel, Sandwich or Indie Heart-warmer', *Mint Magazine*, www.mintmagazine.co.uk/art/submarine-vessel-sandwich-or-indie-heart-warmer).

The film's title, *Submarine*, refers to the bouts of depression suffered by Oliver's father. Lloyd says they make him feel as if he is totally submerged at the bottom of the ocean. Oliver, who in many ways is a carbon copy of his father (see costume in the mise-en-scène section on page 228) experiences similar feelings when he breaks up with Jordana. The idea of being isolated or totally submerged, unable to hear or understand what others think or feel, runs through the whole film. The opening sequence shows Oliver alone looking out to sea over an empty shoreline. Audio-visual references to water or being submerged abound, Oliver and Lloyd are often framed through the glass of the large fish tank in their home especially when depressed. Even Oliver's 'love letter' to Jordana extends the submarine metaphor:

> Dear Jordana, thank you for letting me explore your perfect body.
> I could drink your blood.
> You're the only person I would allow to be shrunk to microscopic size, and swim inside me
> in a tiny submersible machine.

Key term

Coming of age
Term used to describe films that feature young people in the process of growing up or entering into adulthood.

Submarine is a **coming of age** film. The storyline deals with themes from Oliver's perspective. Oliver narrates his own story giving us his 'take' on reality and allowing us to see the contrast between his perception and what actually happens.

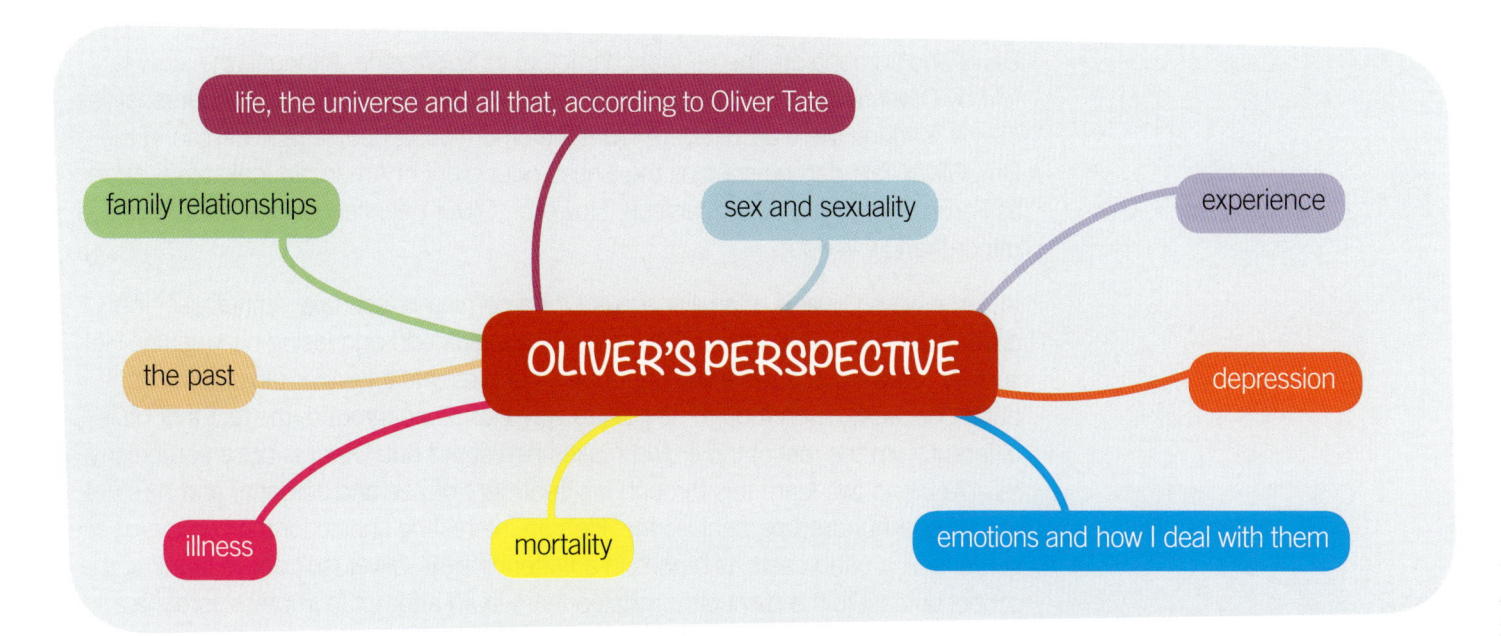

OLIVER'S PERSPECTIVE
- life, the universe and all that, according to Oliver Tate
- family relationships
- sex and sexuality
- experience
- the past
- depression
- illness
- mortality
- emotions and how I deal with them

The themes in the spider diagram above can be seen to work together to deal with even more complex issues about perception, understanding, unspoken issues and communication.

An understanding of the term **intertextuality** will help when analysing and responding to this film. *Submarine* is full of references to other films and the filmmaking process. Obviously, you cannot be expected to recognise all the references to other directors. Besides, Ayoade is keen to emphasise that he is simply trying to present a character who is obsessed with films. So saying, it would be hard to miss the way that Richard Ayoade 'borrows' techniques from other media platforms, for example posters, newspapers, TV news broadcasts or music videos. You may recognise Oliver as a character akin to Adrian Mole (*The Growing Pains of Adrian Mole*, 1985).

If you have chosen *Juno*, *Me and Earl and the Dying Girl* or *Ferris Bueller's Day Off* you may also notice parallels between their leading characters. In terms of audience response the intertextual references serve a variety of different purposes, they add humour and irony (think Oliver's homage to himself when imagining his death). They allow cinephiles the pleasure of identifying directors, films and film techniques that have been incorporated (arguably one of the keys to the recent success of *La La Land*, 2017, Damien Chazelle). More importantly though, in the case of *Submarine* the techniques deepen our understanding of this complex leading character's state of mind.

> **Key term**
>
> **Intertextuality**
> An idea that any text has been influenced and shaped by texts that have come before it (anything read or seen in the case of movies). Therefore, no film exists on its own and consciously or not all films borrow ideas from other films, past or present.

Part 4: Component 2: **Global film**

Mise-en-scène

Oliver and Jordana

Oliver and Jordana are the central characters in *Submarine*. Although the story is told by Oliver, mise-en-scène highlights key aspects of both characters' personalities, clearly marking them as 'different' from the other young people represented in the film. Oliver Tate can be seen as the British equivalent of American indie teens such as Ferris Bueller and Juno MacGuff. However, Oliver definitely comes from Swansea rather than Hollywood.

In some ways Oliver is a familiar subject for a coming-of-age tale: a briefcase and duffle coat clad 'geek' who dreams of getting a girlfriend and losing his virginity. He's socially awkward and generally unpopular. He presents a familiar target for school bullies because, even though he likes to stay in the background, the fact that he is different from the rest of the crowd makes him stand out. Oliver is not a particularly reliable friend (we learn this through his treatment of Zoe and Jordana) and he's not always one-hundred percent likable. He's an interesting choice for the coming-of-age genre, which often casts its heroes in a flattering light. Oliver isn't above taunting the school outcast to the point of humiliated tears in an attempt to impress Jordana and he fails to support his 'new love' when she most needs it.

The 'odd couple' (*Submarine*).

Quick Question 4.22

What do Oliver and Jordana have in common? How are their similarities and differences represented?

Key term

Pyromaniac
A person who has an irresistible impulse to start fires.

Jordana also does not fit in to the stereotypical teen film love interest mould. Usually, the object of the geek's attention is either a female very much like himself or the polar opposite, an unattainable goddess. However, Jordana is no art loving, dictionary reading academic. She refuses to read *The Catcher in the Rye* and forces Oliver to walk out of the cinema before the end of his art house film. She is, at least at the beginning of the film, an emotion-hating **pyromaniac** with scaly hands (she suffers from eczema). She derives pleasure from bullying and blackmailing others and is only marginally more popular than Oliver.

Part 4: Component 2:
Global film

'You've got scaly hands.'
'It's eczema' (*Submarine*).

No more words needed (*Submarine*).

Look carefully at the two stills above.

1. Note down what the framing of each still might suggest.
2. Describe each character's costume. What do the costumes say about the characters?
3. Explain how costume and body language highlight both the differences and similarities between Jordana and Oliver.
4. Describe the setting of each still together with a consideration of what it might suggest about each character and their relationship to each other.
5. Download two more stills from the film that help you to underline the importance of setting in terms of establishing key themes and/or aspects of Jordana and Oliver's situation and personality.

Task 4.30

Costume: Oliver and Lloyd

Clearly, costume is important in *Submarine*. The parallels between Oliver and his dad (a marine biologist) are constantly underlined by their almost matching costumes. On 'date' night Oliver and Lloyd are 'restrained' in slightly oversized blazers, striped shirts with matching ties and 'sensible' brown shoes. Both are studies in fawn and brown, inhabiting a house furnished in beige – beige curtains, beige carpets, beige settees and beige walls – and lit by lamps, which create a depressing sepia glow. Both seem old before their time, when life gets too much for them, they don their matching fawn wool dressing gowns, refuse to leave the house and 'sink ' deeper and deeper into depression. They both spend hours gazing at the fish tank or lying in their respective beds. At one point, Oliver is seen floating away on his bed in a 'sea' of rejection and self-pity.

Date night for dad and Oliver in matching jackets, shirts and ties (*Submarine*).

Depression time for dad, off with the jacket and on with beige wool dressing gown (*Submarine*).

Part 4: Component 2:
Global film

Depression time for Oliver and on goes the beige wool dressing gown (Submarine).

Oliver's mother Jill is also 'trussed up' in overlong skirts and blouses with dainty bows. She is bored rigid and at points in the narrative refers back to the 1960s when she had long hair and more colour in her life. This nostalgia for a different time explains her interest in an ex-boyfriend Graham (Paddy Considine). Graham is a smarmy, new-age guru who sports a formidable mullet, and leather pants and waistcoat. He offers not just colour but flashing neon lights: 'I'm a prism! That's not mad, OK?'

'A healthy glow around you means you are living a "full-filled" life.' (Submarine).

Colour and light play a significant part in the creation of meaning and response throughout the film. Oliver says at one point, when spying on Graham T. Purvis who is giving one of his self-help/life coach sessions, *'If my dad radiated a colour it would be ochre or eggshell.'*

GCSE Film Studies

Task 4.31

Watch the sequence that begins with Graham asking 'What is light?' (0:43:07) and ends with Oliver telling the audience 'Maybe it's time for dad to rip off his vest again' (0:47:55). Answer the following questions:

1. Explore the various ways in which light and colour are used in this sequence.

2. Both Graham and Lloyd have their own performing spaces. Describe each space, what they are doing and what we learn about each character when watching them interact with their audience.

3. Analyse the ways in which costume and body language are used to establish each character, their personalities and motivations in this sequence.

4. As the door closes on Jill we see Oliver peeping out from behind Graham's cardboard cutout figure. The door is covered with ads for Graham's video, what does the mise-en-scène suggest about Oliver and Graham?

Submarine employs a heightened use of mise-en-scène and colour symbolism throughout. Jordana's red coat has obvious symbolism as a dangerous siren (as seen through Oliver's unreliable point-of-view). He views life either through rose-tinted glasses or a blue mist. When he falls in love with Jordana the colour motif of the film changes from blue (for example, in the opening sequence) to red. The film gives us Oliver's romanticised point-of-view. Tinted glasses (his romance with Jordana) or in sepia-tinged melancholy (his home life), blue palette (longing, loneliness and isolation). These colour palettes convey elements of Oliver's emotional world.

'We kiss until our lips are swollen.' Exploding stars, rosy glow, love is in the air (*Submarine*).

Settings are also important, Oliver's room tells us so much about him (and the director – see the style and aesthetics section page 248 of this case study). Water is a recurring motif.

Almost every scene features some reference to water or uses water as a backdrop. As the film opens, Oliver narrates over a shot that shows him sitting in his room just under a mural featuring a submarine. As he sits, the sound of seagulls and the sea can be heard in the background. This is followed by a series of beautiful shots of the hills and valleys around Swansea, which lead us back to Oliver sitting on the shore line looking out to sea (see still below).

'I'm not the kind of fool who's going to sit and sing to you' (Submarine).

In this opening sequence, images combine with narration and song lyrics to introduce Oliver as a loner, a thinker and someone who does not want to seem ordinary. Someone, perhaps, who dramatises a version of himself, which may be at odds with the ways in which others see him. He's not the 'angry young man' we've seen in *Rebel Without a Cause* but we may have seen similar teenagers in *Juno, Little Miss Sunshine*, or *Me and Earl and the Dying Girl* – quirky, funny, angst-ridden young people struggling to understand or fit into their place in society.

The opening raises questions about Oliver; in many ways he's typical of many young British film characters in that he is unlike the archetypes seen in mainstream Hollywood. However, he does resemble teenage characters seen in many teenage films of contemporary US independent cinema (see the style and aesthetic section on page 248).

GCSE Film Studies

Cinematography

> *As much as possible of Submarine was shot using natural light and where there had to be lighting, as in the school scenes, either existing fluorescents were replaced or switched off or other bulbs brought in. The heightened, beautified look comes from diverse visual styles and different types of cameras and recording media. An Arriflex Lite, hired from Take 2 Films and running Kodak Expression 500 stock with a 'nice old Canon lens', was used for the main 35mm shoot, but mixed in with this is Super 8, Video8 and VHS-C.*
>
> *More controversial was an ARRI IIC, the old, small 35mm camera favoured by Stanley Kubrick, who used one on all his films from A Clockwork Orange (1971) onwards. 'We found one somewhere,' says Wilson, 'and no one wanted us to use it but Richard said "We have to use this" So we always had it with us on a tripod and used it for scenic shots, which we did at the weekends. It jumps a bit and is very noisy but the pictures are wonderful and a lot of what we shot on it is in the film.'* (Erik Wilson, 'Suburban Childhood', *British Cinematographer*, https://britishcinematographer.co.uk/erik-wilson-submarine)

> **Top tip**
> When analysing key sequences from your film it can be useful to consider the ways in which cinematography and editing work together to create meaning and response.

The cinematographer Erik Wilson and director Richard Ayoade decided to light as little of *Submarine* as possible, relying on natural light. Oliver's narration, adapted from Joe Dunthorne's book, provided both with opportunities to play mischievously with the codes and conventions of film form, especially in terms of camerawork and editing. The film was shot entirely in Wales: beach scenes at Barry, Oliver's school in Swansea and his family home in the valleys. As many exterior scenes as possible were shot in either the first or last hour of sunlight each day. The light softens at these times and longer shadows were cast giving the outdoor sequences, especially those of Barry's shore line, a soft romantic feeling.

In the opening sequence we move from Oliver's bedroom across the open fields, hills and valleys towards the Barry coastline. Wilson and Ayoade dispense with conventional establishing shots and even connecting shots. Oliver's narration tells us what we need to know. As the narrative progresses we are shown the movies in Oliver's head, giving us touching visual essays on his preoccupations, the incomprehensible nature of his mother and the equally puzzling depression of his father, a man so quiet and passive that he might as well be living underwater with the fish he studies. Oliver also runs down to the sea whenever he can. Sometimes, he tells us, he waits for a darkening sky to equal his morose moods. All of nature reflects his inner life.

> **Quick Question 4.23**
> Describe the effect created by the 360-degree camera turn when Oliver and Jordana kiss for the first time.

Wilson and Ayoade also play with cinematic techniques throwing in tricks, effects and devices such as frozen frames, jump cuts and **action** that is either slowed or speeded up. Oliver, the film's central character, mirrors the filmmaker's passion for French New Wave films and fantasises about both starring in and making a film about his life:

> **Key term**
>
> **Action**
> The story/description in each scene.

> *Sometimes I wish I had a film crew filming my every move. I imagine the camera craning up as I walk away. But unless my life improves my biopic will only have a budget for a zoom out.* (Oliver Tate)

234

Part 4: Component 2:
Global film

'The only way to get through life is to picture myself in an entirely disconnected reality' (Submarine).

The opening sequence and the credit sequence combine to introduce us to Oliver but we are mainly given a picture of what Oliver thinks he is like; this differs markedly from what we learn about him as the narrative unfolds. The mid-shot that shows Oliver looking out to sea reflects his isolation, the blue colour palette and tableau shots connote his isolation from society, the fact that at this point we only see his silhouette and not his face suggests that he is a complex character.

Oliver introduces the Prologue with a rhetorical question 'What kind of person am I?' He then goes on to inform us that the 'only way to get through life is to picture myself in an entirely disconnected reality'. This 'disconnected reality' is then revealed to us via the film he creates in his mind, imagining how people would react to his death.

1. Rewatch the Prologue sequence (00:1:49–00:3:54). Concentrate carefully on Oliver's 'pictures' of how people would react to his death.
   (a) Make a note of the some of the shots used to illustrate the different reactions of his classmates.
   (b) How do the images relate to voice-over (V.O.) and background music?

Task 4.32

Shot	Picture	Time	Audio
1	Panning shot across school foyer to pause on school tannoy loudspeaker	4 seconds	Moving violin music. V.O. (Oliver) 'I picture how people would react to my death.' 'Mr Dunthorne's quavering voice as he makes the announcement.'
2A	Panning mid-shot across classroom	2 seconds	Moving violin music continues. V.O. 'The shocked faces
2B	Panning high angle shot into gym	1 second	'of my classmates.' Music continues
3	Long shot – school gates and playground	2 seconds	Music continues. V.O. 'A playground be decked by flowers.'

235

GCSE Film Studies

2. Look at the outline shooting script on the previous page, which covers the first few seconds of Oliver's imagined tribute to himself.

   Pick two of the following elements of Oliver's tribute:
   - empty school corridor
   - local outdoor TV news report
   - vox pop – giving other students' tributes/views of Oliver
   - tear-stained student tributes at school perimeter fence
   - press conference with Lloyd and Jill
   - candlelit vigil from school, as seen on news
   - female students (including Jordana) lying bereft in school corridor
   - glorious resurrection.

   (a) Re-watch the sequence and note down the audio that accompanies each of your chosen elements and the shots/camera movement that is used.

   (b) Share your findings with the rest of the class.

   (c) Write a short analysis of how cinematography and voice-over combine in order to tell us more about Oliver and to create humour.

Quick Question 4.24

Describe the effect created by the 360-degree camera turn when Oliver and Jordana kiss for the first time.

Key terms

Femme fatale
An irresistibly attractive woman, who causes trouble for men by leading them into difficult, dangerous, or disastrous situations.

Cataclysmic
A term used to describe a violent upheaval that causes great destruction or brings about disastrous change.

This prologue is important, of course it is meant to make us smile but it also helps to illuminate Oliver's character. He's an outsider, uncomfortable with his role in life, he doesn't fit in with the school crowd, and his only friends are 'odd balls' like himself. The tableau-like staging of many shots underline his awkwardness.

Another key sequence takes place under the railway bridge (00:13:26–00:16:08). This is where both the director and cinematographer incorporate tricks, effects and devices from many of their most loved films. *Submarine* is littered with references to the French New Wave (from beaches and bicycles to the *Ma Nuit Chez Maud* poster on Oliver's bedroom wall). Jordana has told Oliver to meet her under the railway bridge. She arrives first, clad in a blood-red coat that gives an ironic take on the danger and qualities of the **femme fatale**. She waits for Oliver under the bridge, a long panning shot follows him walking between the steel bars and sleepers. He looks as if he is walking into a prison. Jordana is revealed standing between the steel bridge supports, a vision in red, smoking a cigarette. The camera zooms in to her face, she smiles, and a close-up of her hand reveals chipped red nail varnish, a lit cigarette and some very scaly eczema! Tate is being lured into Jordana's 'prison'.

Jordana as femme fatale (*Submarine*).

Part 4: Component 2:
Global film

This sequence takes full advantage of cinematic techniques such as jump cuts, zooms and freeze frames. Each of these techniques adds a layer of meaning to the sequence. For example, when Jordana and Oliver first lock lips, Oliver is so happy he keeps his eyes open, and the camera too is so excited it jumps about all over the place. For their second kiss, the camera does a slow 360-degree turn, savouring the moment, making them appear to be at the centre of the world. The flashes of the polaroid camera light up the couple, it records their reactions, they are being watched by two cameras. These techniques combine with the shreeching of the train as it comes over the bridge in order to accentuate the **cataclysmic** nature of the kiss and create a funny, highly charged moment between both characters.

'We kiss until our lips felt swollen, her mouth tasted of milk, polo mints and Dunhill International (Submarine).

The relationship between Jordana and Oliver is beautifully shot; every emotion captured visually on screen. For example, when Jordana and Oliver pass in the school corridor, extreme quick snapshot facial close-ups capture their glances and stares.

Task 4.33

1. In pairs, create a PowerPoint presentation that includes at least two shots of the Swansea countryside or Barry Coast, two shots that show Jordana and Oliver in a romanticised situation, and two shots that use the industrial landscape in an unusual way.
2. Prepare notes to accompany the PowerPoint that describe the cinematography in each shot and consider what meaning and responses are created.

Sound

The voice-over

One of the most interesting uses of sound in the film is Oliver's narration over the action (see more in 'Narrative' section, page 245). Oliver introduces himself to the audience in a monotone, staccato voice-over. He's a 15-year-old Welsh boy with vague literary aspirations, imagining as he stares out to sea that he's 'in a documentary about a prominent thinker who's struggled with unspeakable loss'. Oliver is melodramatic, unreliable both as a narrator and as a friend. His constant narration controls the film and us throughout. This use of the unreliable narrator is inflenced by past British films from the 1960s such as *Billy Liar* (1963, John Schlesinger). The voice-over allows us to weave in and out of Oliver's imagination and subconcious. It leaves us wondering how much of the action is a true record of events or a figment of his imagination. At times, as with *Alfie* (1966, Lewis Gilbert) he breaks through the **fourth wall** and addresses us, his captive audience, directly.

> **Key term**
>
> **Fourth wall**
> Originally a theatrical term for the imaginary wall that exists between actors on stage and the audience. This wall keeps up the illusion of theatre, the actors pretend that they cannot hear or see the audience. This term is also used in films, only the fourth wall in that instance is a camera lens.

Music

Richard Ayoade has stated that *The Graduate* (1967, Mike Nichols) was one of his favourite films. It's clear that Ben Braddock, the film's central character, was an ideal model for Oliver Tate. *The Graduate* was groundbreaking in terms of its experimental look, with jump cuts, long takes and odd camera angles, but it was the ways in which the songs of Simon and Garfunkel moved alongside and deepened the narrative that was to influence films made over the next 60 years.

Task 4.34

Watch 'The Graduate – The Sound of Silence (Soundtrack) *Must See*' on YouTube and 'Despondency' (*Submarine* 1:14:35–1:18:17).

1. In pairs, discuss the similarities between both sequences.
2. Note down particularly effective points where the words and images combine to create a strong emotional response in the audience.
3. Replay part of 'Despondency' without the sound. How is your response to what you see affected?

Richard Ayoade had directed a number of music videos before making *Submarine* and it is clear that the music video aesthetic has influenced his style of filmmaking. The montage imagery used in several sequences accompanied by a complete song (written by Alex Turner of the Arctic Monkeys) strongly portray key themes within the film: isolation, silence, angst, depression, love and mortality.

> *I like using entire songs to suggest a mood and even replace the dialogue rather than just 50-second snatches of some bought in song that tells you literally what you're seeing on the screen. And I like having the same voice for all the songs, Mike Nichols did that in* The Graduate *with Simon and Garfunkel.* (David Gritten, 'Richard Ayoade: Hidden Depths of the Bashful Filmmaker', 10 March 2011, *The Telegraph*)

'You're looking like you're low on energy' (Submarine).

It's like you're trying to get to heaven in a hurry,
And the queue is shorter than you thought it would be,
And the doorman says
you need to get a wristband.

You've got to live between the pitfalls,
But you're looking like you're low on energy,
Did you get out and walk,
To ensure you'd miss the quicksand?

Looking for a new place to begin, …'
('It's Hard to Get Around the Wind', by Alex Turner)

Turner's lyrics convey ideas poetically about social isolation, that nobody knows what anybody else is thinking or feeling, and we're all submerged, travelling under the radar, undetected, and there's nothing anybody can do about it.

Recurring sounds and silence

Sound and silence work together to create meaning throughout the film. At key moments in the narrative, diegetic sound fills the silence in a way that is hard to ignore. Embarrassed silences during conversations between Lloyd and Oliver are frequently punctuated by the heightened sound of water bubbling in the fish tank that looms over them in their exchanges. The water motif that recurs throughout the film is always accompanied by the sound of water moving either above or below both characters. Often, the action that is appearing on screen is silent but the diegetic off-screen noise is heightened, or vice-versa, what can and can't be heard becomes selective, just like memory.

When Oliver asks his dad what his depression is like, he replies 'like being underwater'. Sound works with mise-en-scène in order to communicate just how difficult it is to emerge from an 'ocean of depression' that is six miles deep. Sound accentuates the events and images that are most important in terms of Oliver's social or psychological world.

> **Top tip**
> Download the lyrics to some of Alex Turner's songs used in the film. Note down the sequences they are used in. Pick some especially effective lines that convey key themes. Learn these lines, you may be able to use them in your exam answers.

Part 4: Component 2: **Global film**

GCSE Film Studies

When waiting for Jordana to arrive for 'a wonderful night of lovemaking' his initial manic preparations are followed by a period of stillness as he waits for Jordana to arrive. As the clock hands near 8.30 the ticking becomes louder, accentuating his anxiety. The hands pass the 8.30 deadline, the ticking continues and Jordana's knock, when it finally comes, sounds as loud and startling as a bullet from a gun – Oliver's fears and sexual insecurities are accentuated.

In the sequence where Jordana and Oliver kiss for the first time under the railway bridge (see see 'Cinematography and mise-en-scène', page 264). Jordana's voice is used as a sound bridge, the editing cross-cuts from her close-up to Oliver's journey and arrival under the bridge. Ambient sounds, the sharp wind and traffic sounds, bleed in from this new visual location. The sound of the wind and traffic increases in direct proportion to Oliver's trepidation. When he kisses Jordana a screeching train travels directly above them, the shutter sound of the flashing Polaroid camera is also accentuated, its flashes combine with sound and a camera zoom-in on the couple to create a truly 'climactic' moment. Sound creates humour here and the 'climax' is followed by a period of calm when ambient sound is softer, more gentle and far less threatening.

'Every night I come back to the same place and wait until the sky catches up with my mood' (Submarine).

Task 4.35

Write a short analysis of how sound creates meaning and response in the 'Epilogue' (01:22:29–1:26:45). You should consider:

- the use of diegetic sound and sound levels
- non-diegetic sound
- dialogue and the use of 'poetic' language.

Editing

In Part 2 you will have looked at a range of editing techniques including the jump cut. Simply put, a jump cut is an abrupt transition, typically in a sequential clip, that makes the subject appear to jump from one spot to the other, without continuity.

Most mainstream Hollywood films make use of continuity editing, only breaking the illusion of reality when a certain effect is desired. Conversely, whole movements of independent and art cinema have experimented with new and exciting techniques in film production. Generally speaking though, it wasn't until 1960, when Jean-Luc Godard's first film, *Breathless* (or *À Bout de Souffle*) was released that the jump cut as we know it today would enter the popular film **vernacular**. *Submarine* constantly refers back to the work of directors such as Godard, who pushed the boundaries of filmmaking in many ways but perhaps most importantly in terms of editing and cinematography.

Oliver is frequently framed in isolation, often looking out over a deserted landscape. Extreme long shots, as he roams the empty corridors or lengthy panning shots as he strolls across the deserted beach, highlight his isolation. His commentary suggests that he's happy to be alone but dramatic montages of his imagined death show a need for assurance and a degree of introspection.

Whenever Oliver's thoughts are visualised on-screen, they are edited to look like old cinema reels: the picture is grainy and is bordered. This suggests that teens see their lives as an epic, something everyone should be interested in. They create illusory worlds to escape their changing selves. In Oliver Tate's death **montage** (see 'Cinematography and mise-en-scène', page 264), a low level long shot as he is resurrected gives him a god-like quality. Editing works together with voice-over in this sequence, employing the codes and conventions of a TV news broadcast: outdoor footage, police press appeals, vox-pop soundbites, interviews with friends and quotes from written tributes.

The editing process in *Submarine* also allows Ayoade to explore the visual pleasures of the written word. There is text in almost every frame. The text is used in a variety of ways creating and communicating different meanings. Interesting **typography** is used, the narrative structure is highlighted through subheadings, for example 'Prologue', 'Epilogue'. The montage sequence, which shows Oliver and Jordana's relationship developing, is introduced by a close-up of a compilation tape given to Oliver by his father.

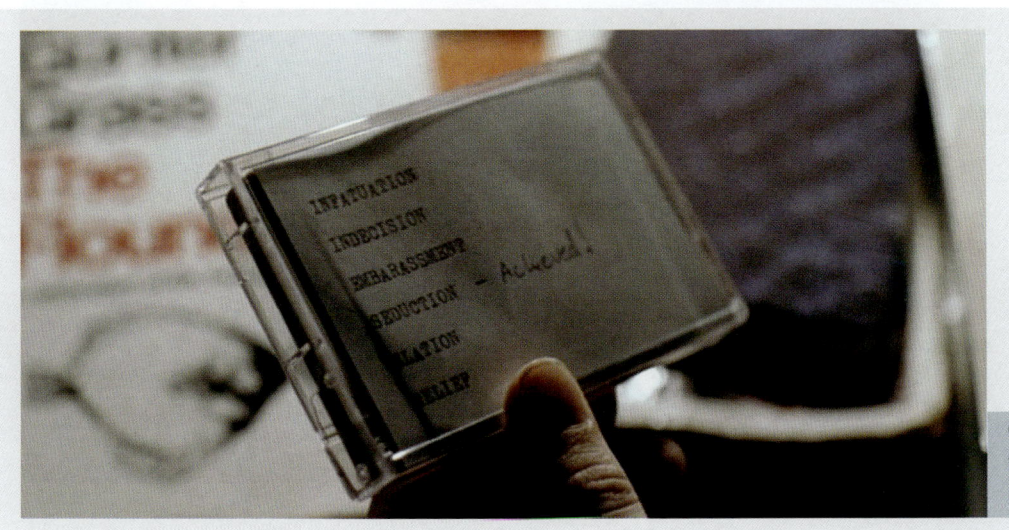

Key terms

Vernacular
Commonly used or spoken language.

Montage
A film editing technique in which a series of shots are edited into a sequence to condense space, time and information.

Quick Question 4.25

What sort of people usually have this kind of TV coverage after they have died? What does tell us about Oliver's 'vision' of himself?

Key term

Typography
The style and general appearance of the printed word.

Cue romantic music for montage sequence (*Submarine*).

GCSE Film Studies

As Oliver starts to listen to the tape, a montage sequence shows the relationship developing. The montage contains many of the typical ingredients of a rom-com film or music video. A familiar illustration of first love remembered is created; the couple laughing by a stream, making paper boats, riding together on a bicycle (*Butch Cassidy and the Sundance Kid*, 1969, George Roy Hill), lighting sparklers, watching fireworks, kissing as they explode into the night sky and (because they are both a little 'alternative') also thrown into the mix is sharing an abandoned bath and singeing Oliver's leg hairs with a match!

The lovemaking 'rules' float away downstream on a paper boat (*Submarine*).

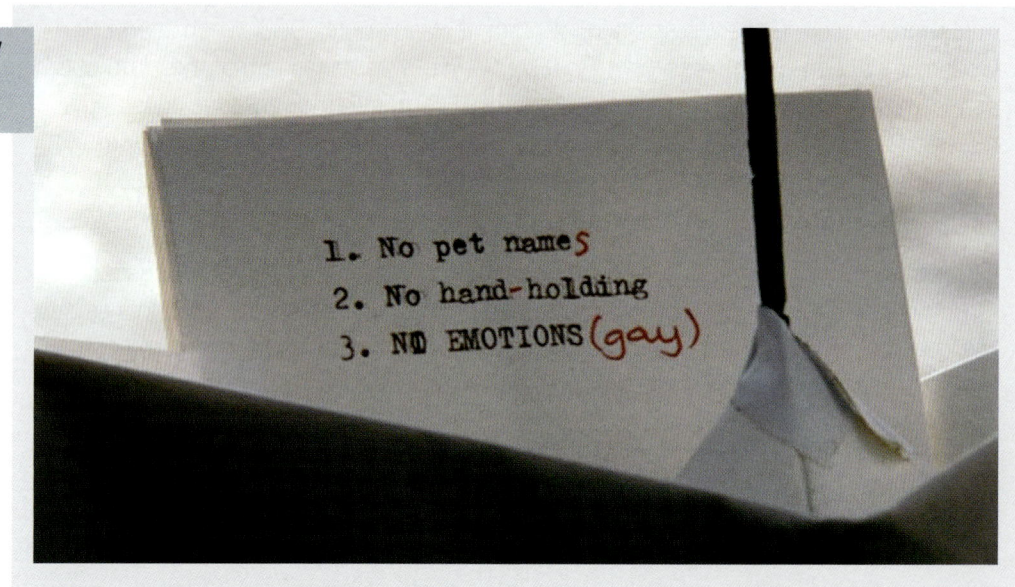

Just in case we are left in any doubt that this is a story seen through Oliver's perspective, the first montage leads into his own, filmed on Super-8 footage and entitled *Two Weeks of Lovemaking*. At the end of the sequence the romantic mood abruptly changes as we cut to the school playground. Oliver is with his mates and Jordana sits on her own under a tree. Chips (the school clown) and the other lads tease Oliver about his relationship and put pressure on him to act in the 'typical' adolescent male way. The atmosphere at this point could not be more different to that created in the previous montage sequence.

Memories already turned into Super-8 footage – Tate–Bevan Productions (*Submarine*).

Part 4: Component 2:
Global film

Task 4.36

Re-watch the montage sequence (0:23:35–0:27:00). Make notes on the following areas:

1. The use of the montage sequence to demonstrate time passing, the references to filmmaking made by Oliver.
2. The effect of using Super-8 footage towards the end of the sequence.
3. The use of sound and the choice of music.
4. The contrast between the montage sequence and the scene back at school. How film form is used to accentuate the difference?
5. What the sequence conveys about central themes such as love, sex and peer pressure.

Critics have commented that *Submarine* contains 'as much texture as cinematography and editing can offer'. The techniques include:

MONTAGES OF STILL AND MOVING IMAGES

VISUALISATIONS OF THOUGHTS AND DREAMS

CHAPTER CARDS

SHOTS RESONATING A STILLNESS AND BEAUTY USING NATURAL LIGHT

SHOTS THAT PLAY WITH ROM-COM CONVENTIONS

SHOTS THAT ECHO OLIVER'S STATE OF MIND

SLOW AND FAST MOTION

FREEZE FRAMES

Task 4.37

When re-watching *Submarine* note down key scenes or sequences that feature any of the above techniques. Describe each technique and explore the ways in which it creates meaning and response.

Keep your findings as revision notes.

Top tip
Several key sequences can be found on YouTube, re-visit these when preparing for your exam.

GCSE Film Studies

Representation

Although the main focus areas in your study of *Submarine* are film form and the film's aesthetic qualities, you should also consider how these elements relate to the film's structure. Many of the representation issues have been covered in the mise-en-scène section of this Case study (see page 228). The checklist below is a handy reference when analysing the representation of characters and setting. (See also 'Cinematography and mise-en-scène', page 264.)

Representation checklist: Oliver

- ✓ **The nerd archetype?** Educated, intelligent and over-analysis of life in general. Seldom seen without his duffle coat and briefcase in school setting. At home 'morphs' into a carbon copy of his father: same dressing gown, clothes for date night. Not conventionally masculine, desperate not to be labelled as gay.

- ✓ **Personality.** A self-conscious intellectual, constantly worried about his parents and his place in the world. Fantasises about his own death and the impact it would have on others. Often the visuals reflect a different story from his reality (hence comedy). Sees himself as 'a solitary Samurai' living alone in a fantasy world. Has problems dealing with other people's emotions (learnt from his parents?). Bullies Zoe and is unable to support Jordana when she most needs it.

- ✓ **Dysfunctional family life.** Parents unable to communicate with Oliver or each other, emotions suppressed by each member of the family. Mother unfaithful, father suffers from depression, copied by Oliver when Jordana finishes with him.

Representation checklist: Jordana

- ✓ **Complex female teen representation.** Goes against female teen archetypes: not a cheerleader/babe/princess /daddy's girl.

- ✓ **Likes to be in control.** Smokes, swears, a bully and pyromaniac, she belittles Oliver at the beginning of their relationship. Purports to hate romance saying 'it's gay'. At first she seems tough, unsentimental and emotionally cold. Shows her vulnerability as the narrative progresses when her mother is diagnosed with cancer and her dog is killed on the railway line. Seems to revert to a more conventional female stereotype towards the end, 'goes gooey', gets emotional; becomes needy, takes Oliver back. Although the Epilogue balances this when we see Oliver following in Jordana's footsteps as she wades deeper into the sea.

- ✓ **Unconventional appearance.** Not idealised or sexualised, the seducer, 'quirky', blunt brown haircut, chipped nail varnish, eczema, no make-up. Seldom seen without her red duffle coat, which initially sets her up as a sex siren/danger/femme fatale.

Task 4.38 Create three-point representation checklists, as above, for the following characters:
- Graham Purvis
- Jill Tate
- Lloyd Tate.

Part 4: Component 2: Global film

Narrative

The audience is left in no doubt about *Submarine*'s narrative structure. It is divided into three parts plus an **epilogue** each of which is signalled by chapter cards.

The **Prologue** gives us background into the oddball character that is Oliver Tate before introducing us to his new obsession, love. The opening sequence in this section is important in terms of establishing Oliver's personality and his unreliability as a narrator. It also allows us to consider how characters are introduced and how we are positioned to think about them. The Prologue begins with a black screen with the word *Prologue* on it. It then cuts to a classroom with the teacher asking the students 'What kind of young person am I, this is the challenge I am giving you this term.' The irony is that we have already learnt quite a lot about Oliver before this and the central theme of self-discovery has been introduced with Oliver's introductory voice-over:

> *Most people like to think of themselves as individuals, that there's no-one on the planet like them. This thought motivates them to get out of bed, eat food and walk around like there's nothing wrong. My name is Oliver Tate.*
> (Joe Dunthorne, *Submarine*)

Key terms

Epilogue
A scene, passage or speech that is added to the end of a film, book or play as a conclusion.

Prologue
Something that comes before an introduction to a book, play or film. It may be an action or situation that leads to something else.

This is immediately followed by an Alex Turner soundtrack played over shots of the beautiful Welsh countryside and coastline, all devoid of people apart from Oliver, with his back to the camera, in silhouette, looking out to sea:

> *I'm not the kind of fool whose gonna sit and sing to you about stars, girl, But last night I looked up into the dark half of the blue and they'd gone backwards.* (Alex Turner, 'Stuck On the Puzzle' [Lyrics], YouTube)

These lyrics and the cinematography work in tandem with his first voice-over to emphasise Oliver's social isolation and ideas of being submerged in a kind of darkness, which recur throughout the film, often in terms of water motifs.

The Prologue is followed by **'Chapter 1'**, entitled **'Jordana'**, the central female character in the film. This section focuses on Oliver's burgeoning relationship with Jordana.

A key sequence in this section features their meeting under the railway bridge complete with Polaroid camera ready to record their first kiss whilst trains flash noisily by (see page 240).

The second key sequence is the Thursday night planned seduction (see pages 239–240) when Oliver's parents go to the movies and Jordana is invited to Oliver's home for 'a wonderful evening of love-making'.

The **'Chapter 2'** is called **'Graham Purvis'**. The name of the long-haired 'Guru' who moved in next door and was Jill's former lover.

'Mum who would you save in a house fire given the hypothetical situation that both Dad and I were equally difficult to save?' (*Submarine*).

GCSE Film Studies

> **Task 4.39**
>
> A key sequence for exploring themes and narrative development in this section begins 00:38:20–00:42:40. Oliver has seen his mother with Graham as he and Jordana leave the cinema. Their closeness (and the fact that the dimmer switch hasn't been used for some time) convinces him they are having an affair. A voice-over then commences with Oliver imagining how the situation is going to develop.
>
> Re-watch this short sequence.
>
> 1. Analyse the ways in which the narrative is developed. You should consider: the contrast between Oliver's internal thoughts and the reality. How is this communicated to the audience and what impact does it have?
>
> 2. What does the sequence tells us about key themes of family relationships, talking/communication, love, loss and fears?

Key term

Juxtaposed
To place side by side.

In Chapter 2 the parallels between Oliver and his father become much clearer. Oliver learns the significance of his father's previous work as a marine biologist. His father describes his depressions as being submerged under water. His father's inability to cope with emotional matters is **juxtaposed** with Oliver's inability to give Jordana the kind of emotional support she needs when her mother is diagnosed with cancer.

Chapter 3 is entitled 'Show down'. At this point Oliver's world starts to crumble. Jordana finishes with him and finds a new boyfriend. His mother admits to having a brief sexual encounter with Graham. Oliver dons the dressing gown that matches his father's and slips into a depression that mirrors his father's. A key sequence, which is more or less Oliver's world crumbling down. Oliver goes to the beach where his mother and Graham are together again and sees that Jordana is with someone else. He finds out that his mother gave Graham a handjob. Adding to his misery, he receives a letter from Jordana stating what he was afraid was true: that their relationship was over and that she had found someone new.

Oliver states rather realistically that none of this will matter when he is 38. Which is him trying to be optimistic but no-one forgets their first love, not even the sophisticated Oliver Tate. He hasn't spoken to Jordana for two months but finds her hard to forget. The Epilogue provides the audience with a 'feel good ending' but also allows the audience to imagine what might happen to both characters next – after all they are still both gazing out to sea and the water is almost up to their knees – life will provide many more waves for them to jump over.

Oliver narrates his own story but the way we see Oliver is markedly different from the way Oliver sees himself. His voice-over narration acts as his inner voice. The opening sequence again is important as it alerts us to key character traits:

- He likes his own company (a loner).
- He has many affectations, for example. reading the dictionary and learning one new word each day.
- He imagines his life as a film playing out before his eyes.

Part 4: Component 2:
Global film

We soon discover that Oliver creates much of the narrative drive in the film. It is fuelled by his two major aims in life:

| 1. To lose his virginity. | 2. To save his parents' marriage. |

Most of the humour in the film stems from his clumsy attempts to do both these things. He monitors his parents' sex lives by checking the dimmer switch in their bedroom each morning. Their relationship is perceived from his point-of-view. He lingers in doorways to overhear what is said, peeps through curtains, hides behind giant cut-outs of his dad's love rival Graham Purvis, and even breaks into Purvis' house. In terms of aim 1 (to lose his virginity) his increasing desperation to 'have his way' with Jordana leads him to engineer what he imagines to be the perfect seduction scenario.

> Watch the sequence that begins just after Oliver has persuaded his parents to go out, leaving him in the house alone and waiting for Jordana to arrive (00:29:50–00:33:44).
>
> 1. Analyse the ways in which cinematography, sound, editing and mise-en-scène combine to create humour in this sequence.
>
> 2. Oliver has achieved his goal to lose his virginity. What might we expect to happen next? What clues are we given about the future of this relationship?

Task 4.40

There are some interesting oppositions within this sequence, all of which create humour. Oliver's anxiety to have sex is set against Jordana's initial indifference. Oliver has dressed for 'date night' (carbon copy of dad's date night attire). Jordana turns up in her same stained, red duffle coat. Oliver has old fashioned ideas about how to seduce a woman. Jordana is a modern female: she is in control and unimpressed by his 'masculine' mating display. Her mockery of his attempts to wine and dine her culminate in the much awaited (by Oliver) bedroom scene. He has decorated the room with balloons and flowers and has lit candles around his bed. He lies on his bed on his side, open legged in a cheesy pose telling Jordana to keep her eyes closed and wait for a surprise. She opens them and deadpans *'Fuckin' hell, you're a serial killer'*.

'Here's to a wonderful evening of love-making.' 'Fuckin' hell, you're a serial killer' (Submarine).

247

Style and aesthetics

A film by Jean-Luc Godard.

Submarine by Richard Ayoade.

Style in Submarine: intertextuality and post-modernism

When researching and thinking about this film you will almost certainly come across two key terms used in the academic study of media/film and by film critics. Don't be frightened by these terms, often explanations of what they mean can be very confusing. Put simply, intertextuality is an idea that any text has been influenced and shaped by texts that have come before it – anything read or seen in the case of films. Therefore, no film exists on its own and, consciously or not, all films borrow ideas from other films, past or present. Perhaps this 'borrowing' is not always brought to the audience's attention but it does provide one of the many pleasures we get from watching films (especially for those of us who like to think of ourselves as 'film buffs'). *Submarine* and many indie films consciously refer to other films, film characters and directors. Critics have attributed much of the recent success of *La La Land* to the ways in which it plays with other musical influences, for example *Singin' in the Rain*.

Part 4: Component 2:
Global film

Understanding **post-modernism** can be equally tricky but again, put simply, it is a term used when the filmmaker uses techniques designed to draw your attention to the fact you're watching a film. *Submarine*, for example, contains several techniques employed in a postmodern way – title cards, jump cuts, montages and frames that are slowed or speeded up, combine to constantly remind us we are watching a media construction. Typically (especially in Hollywood mainstream films), filmmaking techniques are used to draw the audience into the film's world, continuity editing ensures we move 'seamlessly from one scene to the next. Even when presented with monsters, aliens or fantastical worlds we suspend our disbelief and accept their 'reality' in terms of the film's narrative. A postmodern film endeavours to tell the audience a story in a way that changes the meaning of storytelling. It wants to make you aware of how other movies are encoded with meanings and to perhaps challenge the 'accepted' boundaries of film as an important art form.

Richard Ayoade is clearly a cinephile (see page 100 Specialist writing on film, including film criticism). *Submarine* almost submerges under the weight of filmic references ranging from the posters on Oliver's wall, in the cinema and the shop next door, to the narrative structure and its use of particular character types and themes. He plays with stylistic techniques from one of the 20th century's most influential and critically acclaimed film movements, the French New Wave. Even the opening credits feature large, slightly uneven lettering with strong colouring and irregular spaces in between (a reference to Jean-Luc Godard's films – see stills above).

Richard Ayoade is a fan of French New Wave films and he invents a central character who is also an avid fan. Oliver evidences this by having posters on his wall of Jean-Pierre Melville's *Le Samouri* and *Le Cercle Rouge*. Ayoade evidences his cinematic influences in many ways, perhaps most noticeably in terms of cinematic style. He uses the vérité camera (see 'Part 2 Cinéma vérité', page 103) at several points in the film to create a sense of realism that then contrasts markedly from the quirky camera angles, jump cuts and moving freeze frames also used.

> **Key term**
>
> **Post-modernism**
> Refers to techniques used by the filmmaker in order to draw attention to the fact that you are watching a film, e.g. chapter cards in *Submarine*.

'Do you think she looks like me?' (*A Bout de Souffle*, 1960, Jean-Luc Godard).

GCSE Film Studies

Quirky characters directly addressing their audiences (*Moonrise Kingdom*, 2012, Wes Anderson).

Submarine also bears the hallmarks of quirky American indie directors such as Wes Anderson, Noah Baumbach, Woody Allen and Quentin Tarantino.

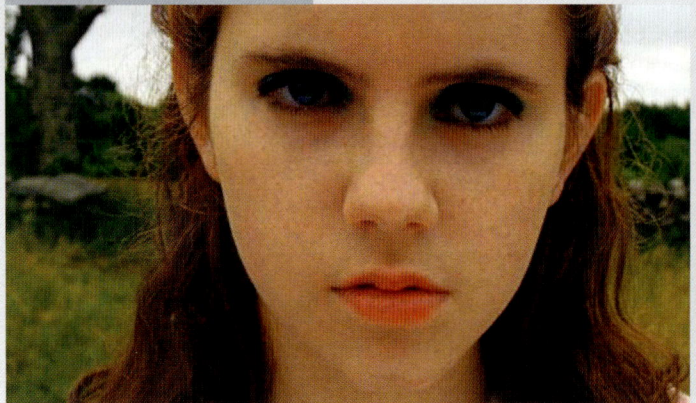

Let's break through the fourth wall (*Submarine*).

Task 4.41

In groups of two, research the work of either Françoise Truffaut, Jean-Luc Godard, Wes Anderson or Quentin Tarantino.

Create a short PowerPoint presentation, which mainly focuses on the director's style and explores where their influence may be seen in short sequences or frames from *Submarine*. You should include some of the following stylistic features:

- Interrupting or toying with the audience's **suspension of disbelief**.
- Breaking the fourth wall – breaking the boundaries normally set up in fiction.
- Examples of intertextuality or postmodern techniques.
- Title cards (draw attention to the fact that it is a 'story').
- Direct address (when an actor turns and speaks directly to the viewer).
- Drawing attention to the 'filmmaking process' within the fictional world of the film.

Key term

Suspension of disbelief
The temporary acceptance as believable of events or characters that would ordinarily be seen as incredible. This is usually to allow an audience to appreciate works of literature or film or drama that are exploring unusual ideas.

When thinking and writing about the aesthetic qualities of film it is important to consider what stylistic influences are evidenced in terms of film form and film structures. In the section on narrative in this case study (see page 245) we have considered the importance of the written word in terms of narrative structure and themes. Ayoade uses chapter titles and captions to draw our attention to the fact that we are watching a fictional construct and techniques can be played or experimented with. He refers back to 'past masters' of cinema but he also uses elements of popular culture and modern technology to create an innovative art work.

Task 4.42

Read through Sukhdev Sandu's *Submarine* critique below.

Ayoade structures Submarine *like a book, configuring its three primary sections as semi-discrete sections. It's one of the many conceits and stylistic tics he borrows from Wes Anderson (*Rushmore, The Royal Tenenbaums*): there's the context of a near dysfunctional family; an attention to costume and styling (Oliver in his cutesy duffel coat, Jordana swathed in red); the tableau-like staging of many shots; the tonal shifts between whimsy, melancholia and euphoria.*

What stops it from being mere **pastiche** *is Ayoade's genuine affinity for Anderson's work; he seems to share the American's belief that emotion in modern cinema should be sparing, oblique, talky. He also bundles in lots of visual references to the French New Wave (especially Truffaut). But, because they're applied to landscapes and social settings often found in British sitcoms, these influences are more often charming than they are hackneyed.*

Charm: Submarine *has lots and lots to offer. Partly this is the result of excellent casting. Roberts, bug-eyed and briefcase-wearing, looks like a cross between Woody Allen and Alex Turner of Arctic Monkeys (who contributes a handful of unexceptional, folky songs to the soundtrack), and is good at the tricky art of being deadpan, a spectator as much as a perpetrator of much of the drama he activates. Oliver may be artless and pompous, but it would take a hard heart not to be touched when he tries to beguile Jordana by taking her to Dreyer's* The Passion of Joan of Arc *on an early date.* (Sukhdev Sandhu, 'Submarine, Review', 18 March 2011, *The Telegraph*)

1. How does Sandhu justify Ayoade's use of ideas and techniques taken from other films or filmmakers?
2. Do you think it is possible to create a work of art that is truly original? If not why not?

Key term

Pastiche
A literary, musical or artistic piece consisting wholly or chiefly of motifs or techniques borrowed from one or more sources.

Submarine as art: the poetry of language

Joe Dunthorne (*Submarine*'s author) is an award-winning, Swansea-born poet. His poetry has been published in magazines and anthologies, has been featured on Channel 4, and BBC Radio 3 and 4. A pamphlet collection, *Joe Dunthorne: Faber New Poets 5*, was published in 2010. One of the great pleasures offered in the film of his novel is Oliver's use of poetic language. Our study of the aesthetic quality of film involves our personal response, how and why certain cinematic techniques, scenes or sounds appeal to our emotions and perhaps stay in our memory.

Oliver looks a little like the very young John Lennon: fresh and hopeful, with the soul of a poet and the self-importance of a teenager who struggles under the weight of his virginity. He may deliver his lines in a staccato monotone but the imagery he uses is beautiful, funny, startling and unusual. His diary entry after having sex with Jordana for the first time is both joyous and funny.

The submarine motif is stretched as far as it can possibly go, venturing boldly into *Fantastic Journey* (1966, Richard Fleischer) territory (watch the trailer of *Fantastic Journey* on YouTube – hilarious). And there's the wonderful irony, that Oliver, who learns a new word from the dictionary each day, can only resort to one the oldest clichés in the world to express the 'depth' of his feelings for Jordana, *'I love you more than words'*.

> *Oh diary, I love her, I love her, and I love her so much. Jordana is the most amazing person I have ever met. I could eat her. I could drink her blood. She's the only person I would allow to be shrunk to microscopic size and explore me in a tiny submersible machine. She is wonderful and beautiful and sensitive and funny and sexy. She's too good for me, she's too good for anyone! All I could do was let her know. I said: 'I love you more than words'. And I am a big fan of words.*

'The flame is the same shape as a falling tear' (Submarine).

Oliver realises Jordana has 'gone all goey in the middle' when she too begins to use poetic imagery to communicate her emotions. He gives her matches as a present because of her previous need to burn objects (and leg hair) but she tells him *'I've noticed that when you light a match, the flame is the same shape as a falling tear'.* She delivers the line in her familiar mumbled monotone but the imagery works alongside a close-up of her expression in order to communicate just how profoundly she has been affected by her mother's cancer and the death of her dog.

The aesthetics of music and poetry

> *Hello Darkness, my old friend*
> *I've come to talk with you again*
> (Simon and Garfunkel, 'The Sound of Silence')

There may be considerable disagreement among academics and critics about whether or not the lyrics of songs can be seen as poetry. However, Bob Dylan was awarded the Nobel Prize for Literature in 2016. Alex Turner, the chief songwriter of the Arctic Monkeys, may not be another Bob Dylan but his songs are poetic, they follow the British social realist tradition of bands such as The Kinks or Pulp, focusing on social issues such as lost chances and wrong choices. His art as a lyricist has been praised by legends such as David Bowie. The poet Simon Armitage says that Turner's

> *Use of internal rhyme exists to be admired and envied. And where some songwriters are never able to get beyond the drama of their own lives and diaries, Turner is more than capable of sidestepping his own experience and producing telling little mini-dramas populated by keenly observed characters.*
> (Simon Armitage, 'Propelled Towards Legend', 27 June 2008, *The Guardian*)

Task 4.43

In the same article Simon Armitage calls Turner *'A story-teller and a scene-setter'*. Re-watch the sequence '2 Weeks of Lovemaking' (00:23:00–00:26:31).

1. Describe the ways in which Turner's music and lyrics help to both set the scene and tell the story.

2. What might the repeated lines 'But I'm quite alright hiding today', But I'm quite alright hiding tonight' suggest about Jordana and Oliver's relationship?

3. Which of the film's central themes are conveyed within the lyrics?

'But I'm quite alright hiding tonight' (*Submarine*).

Quick Question 4.26

Oliver's dad Lloyd says 'I think music can make things a bit more real sometimes' when he gives Oliver the cassette. Do you agree? Have there been times when particular pieces of music have 'struck an emotional chord' in your life?

Film form – working together to create something special

Richard Ayoade has combined all the elements of film form in order to create an almost French New Wave look. He clearly loves old films and the French New Wave in particular, but his style ultimately stems from his central character. It mirrors, interprets or accentuates the way in which Oliver sees himself, which is in the pretentious tradition of French film and of 'cool' male protagonists such as Michel Poiccard (*A Bout de Souffle*, 1960). Ayoade felt that a romantic duffle-coated young man needed to be filmed on digital using a particular type of stock. Most of the action in the film takes place in the time before school and after school, so most of the shooting was done in 'the magic hour'. This is when a soft light that makes everyone more beautiful (see 'Cinematography and mise-en-scène', page 264). It also fits in with the idea that, at that age, key experiences happen in this limbo zone between home and school.

GCSE Film Studies

So, it could be argued that the whole aesthetic is led by Oliver's pretentious tastes, but that so happens also to be a very beautiful way of shooting:

> *I don't know if I've come of age, but I'm certainly older now. I feel shrunken, as if there's a tiny ancient Oliver Tate inside me operating the levers of a life-size Oliver-shaped shell. A shell on which a decrepit picture show replays the same handful of images. Every night I come to the same place and wait till the sky catches up with my mood. The pattern is set. This is, no doubt, the end.*

Love's young dream – Oliver's homage to Jordana (*Submarine*).

Task 4.44

Pick a sequence from *Submarine* that appeals to you because of its aesthetic qualities. Write an analysis that includes a consideration of the following:

- How spectacle engages and compliments the film's narrative (think cinematography).
- The sequence's aesthetic qualities and their significance in terms in terms of themes or narrative.
- How film form helps to create specific emotional responses in the audience.

Part 5
Component 3: Production

Introduction

Production is a vital part of studying film and you will have developed your knowledge and understanding of this area during Components 1 and 2. In Component 3 your ability to apply knowledge and understanding of film to a production and its accompanying evaluative analysis is measured. You must produce either:

- one genre-based film extract (either from a film or from a screenplay), or
- one evaluative analysis of the production.

The production brief, which will be changed every three years, will consist of:

- a choice of genres, which will reflect the genre films set in the specification
- a choice of either a section from the film or an overall effect the narrative will aim to achieve.

The brief

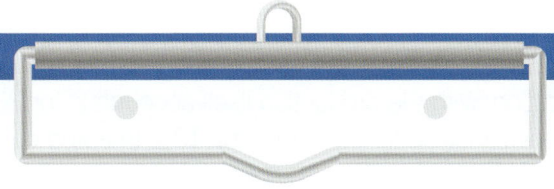

The brief for the first assessment in Summer 2019 and last assessment in Summer 2021 requires you to produce an individual production consisting of:

EITHER

(i) a film extract from one of the following genres of film:

- crime
- science fiction
- war
- horror
- the teenage film
- the musical.

The extract must take the form of one of the following two options:

- the opening of the film, or
- an extract from any part of the film that creates suspense and tension.

The extract must be between two minutes and two minutes 30 seconds in length.

OR

(ii) a screenplay extract from one of the following genres of film:

- crime
- science fiction
- war
- horror
- the teenage film
- the musical.

The extract must take the form of one of the following two options:

- the opening of the film, or
- an extract from any part of the film that creates suspense and tension.

The extract must be between 800 and 1,000 words in length. It must be accompanied by a shooting script of a key section from the screenplay (approximately one minute of screen time, corresponding to approximately one page of screenplay).

GCSE Film Studies

Evaluative analysis

You must complete an evaluative analysis of your production that is between 750 and 850 words. This will consist of:

- the aims of the genre film extract (the chosen genre of the production, its main audience), approximately 50 words
- a brief indication of how key aspects from approximately three genre films have influenced the production (which may include genre films studied during the course), approximately 200 words
- an analysis of how at least three important parts of the production compare with similar genre films (which may include those influencing the production), approximately 500 words.

The evaluative analysis must be mainly in the form of extended writing (which may include subheadings and some bullet points). You are advised to word-process the work, which may be illustrated with screen shots or screenplay extracts.

Assessment

This area of study is non-exam assessed and is worth 60 marks or 30% of your overall qualification, with the production itself accounting for 20% (marked out of 40) and the evaluative analysis for the remaining 10% (marked out of 20).

The work you produce will assess:

- Assessment objective two (AO2): your ability to apply knowledge and understanding of elements of film, including analysing and comparing films and analysing and evaluating your own work in relation to other professionally produced work.
- Assessment objective three (AO3): your ability to apply knowledge and understanding of elements of film form to the production of film or screenplay.

Suggested approach

You will have developed your knowledge and understanding of genre, genre conventions and narrative through your study of films in Components 1 and 2. You may supplement this by researching additional genre films and their screenplays in preparation for the production.

Try keeping a portfolio or notebook during your studies consisting of:

- examples of genre films and their conventions that could inform your own production work
- character(s) and narrative ideas for your genre-based extract
- examples of screenplay techniques
- examples of shooting scripts.

> **Top tip**
> Utilise technology by making your portfolio electronic. You could keep a blog or create a Pinterest board of genre films with ideas that will assist you with your own production. This will help you immensely when you come to write your evaluative analysis.

Part 5: Production

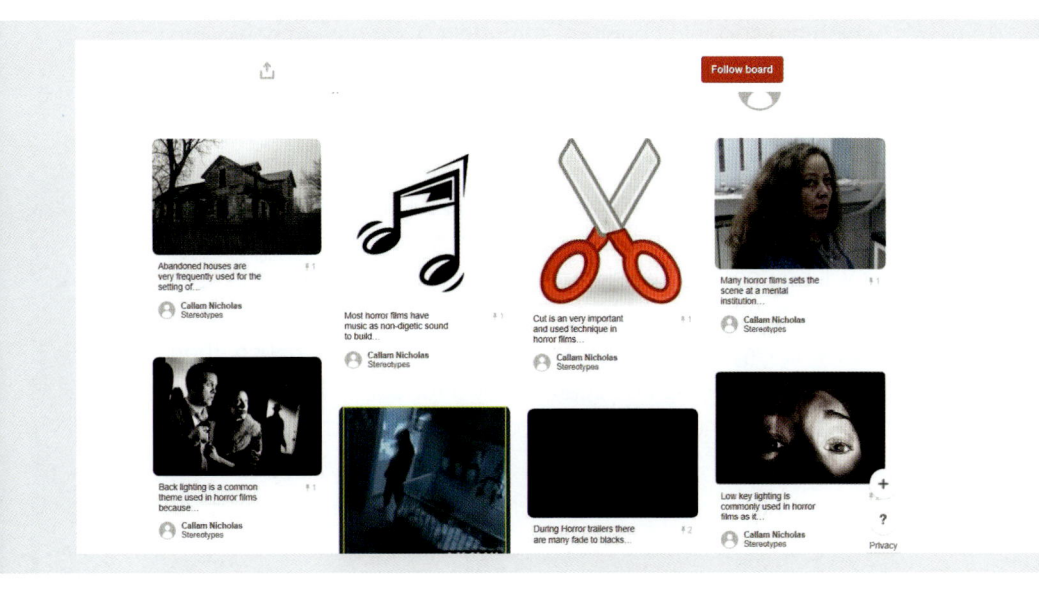

Pinterest board of horror genre stereotypes.

Screenwriting option

If you are choosing the screenwriting option, one of the first things you will need to do is decide the genre of your film (from the given list) and come up with a basic narrative. Once you have this, you can select which part of the plot you think would be most suitable for your extract. Will you be writing the opening of the film or a sequence that creates tension and suspense?

> Once you have chosen which part of the plot you are going to focus on get it down on paper in a draft form. Don't worry about formatting or film conventions at this point and don't make it too detailed; just get the basic story down. It is advisable to word-process your work for this task, as you will be going back and amending it throughout the chapter.

Task 5.1

Your work will probably resemble an extract from a book rather than a screenplay and for the moment that is fine. Screenplays and novels share many characteristics – after all, they are both pieces of writing that tell a story and, just as books need to 'play' in the reader's mind, a screenplay must do the same.

Formatting

Formatting a screenplay correctly is vital. If formatting is wrong some companies may not even read your screenplay so it is worth getting it right so your script looks professional. If you have access to screenwriting programs then the formatting will be done for you; however, if you are word-processing your work, then scripts should always be written in 12-point courier font and margins should be one inch (slightly larger on the inside for binding).

Top tip

When you first write your basic idea, try to do it without any dialogue. This will help you create a more visual piece and will also ensure any dialogue you add later is more character specific.

257

GCSE Film Studies

> **Top tip**
> To get a very professional look try using a screenwriting software. You can invest in a program such as Final Draft or even use free ones such as Celtx, which is available to download online.

> **Key term**
> **Slugline**
> The scene heading.

Unlike novels, which are split into chapters, screenplays are broken down into scenes. Every time the story moves into a new location (when the camera needs to be moved) a new scene is required. Scenes should be numbered.

Each scene will need a heading (or **slugline**) that should be in block capitals in order to distinguish it from the rest of the action. This sits to the left of the page and is useful for directors and potential investors as they can skim through the script and see what kinds of settings will be needed. The slugline should specify whether the scene takes place inside (INT for internal) or outside (EXT for external) and should describe the setting from smallest to largest area (just like writing an address – house, then street, then city). These elements should be separated by a full stop. The last word of the slugline should specify the time of day and should be separated by a dash.

```
EXT. HOUSE — DAY
```

The above example is correct but it doesn't tell the reader that much about the setting. It could be any type of house. Is it a shack or mansion? Is it 5am or 3pm? The slugline should include as much information as possible (whilst remaining succinct) to help create that picture in the readers' minds.

```
EXT. QUAINT COUNTRY COTTAGE — MIDDAY
```

Just by adding a few extra details we are already helping to create a certain visual for the reader. The scene instantly creates a picture of the type of house we are looking at and we can see it in our imagination. The time of day and the wording chosen suggest a happy, bright scene.

Task 5.2 Open the draft story you wrote in Task 5.1 and go back through it creating sluglines for each scene.

Writing action

> **Key term**
> **Shooting script**
> A version of the screenplay that is used during filming.

The majority of your screenplay will be action. This is the story, the description. Action in a screenplay should not include camera directions or film-specific language. These are things that will be added in later when the director is involved and a **shooting script** is written. A screenplay, however, should be written as a concise story that anyone would be able to understand.

Although screenplays are telling a story just like a novella, this particular story is one that needs to be envisaged and interpreted by a director, thus detail must be included but also must be kept short and to the point. Good action is detailed but not descriptive. It is concise and paints a picture in the readers' minds in as few words as possible. Whilst a book may spend several pages describing a new location, a screenplay must do it in a few lines. The best action tells the audience about the story and/or character and does this in a non-verbal way.

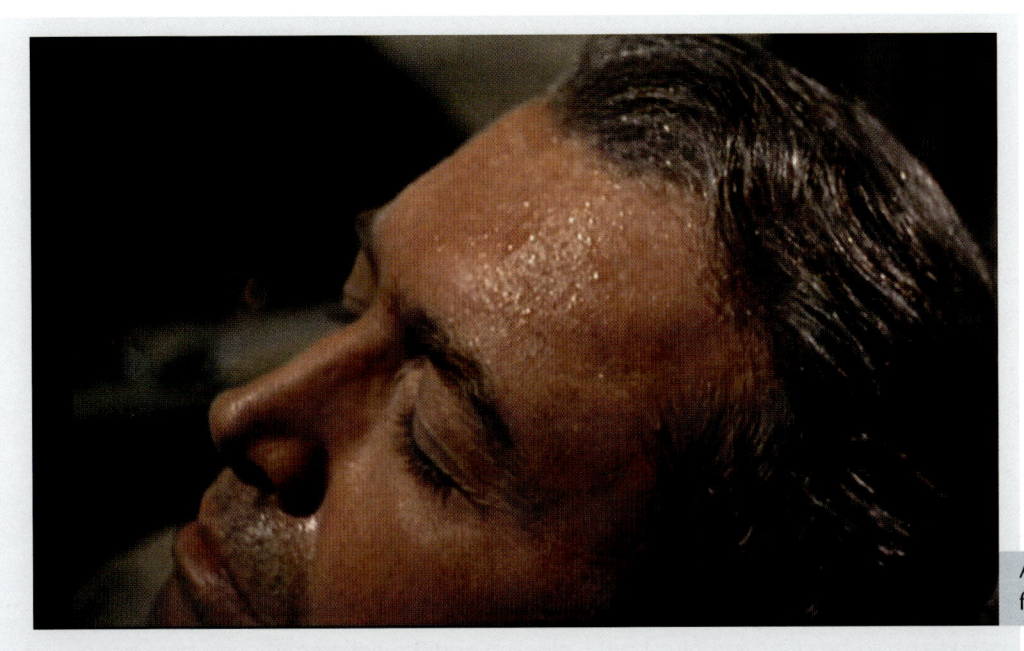

Top tip

Read scripts. The best way to learn the proper layout and formatting is to look at other peoples' work. This will also help with your own writing style and improve your ideas and imagination. There are hundreds of websites that you can use to download feature film scripts – you should never have to pay for them.

A large sleeping profile of a man fills the screen (*Rear Window*).

```
INT. JEFFERIES' APARTMENT - DAY

Although we do not see the foreground
window frame, we see the whole background
of a Greenwich Village street.

We can see the rear of a number of
assorted houses and small apartment
buildings whose fronts face on the next
cross-town street, sharply etched by the
morning sun.

Some are two stories high; others three;
some have peaked roofs, others are flat.
There is a mixture of brick and wood and
wrought iron in the construction.

The apartment buildings have fire escapes,
the others do not.

The neighborhood is not a prosperous one,
but neither is it poor. It is a practical,
conventional dwelling place for people
living on marginal incomes, luck -- or
hope and careful planning.
```

GCSE Film Studies

```
          The neighborhood is not a prosperous one,
          but neither is it poor. It is a practical,
          conventional dwelling place for people
          living on marginal incomes, luck -- or
          hope and careful planning.

          The summer air is motionless and heavy
          with humid heat.

          It has opened windows wide, pushed back
          curtains, lifted blinds and generally
          brought the neighborhood life into a
          sweltering intimacy. Yet, people born and
          bred to life within earshot and eye glance
          of a score of neighbors have learned
          to preserve their own private worlds by
          uniformly ignoring each other, except on
          direct invitation.
```

> **Top tip**
> To create more white space, try to keep action to a maximum of three lines per paragraph. A paragraph can even just be one word if necessary!

(https://the.hitchcock.zone/wiki/Scripts:_Rear_Window_(final_draft,_01/Dec/1953)_-_part_1)

Format-wise action should be positioned to the left and should continue to be 12-point courier font. If you look at an extract from a book compared to a screenplay extract you will see that there is a lot more 'white space' on the page when it comes to screenplays and this is something you must aim to adopt. In order to assist with this, a line should be skipped between the slugline and the action and each paragraph of action thereafter should be short. Each paragraph should be followed by another blank line. This will keep the story flowing and ensure a lot of 'white space' is created.

```
          EXT. QUAINT COUNTRY COTTAGE — MIDDAY

          A picture-perfect cottage surrounded by
          flowers and shrubs. Roses decorate the
          walls.
          Behind the cottage, woodland as far as
          the eyes can see. Trees with sun-blushed
          leaves dance slightly in the breeze.
```

Task 5.3 — Go through your draft story now and under each slugline separate your action to create more white space.

Part 5: Production

Introducing characters

When introducing a new character to the story, that person's name should be in capitals, their age in brackets and a short description included as in the example below. This is done so that the reader can get an instant picture of what this person is like. Names only need to be in capitals when we first meet the character. This helps potential investors as they can skim through a screenplay and see how many actors will be needed and therefore how much casting is likely to be. The description of the character not only helps the reader picture the person in the film, it also assists with casting later on.

```
EXT. QUAINT COUNTRY COTTAGE — MIDDAY

A picture-perfect cottage surrounded by
flowers and shrubs. Roses decorate the
walls.
Behind the cottage, woodland as far as
the eyes can see. Trees with sun-blushed
leaves dance slightly in the breeze.

EMILY (30) a pretty, thin-framed lady with
long golden hair and flowing floral dress
and wellies digs in the soil.
```

> Go through your story draft. Wherever a new character enters, amend your story to follow the above character introduction conventions.

Task 5.4

Writing style

The basic story you created in Task 5.1 should be looking a lot more like a screenplay instead of a novel extract. Now you need to make sure it sounds like one too.

Screenplays are written in the present tense so that the action unfolds in the reader's mind as if it were happening right there in front of them. One way to help the story flow in the reader's mind is to minimise interruptions. Do this by limiting the number of camera directions.

Although essential camera directions can be included in your screenplay, try and keep them out if possible and save them for your shooting script. If you really need something to be from a particular angle, then use POV (point-of-view) instead.

For example, if you really must have a close-up of the killer's hand so that the audience see a distinctive ring on his finger, then instead of writing the camera directions just write it as a POV:

```
A hand reaches for the doorknob. A BLACK
RING on the index finger.
```

GCSE Film Studies

Although you haven't actually stated it is a close-up, the way you have written it implies that is the way you would like it to be shot. Capitalising the significant prop also brings it to the reader's attention and highlights the fact that it will probably be significant later in the plot.

The biggest tip for writing a screenplay is – show, don't tell. If your main character is bored of his job it is better to show us this in a quick scene such as the below rather than have him tell another character 'I hate my job.'

> **Top tip**
> Just like this shot, action should be visual and it should always forward the story or reveal something about the character. Ideally, it should do both. Although you want scenes you write to be visually striking and affect our senses, emotions and intellect, you should never write a scene just to create a mood or because you like it. Scenes need to have a purpose or they will be cut when it comes to filming.

```
INT. OFFICE — DAY
Tweezers pluck spikes from a cactus. A
voice counts them off as they are placed in
a pile.

DAVE (50s), just one suit in a sea of
many, slumps at his desk. He brushes the
cactus spikes off his desk and into the
bin.
```

This short scene ticks several boxes. It tells us about the character Dave, his job and his state of mind. The fact that he is carrying out such a tedious task shows us his boredom. The scene also sets up where he works and, just like the previous example, it implies the use of a close-up, this time followed by a long shot.

Task 5.5 Below is an example of writing where the author is telling us rather than showing us. Re-write it to make it more visual.

```
                LIZZIE

    Hello dear. How was your day working in
       the city where you have a high-level
     executive job and are very well paid as
         you have just received a promotion?

                 NEIL

    Fine thank you. How was your day? Did you
      manage to find a house we would like now
    that our marriage is back on track after
       my affair and we have decided to start
     afresh somewhere we can have a family?
```

262

Part 5: Production

Where did you put the characters? Was the female in the kitchen? Cooking dinner? Was it all done in just one scene or several? Was there a lot of dialogue in order to get the information across?

Don't just write the first thing that comes into your head. This information could be shown to us in several quick and visual scenes. Ask yourself, what information does the writer need to get across here? How can this be done visually?

Quick Question 5.1

Think of some creative and visual ways you could write the following:
- a customer in a restaurant that you want the audience to dislike
- a woman who has a split personality you want to hint to.

INFORMATION:
Neil works in London. He is a well-paid businessman.

→

POSSIBLE VISUAL:
Neil, in an expensive suit, runs down a flight of stairs outside an extremely large building. A valet brings his sports car. Big Ben is in the background. Perhaps he glances at his Rolex.

INFORMATION:
They are looking for a new house and plan to start a family.

→

POSSIBLE VISUAL:
The sports car now sits outside an imposing, double-fronted house, a 'for sale' sign in front. Lizzie and an estate agent accompany Neil as they exit the house. The estate agent mentions space for a nursery. Neil and Lizzie exchange a knowing look.

INFORMATION:
Neil has had an affair.

→

POSSIBLE VISUAL:
Neil's phone rings. The caller ID says 'Jenny'. Neil silences it and slinks away to answer it. He is hushed and secretive. Lizzie watches with worry in her eyes.

Task 5.6

Go through your screenplay and make sure it is in present tense. See if you can re-write any of your action to make it more visual. Is there a better way to get across the information you need?

The key elements of film form

Your screenplay should now be looking and sounding like a professional one; however, you need to remember you are working to a set brief. Your script must be a genre-based extract. This means the reader must be able to get a sense of that genre from what you have written and your work should adhere to at least some genre codes and conventions. Say you have chosen horror genre – there are several codes and conventions you could follow. The easiest way to do this is to use the framework of study you have already used when studying films in Components 1 and 2:

- cinematography including lighting
- mise-en-scène
- editing
- sound
- genre and narrative.

Quick Question 5.2

Create a list of codes and conventions for your chosen genre using the framework of study bullet points above as headings.

Cinematography and mise-en-scène

Continuing with our example of horror, you may have noted that cinematography codes and conventions for this genre typically include some of the following:

- low angle shots usually to emphasise the power of the monster/killer and can also be used to show the power of the hero
- high angle shots to connote the victim's lack of power
- wide/long shots of isolated areas to show there is no escape
- close-up shots to show victim's fear or to connote entrapment
- medium shots to show the distance between the monster/killer and the victim
- point-of-view shots to allow the audience to empathise with the victim
- pans, canted angles and tracking shots during chase sequences.

Lighting for horror films will usually be dark, under-exposed or set at night. Low-key lighting will generally be used on the villain whilst the hero or damsel in distress may require more high-key lighting. You may have lighting that creates shadows or silhouettes to add to the dark atmosphere.

Ideally your screenplay should include a mix of these where possible to add variety and to keep your visuals exciting.

Horror codes and conventions (*The Shining*, 1980, Stanley Kubrick).

Part 5: Production

Halloween (1978, John Carpenter).

Nosferatu (1922, F.W. Murnau).

> Go through your screenplay and see if you have included a range of these cinematography and lighting codes and conventions. If you have not, write some in now. Remember, don't write the camera angles themselves in yet (this is for the shooting script) but make sure they are implied. You want a mix of these where possible to add variety to your screenplay and to keep your visuals exciting.

Task 5.7

Mise-en-scène for horror genre films tends to include settings and locations that are dark and isolated, such as woods or abandoned buildings/houses in the middle of nowhere or they take familiar places and make them seem less familiar to us somehow. There are the usual props of weapons, torches, blood and gore, and the villain usually wears darker clothing and is positioned higher in the frame (or fills more of it) than victims in order to show his or her power. Of course, these conventions can be and are changed and subverted to make horror films less predictable for audiences.

GCSE Film Studies

Horror movie villains.

Freddy Krueger (*A Nightmare on Elm Street*, 1984, Wes Craven).

The Ring (2003, Gore Verbinski).

Friday the 13th (1980, Sean S. Cunningham and Steve Miner).

Scream (1996, Wes Craven).

Editing

Editing for horror films ranges from slow-paced scenes to help build tension and establishing shots to connote isolation and danger, to faster cuts to provide tension and suspense. Jump cuts will help create shock for the audience. Whilst much of this aspect will be covered in the shooting script as you will be able to add in types of edit to show how scenes and shots are joined together, you can still use these conventions in your screenplay.

The speed of the shots affects the pace and rhythm of a film sequence and helps to create certain moods and atmospheres. Although you cannot dictate shot durations in your screenplay you can imply them.

Thrillers and horrors often use urgency and pace by shortening scenes as the tension increases. The way you write the action will also indicate tension and suspense.

See how the pace and feel of the below scene changes with a quick rewrite.

Example 1

```
INT. SLEEK SPORTS CAR — NIGHT

Dan and Lucy get into the car. Lucy puts
on her seatbelt as Dan starts the engine.

                LUCY

             Drive!

Dan activates the central locking and
pulls away sharply. He begins to drive
faster and faster.
```

Example 2

```
INT. SLEEK SPORTS CAR – NIGHT

Dan, shrouded in a black hoody, jumps into
the car. He is out of place amongst the
expensive black leather. Lucy, running on
adrenaline, slides in behind him.

Seatbelts slam into holders.

Central locking activates.

The key turns. The engine roars.

                    LUCY

              Drive!

The screech of tyres on tarmac.

Speedo: 50, 60, 70, 80 …
```

Another way to control pace and rhythm is to have high emotionally intense scenes followed by calmer scenes. Audiences wouldn't enjoy a lot of high tension scenes one after the other. They need the rollercoaster ride with the ups and the downs.

You can also use clever and stylish cuts to increase or slow the pace. For example, you could have person A placing a glass on a table in one scene and in the next scene person B picking up a glass.

Editing techniques such as **graphic matching** and **cross-cutting** don't need to be named but can be implied in your writing and will help create a visually stunning piece.

> Get your screenplay out again and now go through it and make sure you are adhering to mise-en-scène and editing codes and conventions for your genre. If you are not, try rewriting scenes with these aspects in mind. This is easily done as can be seen in the example below.

Key term

Graphic matching
An editing technique that involves matching shots in terms of their composition either in a scene or in a transition between two scenes.

Cross-cutting
An editing technique that involves moving from one sphere of action to another, often for extended periods.

Task 5.8

Using the scene we wrote earlier, we can see that this is currently not adhering to the codes and conventions of our chosen genre – horror.

```
EXT. QUAINT COUNTRY COTTAGE – MIDDAY

A picture-perfect cottage surrounded by
flowers and shrubs. Roses decorate the walls.
```

Part 5: Production

267

GCSE Film Studies

```
Behind the cottage, woodland as far as
the eyes can see. Trees with sun-blushed
leaves dance slightly in the breeze.

EMILY (30) a pretty, thin-framed lady with
long, golden hair and flowing, floral dress
and wellies digs in the soil.
```

There isn't too much that is scary about a pretty lady and a quaint country cottage, so let's change it. Instead of being a quaint cottage, let's make it an abandoned one. Instead of being set in day, let's move it to night.

```
EXT. ABANDONED COTTAGE — 3AM
A dilapidated and ramshackle building sits
draped in cobwebs and weeds.
Behind the cottage, woodland as far as
the eyes can see. Bare skeleton trees
stand like bars on a cage surrounding
the building. The moonlight casts eerie
shadows that dance across their twisted
branches.
```

We have kept all of the same features (the cottage, the trees) that we were writing about but a quick change of the description and the whole feel of the scene has changed.

Of course, Emily as she currently stands does not quite fit the genre. We could make her the damsel in distress – `EMILY (30), a pretty, thin-framed girl in a white dress and with eyes that have seen too much` – or we could make her the villain – `EMILY (70), a haggard, thin-framed woman with pale, leathered skin and vacant eyes stands dressed all in black.` Either way we are using what we know about our chosen genre to make sure that all aspects of our screenplay follow the codes and conventions.

Sound

Have you ever watched a scary movie without the sound? Sound is one of the key things in creating mood in films – especially in horrors and thrillers. Whether it is eerie, tension-building music or **pleonastic sound effects** that add to scares, sound will be very important in your screenplay. Even silence helps build tension. It is recommended that sounds are capitalised and if you want to add extra tension by prolonging a moment in your screenplay, then add a beat.

```
EXT. ABANDONED COTTAGE — 3AM

A dilapidated and ramshackle building sits
draped in cobwebs and weeds. Wind WHISTLES
through the empty windows.
```

> **Top tip**
> You may not want to conform to all the codes and conventions of your genre. Perhaps you want to set your final battle scene in broad daylight to subvert the conventions. This is something that is perfectly acceptable and will give you something extra to discuss in your evaluative analysis.

> **Key term**
> **Pleonastic sound effects**
> Sound that is heightened in order to appeal to the emotions or draw attention to a significant action or prop.

```
Behind the cottage, woodland as far as
the eyes can see. Bare, skeleton trees
stand like bars on a cage surrounding
the building. The moonlight casts eerie
shadows that dance across their twisted
branches.

The wind fades.

SILENCE.

Beat.
```

Task 5.9 — Go through your screenplay and add in any sounds or periods of silence that may add to your extract.

Representation

When writing your screenplay keep in mind the representation of people and place. Have you got archetypal characters in your screenplay? The damsel in distress. The hero. The villain. Have you got stereotypical characters? Is the dumb blonde the first victim, for example?

Think about how you represent different social groups such as gender, ethnic, culture and social class. These are areas you may wish to subvert or change from the norm. Killers are typically represented as lower class males but perhaps yours will be upper class and highly educated? Maybe your hero will a strong female and the men will be the victims?

Adding dialogue

Make adding dialogue to your screenplay one of the last things you do. This will ensure that your work remains visual and that any dialogue is relevant and required. Never just add dialogue for the sake of it. Speaking parts cost filmmakers more than non-speaking parts so any dialogue that is not needed will be cut.

Real-life dialogue has interruptions, false starts, is digressive and often banal. It would not work well on-screen. Silence in real life makes people feel uncomfortable but it can be good on-screen to create atmosphere and tension. Therefore, when writing screenplays, we have to change the way we use dialogue. Audiences obviously do not want to watch a two-hour film with absolutely no dialogue and an abundance of silence; however, we need to make sure whatever dialogue we have is functional. Dialogue should give the impression of real life but take out the boring bits. It should be compressed, economical, have clear purposes and be satisfying. It works least well when it tells you what is going on or has no real point to it, so it is important to remember that it should only be used when necessary. Many students' scripts fall down because their screenplays become too dialogue heavy and contain unnecessary conversations that are irrelevant and lengthy. If the dialogue isn't needed – scrap it! It should only be there if it helps progress the story or if it reveals character.

GCSE Film Studies

When adding dialogue, remember that it is the only part of the action that will be centred. The speaker's name should be in the middle of the page and capitalised. This will make it stand out from the bulk of the text so the reader can immediately identify it as dialogue.

```
EXT. ABANDONED COTTAGE — 3AM

A dilapidated and ramshackle building sits
draped in cobwebs and weeds. Wind WHISTLES
through the empty windows.

Behind the cottage, woodland as far as
the eyes can see. Bare skeleton trees
stand like bars on a cage surrounding
the building. The moonlight casts eerie
shadows that dance across their twisted
branches.
The wind fades. Beat.

SILENCE.

EMILY (30), a pretty, thin-framed girl in
a white dress and with eyes that have seen
too much, hugs herself against the cold as
she heads towards the front door.

                    EMILY

              Hello?
```

Task 5.10 — Go through your script and add in any dialogue that is needed. Remember to keep it economical and relevant.

Final checklist

Your screenplay should now be looking pretty good and it is almost time to give yourself a pat on the back and print out your masterpiece. Just one final task!

Use the following handy checklist to make sure your screenplay ticks all the boxes.

Part 5: Production

Format features:

- [ ] single column with wide margins
- [ ] sequential page numbering (top right)
- [ ] mf (more follows) (bottom right)
- [ ] dialogue centred, with speaker's name in upper case
- [ ] parentheticals in brackets under speaker's name
- [ ] sluglines and sound in upper case
- [ ] character name in upper case on first appearance only
- [ ] font – courier, 12 point

Content:

- [ ] each scene is numbered and accompanied by a slugline

The slugline consists of:

- [ ] an indication of where the action takes place – INT or EXT
- [ ] location descriptor
- [ ] lighting descriptor – DAY or NIGHT or TIME
- [ ] scene/action descriptor (with succinct description of character on his/her first appearance)
- [ ] essential camera instructions (in upper case within scene descriptor) or essential edit instructions (in upper case, range right) only
- [ ] action written in present tense

Genre codes and conventions:

- [ ] cinematography including lighting
- [ ] sound
- [ ] mise-en-scène
- [ ] narrative features
- [ ] editing
- [ ] representation

271

GCSE Film Studies

Shooting script

If you chose the screenwriting option, then you will also need to produce a shooting script extract as part of your work. Producing a shooting script will help demonstrate your visualisation skills. You have written a fantastic screenplay but now you must show you understand how it will be filmed.

For this additional task, you must create a shooting script for a key section of your screenplay. You should aim to write a minute of screen time for the shooting script, which equates to about a page of script.

> **Task 5.11**
>
> Read over your now complete screenplay and pick a scene or sequence you will use for your shooting script. Which scenes jump out at you as being the best to use for the shooting script? Which do you picture most clearly in your head? Make sure you select a scene that will have a variety of shots in it.

Once you have selected your scene or sequence you need to re-write it as a shooting script. Whilst shooting scripts can and do vary, the generally accepted conventions must be used. They should include:

- standard conventions of a screenplay as above
- a numbered sequence of shots to demonstrate how the key section of the screenplay will be filmed (positioned on the right side of the page).

> **Task 5.12**
>
> Copy your chosen scene to a new document and save as 'shooting script'. Now go through the scene and add in all the things that you were not allowed to add when writing your screenplay. Put in all those camera directions and editing transitions. Make sure they are in capitals such as in the example below and that transitions are aligned right.

```
BLACK.

The sound of HEAVY RAIN and WIND.

                              FADE IN:

EXT. ABANDONED COTTAGE — 3AM

ECU of a spider on a web. SLOW ZOOM OUT
to ESTABLISHING LONG SHOT. LOW ANGLE A
dilapidated and ramshackle building sits
draped in cobwebs and weeds. Wind WHISTLES
through the empty windows.

LOW ANGLE PAN L–R Behind the cottage,
woodland as far as the eyes can see. Bare
skeleton trees stand like bars on a cage
surrounding the building. The moonlight
casts eerie shadows that dance across
their twisted branches.

The wind fades. Beat.
```

```
SILENCE.

ECU bare feet trample twigs and weeds.
SLOW ZOOM OUT to see white, tattered dress
hanging at the bare feet. OTS LOW ANGLE
LONG SHOT EMILY (30), a pretty, thin-
framed girl in a white dress stands in the
grounds of then shack. CU Emily's eyes -
eyes that have seen too much. LONG SHOT
she hugs herself against the cold as she
heads towards the front door.

CU Emily pushes the door open slowly.

                    EMILY

                Hello?
```

Filmmaking option

If you are choosing the filmmaking option, just as in the screenwriting option, one of the first things you will need to do is decide the genre of your film (from the given list) and come up with a basic narrative. Once you have this, you can select which part of the plot you think would be most suitable for your extract. Will you be filming the opening of the film or a sequence that creates tension and suspense? Remember that the extract is only going to be between two minutes and two minutes 30 seconds so pick a sequence that will involve enough action to make it exciting but that is not so complicated that it will be difficult to film.

Once you have chosen which part of the feature you are going to film get it down on paper in a draft form. Don't make it too detailed. It is advisable to word-process your work for this task, as you will be going back and amending it throughout the chapter.

Task 5.13

One of the biggest tips when making a film is don't rush. For many students, it is a very exciting prospect that they are about to make a film and they cannot wait to start. However, the key to succeeding in this task is planning and preparation.

You have your basic film idea and have chosen the part of that story you will film. Let's say I want to make a film about a video tape that kills you exactly seven days after watching it – sound familiar? I am going to film the opening of this film, which should get across certain information – the genre, the main characters or problem, for example. Does my opening do this? If it does it may be tempting to jump right in and start shooting but time won't allow for many re-dos and it's hard getting all my actors and equipment together for one day let alone several, so I must plan! You need to do this too! Make sure you are going into the actual shoot completely organised, knowing exactly what you want! One way to ensure this is the case is to plan each element of film form in detail before you start.

> **Top tip**
> Consider the equipment and resources you have access to when choosing which sequence to film. You might have an excellent car crash scene but how will you realistically film this? You might have a great scene set on top of a cliff but do you have a location such as this near you?

> **Top tip**
> Keep it simple! You may be tempted to go all out and choose the most action-packed scene of your film, but often less is more. Choosing a scene with a simpler story will allow you to really focus on the elements of film form and will help you demonstrate your knowledge and understanding.

Part 5: Production

GCSE Film Studies

> **Top tip**
> If you can try to pick a sequence that won't need any dialogue. Always try and show the audience what is happening, rather than telling them. This will help you create a more visual piece and, although actors' performance is not assessed, if the actors remain silent it will help make any amateur actors look more believable.

The key elements of film form

Your brief says the sequence must be a genre-based extract. This means the reader must be able to get a sense of that genre from what you film and your work should adhere to at least some genre codes and conventions. You must also show your knowledge and understanding of how to create meaning using the elements of film form and you are encouraged to use an appropriate range of camera shots, sounds, props, lighting and editing techniques in your production.

Framework of study:

- cinematography including lighting
- mise-en-scène
- editing
- sound
- genre and narrative
- representation of people and ideas.

Task 5.14

As you are producing a horror film, you need to know how horror films utilise the above elements of film form.

1. Watch the opening sequences of some horror films you like. Note down the types of things you see and hear.

2. Discuss with a partner how horror genre films use the above elements of film form. What kind of places are they usually set in? What props or characters do you expect to see? What is the sound like?

3. What does the opening of a horror film usually do in terms of setting up the narrative?

4. Add these findings to your portfolio/notebook if you are keeping one, making a note of any particular shots or ideas you liked and which film they were from. These will come in handy when you come to do your evaluative analysis.

Going back to our example – the film about the killer video tape is obviously *The Ring* (2002, Gore Verbinski). Let's pretend this is my film. I am going to film the opening sequence that sets up the genre and the problem by showing a death caused by this video tape. So far, I have planned that it will be two school friends talking about the video and then one admits to watching it. Spooky things happen until ultimately the girl who has watched the tape is killed.

This is the basic idea but before I can start filming anything I need to know exactly what is going to happen in the sequence. Bear in mind that the opening we are looking at here is much longer than the one you will need to produce. First I need to plan what will happen step by step.

- Shot of house
- Katie and friend in bedroom – tale of the tape – Katie has seen it – spent last weekend with boyfriend
- Phone rings – it's 10pm!
- Answer phone – just mum
- Go to kitchen to get drink – TV turns on
- Remote is there. Turn TV off
- TV back on. Pull plug
- Go upstairs. See water
- Open door. TV screen on
- Katie dies

> **Task 5.15**
>
> 1. Create a list of bullet points like the above that detail what is going to happen in your sequence.
> 2. Write your bullet points out like a script. Don't worry about formatting at this point. You just want to have the full sequence in front of you. You should word-process this as you will be amending it several times.

Now you need to make it visual and show your understanding of the elements of film form and of narrative and genre. The easiest way to do this is by going through the elements one at a time. Let's look at *The Ring* opening for inspiration.

Cinematography and mise-en-scène

The first shot of the opening of *The Ring* immediately suggests the genre to the audience (as well as setting up where we are) through the carefully considered cinematography, mise-en-scène and lighting.

The establishing shot sets the genre (The Ring).

A long, low angled shot captures the house and the low angle used makes the house look imposing and dangerous. It is set at night. It is dark and raining. An overhead diffused, high key light highlights the twisted branches of a tree and casts a lot of the shot into shadow. The house itself is double fronted and imposing with twisted vines and branches covering its front, as if trapping it. This is definitely not going to be a happy comedy or a romance. A slow zoom takes us towards the house apprehensively and this zoom continues when we cut to a teenager's bedroom and meet the two school girls.

The interior of the scene uses dull low key lighting to continue with the eerie tone set up earlier. The girls are normal school girls wearing school uniform (to highlight their age). There are school books and shoes on the floor. It is a typical girl's bedroom.

After a brief conversation between the girls, which sets up the idea of the tape and the fact that it kills you exactly seven days after watching it, one of the girls (Katie) admits she has seen the film and when the house phone rings the action begins.

Close-ups are used to show reactions and the fear on Katie's face and a fast zoom into the clock face suggests that Katie watched the film exactly seven days ago to the minute. This heightens the tension for the audience.

Reaction shot to show fear (*The Ring*).

Fast zooms to create tension (*The Ring*).

The girls make their way to the phone downstairs and the way the cinematography is used keeps the tension heightened. As the girls approach the phone, it is kept in the immediate foreground and the focus is kept on the girls in the background as they approach. This long shot makes the girls look weak and in danger as they approach the phone, which fills the majority of the frame. This also shows the girls walking through the narrow hallway, suggesting ideas of being trapped and being unable to escape.

There is a false scare when Katie realises it is just her mum on the phone (this information also answers the enigma code of why these girls are alone in the house at night). Her friend heads back upstairs as Katie goes to the fridge. Opening the fridge and getting a drink is captured in an extreme close-up. The filmmakers are playing with the conventions here and playing on the audiences' expectations. We have all seen horror movies where a door is opened and then once it is closed again the monster appears behind it to give us a jump scare.

However, here the door is opened and, although we expect something or someone to be behind it, when it is closed again there is no-one there. This false scare acts to keep the audience on edge. We are waiting for something to happen and we don't know when it will.

The girls approach the threat in a long shot (*The Ring*).

The camera is constantly moving and only stops when something happens. For example, as Katie is pouring a drink the camera zooms slowly into the kitchen. The camera only stops when the television comes on in the next room. The camera is almost mimicking the audience here – the TV coming on makes us jump and hold our breath.

Setting up a false scare (*The Ring*).

More extreme close-ups are used to capture Katie's fear and then a Steadicam POV is used as we enter the living room. This is putting us in Katie's shoes and making us feel her fear. What are we walking into?

Close-ups are used to show the remote control and the plug being pulled so that the audience is aware it is not her friend messing about and turning the television on, but is something more sinister.

GCSE Film Studies

POV shot puts us into the shoes of the victim (*The Ring*).

A good use of close-ups (*The Ring*).

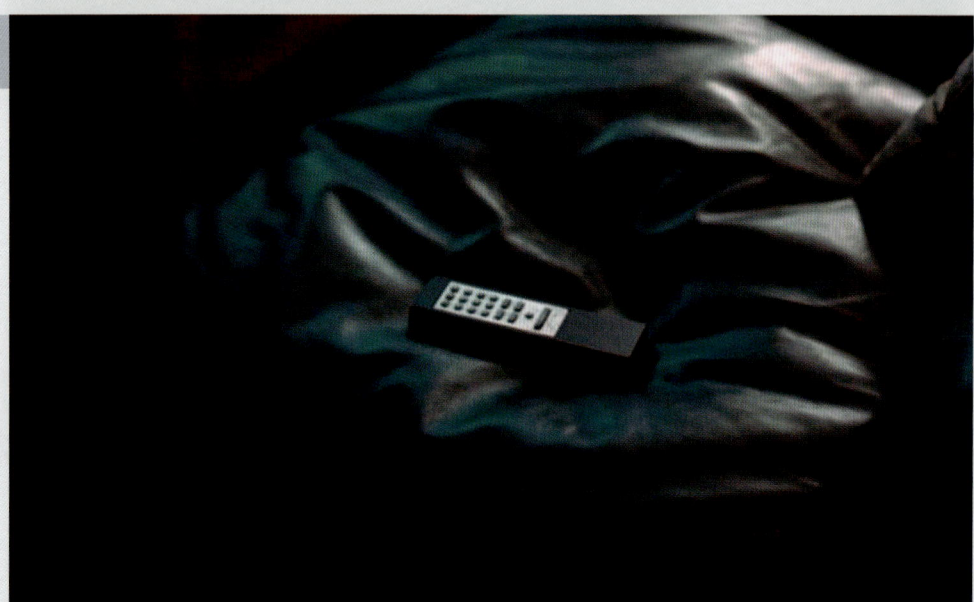

Another good use of a close-up (*The Ring*).

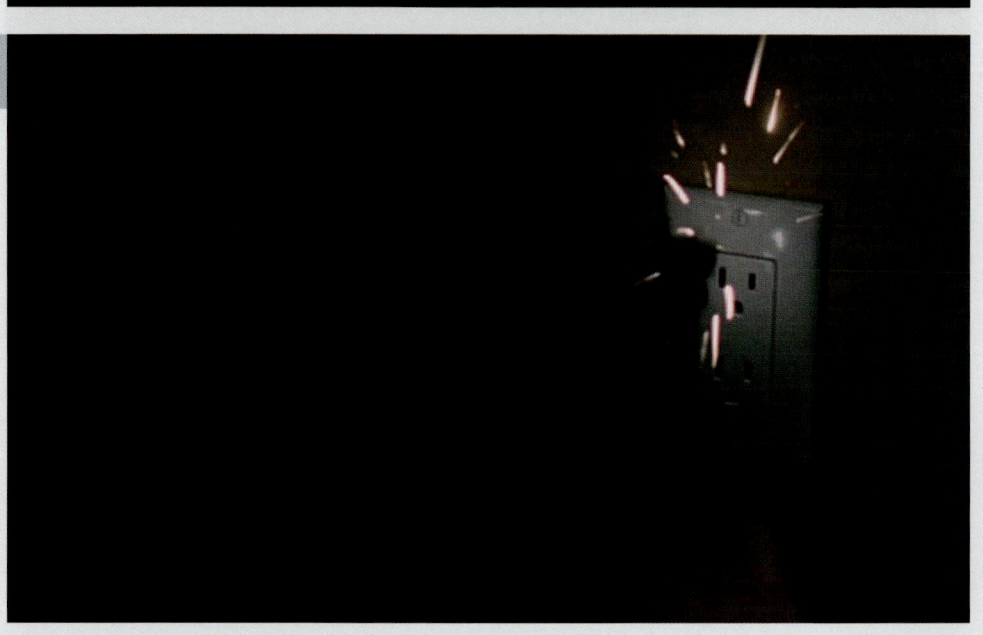

Part 5: Production

A mid-shot of Katie facing the television screen sets up the victim and the killer (as we later find out the killer comes through the television screen). It is also used again after the plug is pulled to give Katie a mini victory. However, this turns into a scare again when a figure appears to run behind her in the television reflection.

A two-shot of Katie and the killer (*The Ring*).

Quick Question 5.3

There are lots of shots of windows or glass in the opening. Why do you think this is? What could it be suggesting?

As Katie heads back upstairs, the camera is in an extreme high angle long shot for the first time. This makes Katie look very small and weak. She is the victim and as she walks up the stairs we feel she is walking into danger. Note also that the lighting is still very low key, creating a more sinister feel to the scene.

The victim in a high angled long shot (*The Ring*).

As she reaches the top of the stairs a low level shot highlights the water on the stairs. We see Katie once more at the end of the long shot. She is the victim once again approaching the danger.

Katie's bare feet make her look very vulnerable as she walks towards the water, which itself is often a symbol of life and death. As Katie opens the door we have two very fast zooms, one out from the television screen and one in to Katie's screaming face. This suggests the movement of something or someone coming out of the television screen and lunging towards Katie.

GCSE Film Studies

Task 5.18 — Go through your screenplay and look at the shots you are using. What kind of pace will this create? Is it the type of pace you want? If it isn't, think of ways you can change it.

There are many ways you can control and change the rhythm and pace of a film. Different types of edit such as cuts, dissolves and fades can do this. At the start of *The Ring* the film fades in to the establishing shot, almost like a slow reveal. At the end of the sequence fast cuts speed up the pace.

The pace of *The Ring* also goes up and down throughout the sequence. As previously suggested, audiences cannot cope with one high intensity scene after another so it is a good idea to try and raise the tension then lower it with a calmer scene before raising it again. One way *The Ring* did this was with the false scares, but it can also be achieved with the use of stylish cuts such as cross-cutting or graphic matching or even just by mixing longer scenes in with short ones.

Task 5.19 — Go through your screenplay and see if you have planned to use a variety of editing techniques. Use the checklist below to see if you can add any more. Keep notes in your portfolio to use in the evaluative analysis. Remember you must solely responsible for the editing of your sequence.

- ✓ Types of edit (cut, dissolve, fade)
- ✓ The principles of continuity editing (shot-reverse-shot)
- ✓ Cross-cutting
- ✓ Pace of editing
- ✓ Visual effects created in post-production
- ✓ The typical meanings associated with all of the above
- ✓ How continuity editing establishes relationships between characters
- ✓ How cross-cutting contributes to the portrayal of character
- ✓ How editing contributes to narrative development
- ✓ How editing generates response

Top tip

Don't be tempted to just pick a relevant song and play the track over your entire sequence. This won't show your knowledge and understanding of sound. Think about the sounds you want in your film and plan them in advance. Remember silence is a good use of sound.

Sound

Apart from the conversation between the girls at the beginning of the opening, there is not much dialogue in the sequence we have studied. That is good. It means the tension and suspense created is coming from the visuals and the sound alone. The film even opens on a black screen with just the sound of rain – what better way to introduce the genre?

The lack of background sounds in the opening make the sounds that do occur all the more heightened. When the phone rings, for example, it is very loud and cuts through the silence making the audience jump. This is the same when the white noise from the television stops Katie in her tracks in the kitchen.

Silence is used a lot in the opening as it keeps the audience holding their breath.

They are waiting for something to happen. When things make Katie jump, such as someone running behind her in the television reflection, sound effects are used to make the audience jump and feel the same fear Katie feels.

As the tension builds, electrical sounds echo faintly in the distance suggesting that something more supernatural is present. When Katie ascends the stairs, we hear the screeching violin aural motif for the first time. The audience will become familiar with this motif and quickly pick up that every time we hear this something bad happens.

The sounds of breathing and dripping water are heightened as Katie opens the door to the bedroom. We are at the peak of the suspense here. When she opens the door we are met with a very loud, exaggerated screech as Katie dies. The sound resembles the aural motif and mimics Katie's scream.

> **Task 5.20**
>
> Go through your screenplay and add in any sounds or periods of silence that may add to your extract. Think about the diegetic and non-diegetic sounds you want to incorporate. What sound effects will you use? Will you have any music? Any orchestral scores? What about an aural motif?

Representation

Think about how your will film portray your views about certain places, people or issues. How are the characters in your film represented? Have you got any archetypal or stereotypical characters in your film? *The Ring*'s first victim, Katie, is the usual young girl who has sex and ends up being a victim. Does your film follow any of these predefined conventions? Is your film saying about society? Is your film offering certain perspectives on gender, ethnicity, age and cultures?

Evaluative analysis

Whether you chose to do a screenplay or a film extract for your production, you must now produce an evaluative analysis. Unlike the production, the brief for the evaluative analysis will remain unchanged. It must be between 750 and 850 words and consist of three things:

- the aims of the genre film extract
- its influences, and
- an analysis of how at least three important parts of the production compare with similar genre films.

The first part is the shortest and should be easy enough. You know what genre your production is so state this. The intended audience you should have learnt through earlier studies in Components 1 and 2 as well as your own research.

This area of the evaluative analysis should be no more than two or three sentences as it is only intended as an introduction. If you have room you can always offer a little bit of information about your film.

> **Top tip**
>
> The example film used here (*The Ring*) was chosen specifically to show the kinds of thing you can achieve. There is nothing in this opening that you could not reproduce yourself. The opening is shot entirely in one house, the costumes are basic school uniform, the main props consist of a television, a phone, water and a fridge. It is the way the elements of film form have been combined that make the opening so effective. Planning properly will allow you to achieve similar results. Remember less is often more!

GCSE Film Studies

> For my production, I filmed the opening to a horror film entitled The Ring, which is about a video tape that kills you exactly seven days after you watch it. My film is aimed at predominantly male 18–24-year-olds and in the opening I aimed to set up the genre of the film and the main storyline/problem by showing the first death.

Task 5.21 Write your introduction to the evaluative analysis, identifying the genre and intended audience.

The next part of the evaluative analysis needs to give a brief indication of how key aspects from approximately three genre films have influenced your production. These can be films you have studied throughout the course.

This is where your portfolio or notebook will come in very handy, as you will be able to look back and see what types of things you liked when you watched other films of a similar genre. Perhaps you liked the found-footage style of films like *REC* (2007, Jaume Balagueró and Paco Plaza) *and The Blair Witch Project* (1999, Eduardo Sánchez and Daniel Myrick). Maybe you were influenced by the all-female cast of *The Descent* (2005, Neil Marshall) or the way Paris Hilton subverted the stereotype of the female victim in *House of Wax* (2005, Jaume Collet-Serra).

Whether you were influenced by the lack of music in Hitchcock's *The Birds* (1963) or the subverted meanings of light and dark in *Let the Right One In* (2008), this is the place to talk about it. You can also supplement your findings with stills from various films. You should aim to write a couple of paragraphs on this section totalling about 200 words in length.

If it suits your writing style, you may wish to combine sections two and three of the evaluative analysis. This may also be helpful if you want to include stills from a film that influenced you and your film so that comparisons can be drawn.

Task 5.22 Go through your portfolio/notebook and identify several influences you may like to discuss in your evaluative analysis. If applicable, source some screenshots or images that you may wish to include.

The final, and longest, part of the evaluative analysis is the third area where you should analyse how at least three important parts of the production compare with similar genre films (which may include those influencing the production). This section should be approximately 500 words.

Part 5: Production

For this section, don't fall into the trap of reliving the production experience. Moderators do not need to know a step-by-step account of what happened. Similarly, they do want more than a description of what you thought went well or didn't go well.

Let's take the opening of *The Ring* as our example. One of the areas I am going to analyse is the opening shot of the house.

> I wanted to get across the genre of the film right from the outset. I decided to open the film on a black screen with just the diegetic sound of heavy rain. This would immediately set up the negative tone and also suggest that there is something there that we can't see. I liked the slow pace used in *Let the Right One In* (2008) as I felt that a slow pace in a horror was more unusual and helped to slowly build tension, so I used a slow fade into the first shot.
>
> I then slowly zoomed into the establishing shot of the house to again slowly build the tension. I wanted to make the audience feel as if they were apprehensively walking towards this eerie looking building. I decided to zoom for eight seconds so that the slow pace was maintained and the audience could take in all the surroundings.

Top tip

Don't fall into the trap of saying you wanted a *Blair Witch Project* feel to your film so you have lots of shaky camera movements. By all means include some shaky footage but you should be aiming to incorporate several different types of camera movement.

Putting danger into a place that should be safe (*The Ring*).

GCSE Film Studies

> **Top tip**
> The best way to approach the third part of the evaluative analysis is to think of your production as a film that someone else has made. You are going to identify the elements of film form used and discuss what meanings and responses they generate.

> **Top tip**
> Use as much subject specific language in your evaluative analysis as you can. Correctly identify elements of film form.

The house itself I chose because, when filmed at a low angle this double-fronted building seems very imposing. The twisted, dead-looking vines on the house also connote ideas of entrapment and danger. The vines almost look red in the dull light giving the impression of blood and veins, suggesting there may be blood spilt in this house. Although it is a nice, middle-class house, because I chose to film it at night, in the rain, it seems a lot more intimidating and the audience knows the genre is going to be horror. The overhead high key light behind the tree is diffused and casts eerie shadows, whilst also highlighting the twisted branches of the tree. I was aware from my research that a lot of horror films take place in isolated locations, in the middle of nowhere such as woods; however, I wanted to put the danger into a place that is supposed to be safe – your home.

However, to keep that sense of isolation, the house doesn't appear to have any neighbours as I positioned the long shot so that they could not be seen. I also heightened the sound of the rain in post-production so that all other sounds were drowned out by the heavy rain. This makes the occupiers of the house seem very alone and vulnerable.

As you will notice I have combined sections two and three of the evaluative analysis here and have referred to my influences whilst analysing my film.

Task 5.23

Pick three shots that you would like to discuss in your evaluative analysis. One at a time, work through the following points to help write your analysis of each shot.

1. Using the framework of study, identify and discuss each applicable element of film form. Why did you make the decisions you made? What meaning or response has the element of film form created?

2. How did any of your portfolio work influence your decisions here?

3. Would you do anything differently if you could do it again?

Part 5: Production

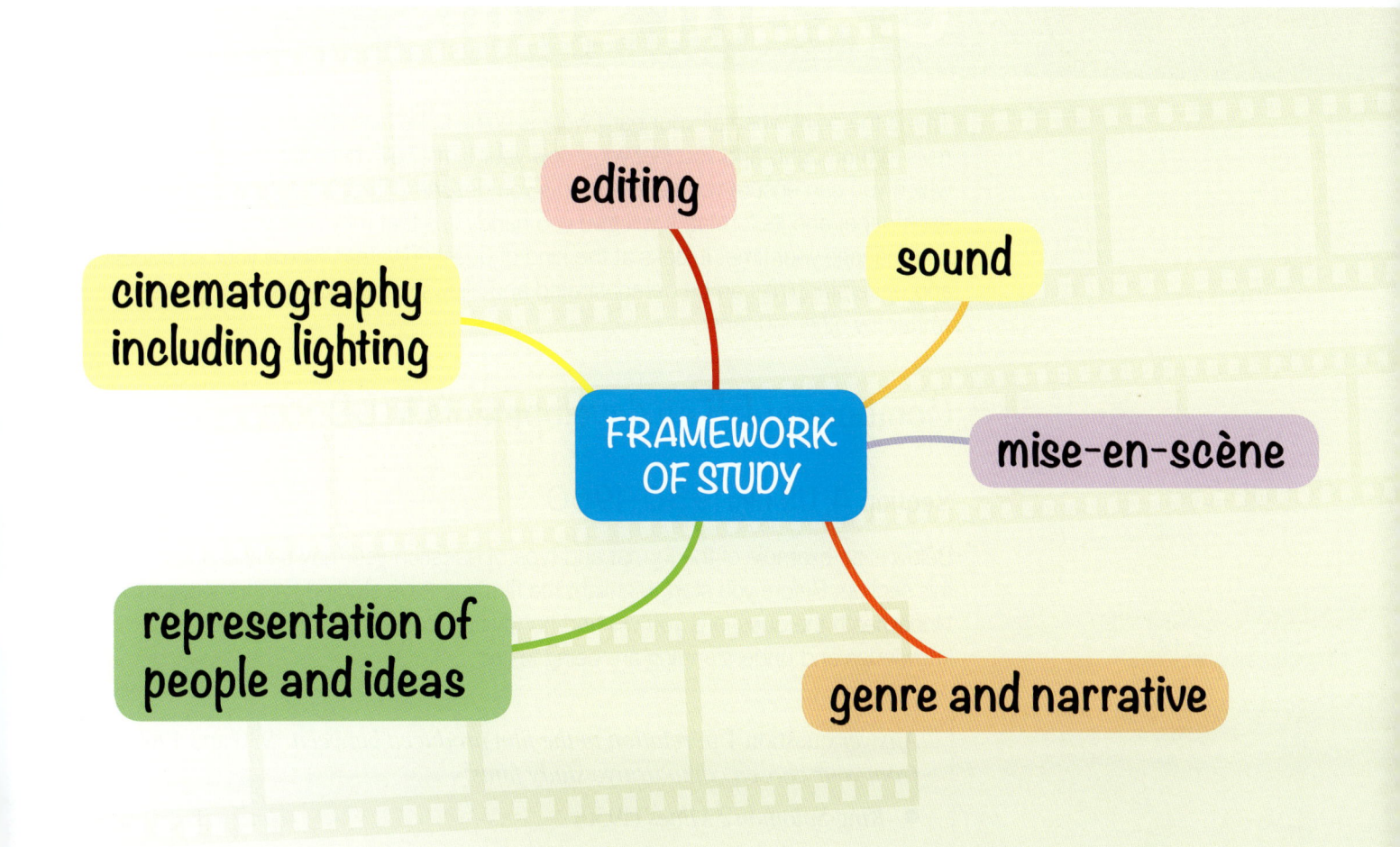

FRAMEWORK OF STUDY

- editing
- sound
- mise-en-scène
- genre and narrative
- representation of people and ideas
- cinematography including lighting

287

Part 6

Exam skills

This is the point when all your hard work is going to be tested! Even though you have revised thoroughly and you feel you know your films well, there are many ways in which you can ensure you get the marks you deserve. This part takes you through each paper and its format. It will give you handy tips that may help you to gain marks and manage your time. It looks at the kind of questions/areas where your knowledge and understanding can be demonstrated and allows you to examine responses written by other students.

Component 1: Key developments in US film

Section A: US film 1930–1960

Below is an example of the format and type of question you may be asked for this section. Before you start, highlight the film you have studied for this section. Underneath the questions you will find handy tips that will clarify which areas of knowledge and understanding are being tested.

> *Answer* question 1 *in relation to the film produced between* 1930 and 1960 *from your chosen comparative study films:*
> - *King Solomon's Mines* (1950)
> - *Singin' in the Rain* (1952)
> - *Rear Window* (1954)
> - *Rebel Without a Cause* (1955)
> - *Invasion of the Body Snatchers* (1956).
>
> 1. (a) Identify **one** genre convention used in your chosen film. [1]
>
>   (b) Briefly outline why conventions are used in genre films. [4]
>
>   (c) Explore how the convention you have identified is used in **one** sequence from your chosen film. In your answer, refer to at least **one** key element of film (e.g. cinematography, mise-en-scène, editing or sound). [10]

1. (a) Although this question is only a 1 mark question you will have to be specific in your answer. The genre convention will need to be a recognised one, for example setting. It will also need to be specific to your chosen film, for example *King Solomon's Mines* uses the adventure film typical protagonist of the swashbuckling hero, Allan Quartermain (Stewart Granger). In making a point about any genre convention it is important to stress typicality.

A 1950s hero (*King Solomon's Mines*).

1. (b) For 4 marks, here you should consider typicality in more detail: you could talk about how conventions act as the typical 'ingredients' of a genre film, or how they establish films as being in a particular genre. Going further you should also consider how these 'ingredients' become attractive to audiences both general and specific (fans). Again, examples from your chosen film should also be included, for example the typical use of expertly choreographed song and dance productions in musical films such as *Singin' in the Rain* when Gene Kelly dances with the umbrella to the film's title song.

Gene Kelly: *'laughing at clouds'* (*Singin' in the Rain*).

1. (c) To score in the top band here (9–10 marks) it is the demonstration and use of detail from your chosen film that will be the key to success. Sticking with the scene from *Singin' in the Rain*, you could talk about how the mise-en-scène and performance elements of film form are used to emphasise the mood and emotion of Gene Kelly's character. Describing that he is so happy at being in love with his girlfriend that not even the pouring rain of the sequence can dampen his mood. Gene Kelly further makes this meaning by the use of movement, from the very start his body seems to be light and relaxed – almost walking on air. As the tempo of the music increases he begins to dance in a joyful way, using aspects of the mise-en-scène like the lamp-post to demonstrate his playful and happy mood, as he jumps up and swings on it while telling us that he is *'laughing at clouds'*. Even the rain itself is used to further highlight his joy, as he emphasises beats in the song with spirited splashing. The two key aspects of your answer here would be the understanding of the meaning of the sequence and how the typical, or conventional, use of the elements of film form have been used in detail to create it for the audience.

GCSE Film Studies

Section A: US film 1961–1990

Question 2 in Section A focuses on a US film made between 1961 and 1990. Firstly, highlight the film you are going to write about. Again, under each question there are valuable hints on ways in which to demonstrate your knowledge and understanding.

Answer question 2 in relation to the film produced between 1961 and 1990 from your chosen comparative study films:

- *Raiders of the Lost Ark* (1981)
- *Grease* (1978)
- *Witness* (1985)
- *Ferris Bueller's Day Off* (1986)
- *E.T. the Extra-Terrestrial* (1982)

2. (a) Identify **one** example of cinematography used in your chosen film. [1]

   (b) Briefly explain what this example of cinematography typically suggests. [4]

   (c) Explore how this example of cinematography is used in **one** sequence from your chosen film. [10]

2. (a) Here again the need to be specific to your chosen film is important. To score the mark you will need to use the correct terminology in describing the example you choose from your film. Try to remember that cinematography includes any camera shot (relating to its distance, angle or movement) and/or any example of lighting (relating to direction or intensity of lighting). For example, the low angle shot used in *E.T. the Extra-Terrestrial* to show the men who are hunting E.T. in the woods at the beginning of the film.

You should take extra care here with your choice of example as you will have to discuss it, and other examples of it, in parts (b) and (c). So don't pick one that is so rare as there may be no other examples you can remember, and pick one where you are confident about the meaning the director is trying to convey to the audience through its use.

Low angle shot from *E.T. the Extra-Terrestrial*.

2. (b) Here you should begin to reap the benefits of carefully choosing your answer to question 2. (a). To score 4 marks you must be as clear as you can about the meaning behind your selection. You should discuss how a low angle shot such as this typically emphasises the threat of what we see: in this case the strange men. As it is a point-of-view (POV) shot it also serves to allow the audience to share the character's, E.T.'s, vulnerability.

Hopefully, you can see now how carefully choosing a camera shot that is used in the film to express a clear meaning throughout gives you both plenty of examples to use in discussing this, and other, meanings.

2. (c) In this final 10 mark question, to score in band 5 (9–10 marks) you must be as clear as you can about the meaning(s) behind your selection. In this example from the opening sequence you could talk about how E.T. is scared and hiding in the bushes at this point in the scene and that the low angle shot does two main things for the audience. Firstly, it allows us to share E.T.'s POV, so we share in his feelings. Secondly, by looking up at the men and only being able to see them from below the waist it conveys E.T.'s feeling of powerlessness and fear, as well as creating an air of unknown danger around these men. In your answer you should emphasise that this is a typical way to use a low angle POV shot, but also discuss how this sets up its use during the rest of the film that is less typical. Discussing how much of what we see is shot using this type of cinematography is unusual but it is used by Spielberg to show us the shared viewpoint of both Elliot and E.T. in a film that looks at the world and its adults from their young and innocent eyes.

Hopefully by now you can see the full benefit of carefully choosing an aspect of cinematography that is used throughout the film in both typical and non-typical ways, so you have plenty of ideas to talk about. This is a key skill to practise to make sure you can show a clear knowledge and understanding of the key aspects of film form.

Section A: The US film comparative study

The final question in Section A asks you to compare each of the films you have studied. In order to make sure you do this, first highlight your film pairing on the exam paper. Below are handy tips that will help to improve your exam technique.

Answer question 3 *in relation to* **both** *your chosen comparative study films:*
- *King Solomon's Mines* (1950) and *Raiders of the Lost Ark* (1981)
- *Singin' in the Rain* (1952) and *Grease* (1978)
- *Rear Window* (1954) and *Witness* (1985)
- *Rebel Without a Cause* (1955) and *Ferris Bueller's Day Off* (1986)
- *Invasion of the Body Snatchers* (1956) and *E.T. the Extra-Terrestrial* (1982).

3. Compare how the same theme is explored in each of your comparative study films.

   In your answer, you should consider:
   - how characters and narratives illustrate the theme you have identified
   - similarities between the way the theme you have identified is explored in each of your films
   - differences between the way the theme you have identified is explored in each of your films. [20]

GCSE Film Studies

> **Top tip**
> Make sure you compare and contrast both films and use terminology accurately. When exploring themes show what you have learnt by relating them to the context.

> **Top tip**
> Good answers will analyse the ways in which particular scenes connect with other moments in the film to create a coherent view if a particular issue.

3. In answering this question you must remember two things that will be true of any comparative question you may be asked. Firstly, make sure you discuss both the films you have studied, giving equal weighting if possible. Secondly, make sure you discuss the same theme for each film. If you don't do this then you are limiting your mark to a maximum of 10.

Two useful ways to approach comparing a theme in two films are by asking: what does the film say about this theme and how does it say it through the use of the key aspects of film form? Do not be afraid of using the obvious, in the case of *Invasion of the Body Snatchers* (1956) and *E.T. the Extra-Terrestrial* (1982) the main theme is our attitude to aliens. If we choose to discuss the theme of 'the alien' it is useful as both films have a very different attitude to the theme, which will make the comparison more straightforward.

You would start by pointing out that in *Invasion of the Body Snatchers* the alien is the threat to us compared to *E.T. the Extra-Terrestrial* where it is the people that are the threat to the alien. To make your point you should describe at least one example of film language from each film where this is shown. To aim for the band 5 marks you should explore this friend/enemy approach to aliens in as many different ways as you can. In exploring why the films take such differing approaches you could cover the different kinds of narratives each director wanted to construct – *Invasion of the Body Snatchers* is about thrilling the audience with a scary story, whereas *E.T. the Extra-Terrestrial* is about exploring the emotions most of us share from our childhood. In discussing the theme in this way you should also touch on how each of them reflects in some way the context of their production. In other words, in *Invasion of the Body Snatchers* people in America were scared of communism and the aliens tried to take over the world, reflecting these Cold War feelings. In *E.T. the Extra-Terrestrial*, although the Cold War is still going on, people were more concerned with the 1980's changes in the American family, and the film reflects on some of these.

Above all, when making a comparison make sure you cover both differences and similarities, referring as directly as you can to the ways the key aspects of film form are used to create these meanings.

An alien invader (*Alien*).

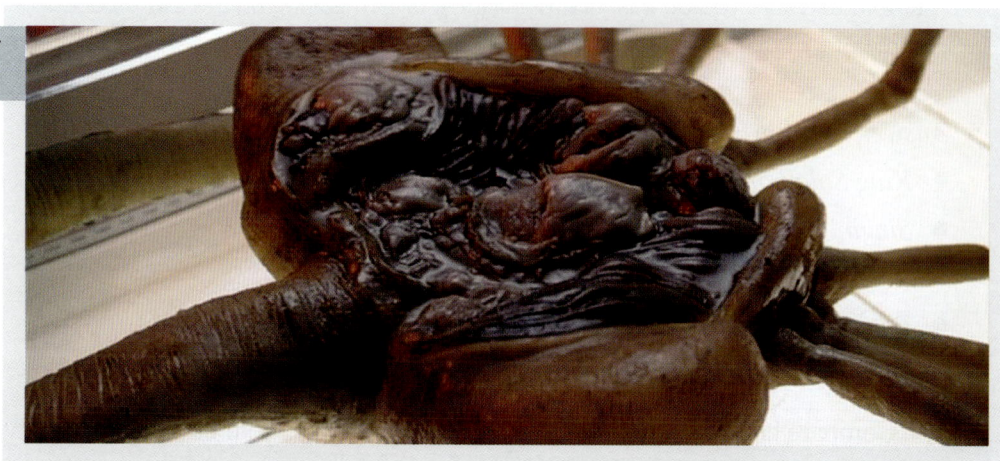

Part 6:
Exam skills

An alien invader's opposite (*E.T. the Extra-Terrestrial*)?

Section B: Key developments in film and film technology

In this part of the paper you will have to make sure that you have done your revision. Using the timelines in this book, revision notes and practice knowledge tests from you teacher will be essential.

> 4. **(a)** In which decade was the first full colour feature film produced? [1]
>
>   State the correct answer in your answer book: 1930s 1940s 1950s.
>
>   **(b)** Name **two** of the five major studios operating in Hollywood in the 1940s. [2]
>
>   **(c)** Give **two** examples of how film technology **is** used in **one** of the US films you have studied. Name the film you have chosen. [2]

4. (a) The answer is the 1930s, for 1 mark. Even if you cannot remember this straight away you can try to use other knowledge to help you work it out. You might remember that the 1920s was the time of silent films so maybe sound comes just after that. Or you might know that the 1950s was all about the rise of television, so films would have had sound by then. The 1940s were when World War II happened and films were 'talkies' before then. All these clues should help you to find the right answer. But remember there is no substitute for good revision and at the very least a guess, never miss questions such as this out – what have you got to loose?

4. (b) The possible answers here are Paramount, Warner Brothers, 20th Century Fox, MGM or Metro-Goldwyn-Meyer, and RKO. Again, if you are not sure here you need to try and use what you do know in the best way you can. Four of these are still around today so naming a big modern studio gives you a chance. Revision again is key, as you will be wrong if you say Universal, United Artists or Columbia (the so-called 'little three') or Disney, as none of these were part of the big five studios that owned their own cinemas.

4. (c) Do not be scared by the phrase 'film technology', as it sounds more complicated than it is. When you look at the list of technologies you can use to answer this question there are lots of things you will recognise. You could use:

293

GCSE Film Studies

> - widescreen technology (for most of the 1950s Hollywood films)
> - Steadicam technology used, for example in the US independent films
> - the use of some CGI – computer generated imagery (used in US mainstream films)
> - a reference to colour processing rather than just 'colour', e.g. Eastmancolor or Technicolor
> - sound technology such as synchronised sound, Dolby sound, post-production sound effects.
>
> So, to get both marks you might say, 'In my film, *Ferris Bueller's Day Off*, it was filmed in 2.35: 1 (CinemaScope) widescreen in Metrocolor.'
>
> Remember, also, the instruction to the examiner, 'All valid explanations must be credited', which means that any film technology can be used here, not just the examples from the list.

Section C: US independent films

Your final question focuses on your study of US independent film. There is just one question, which carries 15 marks. You will have been provided with stimulus material in order to inform your responses to this question before the exam.

Answer question 5 *on* one *of the following films:*

- *Little Miss Sunshine* (2006, Dayton/Faris)
- *Juno* (2007, Reitman)
- *The Hurt Locker* (2008, Bigelow)
- *Whiplash* (2014, Chazelle)
- *Me and Earl and the Dying Girl* (2015, Gomez-Rejon)

5. Explore how **one** example of specialist writing on the chosen film you have studied has deepened your understanding of the film. Refer to at least **one** sequence from your chosen film to illustrate your answer.

   In your answer, you should:
   - identify the example of specialist writing you are using in the box provided in your answer book
   - briefly describe **one** key idea from the example of specialist writing you have studied
   - outline what this key idea suggests about your chosen film
   - show how this idea compares with your own views on the film (use **one** sequence from your chosen film to illustrate this).

   [15]

> Another big mark question and the best advice here is to use the bullet points. If you do this then you should have something to talk about and the bullet points will help you to structure your discussion in such a way as to give you a good chance at a band 5 mark (9–10). Equally important is to refer directly to a sequence from your film; if you don't then the most you can get is 6 marks. Your teacher will have discussed examples of specialist writing on your chosen film with you and you should have focused on the ones you found most interesting in your revision.

Remember, specialist writing is often more interesting when it either includes ideas brand new to you or ones that really differ from your own. If you can prepare ones such as this then you should have more to say in answering a question such as this.

Taking it step by step, make sure that you give a clear identification of the specialist writing you have studied, naming the author, publication, year and title – as much information as you can really. It is also important to remember that an idea can include any aspect of the film – its key and structural elements, its narrative and themes, its contexts.

Choose the idea you want to discuss carefully, it may be one that you want to argue with as you only agree with it in part, this should help develop your answer. Don't spend too much time describing it (you may well be short of time at this point) but do make sure you state it as clearly as you can and make sure you only discuss one idea as there is not time or space for any more. In the next step of outlining what this key idea suggests about your chosen film you should take more time and use examples from the film to make your explanations clear. The final, and perhaps most important, step is to talk about both the similarities and differences between your view and the writer's. This may reflect what you have thought about, discussed in class or written in essays in preparation for this type of question.

The ways you can discuss the specialist writing can vary but commonly it may be about the things in the film you may not have noticed at first; in other words, what the specialist writing has helped you to realise. Examples of these could be: uses of key elements of film form you missed; new information about the making of the film; suggested interpretations of the characters; analysis of the narrative; different contexts of the film; and the themes and issues it raises for the author. This list contains very specific topics; it is also acceptable to take a more overall approach and offer an interpretation of the film you have achieved as a result of the specialist writing. You can challenge or question the specialist writing but you will have to make sure you have good evidence from the film and your chosen sequence to back this up.

This brings us back to the most important aspect of answering the question, after using the bullet points – the use of a sequence to support your answer. When you write your answer, discussion of a sequence from the film will support the deeper understanding you have gained of the film. Preparing at the very least one sequence as part of your revision is key here. You should be very familiar with it and have made clear notes on its use of key elements of film form, its relevance to the structural elements of film form and any relevant contexts it may have. If you have made this preparation, then aiming for a band 5 mark will be much more straightforward.

A short plan of how to approach the bullet points for this question for *The Hurt Locker* is shown below:

- My specialist film writing: From the *Journal of War & Culture Studies*. Embodiment in the war film: *Paradise Now* and *The Hurt Locker*. War as a medium of experience by Robert Burgoyne.
- The idea put forward by Robert Burgoyne of how the physical vulnerability of both the suicide bomber and the leader of the bomb deactivation squad contrasts with the modern trend in war for drone strikes and the distance, both moral and physical, of remote targeting and weaponry.
- It helps to explain how powerful the film is and how real war is at this level, and how far away from video games it is unlike the use of drones.

> **Top tip**
> Make sure that you have fully understood what has been said in the specialist writing stimulus. If initially there are words you are not familiar with, or terms used that you don't understand, make sure that you find out what they mean.

GCSE Film Studies

- This idea of physical distance making it more or less real for participants is a really interesting idea to think about in the film but wider context of what war really is and means for both sides should also be considered.
- The sequence I would use is where the squad is called to a car bomb outside the UN building. Here we have the close-up element of the disposal and the more distanced element of the helicopter overhead and the sniper on the roof top. These are two key aspects to explore the idea suggested by Robert Burgoyne.

The Hurt Locker – the distance of war, both moral and physical.

Component 2: Global film: narrative, representation and film style

This second exam paper gives you the chance to demonstrate just how much you know about your chosen 'global' films and to consider the ways in which they create meaning and response through film form and film structures. It also allows you to focus on the ways in which your study films communicate ideas and issues – their style and aesthetic qualities.

Each of the films you have studied present contrasting social and cultural film worlds. They offer a wide variety of representations of different people and places. They present important ideas about, for example, gender, ethnicity, age or different cultures. They may reflect the social, cultural or political context in which they were made. They also may have challenged you to think about groups of people and their situation in a different way.

> **Top tip**
> Choosing an appropriate key scene is very important. When you are asked to do this in your exam make sure you spend time choosing an appropriate sequence. If asked to only refer to one sequence do not talk about the whole film.

Time management

You will have just 90 minutes to complete the exam.

There are three question sections. This means you should spend no more 30 minutes on each section.

Each section contains stepped questions:

a) A simple 1 or 2 marker. This requires you to make one or two simple points.

b) A follow-up question to (a). It's worth between 3 or 4 marks so try to make at least three points but don't repeat what you have already said in (a). Try to make sure you only spend a maximum of five minutes on these brief questions.

This this leaves you 25 minutes for the big mark question or questions. **The final question is worth 15 marks so give this priority – at least 15+ minutes.**

> **Top tip**
> Read through all of the stepped questions before starting on a section. Often your initial choice for a 1 or 2 mark question will affect your ability to give good answers for (c) or (d) questions.

GCSE Film Studies

Section A: Global English language films (produced outside the US)

The question in this section will focus on film form, context and **narrative**. Below is an example of the possible ways in which your knowledge and understanding of some of the focus areas will be tested. The questions are stepped; you should make sure you read through (b) and (c) before answering question (a).

The writing in red is an example of one student's responses – Amy – to each part of Section (A). She has studied *Rabbit-proof Fence*.

Section A: Global English language film (produced outside US)

Answer question 1 *on* one *of the following films:*

- *Rabbit-proof Fence* (2002, Noyce, Australia)
- *Slumdog Millionaire* (2008, Boyle, UK)
- *District 9* (2009, Blomkamp, South Africa)
- *An Education* (2009, Scherfig, UK)
- *Song of the Sea* (2014, Moore, Eire)

1. **(a)** What do you understand by the social context of a film? [2]

The social context of the film could be where and when it was set or where or when it was made. It's how films reflect parts of society, perhaps in terms of racism or other forms of social inequality.

1. **(b)** Briefly describe the main social context of your chosen film. [3]

The film is set in the Australian outback in the mid-1930s. It shows how badly the Aboriginal people were treated at that time. Molly, the central character, is taken from her home by the police and put in a settlement because she had a white father and a black mother. The aim was to breed the blackness out of her.

1. **(c)** Explore how the narrative of your chosen film reflects its social context.

   In your answer, you should consider:
   - how key characters reflect the social context
   - how the social context is built into the narrative
   - at least one example from the film's narrative that demonstrates its social context. [15]

The key characters are Molly and Mr A.O. Neville and Moodoo. Molly drives the narrative. She begins the story with a voice-over (as an old woman) telling us what we are about to see is a true story. She gives us some facts about how her family has become dependent on the store in Jigalong for supplies. This builds on the facts given after the title sequence that tell us about the law that allows young half-caste Aboriginal children to be taken away from their families in order to 'breed the blackness' out of them. Although we hear the older Molly as the film begins, most of the narrative is linear. We follow young Molly, Daisy and Gracie when they are taken from their home at Jigalong, to the River Moore settlement. When there they are inspected by Mr Neville so he can judge just how white they are.

> They are treated like aliens in their own land. Neville seems to have no understanding of racism as we think about it today. The narrative takes the form of a journey. We see what happens to the girls when they escape. The events that take place during the escape keep us interested in their long journey home. Moodoo, another key character, is an Aboriginal tracker; it is his job to catch Molly but we are never sure where his loyalties lie. He is employed by Mr Neville and has to obey orders but he is also an Aborigine and has respect for Molly and her fierce need to go back to her family and her true culture. Mr Neville is the British Chief Protector; the film shows him in a negative light. The first time we see him he is giving a lecture to a group of elderly white women. His power and importance is underlined by a low angle shot looking up as he is on the stage. He is shown as powerful and threatening, his lecture talking about all the Aboriginals being under his protection is used as a sound bridge over the images of Molly's mother and grandmother as they lie in the dust after Molly has been taken away. Neville also drives the narrative, Molly is trying to escape and he is determined to bring her back and 'civilise' her. The fact that this is a true story, its real social context is reinforced after the credits when we see actual footage of the old Molly and are told that she was taken back to the River Moore settlement many times only to escape again.

Amy is obviously a good candidate. She is succinct when answering parts (a) and (b). She shows a good understanding of social context and how it might be evidenced in film and describes the social context clearly – Australia in the 1930s and the racist treatment of the Aboriginal community under British rule.

Part (c) addresses each of the three bullet points in a coherent, well-argued way. The candidate selects three relevant characters and describes their role within the film's narrative. All three, Moodoo, Molly and A.O. Neville, are considered in terms of their social context. Moodoo is the Aborigine man caught between two cultures, Molly refuses to give up her culture and will not be forced into becoming something else and Neville is considered as the powerful aggressor who has absolute belief that what he's doing is right. Several relevant examples from the film's narrative are given in order to demonstrate social context. She demonstrates an excellent knowledge and understanding of social context is shown and excellent points are used in order to develop a strong point-of-view – terminology is used accurately throughout.

Section B: Global non-English language films

The question in this section will focus on film form, context and the representation of people, places and ideas. Below is an example of the possible ways in which your knowledge and understanding of some of the focus areas will be tested. The questions are still stepped so you should make sure you read through (b), (c) and (d) before answering question (a).

Top tip
Make sure that you maintain your focus on the areas of knowledge and understanding being tested by the questions. Section A requires a focus on context and narrative underline or highlight these terms before you complete your answers.

GCSE Film Studies

In this section you must answer question 2, focusing on one of the following films:
- *Spirited Away* (2001, Miyazaki, Japan)
- *Tsotsi* (2005, Hood, 2005)
- *Let the Right One In* (2008, Alfredson, Sweden)
- *The Wave* (2008, Gansel, Germany)
- *Wadjda* (2012, Al Mansour, Saudi Arabia).

Below is an example of one student's answers, Connor.

2. (a) Name and briefly describe **one** young character in your chosen film. [2]

Tsotsi

2. (b) Briefly describe the costume of this character on their first appearance. [3]

He's got a black jacket and red T-shirt on.

2. (c) Briefly explore how other aspects of mise-en-scène (setting, location and props) are used to create your first impression of this young character in **one** sequence from the beginning of your chosen film. [5]

He's in his house and it looks poor. He don't say anything just look out of the door. When he goes out the gang follow him and he still don't say anything, he's the boss. He walks through the town, it's got lots of shacks and a dusty road. People are lined up to get water from a tap. Another gangster shouts at him but he just lift his finger and carry on walking.

2. (d) Explore how young people are represented in your chosen film. Refer to at least **one** sequence where young people are shown.

In your answer, you should consider:
- how at least two young people are represented in your chosen film
- how two of the following contribute to the representation of young people in your film – cinematography, mise-en-scène, editing or sound
- how at least one sequence demonstrates the representation of young people. [15]

Tsotsi is a thug. He is the leader of a gang who kill a man on a train in order to get money. Boston is a member of his gang but he has gone to school and didn't want to kill anybody. He has a fight with Tsotsi but Tsotsi feels bad after and wants to make it up to him. We don't know at the start what has happened to Tsotsi but later on flashbacks show his mum dying of aids and his dad beating a dog. Lots of close-ups are used for him and at first he looks blank but at the end he cries and shakes as he give the baby back. In the start all of his gang are with him in his shack. They are gambling and shouting, they have dirty clothes and one of the gang has a sharp spike. Boston wears glasses to make himself look more clever. At first they all look bad but at the end Tsotsi has a white shirt on and he does the right thing.

300

Part 6:
Exam skills

Read through Conner's paper once again.

Task 6.1

1. Go through each question and make notes on where he may have lost marks and where he might have gained marks.
2. In pairs write an examiner's report on Conner's paper outlining what he has done well. Finish with a paragraph giving some simple advice on how he could have gained higher marks.

Section C: Contemporary UK films (produced after 2010)

The question in this section will focus on film form, context and style, and the aesthetic qualities of film. There are a number of ways of talking, writing and thinking about your film's aesthetic qualities. You could consider the 'look' of the film – are there any beautiful, shocking, surprising images? You could consider the artistic influences on your film – other filmmakers, writers, musicians, etc. You could consider style – interesting or innovative ways of using elements of film form. The questions in the exemplar paper below ask you to consider how one element of cinematography, lighting, is used in your focus film. It then broadens out in order to allow you to think about the ways in which all the elements of cinematography work together to create a particular 'look'.

Advice about the ways to tackle questions (a) to (d) is given in red underneath each question. Make sure you have read through all the questions before starting as your choice for question (a) will influence your response to (b), (c) and (d).

Answer question 3 *on ONE of the following films:*

- *Submarine* (2010, Ayoade, UK)
- *Attack the Block* (2011, Cornish, UK)
- *My Brother the Devil* (2012, El Hosaini, UK)
- *Skyfall* (2012, Mendes, UK)
- *Brooklyn* (2015, Crowley, UK).

GCSE Film Studies

3. (a) Identify **one** example of lighting used in your film. [1]

A simple 1 mark question on one element of cinematography. Just make sure you use appropriate terminology for whichever **one** you choose, for example high/low key lighting, backlighting, top lighting, diffused lighting, reference to filters (possibly colour filters).

3. (b) Briefly outline what this example of lighting typically suggests. [4]

You named the type of lighting in (a) now refer to the effect it typically creates and the response it aims to get from an audience. For example, low key lighting is typically used to create an atmosphere of mystery or suspense. It may suggest a particular character has dark secrets. It casts shadows that can give characters places to hide or spy on others. It can help to create a dark environment where all kinds of dark deeds take place. 4 marks – four quick points made.

3. (c) Briefly explore how your example of lighting is used in **one** sequence. [5]

Begin by identifying your **one** sequence! Make sure you make a number of different points about the use of lighting in the sequence. You may want to pick a sequence that moves from one location to another. For example, the sequence in Skyfall that begins in the Art Gallery (see Conner's response to (d) below) when high key lighting in the Gallery creates a very different set of meanings to the low key lighting of Shanghai at night.

3. (d) Explore how cinematography and lighting help to create the film's 'look'.

Refer to at least **one** sequence in your answer.

In your answer, you should refer to:

- camera shots and movement
- framing including lighting
- relevant aspects of mise-en-scène. [15]

You could focus on the same sequence that you used for (d), as this question asks you about the role of cinematography (including lighting) and how it helps to create a particular style or 'look' in your film. However, you may then find it difficult not to repeat points made in (c). So make sure you are confident that you can say enough for this big 15 marker without repeating ideas if you do opt to use the same sequence.

The question says you **should** refer to each of the bullet points, this means you will lose marks if you don't consider each of them in your answer. That doesn't mean you have to deal with them separately as we know all the elements of film form work together to create meaning and response. For example, when considering mise-en-scène you will also think about framing, lighting and the kind of camera shot used. In order to reach the higher bands you should be able to refer to at least one key sequence and to:

- describe what you think the 'look' of the film
- consider the selection of shots and how they are emphasised through framing and lighting
- refer to the ways cinematography and lighting work together with mise-en-scène.

Part 6: Exam skills

Light, shadows, reflections, where are they, who are they? (*Skyfall*).

Top tip
When considering mise-en-scène think of how the objects and people in the frame have been positioned. It will be lit in a certain way, contain important props and costumes, some things will be in the background others in the foreground.

Below are excerpts from Amy and Conner's responses to part (d) and a copy of the marking scheme for this question. Look carefully at the annotation that highlights where knowledge and understanding is demonstrated by each candidate. Amy has studied *Submarine* and Conner has studied *Skyfall*.

---

4. (d) *Submarine* uses many different techniques in order to create different 'looks' in different parts of the film. Oliver Tate likes to imagine his life as a film and near the beginning of the film he imagines how people will react when he dies so we see the reactions of his school mates, a news broadcast, a vigil, a press conference all giving tributes. When he begins his relationship with Jordana he makes a grainy film of their days together. Oliver is obsessed with filmmaking and so is the director Richard Ayoade who uses many techniques from early famous film directors such as Jean-Luc Godard. For example, in the scene under the bridge when Oliver meets Jordana there are frequent jump cuts from one to another as they meet and finally kiss. This gives a feeling of unreality and humour. The opening sequence of Submarine begins in Oliver Tate's bedroom. He is sitting on the floor and a mid-shot shows us that his walls are full of posters. He is sitting on the floor and a submarine is painted on the wall next to him. The film posters signal his interest in film and the submarine is one of lots of references to water and the bottom of the sea that happen throughout the film. Oliver and his Dad, a marine biologist, both suffer from depression and his Dad says it makes him feel like he is underwater.

When Oliver gets up to look out of his window to look outside we see a series of long shots sweeping over the hills and valleys giving a sense of place and remoteness. The images are slightly grainy as natural light was used, the cinematographer uses natural light a lot during the film because he thought the natural light gave the film a special soft quality. Oliver's voice-over the landscape shots tells us about himself but from his own point-of-view. We are given a picture of what Oliver thinks he is like, this isn't real. After the long shots of the countryside an over-the-shoulder shot shows Oliver looking out to sea, he seems isolated. The blue colour palette adds to the feeling of sadness and isolation.

Annotations:
- Identifies how different techniques can create a different look.
- Begins to develop a point-of-view.
- Describes the different elements of tribute sequence.
- Cinematography.
- Influences on directorial style.
- Terminology and meaning identified in key sequence.
- Shot identified plus meaning.
- Mise-en-scène linked to key themes.
- Shot identified plus meaning.
- Use of light and its effect.
- Shot identification and meaning.
- Colour filter and meaning.

303

GCSE Film Studies

Task 6.2

1. Copy the following excerpt from Conner's answer and underline the parts that you think will gain him marks. Write brief annotations in the margins (as in Amy's response).

2. Answer question (d) using your own focus film. Ask a classmate to underline and annotate it and write brief constructive comments on how you might improve your response.

In the sequence when Bond meets Q for the first time in an Art Gallery both sit down on a bench in front of some old paintings. When they talk to each other there are a lot of mid shots, they are both at the front of the frame looking straight ahead. The lighting is bright so they can be seen clearly and they both seem on the same level. There are some close-ups of important props such as Bond's new gun and a transmitter this shows us he is going to need them later on. The gallery has a glass roof, which gives extra light from above. When the scene moves to abroad it's night, a bird's-eye view shows the city from above and there's lots of skyscrapers and signs all lit up. Bond follows the bad man into a big building, when Bond gets into the building its dark and the light seems to come from outside so lots of shadows are made. This gives him places to hide when he's looking for the bad man. The top floor of the building is dark, because it's got so many glass windows but the flashing lights from outside light up the fight when Bond finally gets to face the man. It's hard to make out which is Bond cos you can only see their outline so we are kept guessing.

Glossary

16mm film A frequently used, economical gauge of film. 16mm refers to the width of the film. It is not generally used for mainstream films unless the filmmaker wants to create a gritty or grainy look for the film.

35mm The film gauge or width most commonly used for motion pictures and chemical still photography. It is significantly more expensive than 16mm film but is seen as the cost-effective option for mainstream films producing a good trade-off between price and quality of image.

180-degree rule A general rule used in cinematography and editing that aims to ensure that the camera is kept on one side of the action and the audience does not feel disorientated. For example, when two characters are having an on-screen conversation and we only see one character as he/she speaks, this rule ensures that the on-screen character keeps looking towards where the other (off-screen) character is standing or sitting.

Academic study Usually used to describe work carried out in schools, colleges, and universities, especially work that involves studying and reasoning skills rather than practical skills.

Action The story/description in each scene.

Action codes Significant events that move the narrative on in a particular direction, e.g. Mr Neville's phone call to the police in Jigalong to take Molly, Gracie and Daisy to the River Moore settlcment.

Aesthetic Concerned with beauty or the appreciation of beauty. Designed to give pleasure through beauty. Of, or relating to, art or beauty.

Aestheticised To depict as being pleasing or artistically beautiful; represent in an idealised or refined manner.

Affluent Having a great deal of money or other material goods.

Allegory A story, poem, picture or film narrative that can be interpreted to reveal a hidden meaning, typically a moral or political one.

Ambient sound Sounds used to create a sense of place, e.g. birds singing and trees rustling in a woodland.

Ambiguity Something that is unclear or confusing, or can be understood in more than one way.

Anamorphic The creation of a distorted image that appears normal when viewed with an appropriate lens. Typically used when shooting a widescreen picture on standard 35mm film with its non-widescreen aspect ratio.

Androgynous Having both masculine and feminine qualities.

Archetype An easily recognised representation of a character that has been used over a long period of time.

Art house classics An art house film is a film that is intended to be a serious artistic work rather than a piece of popular entertainment aimed at a mass market. Art House Classics are the most highly regarded of these, often made during the 20th century.

Artistic merit A term used by critics to judge, appreciate or evaluate a cultural product (in this case film) as a work of art. Critics and academics frequently view a film's artistic merit as more important than its entertainment value.

Aspect ratio The ratio of the width to the height of an image or screen.

Audio-visual Using both sight and sound, typically in the form of images and recorded speech or music.

Aural Relating to the ear and hearing.

Auteur A filmmaker whose individual style and complete control over all elements of production give a film its personal and unique stamp.

Authenticity Real or genuine: not copied or false, true and accurate, made to be or look just like an original.

Baby boomer A person who was born between 1946 and 1964.

Back projected Sometimes also called a rear projection. Way of projecting images onto a translucent screen so that they are viewed from the opposite side. Used to create the illusion that the characters in the foreground are moving. It was widely used for many years in driving scenes, e.g. *Psycho* (1960, Alfred Hitchcock) or to show other forms of distant background motion, e.g. *King Solomon's Mines*.

GCSE Film Studies

Binary oppositions   Characters or ideas that represent sets of opposite values, e.g. good and evil, light and dark.

Bird's-eye view   The camera is placed directly above a subject, looking straight down.

Blockbuster   Any film that takes over 100 million dollars at the American box office. Usually created with both huge production and marketing budgets.

Blocked or blocking   Originally a theatre term referring to the positioning and movement of the actors on the stage. In cinema, blocking a scene entails working out the details of an actor's moves in relation to the camera and lighting.

Box office   The financial success or failure of a movie measured by the total value of ticket sales.

Brand recognition   How easily a consumer can correctly identify a particular product or service just by viewing the product's or service's logo tag line, packaging or advertising campaign. How famous a business is.

Canted angle   When the image is on an angle rather than on a straight horizontal line.

Cataclysmic   A term used to describe a violent upheaval that causes great destruction or brings about disastrous change.

Catharsis   The process of releasing strong emotions through a particular activity or experience, e.g. watching a moving film or listening to sad music.

Cause and effect   Something that triggers an event or action (cause) and the effect of the event or action.

CCTV   Closed-circuit television is a TV system in which signals are not publicly distributed but are monitored, primarily for surveillance and security purposes.

Celtic mythology   The ancient Celts had a vibrant mythology made up of hundreds of tales featuring romance, magic and heroism. The Celts did not record their myths in writing but passed them down through the generations orally.

Characters   The people who feature in the film's world.

Chiaroscuro   An Italian term originally used in art to refer to the high contrast light and darkness in Renaissance paintings. Later used in in cinema to describe the use of high and low key lighting in, for example, film noir films.

Chinese lanterns   A great low-budget method for creating soft, diffused light in a number of directions.

Chronological   The arrangement of things following one after another in time.

Cinematic   Does it feel like we are watching a film? Having qualities characteristic of films – big screen, big sound, big drama, a feeling of created or designed intensity. Adding additional layers of meaning, making the viewer involved and the ability to create a story in a viewer's mind.

Cinephile   A devoted moviegoer, especially one knowledgeable about the cinema.

Circular narrative   A narrative that starts at the end then goes back in time to return to this point later on.

Classic Hollywood three-act structure   A narrative structure based on cause and effect. Occurrences are organised along a line of action and connected through a theme or themes.

Claustrophobic   A fear of being in closed or small spaces or an unsettling, uncomfortable feeling caused by being in a situation that limits or restricts you.

Cliché   A stereotyped expression; a sentence or phrase, usually expressing a popular or common thought or idea, that has lost originality.

Codes and conventions   The detailed 'rules' of a genre – the elements of film form and structures we come to expect when we hear a genre name.

Cold War   The non-violent conflict between the US and the former USSR after 1945 that would last until 1990.

Collective memory   The memory of a group of people, passed from one generation to the next.

Coming of age   Term used to describe films which feature young people in process of growing up or entering into adulthood.

Composition   How the elements of a shot are arranged, including sets, props, actors, costumes, and lighting.

Connotation   The meanings we may associate with what we see on the screen.

Context   The background, environment, framework, setting or situation surrounding an event or occurrence.

Context (film)   Where and when a film is made and set. What is communicated about culture, history, society, institutions or politics.

Contextualise To think about or provide information about the situation in which something happens.

Continuity editing A style of editing that gives the viewer the impression that the action unfolds consistently in space and time. In most films, logical coherence is achieved by cutting to continuity, which emphasises the smooth transition of time and space.

Contrapuntal sound Sound that does not seem to 'fit' with the image on screen. It often works to add another layer of meaning or irony to what we see. For example, in Mike Moore's *Fahrenheit 9/11* (2004) a montage of horrific scenes showing wars across the globe is shown while Louis Armstrong sings 'I think to myself what a wonderful world'.

Cross-cutting Moving from one sphere of action to another often for extended periods. For example, A.O. Neville in Brisbane directing the search for Molly and Molly's progress on her long walk home in *Rabbit-proof Fence*.

Cross-generic A cross-genre (or hybrid genre) is a genre in fiction that blends themes and elements from two or more different genres.

Cultural norms The accepted behaviour that an individual is expected to conform to in a particular group, community, or culture.

Cultural tropes When a character holds up one culture or element of that culture (often but not necessarily their own) as a shining example of development and progression. The evidence for their assertions is invariably flawed or fictitious (think Donald Trump).

Culture The customs, standards and beliefs of a particular community or civilisation.

Debate Discussions between people in which they express different opinions.

Deep focus When all of the background and foreground details are in focus.

Dehumanise Make less human.

Democratic Party One of the two main US political parties (the other being the Republican Party), which follows a broadly liberal programme, tending to support social reform and minority rights (en.oxforddictionaries.com).

Denotation What we see on the screen.

Diegetic sound Sound that is a part of the film's world, e.g. birds singing, traffic passing.

Dissolve An editing technique that creates a gradual transition from one image to another. Often used to connect the images in some way.

Documentary A non-fictional film intended to document some aspect of reality, for the purpose of maintaining a historical record. To be real.

Dutch angle A tilted camera angle that causes the horizon in the shot to be diagonal to the bottom of the frame. It can be used to express a character's drunken state (as in *Rebel Without a Cause*), mental state, disorientation and anxiety.

Dystopian A fictional world or place in which everything is unpleasant or bad and people are oppressed, unhappy and afraid.

Educate The knowledge and understanding acquired by an individual after studying particular subject matters or experiencing life lessons.

Ellipsis The most basic idea in filmmaking, it refers to the omission of a section of the story that is either obvious enough for the audience to fill in or concealed for a narrative purpose, such as suspense or mystery.

Engima codes Questions or puzzles posed that invite/encourage an audience to become involved with a film, curious as to what will happen next, they also help to move on the narrative.

Epilogue A scene, passage or speech that is added to the end of a film, book or play as a conclusion.

Episodic narrative A narrative that has clearly separated sections, often broken up by a title, date or by the cut back to a narrator.

Establishing shot A shot usually taken from a distance that typically shows where the film is set.

Ethnicity How people are identified in terms of their ancestry.

Eye-level shot The camera is placed at the same eye level as a character.

Fade Where a shot gradually turns black or white.

Femme fatale An irresistibly attractive woman, who causes trouble for men by leading them into difficult, dangerous, or disastrous situations.

Film budget The money made available to make a film.

GCSE Film Studies

Film festivals Organised, extended presentations of films in one or more cinemas or screening venues, usually in a single city or region.

Film noir A term originally used to describe films produced in the 1940s, which is now used to describe films with some of the lighting and narrative conventions of the period, e.g. low key lighting creating shadows, dark, urban cityscapes and dark, shadowy characters.

Film production budget The money allowed to be spent on making the film project.

Film score Original music written specifically to accompany a film.

Film A story or event recorded by a camera as a set of moving images.

Foreground The front of the frame.

Foreshadow An event or clue in the narrative that signals a major event.

Found footage Fictional, filmed material presented as if it is a documentary or factual footage.

Fourth wall Originally a theatrical term for the imaginary wall that exists between actors on stage and the audience. This wall keeps up the illusion of theatre, the actors pretend that they cannot hear or see the audience. This term is also used in films, only the fourth wall in that instance is a camera lens.

Framework A supporting structure around which something can be built. A system of rules, ideas, or beliefs that is used to plan or decide something.

Gaze of the medium Seeing the world through the eyes of the camera.

Gender What is expected of a man or woman in a particular society or culture.

Genre A type or category. The characteristics that distinguish, for example, a science fiction from a romance.

German Expressionism A film movement originating in Germany just after World War I, using mise-en-scène to express the inner thoughts or emotions of particular characters or their situations.

Global society A society that has been created in modern times where people of the world acknowledge that they have a good deal in common with one another. The idea of a global society helps people to understand the links between their own lives and those of people throughout the world.

Globalised conglomerate A large business made up of many smaller businesses and brands that are large enough to trade on a worldwide basis.

Graphic matching An editing technique that involves matching shots in terms of their composition either in a scene or in a transition between two scenes.

Hand-held camera When the shot does not remain still but is shaky.

High angle shot The camera is positioned above the subject to make it look smaller and therefore weaker.

High key lighting When bright colour is created through the use of lots of filler lights.

High-concept films Movies with simple ideas at their heart that could be pitched in one or two sentences making them easily marketable and understandable to the mainstream audience.

Hollywood Ten Of the 41 screenwriters, directors and producers called to testify by the US government about Communists working in Hollywood ten refused to cooperate. They were 'blacklisted' by Hollywood and not allowed to work in movies due to their stand on free speech.

Hook An exciting scene early in the script that grabs the audience's interest.

Hurt locker The term 'hurt locker', according to the writer-producer Mark Boal, is military slang that means 'a bad and painful place'. The online Urban Dictionary defines it as 'a period of immense, inescapable physical or emotional pain', citing usage examples: 'This recession has been a real hurt locker.' 'She did not foresee her actions as contributing to the hurt locker she would soon be in.' 'That last track meet – Man, what a hurt locker!'

Hybrid genre A film that combines two or more distinct genre types. It cannot be easily categorised by a single genre or sub-genre type.

Hybridity Concepts that can be evidenced in a film, making it difficult to fit easily into a particular genre category.

Icon An image, emblem, idol or hero.

Iconography A symbolic representation. It is used within film to describe the visual language of a film, particularly within specific genre. We expect to see certain objects on-screen when we see a particular genre; for example, in a horror film, we may expect monsters, haunted castles, gravestones and dark, scary woods.

Ideologies A collection of beliefs held by an individual, group or society.

Imbues Fills someone or something with a particular feeling or idea.

Improvised explosive device (IED) A homemade or makeshift bomb.

Independent film One that received less than 50% of its funding from one of the 'big six' major film studios; typically, with a relatively small budget, where the filmmaker gets to tell the story they want to tell in the way they want to tell it.

Innovation The creation of something new or the development of a new method of doing something, e.g. computer generated imagery (CGI).

Institutional The organisations created to pursue, promote or produce a particular type of endeavour, e.g. filmmaking.

Insurgency A movement within a country dedicated to overthrowing the government. An insurgency is a rebellion.

Integrated studio system The system of organisation where studios controlled production, distribution and exhibition. This enabled the studios to apply assembly-line manufacturing and cost control methods to film production.

Interior monologue Expressing a character's inner thoughts.

Internalised/inner turmoil If you internalise your emotions or feelings, you do not allow them to show although you think about them while experiencing a state of confusion, disturbance and agitation.

Intertextuality An idea that any text has been influenced and shaped by texts that have come before it (anything read or seen in the case of movies). Therefore, no film exists on its own and consciously or not all films borrow ideas from other films, past or present.

Intertitle Printed text or narration shown between scenes.

Introspection Observation or examination of one's own mental and emotional state, mental processes; the act of looking within oneself.

Jeopardy Hazard or risk of or exposure to loss, harm, death or injury; peril or danger.

Jump cut Is an abrupt transition, typically in a sequential clip that makes the subject appear to jump from one spot to the other, without continuity.

Juxtaposed To place side by side.

Key demographic A term used by government agencies, political parties and manufacturers of consumer goods to describe particular groups in society. Films are often aimed at a 'key demographic', e.g. a particular age group or gender grouping.

Kino Flo tube `An LED and fluorescent lighting system.

Lense flare The effect created when light is scattered or flared in a lens system, often in response to a bright light. It usually produces an undesirable effect on the image but has increasingly been used by filmmakers to create an aesthetic effect, e.g. Oliver Tate's '2 Weeks of Lovemaking' video in *Submarine*.

Linear narrative A narrative told in chronological order.

Long shots Enable us to view a character, or group of characters, within a setting, so we gain clues as to the coming action within the narrative and their role within it. There may be a number of things happening relevant to the plot within a long shot. A long shot can also show the whole of a person from head to toe, or the equivalent view of a building, landscape or prop.

Low angle shot The camera is placed below the subject making it look bigger and dominant.

Low key lighting When less filler lights are used to create pools of shadows.

Mainstream Mainstream films can be defined as commercial films that know a wide release and play in first-run cinemas. Hollywood films are usually considered mainstream and blockbusters are mainstream films.

Major film studio A production and film distributor that releases a substantial number of films annually and consistently commands a significant share of box office revenue in many markets. The current big six are considered to be: Warner Brothers, 20th Century Fox, Paramount Pictures, Universal Pictures, Sony Pictures Entertainment (earlier known as Columbia-Tristar Pictures) and Walt Disney Studios.

Meaning   What the director intends you to think and feel while watching the film.

Melodrama   A film or literary work in which the plot is typically sensational and designed to appeal strongly to the emotions.

Mid-shot   Frames the character from the waist up or down.

Montage   A film editing technique in which a series of shots are edited into a sequence to condense space, time and information.

Motif   A recurring idea or symbol in a film, e.g. dogs in *Tsotsi*, the spirit bird in *Rabbit-proof Fence*, water in *Submarine*, phones in *E.T. the Extra-terrestrial.*

Motivation   A reason or reasons for acting or behaving in a particular way. For example, the reasons (motivations) for Tsotsi's criminal behaviour is his poverty and/or because he is unemployed.

Multiplex   A cinema with several separate screens.

Musical motif   A short repeated pattern of music.

Narrative function   The importance of, for example, a particular type of character to the ways in which the story is told and understood .The predictions we can make about their actions once we have identified what type of character they are.

Negotiated reading   When a spectator agrees with some but not all messages and values in film.

Newsreel   A short film of news and current affairs, formerly made for showing as part of the programme in a cinema.

Non-diegetic sound   Sound that is not a part of the film's world, e.g. musical score or voice-over narration.

Nuclear family   A family unit that includes two married parents and their children living in the same residence.

Omniscient/unrestricted narrative viewpoint   The audience see aspects of the narrative that the main character does not.

Oppositional reading   When a spectator disagrees with or dislikes a film's messages or values.

Panavision   Company that produced a camera with a type of wide-screen lens, the word is formed from elements of panorama and vision.

Panning   The camera moves slowly from one area of the setting to another. If done quickly this is known as a whip pan.

Paradox   A situation where two contradictory ideas exist at the same time.

Parallel editing   An editing technique of alternating two or more scenes that happen simultaneously but in different locations. If the scenes are simultaneous, they occasionally culminate in a single place, where the relevant parties confront each other.

Parallel sound   Music that matches the action on-screen.

Pastiche   A literary, musical, or artistic piece consisting wholly or chiefly of motifs or techniques borrowed from one or more sources.

Pleonastic sound effects   Sound that is heightened in order to appeal to the emotions or draw attention to a significant action or prop.

Political   Of or relating to the government or public affairs of a country.

Post-modernism   Refers to techniques used by the filmmaker in order to draw attention to the fact that you are watching a film, e.g. chapter cards in *Submarine*.

Post-traumatic stress disorder (PTSD)   A mental health condition that is a result of a terrifying event – either experienced or witnessed. Symptoms may include flashbacks, nightmares and severe anxiety.

Precociousness   Being very clever, mature or especially good at something, often in a way that is usually only expected in someone much older.

Preferred reading   When the spectator understands and largely agrees with the messages and values evident in a film.

Pre-sold property   A basis for a film that the producers have paid exclusivity to use. Pre-sold as it comes with its own audience. For example, the Harry Potter books film rights were sold to Warner Brothers and had sold millions of copies before the movies were made.

Prologue   Something that comes before an introduction to a book, play or film. It may be an action or situation that leads to something else.

Pseudo-documentary   Having the appearance of but is not actually a real documentary.

Pyromaniac A person who has an irresistible impulse to start fires.

Re-boot To discard all continuity in an established series in order to recreate its characters, timeline and back-story from the beginning.

RED One camera A new camera used in a number of Oscar winning films, which is able to capture sharp, high quality images.

Renaissance A new growth of activity or interest in something, especially art, literature or music.

Republican Party One of the two main US political parties (the other being the Democratic Party), favouring a right-wing stance, limited central government, and tough, interventionist foreign policy (en.oxforddictionaries. com).

Restricted narrative viewpoint The audience only know as much as the main character.

Self-effacing Being modest about what you have done. Not encouraging praise and not trying to get the attention of other people.

Shallow focus When the camera only focuses on the subject in the foreground and the background is blurred out.

Shooting script A version of the screenplay that is used during filming.

Shot-reverse-shot A convention for showing dialogue that gives the audience the feeling that they are watching the conversation in a 'real-life' way.

Slugline The scene heading.

Social The interaction of the individual and the group, or the welfare of human beings as members of society.

Sound bridge Used to link two frames together, even if the setting has changed or the narrative action. They are often used to give a sense of continuity, to keep the connection in the audience's mind.

Sound effects Diegetic sound that is created artificially to emphasise action, for example tyres screeching, punches and explosions.

Soundscape A sound or combination of sounds that forms or arises from an immersive environment.

Speed of editing Refers to how many consecutive shots are used in a period of time. Fast cutting involves several consecutive shots of a brief duration (e.g. three seconds or less). It can be used to convey a lot of information very quickly, or to imply either energy or chaos. Slow cutting uses shots of longer duration (any shot longer than 15 seconds depending on context). This often has the effect of slowing down the action and allowing the audience to concentrate for longer on key events within the movie.

Staged or staging The process of selecting, designing, adapting to, or modifying the performance space for a film.

Stereotype A simplified representation of a person, or group of people, repeatedly used so it becomes seen as the norm.

Straight cut A smooth cut between one shot and the next.

Stylised Has a particular 'look' or style.

Sub-genre A sub-category within a particular genre: they are identifiable sub-categories of the larger category of main film genres, with their own distinctive subject matter, style, formulas, and iconography.

Subverted Undermine the usual way of doing something.

Superpower A country with a dominant position in international relations that has the power to exert influence on a global scale. This is done through the combined-means of technological, cultural, military (conventional and nuclear) and economic strength, as well as diplomatic influence.

Suspension of disbelief The temporary acceptance as believable of events or characters that would ordinarily be seen as incredible. This is usually to allow an audience to appreciate works of literature or film or drama that are exploring unusual ideas.

Symbolically A mark, sign or word that indicates, signifies or is understood as representing an idea, object or relationship, e.g. In *Rabbit-proof Fence* the hawk symbolises freedom and the spirit world.

Talking head When a person addresses the camera directly, viewed in a close-up.

Tilt (up and down) The shot moves up or down.

Time lapse photography A way of filming that makes slow action, e.g. a flower opening appear to happen quickly (often used in wildlife programmes).

Tracking shot The camera moves alongside the subject it is filming.

Typicality The ways in which certain elements of film form are used repeatedly to create meaning and response, e.g. exciting, fast-paced music is typically used in the action/adventure genre to mirror or accentuate the action.

Typography The style and general appearance of the printed word.

Verisimilitude Establishing the truth and reality of a fictional world, believability, successfully suspending an audience's disbelief.

Vernacular Commonly used or spoken language.

Vertical integration The ownership of the chain of production by one business. In the case of filmmaking this involved the studios producing, distributing and exhibiting their films.

Visceral Affecting internal feelings.

Wipe A type of film transition where one shot replaces another by travelling from one side of the frame to another or with a special shape.

Xenophobia A dislike of or prejudice against people from other countries or places.

Zeitgeist The spirit of the time; general trend of thought or feeling characteristic of a particular period of time.

Zoom in or out The camera shot moves closer to or further away from the subject.

Index

16mm film 111, 135, 162
35mm film 81, 123, 133, 135, 162, 234
180-degree rule 164
3D film 87, 111–112, 116, 120–123
academic study 178, 180, 248
action 14, 18–20, 22, 24–26, 28–30, 34, 44–45, 47, 49, 55–56, 63, 66, 71, 80–81, 110, 116, 120–121, 133–134, 139, 142, 162–176, 212–213, 234, 238–239, 245, 253, 258–263, 266, 268, 270, 273, 275
action code 63
action/adventure genre 24, 29, 43–44, 46–47, 49, 62, 71, 74, 98, 118, 162–176, 179
actual sound 22
aesthetic qualities 20, 41, 65, 76–83, 92, 107, 136, 144–145, 162–163, 238, 244, 250–254
aestheticised 162
affluent 86, 96
age 65–66, 71–72, 74–75, 98–99, 152–153, 203, 216, 221, 224, 226–228, 254, 261, 275, 283
allegory 91
America 35, 40, 85–88, 97–99, 102, 107–108, 110, 112–115, 117, 123, 126–134, 137, 139, 141, 144, 151–153, 155, 157–159, 165, 173, 179, 224, 228, 233, 250–251
ambient sound 11, 22, 24, 240
ambiguity 138
An Education 57, 59
anamorphic 112, 133
androgynous 213
anti-narrative films 64
archetypes 44, 67–68, 233, 244, 269, 283
art house classics 102
artistic merit 21
aspect ratio 133, 135
audio-visual 8, 226
aural interior monologue 207
aural motif 283
auteur 108, 220
authenticity 46, 92, 159, 162–163, 170, 172–173, 175–176
Avatar 160–161

baby boomer 129
back projected 134
Barthes, Roland 63
Bigelow, Kathryn 29, 88, 155–156, 158–163, 165, 168–170, 173, 175–176, 178
binary oppositions 53, 63, 203–204
bird's eye view 12, 18, 34
blockbuster 92, 108, 113, 115, 117–118, 120, 125, 155, 160, 172, 220
blocked/blocking 172
body horror 194–195
body language 32, 38–39, 66–67, 73, 172
Boyle, Danny 12, 20, 55, 80, 83
brand recognition 114
Brooklyn 35, 98–99
Burgoyne, Robert 180

canted angle 19–20, 80, 264
cataclysmic 236–237
catharsis 103
cause and effect structure/narrative 49, 53, 55–56
CCTV 163, 190
Celtic mythology 91–92
centre frame 38
chapter cards 243, 245, 249
character
    agents of cause and effect 56
    types 61–63, 68–70
chiaroscuro 144
Chinese lantern 169
chronological 55
cinematic 9, 42, 76, 79, 83–84, 89, 97, 155, 162, 234, 237, 249, 251
cinematography 10–12, 16, 18, 20, 41, 43–44, 47, 64, 73, 76, 79–83, 97–98, 100, 102, 107, 115, 133–136, 162, 164, 169, 184, 190, 194, 204–206, 214, 234–237, 241, 243, 245, 264–265, 274–280, 287
cinephile 102–103, 179, 227, 249
circular structure/narrative 53–54
Classic Hollywood three-act structure 49
claustrophobic 152, 166

close-up 11–14, 47, 133–135, 140, 163, 166, 194–195, 236–237, 240–241, 252, 261–262, 264, 276–278
cliché 74, 103–104, 176, 191, 252
Cold War 114, 118, 127–128, 130
collective memory 79
colour 10–11, 16–18, 32–33, 37, 42, 76, 81, 87, 110–112, 121, 135, 184, 205, 224, 231–232, 249
colour film 87, 110–112, 121, 135
colour palette 16–18, 33, 76, 81, 232
coming of age 98–99, 203, 224, 226–228, 254
commentary sound 22
comparative study 40, 43, 51, 85, 106–107, 144, 151
composition 80, 173, 267
computer-generated imagery (CGI) 10, 34, 46–47, 84, 87–88, 116, 120–121
connotation 66, 68
contextual 6, 10, 57–58, 85, 88, 90, 96
continuity editing 27, 139–140, 175, 241, 249
contrapuntal sound 11, 26, 207
costume 11, 21, 32, 35–39, 66, 71, 137–138, 173–174, 230, 251, 283
crime/thriller genre 43, 46–48, 52, 59, 85, 121
cross-cutting 27, 29, 31, 175–176, 240, 267, 282
cross-genre 42
cultural norms 204
cultural tropes 104
culture 8–9, 18, 21, 34, 36–37, 65–66, 68, 72–73, 77–79, 84–85, 88–89, 92–97, 104, 107, 126, 129, 152, 179, 186–187, 202, 204, 222–223, 251, 269, 283

Dancer in the Dark 50–51
Dean, James 77–78, 114, 118
debate 8, 67, 88–89, 149
deep focus 18
dehumanise 195, 200
Democratic Party 127, 130
denotation 66, 68
denouement 49
depth of field 12
dialogue 9, 15, 18, 21–24, 27, 52–53, 73, 141–142, 172, 238, 257, 263, 269–270, 274, 280, 282
diegetic sound 11, 22–25, 141–142, 176, 239
dissolve 11, 27–28, 139–140, 282
District 9 58, 91, 98, 185–201

documentary 20, 58, 111, 121, 133, 162, 165, 168, 170, 175, 187, 195, 238
Dutch angle 19, 165
dynamic paradigm 50–51
dystopian 195

Ebert, Roger 52, 104
educate 8–9
ellipsis 60, 200
enigma codes 53, 63, 200, 276
Epilogue 241, 244–246
episodic structure/narrative 53–54
equilibrium 63
establishing shot 34, 133, 136, 204, 234, 266, 275, 281–282
E.T. the Extra-Terrestrial 10, 27–28, 36, 43, 83, 85, 91, 106–107, 116–118, 124, 130–132, 135–136, 138, 140, 142–146, 149, 151–154
ethnicity 36, 65–66, 68, 72, 75, 99, 151–152, 269, 283
evaluative analysis 283–287
expressionism 64
eye-level shot 18

facial expressions 13, 38
fade 11, 24, 27–28, 157, 282
fast-paced editing 11, 27, 29, 47, 168, 266, 281–282
Ferris Bueller's Day Off 43, 85, 106, 118, 227–228
femme fatale 236, 244
fill light 17
film
　1950s 113–114, 125
　1980s 117–119, 125
　21st century 124–125
　budget 67, 108, 114, 116, 118, 121, 124, 132, 155, 157–158, 161, 190–191, 223–224
　critics 52, 100–101, 243
　definition of 11
　editing 11, 21, 27–30, 34, 41, 43–44, 47, 52–53, 55, 60, 64, 76, 80, 107, 139–140, 162, 164–165, 168, 172, 175–176, 194, 208–213, 234, 240–243, 249, 264, 266–269, 274, 281–282, 287
　elements of form 11, 41–64, 132, 264
　festivals 156, 159, 224
　noir 133, 144–145
　reasons for studying 8–9

reviews 52, 74, 100–101, 103–104, 178–179
score 23–24, 26, 141–142, 175, 204, 207
timeline 110–112, 114–116, 120–123, 158
use of form 65–76
filmmaking option 273–283
first-person narration 57
flash forward 53
flashback 53–56, 139, 160
foreground 18, 36, 38, 73, 134, 180, 276
foreshadow 14, 49, 134, 171
found footage 20, 163, 284
fourth wall 238, 250
framework 84
framing 11–12, 15–18, 32, 38–39, 47, 73, 76, 81–82, 133–136, 141, 163–166, 172–173, 175, 205, 209, 226, 241, 265, 276
freeze frames 237, 243, 249

gaze of the medium, 195
gender 65–70, 72, 75, 94, 129, 134, 152, 213–214, 216, 269, 283
genre 15, 17, 20, 24–25, 29, 39–53, 62, 65, 67, 85–86, 88, 91, 94, 100, 102, 107–108, 113–114, 117–118, 124–125, 131–132, 142, 144, 146–150, 160–161, 186, 193, 195, 203–204, 206, 214, 228, 255–257, 264–265, 267–268, 273–275, 280, 282–284, 287
  codes 40, 42, 44, 98, 203, 224, 234, 241, 264, 267–268, 274
  conventions 40, 42, 44, 86, 88, 98, 147, 150, 194–195, 203, 218, 224, 234, 241, 243, 256, 264–268, 274, 283
  importance of 150
  narratives 49
  writing about 52
German Expressionism 64, 144
global society 9
globalised conglomerates 108
golden age/era 108, 114, 123, 220
graphic matching 11, 267, 282
Grease 38–39, 43, 50–51, 78, 86, 106, 118

hair 11, 38, 69, 71, 173, 200, 203–205, 213, 222–223, 231, 244–245
hand-held camera 12, 19–20, 163–165, 190, 211, 224
high angle shot 11–12, 15–16, 18, 36, 134, 164, 264, 279

high-concept films 117
high key lighting 16, 47, 144, 264, 280
Hitchcock, Alfred 13, 34, 46, 52, 59, 79, 106, 114, 118, 134, 284
Hollywood Ten 114
hook, bell 49
horror genre 25, 45, 59, 94, 112, 118, 141, 148–149, 202–219, 257, 264–268, 276, 280–281
The Hurt Locker 29, 34, 88, 155–181
hybrid genre 42, 146, 148
hybridity 203

iconic 77–79, 83, 103, 129, 140, 177, 224
iconography 45, 144, 146–148
imbues 138, 140, 145
immigrants/immigration 35, 151, 153, 187, 203–204
improvised explosive device (IED) 159, 174
indie/independent 88–89, 92, 98, 104–105, 119, 123, 155, 157, 224, 228, 248, 250
innovation 10, 42, 120, 223, 251
institutional context 41, 84, 88, 92, 107, 186, 223
insurgency 128, 159, 174–175
integrated studio system 108
internalised/inner turmoil 32, 98, 171
intertextuality 227, 248
intertitle 58, 102
Invasion of the Body Snatchers 10, 40, 43, 85, 87, 91, 98, 106–107, 112, 114, 130, 131–133, 137, 139–141, 144–146, 149, 151, 154
introspection 171, 241
Iraq 155, 159–161, 170, 173, 178–179

jeopardy 174
jump cut 11, 27–29, 222, 224, 234, 237–238, 241, 249, 266, 281
Juno 12, 17, 34, 39, 66–68, 70, 88–89, 97, 155, 158, 224, 227–228, 233
juxtaposed 246

key demographic 125, 152
key lighting 16–18, 47, 133, 136, 144, 264, 280
King Solomon's Mines 34, 40, 43, 45–46, 62, 86, 106, 114, 134
Kino Flo tube 169

lens flare 136
Let the Right One In 67, 82, 94, 182, 202–220, 284, 286
Lévi-Strauss, Claude 63
lighting 9–12, 16–18, 20, 32, 36, 45, 47, 80–81, 96, 105, 123, 133–136, 140, 144, 162, 168–169, 172–173, 190, 203–208, 214, 224–225, 231, 234, 237, 243, 253, 264, 268, 274–275, 279–280, 284, 287
linear structure/narrative 53–55
location 20, 32, 34, 42–44, 46, 81, 137, 164, 175, 190, 222, 240, 258–259, 265, 273
long shot 11–12, 14, 96, 133–135, 138, 140, 164, 194, 210–211, 241, 262, 264, 276–277, 279
low angle shot 11–12, 15–16, 134–135, 164, 264, 275
low key lighting 16, 18, 47, 133, 136, 144, 264

major film studio 118, 155, 157
make-up 11, 32, 35, 38–39, 67, 71, 173–174, 244
meaning 9, 11, 15–16, 21, 26–27, 32, 38, 40, 42, 44, 64, 66–67, 76, 81, 91, 100–102, 144–145, 150, 162, 204, 206, 226, 231–234, 237, 239, 241, 249, 274, 280, 284
Memento 49, 158
mid-shot 11–12, 15, 73, 133, 235, 278
mise-en-scène 11, 29, 32–40, 43, 76, 96, 107, 137–138, 144, 147–148, 162, 170–176, 184, 190, 194, 204–205, 224, 226, 228–233, 239, 264–265, 274–280, 287
monologue 207
montage 27, 60, 64, 80, 225, 238, 241–243, 249
motif 26, 36, 51, 208–210, 232, 239, 245, 251
motivations 13, 38, 47, 56, 63, 74, 96, 245
multiplex 103, 114–115, 123
music 8–9, 21–23, 25–26, 41, 43–44, 47, 53, 79–83, 86–89, 98, 103, 112, 114, 118, 141–142, 176, 193, 204, 207, 218, 222–225, 227, 238, 241–242, 248, 251–253, 268, 283–284
musical instruments 25
musical motif 26
musical genre 43, 79, 86–88, 112, 114, 118, 248

Nathan, Ian 178
narrative
  alternative 64
  analysis 64
  codes 58, 63
  conventions 51, 53, 58, 133
  function 36, 38, 45–46, 56, 62, 64, 71

theory 61–64
  time and space 59–60, 139
  viewpoint 56, 59
negotiated reading 73
newsreel 111, 175
non-diegetic sound 11, 22–25, 141–142, 207
nuclear family 129–130
nuclear weapons 126–128

omniscient narrative viewpoint 53, 57, 59
oppositional reading 73

Panavision 135
panning 11–12, 14, 19, 133, 135, 211, 236, 241
paradox 127–129
parallel editing 60
parallel sound 26
pastiche 251
pleonastic sound effects 268
plot 9, 13–14, 21, 41–44, 47, 49, 53, 55, 62, 92, 98, 257, 262, 273
point-of-view (POV) shot 11, 18, 56, 65, 122, 135–136, 153, 198, 232, 247, 261, 264, 278
political issues 58, 65, 73, 84, 88, 91, 94, 97–98, 107, 126–127, 130, 151–152, 186, 220, 222
popular culture 77–79, 85, 202, 251, 283
post-modernism 195, 248–249
post-traumatic stress disorder (PTSD) 160
poverty 34, 65, 91–93, 95–97
precociousness 102
pre-sold property 109
preferred reading 73
Prologue 235–236, 241, 245
Propp, Vladimir 61–63
props 11, 21, 32, 35–36, 42–44, 47, 51, 137–138, 173–175, 190, 265, 274, 283
pseudo-documentary style 195
pyromaniac 228, 244

Rabbit-proof Fence 14, 18, 24, 28–30, 32–34, 36, 55–58, 64, 72, 90, 93
Raiders of the Lost Ark 34, 40, 43, 45–46, 49, 62, 86, 106, 117–118
Rear Window 13, 15, 34, 43, 46, 48, 52, 79, 85, 106, 114, 259–260

Rebel Without a Cause 10, 43, 77–78, 85, 106, 113–114, 165, 233
recurring sounds 239, 268–269, 282
RED One camera 190
renaissance 89, 144
representation 10, 41, 45, 65–74, 86, 107, 139, 151–153, 198–199, 203, 205, 213–218, 222, 244, 269, 274, 283, 287
Republican Party 127, 130
restricted narrative viewpoint 53, 59
romance 52, 91–92, 203, 206, 214, 224, 232

Saturday Night Fever 78, 118
science fiction genre 43, 45–46, 50, 91, 98, 112, 114, 118, 130–150, 185–201
screenwriting option 257–273
self-effacing 102
setting 11, 14, 17–19, 28, 30, 33–36, 40, 42–46, 51, 68, 72–73, 84, 90–91, 137–138, 168, 170–171, 184, 186, 190, 193–194, 232–233, 244, 251, 258, 265
shallow focus 18
shooting script 256, 258, 261, 266, 272
shot reverse shot 27, 133–134, 139
silence 23–24, 176, 207, 238–239
Singin' in the Rain 10, 22, 43, 50–51, 78–79, 84, 86–88, 106, 114, 248
Skyfall 14, 16, 20, 24–25, 29, 34–35, 37, 69–71, 74, 98, 220
slow motion 167–168, 243
slow-paced editing 11, 27, 29, 47, 139–140, 210, 212, 266–267, 281
Slumdog Millionaire 12, 18, 20, 23–24, 26, 31, 34, 41, 54–57, 60, 62, 76, 80, 92–93, 161
sound 8, 11, 13, 21–26, 29–30, 43, 64, 73, 76, 83, 87, 107, 110–112, 120, 141–142, 162, 176, 184, 193–194, 206–208, 233, 238–240, 245, 251, 264, 268, 274, 282–283
social context/society 8–9, 34, 43, 51, 58, 64, 66, 68, 71, 76, 84–89, 94, 97, 107, 129, 131–132, 152, 155, 186, 195, 203–204, 222, 233, 235, 283
slugline 258, 260
society, changes in 34, 43, 51, 68, 222
Song of the Sea 55, 91–92
sound bridge 11, 30, 176, 240
sound effects 22–24, 207, 268, 283

sound levels 23
soundscape 176
soundtrack 23, 98, 112, 141–142, 207, 245, 251
Soviet montage cinema 64
specialist writing 102–105
speed of editing 11, 29, 34, 47, 140, 166, 168, 281
Spielberg, Steven 34, 83, 106, 115, 117–118, 120, 124–125, 131, 135–136, 138, 140, 144–145, 154
spray light 206
staged/staging 52, 153, 172, 236, 251
Star Wars 117–118, 121, 124–125, 149, 220
stereotypical 44, 46, 63, 65, 67–68, 74, 103, 213, 228, 244, 257, 269, 283–284
story, difference from plot 53
straight cut 11, 27, 139–140, 175
style 10–11, 20, 27, 34, 42–45, 47, 51–52, 55, 58, 76, 79–80, 83–84, 87, 92, 98, 102, 108, 121, 139–142, 144–146, 163–165, 172, 175–176, 187, 193, 195, 205, 222, 225, 234, 238, 241, 248–249, 253, 284
 of editing 11, 27, 140, 165, 175–176
stylised 102, 205
sub-genre 146–148, 160
Submarine 37–39, 57, 98, 103, 136, 221–254
superpower 126, 128
suspension of disbelief 250
surrealism 64
synchronised sound 22

talking heads 190, 195, 198
The Ring 266, 274–286
The Thing 114, 118, 149
tilting 11–12, 19, 136, 165
time lapse photography 133
Todorov, Tzvetan 63
tracking shot 11–12, 19, 43, 133, 140, 163, 211, 264
Tsotsi 13–14, 24, 36–37, 56, 67, 75, 80–81, 91, 94–98
typicality 44–47, 49–51, 62, 67–69, 73, 79, 92, 98, 103, 134, 139, 142, 146–147, 152, 170, 175, 213, 224, 233, 242, 264, 269
typography 241

UK 98–99, 220–225, 234
unrestricted narrative viewpoint 53, 59

vampire genre 94, 202–204, 206, 214, 218–219
verisimilitude 133, 135, 141
vernacular 241
vertical integration 114
visceral 168, 175, 180, 204
visual motif 208–210, 232
voice-over 22–24, 53, 55–58, 102, 141, 238, 241, 245–246

Wadjda 62, 67, 77, 94
Westwell, Guy 179
whip pan 14, 135
Whiplash 26, 41, 70, 88–89, 155
wide-angle 80, 264
Williams, John 83, 142
wipe 11, 27–28

xenophobia 188

youth film genre 43

zeitgeist 129
zoom 12, 19, 163–165, 168, 236–237, 240, 275–277, 279–280

Acknowledgements

Screenshot acknowledgements

A Bout de Souffle, dir. Jean-Luc Godard [DVD], 1960, Optimum Releasing [2000]. *A Nightmare on Elm Street*, dir Wes Craven, [DVD], 1984, New Line Home Video. *Alien*, dir. Ridley Scott [DVD], 1979, Twentieth Century Fox Home Entertainment. *Brooklyn*, dir. John Crowley [DVD], 2015, Lionsgate.

Dancer in the Dark, dir. Lars Von Trier [DVD], 2000. Film 4. *District 9*, dir. Neill Blomkamp [DVD], 2009, Sony Pictures Home Entertainment. *Dracula*, dir. Terence Fisher [DVD], 1958, Optimum Releasing [2008]. *Earth vs the Flying Saucers*, dir. Fred F. Sears [DVD], 1956, Columbia Pictures Industries Inc. *E.T. the Extra-Terrestrial*, dir. Steven Spielberg [DVD], 1982, Universal Studios [2012]. *Forrest Gump*, dir. Robert Zemeckis [DVD], 1994, Paramount Home Entertainment (UK). *Friday the 13th*, dir. Sean S. Cunningham [DVD], 1980, Warner Home Video. *Grease*, dir. Randal Kleiser [DVD], 1978, Paramount Home Entertainment. *Halloween*, dir. John Carpenter [DVD], 1978, Anchor Bay. *Invasion of the Body Snatchers*, dir. Don Siegel [DVD], 1956, Universal Pictures UK. *Juno*, dir. Jason Reitman [DVD], 2007, Twentieth Century Fox Home Entertainment [2008]. *King Solomon's Mines*, dir. Compton Bennett and Andrew Marton [DVD], 1950, Warner Bros Home Entertainment. *Let the Right One In*, dir. Tomas Alfredson [DVD], 2008, Magnolia Picture Entertainment. *Me and Earl and the Dying Girl*, dir. Alfonso Gomez-Rejon [DVD], 2015, 20th Century Fox. *Moonrise Kingdom*, dir. Wes Craven [DVD], 2012, Universal Pictures UK. *Nosferatu*, dir. F.W. Murnau [DVD], 1922, Eureka Entertainment. *Oklahoma!*, dir. Fred Zinnermann [DVD], 1955, Twentieth Century Fox. *Rabbit-proof Fence*, dir. Phillip Noyce [DVD], 2002 Buena Vista Home Entertainment. *Raiders of the Lost Ark*, dir. Steven Spielberg [DVD], 1981, Paramount Home Entertainment. *Rear Window*, dir. Alfred Hitchcock [DVD], 1954, Universal Pictures UK Ltd. *Rebel Without a Cause*, dir. Nicholas Ray [DVD], 1955. Warner Bros. Home Video. *Scream*, dir. Wes Craven [DVD], 1996. *Singin' in the Rain*, dir. Gene Kelly and Stanley Donen [DVD], 1952, Warner Bros. Home Video *Skyfall*, dir. Sam Mendes [DVD], 2012, Columbia Pictures Industries Inc. *Slumdog Millionaire*, dir. Danny Boyle [DVD], 2008, Celador Films, Channel4 & Twentieth Century Fox. *Song of the Sea*, dir. Tomm Moore [DVD], 2014, Studio Canal. *Star Trek II: The Wrath of Khan*, dir. Nicholas Meyer [DVD], 1982, Paramount Home Entertainment. *Submarine*, dir. John Crowley [DVD], 2015, Warp Films, Optimum Home Entertainment. *The Day the Earth Stood Still*, dir. Robert Wise [DVD], 1951, 20th Century Fox Home Entertainment. *The Hurt Locker*, dir. Kathryn Bigelow [DVD], 2008, Lions Gate Home Entertainment UK Ltd. *The Lone Ranger*, dir. Gore Verbinski, Walt Disney Studios, 2013, Buena Vista Home Entertainment. *The Lost Boys*, dir. Joel Schumacher [DVD], 1987, Warner Home Video. *The Ring*, dir. Gore Verbinski [DVD], 1984, Dreamworks Video. *Tsotsi*, dir. Gavin Hood [DVD], 2005, Momentum Pictures. *Wadjda*, dir. Haifaa al-Mansour [DVD], 2012, Soda Pictures Ltd. *Wall Street*, dir. Oliver Stone [DVD], 1987, 20th Century Fox Home Entertainment. *Whiplash*, dir. Damien Chazelle [DVD], 2014, Sony Pictures Home Entertainment. *Witness*, dir. Peter Weir [DVD], 1985, Paramount Home Entertainment.

GCSE Film Studies

Photo acknowledgements

p1 iStock.com / baronvsp; p5 Sylverarats Vctors; p7 (top) charnsitr, (middle) Panda Vector; (bottom) LuckyImages; p7 (top to bottom) Quarta; p8 Vectomart; p17 IADA; Lutsina Tatiana; Leremy; Alex Pin; p21 Photo 12 / Alamy Stock Photo; p52 Public domain; p62 (bottom) Public domain; p63 Tzvetan Todorov no Fronteiras do Pensamento São Paulo 2012; p68 SeneGal; p78 (top) www.tumblr.com/search/andy%20warhol%20james%20dean; p78 (bottom right) Mirramax; p83 Public domain; p100 Library of America; p101 Sabelskaya; p101 Konstantin Faraktinov; p105 (top) Denis Makaraenko / Shutterstock.com; p105 (middle) Featuaaareflash Photo Agency / Shuttersock.com; p105 (bottom) Featuaaareflash Photo Agency / Shuttersock.com; p106 Gabriele Maltinti / Shutterstock.com; p107 barteverett / Shutterstock.com; p110 www.we-heart.com; p111 Public domain; p113 Photo 12 / Alamy Stock Photo; p115 Public domain; p119 Public domain; p121 (top) samzsolti / Shutterstock.com; p121 (bottom) Photo 12 / Alamy Stock Photo; p122 (top) Collection Christophel / Alamy Stock Photo; p122 (bottom) LuckyImages; p123 Diabluses / Shutterstock.com; p124 PHILIPPE LOPEZ / Staff Editorial; p126 H. Armstrong Roberts / Stringer Editorial / Getty; p128 (left) Joseph Sohm / Shutterstock.com; p128 (right) Tymonko Galyna; p130 graysolid; p131 (right) Everett Collection / Alamy; p131 (left) Everett Collection / Alamy; p144 A.F. Arhive / Alamy; p145 ScreenProd/Photononstop/Alamy Stock PhUnited Archives GmbH / Alamy Stock Photo; p150 Public domain; p152 (left) INTERFOTO / Alamy Stock Photo; p156 Everett Collection Inc. / Alamy Stock Photo; p161 Everett Collection / Shutterstock.com; p189 (bottom) Gianluigi Guercia / Staff; p220 chamsitr; p257 https://nz.pinterest.com/callamn/stereotypes/; p297 CoralMax; p297 Charis Estelle

Text acknowledgements

p74 Copyright Guardian News & Media 2017; p102 Copyright Independent; p104 Ebertdigital.com; p105 Copyright Guardian News & Media 2017; pp110–112, 113, 114–117, 120–123 Courtesy of Filmsite.org; p220 Copyright Guardian News & Media Ltd 2017; p224 Copyright Independent; p228 © Telegraph Media Group Limited 2011; p239 Alex Turner; p251 © Telegraph Media Group Limited 2011